Global Government

Creating a System for Conducting the Planet
(The Global Union of Commonwealths)

Alan Wittbecker

Books by Alan Wittbecker
- Eutopias: A Poetic Commonwealth of Earth
- Ordering Spaces and Living Places: Aesthetic & Ecological Dimensions of Place
- Poetic Archaeology of the Flesh: Creative Language, Physics & the Ecology of Being
- One Earth Many Worlds: The Role of Cosmologies on Ecological Impact & Accommodation
- REviewing REthinking REturning: Essays of Life, Ecology, and Ecological Design (2 ed.)
- Good Forestry from Good Theories & Good Practices (2 ed.)
- Eutopian Essays: Towards Making Good Places
- [O]utopias Or [E]utopias (Eutopias Part 1)
- Topopoetics (Eutopias Part 2)
- Global Emergency Actions (Eutopias Part 3)
- Eutopias: Making Good Places Culturally & Ecologically (3 ed.)
- Foundation for Redesigning Places Regions & Planet
- Redesigning the Planet (Version 3)
- Redesigning Regions in the Planet (Version 2)
- Redesigning Local Systems in the Planet (Version 1)

Global Government

Creating a System for Conducting the Planet
(The Global Union of Commonwealths)
A Rough Outline of a Preliminary Proposal

Alan Wittbecker

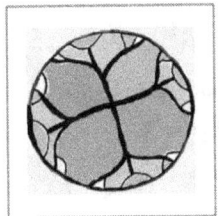

20th Anniversary edition
2011

Clio Press
Sarasota

For more information on sites and projects in text:
   SynGeo ArchiGraph Co.: www.syngeo.org
   Ecoforestry Institute: www.ecoforestry.net
   G. P. Marsh Institute: www.marshinstitute.net
   Pan Ecology: www.panecology.net
   Rian Garcia Calusa: www.riangarciacalusa.com
   Eutopian Ecologists: www.eutopias.net

Copyright © 1971, 1991, 2011 Alan Wittbecker

All rights reserved under International and Pan American Copyright Convention. No part of the book may be reproduced in any form or by any means, including information storage and retrieval systems, without the prior written consent of the Author or Publisher, excepting brief quotes used in reviews:
Clio Press, Mozart & Reason Wolf
SynGeo ArchiGraph, P.O. Box 370, Tallevast, Florida 34270

Publisher's Cataloging in Publication Data
Alan Wittbecker 1946-
   Global Government
   p.   cm.
   Includes Bibliographical References and Index.
   1. Human Ecology. 2. Radical Philosophy. 3. Ecological Design
I. Title.
JZ 5170.W5851
ISBN 9781467900034 (paper)

Book Design by Rian Garcia Calusa
Manufactured in the United States of America
10 9 8 7 6 5 4 3 2

Contents

1.0. Introduction to Global Government   9
    1.1. Who Needs Governing   10
    1.2. Tools for Understanding Governance: Gigatrends   11
    1.3. Examining Possibilities of Governance with Thought Experiments   16
    1.4. Other Tools for Addressing Governance: Analysis to Questioning   18

2.0. Experimental Images of Government—Utopias   27
    2.1. History of Human Cultures   29
        2.1.1. Copying & Animal Culture
        2.1.2. Imitation & Human Culture   30
        2.1.3. Effectiveness of Culture   39
        2.1.4. Diversity & Universals of Culture   41
        2.1.5. Cultural Transformations   42
        2.1.6. Is There a Global Culture?   43
    2.2. Designing Ideal Cultures (Utopias)   46
        2.2.1. Images Cast Shadows   48
        2.2.2. One World Through Reason (Formation of United Nations)   50
        2.2.3. Ending Up Nowhere (Competition & Conflict)   52
            2.2.3.1. Trapped in Images   53
            2.2.3.2. Committed to War   54
            2.2.3.3. Fear of Peace   56
    2.3. The Potential of Good (Eutopias)   58

3.0. Recognizing Challenges & Problems for Government   61
    3.1. Environmental Challenges
        3.1.1. Ecosystem Properties   61
        3.1.2. Ecosystem Change   65
        3.1.3. Ecosystem Problems: Drought   67
    3.2. The Challenge of Population   68
        3.2.1. Population Growth
        3.2.2. Population Size   69
        3.2.3. Cultural Status   70
        3.2.4. Equity & Distribution   71
    3.3. The Problem of Cultural Dominance   72
        3.3.1. The Use of Slavery   72
        3.3.2. Colonialization   74
        3.3.3. Humanity as Pandominant Agent   76
    3.4. Challenges & Traps   77
    3.5. Problems: Conflict & Collapse   78
        3.5.1. Intensification & Civilization   81
        3.5.2. Patterns & Renewal   82
    3.6. Habit & Hope   83
        3.6.1. Hope & Science   84
        3.6.2. Implications of Good & Evil   84
    3.7. The Possibility of Good   85
        3.7.1. The Necessity of Evil
        3.7.2. Intention & Evil   87

4.0. Reviewing Cultural Adaptations to Challenges & Problems   89
    4.1. Agriculture Cities & Civilizations
        4.1.1. Adopting an Agricultural Style   91
        4.1.2. Concentrating in Cities   93
        4.1.3. The Complex of Civilization   99
    4.2. Using the Environment: Economics   101
        4.2.1. Traditional Economics
        4.2.2. Modern Economics   104
        4.2.3. Holeconomics   106
    4.3. Playing with Possibilities: Politics of Cities & Nations   109
        4.3.1. Forms of Leading & Governing   110
        4.3.2. Functions & Branches of Government   120
        4.3.3. Functions of Politics   122
    4.4. Expanding Ethics to Encompass the Global   130

5.0. Creating Ecological Patterns for Developing Global Government   132
    5.1. Creating a Good Society   132
        5.1.1. Properties of a Good Society (Method to Harmony)   133
        5.1.2. Thoughts on Social Design
    5.2. Making Good Places in Ecosystems   136
        5.2.1. Properties of Good Places
        5.2.2. Dynamics of Good Places   139
    5.3. Expanding Possibilities with Ecological Politics   139
        5.3.1. Deciding on the Goals   139
        5.3.2. Applying Ecological Planning & Limits   144
        5.3.3. Controlling Political Issues & Areas of Concern   146
        5.3.4. Rights Justice & Law as Political issues   149
        5.3.5. Moderating Cultural Interactions   150

6.0. Describing a Thought Experiment in Government (Eutopian Framework)   152
    6.1. Describing a Eutopian Framework for Government   155
        6.1.1. Properties of Eutopian Framework   155
        6.1.2. Describing the Dynamic Structure of Eutopian Go   158
    6.2. Participating in Government   159
        6.2.1. Participating as Individuals   159
        6.2.2. Participating in Communities & Nations   159
        6.2.3. Participating in Global Government   159
            6.2.3.1. Necessity of Framework (United Nations Currently)   160
            6.2.3.2. Responsibilities of a Framework   175
        6.2.4. Needs for Real Global Government   175
            6.2.4.1. Potential Strengths   175
            6.2.4.2. Possible Weaknesses   177
            6.2.4.3. Responsibilities of Global Government   178

7.0. Getting to Global Government of Commonwealths   189
    7.1. Finding Workable Divisions & Sizes   189
        7.1.1. The Stage of Nations   189
        7.1.2. Limits of Nations   190
        7.1.3. Discord Conflicts & Nations   190
        7.1.4. Nations & Disarmament   191
        7.1.5. Decline & Breakup of Large Artificial Nations   192
    7.2. Transitioning to Global & Local Politics   193

    7.2.1. Adopting a Psychology of Catastrophe 193
    7.2.2. Taking Immediate Actions 197
  7.3. Taking Coordinated Actions 198
    7.3.1. Acting as an Individual in Community 198
    7.3.2. Contributing at a National Level 199
    7.3.3. International Level Actions 200
      7.3.3.1. Implementing Immediate Steps 202
        7.3.3.1.1. Creating the Union Framework 202
        7.3.3.1.2. Starting Catastrophic Measures 204
        7.3.3.1.3. Starting a year of Consideration 206
        7.3.3.1.5. Pressing Equity Measures & Goals 207
      7.3.3.2. Managing Nations 208
        7.3.3.2.1. Creating a Charter & Constitution
        7.3.3.2.2. Creating New Structures
  7.4. Managing Itself as Global Government 209
    7.4.1. Collecting Revenue or Income 211
    7.4.2. Issuing Expenditures or Payout 225
  7.5. Expanding Global Responsibilities 227
    7.5.1. Executive Branch 227
    7.5.2. Special Offices & Agencies 231
    7.5.3. Judicial Branch & International Courts 237
    7.5.4. Commission on Earth 239
    7.5.5. Commission on Cultures & Religions 243

8.0. Creating & Maintaining Global Government 245
  8.1. Dance of Art Money and Ethics: Advertising Good 246
    8.1.1. Monetary Lies 248
    8.1.2. Ecological Persuasion 248
  8.2. Creating & Maintaining Global Government 250
    8.2.1. What a Global Government Can Do 251
    8.2.2. Moving Forward Backward Outward & Inward Wisely 261

9.0. Appendix 264
  9.1. Ecodex: Properties Principles Standards & Practices 265
  9.2. Endnotes 270
  9.3. Bibliography 273
  9.4. Biography & Author's Note 290
  9.5. Index 291

Dedications

My continued gratitude to colleagues Michael Barnes, George Carroll, Christyann Helm, Amy Ihrke, Twila Jacobsen, Neil Keefe, Nadya Kristoforova, Devorah Levy, Boyd Martin, Linda Martin-Schapf, William Odum, Nela Rachevitz, Karen Walter, Janet Wampler, and Precious Woulfe for their unselfish criticism, suggestions, support, or assistance. To my colleagues at International College, Los Angeles: Michael W. Fox, John B. Cobb, Jr., Paolo Soleri, Neil Evernden, David Klein, Paul Shepard, Buckminster Fuller, and Henryk Skolimowski. Finally, if I had not been trapped in a mountain snowstorm for a month at the observatory on Mt. Lemon, Arizona in early 1973, I might not have read books by Theodore Roszak, Ivan Illich, and Leopold Kohr, and become inspired and more determined to continue exploring these topics.

Author's Notes

The form of this work reflects an effort to describe the ideas and creation of good places under a good government. It is not a linear path leading to a definite conclusion. It is a dialectical spiral, which gathers facts and ideas and reforms them in wider contexts, then tries to use repetition and charm to lead readers to agreement. But, it also requires more effort from you, the reader. The work presents its subjects in a loose form. If the metaphors and ideas stretch too far to hold, perhaps they are, as Ludwig Wittgenstein wrote of his own propositions, all nonsense, to be read and left behind.

To repay some of the costs of putting these adventures in ideas (the term was used nicely by A. N. Whitehead) into print on paper, I have replanted tens of thousands of trees to contribute to forest restorations in Idaho, Washington and Oregon starting in the 1970s. The next plantings in 2012 will be at River Forest on the north branch of the Shenandoah River in Virginia. Now that I am no longer paid by the plug or by the hour, the work is much more fun and involves more picnics and naps (and praise to Artemis). I name the trees now and watch them more closely as they grow and mature.

1.0. International Governance

Humanity has not ever assembled, or been dominated by, a global governing body. Several attempts have been made to include all or most nations in a body to discuss world peace, most recently in the United Nations (UN). The UN, however, despite its good objectives and attempts to broker peace, has been hampered by the limits imposed by jealously sovereign nations.

The accidental ascension of global capitalism, as a basis for global politics, is unsustainable. Under its current rules, global trade is unsustainable; at its core is the unrealistic requirement for growth. The inequities and breakdowns of capitalism are already part of the problem. Global integration crudely repudiates the role of labor in capital, leaving it out of 'free trade,' unless it offers some violence through protest marches or strikes. Ecological capital in ecosystems gets left out, unless it becomes the lowest common denominator. Community capital erodes when costs are ignored or eliminated. Human economic activity compresses its time frame below that of biological adaptation or evolution, even below that of most cultural change. The activity and comprehension of the market is not good at the global scale because it does not inventory or monitor resources at the global scale, especially those in a commons. No framework exists internationally to moderate absolute advantages from trade. There are no international community ethics or rules, or laws or customs.

Many people are warning of imminent doom, and they are surely correct. Others are praising a glowing future, and they are certainly right. But, either way, we have to create those circumstances through our intentions and actions. We need a lot of information and the wisdom to apply it to our actions. There are so many streams of information, so many different forces. There will be too much information and force, and too many options. We will have many choices, some easy, others less easy. Civilization has become complex and global, so its continuity requires us to work together on global problems and even on local problems. More people will be happier if we can work on a common future that they participate in and help shape. We need to be determined to start acting.

Our challenge is to deconstruct economics and large-scale politics, then to reconstruct the ecological and basic human communities to fit the limits of productivity, resources and growth. Our challenge is to reshape governing rules and institutions of globalization, to reshape sustainable adaptations such as agriculture and industry, to recognize ecological and social values, and to create ecological designs based on them, designs of technologies, cities, and industries, as well as ways of living and conserving. Design diverts some flows of energy and matter for human use, but it has to mesh with the limits and processes of the whole system; it has to be based on natural principles of organization, especially those derived from physics, chemistry, biology, ecology, psychology, and sociology.

We need to create a global government that can recognize and emphasize the shared interests of all living communities. The community has to set the goals and limits first, before the economy can design a path to get there and before politics can propose how things are shared. Then, a global government can coordinate the global inputs and outputs of the communities. First, however, it has to identify all of the stakeholders in the global government.

1.1. Who Needs Governing?

The United Nations coordinates some help for nations, but it does not govern them. Perhaps nations are not the only level that needs to be governed. Who should be governed? Human beings in small groups often relate well in a genetically-related group or in a creative anarchy. But, larger groups of people tend to drift into hierarchical patterns. Larger groups tend to follow leaders. At the global level, on a complex and limited planet, people need to have more specific structures and rules. National balances have not proved to be useful or effective. A league of national voices has not been able to provide harmony for humanity or the wild planet—partly because so many other voices have no representation in a human system. A global governing body would need to be independent of nations of economic interests. Therefore, it would need an economic base, with political and military power for enforcement if necessary. It should also be located in neutral territory, such as a specially-built arcology in Antarctica.

A truly global system would address the problem of membership by allowing representation for every placeholder or stakeholder in one governing system and then by providing different levels of influence or control. For instance, every community, starting with ecological communities and extending to every kind of human community, would be represented: Habitats, landscapes, and bioregions; human cultures, ethnic nations, voluntary federations, political or economic empires; cities, urban states, unions; incorporations, whether financial, conservative or nongovernmental; and groups, such as religions or totems.

And each of these kinds of membership would have different authorities, powers and responsibilities. Some, such as defined ecological communities, nations, or cities, would have voting status. Others, such as large confederations or nonprofit incorporations would be contributing members. And, still others, such as unions, business corporations, or totems, would have status as advisors. There might be some overlap, or there might not. Table 11-1 offers one possible configuration of memberships.

Table 11-1. Possible Kinds and Levels of Membership

Automatic (voting):	Communities: Ecological Communities, Human Cultures. This would include all landless cultures or some of those now subsumed by nations.
Contributing:	Large confederations, such as nations, cities, or special interest communities, such as Unions or Conservation organizations
Advising:	Totems, financial power interests, such as corporations. Other forms of incorporations and NGOs

But all levels could not vote due to overlap, so they might be like registered, limited lobbyists. Some cultures might prefer to be represented in a nation, but all would have equal votes, so a nation might not have any advantage. Voting memberships would be most powerful, but there would be other levels of membership that would contribute or advise.

To enforce or persuade nations to peace, a global governing body needs to have a larger fighting force than the largest single nation. To secure its own independence and income, such a body needs to be able to control all global commons.

The immediate possibility of such a body tends to be indicated by historical gigatrends. And, certainly, we can describe it in some detail as a thought experiment.

1.2. Tools for Understanding: Gigatrends

Human groups create organizations based in natural ecological systems. They expand or simplify the systems for their own benefit. The unconsidered use of ecosystems results in still more long-term trends:
- Human interactions are becoming more global. We dominate many ecosystems; even our pollution influences virtually all systems now.
- Humans are taking over the productivity of nature. Mathis Wackernagel estimates all human demands on the environment surpassed the planet's regenerative capacity in 1980. By 1999, it surpassed it by twenty percent. What happens if we extrapolate this to 100 or 200 percent?

These trends contribute to a shifting planetary system that has less flexibility. Some of these negative gigatrends are hard to see, much less stop or reverse, because they are based on misunderstandings, fallacies, discredited myths, and psychological blinders.

These trends are partly the result of our unconsciousness of large-scale, long-term events, partly the result of our cultural amnesia about things that make us unhappy, and partly the result of our cultivated indifference—doubtless from our remoteness from wild nature, remoteness as a result of our tools and the general abstraction of civilization. Many of these trends have to do with war and conflicts.
- Trends in war from amateurs to specialists, from special days to every day, even holy days, from soldiers to noncombatants, from fields of killing to any fields and any places, from destruction of soldiers to destruction of civilians, fields and ecosystems.
- Disarmament of civilian populations. In England recently (1995), murder rates were only a tenth what they were 800 years ago and half what they were 300 years ago. The disarmament took place in many small steps from seizures to licensing, production controls, and fewer public exhibitions.
- Stress between countries polarized by wealth.
- Overmilitarization by wealthy countries. Overmilitarization by poor countries.
- The transition of states, from surplus distributors, to tribute-driven, and then to commercial exchanges.
- The political transitions from leaders, to chiefs, to tribute systems, to economic and political trade systems.
- The reach of the state into individual lives. From tribute to lack of arms, ownership, and licensing, to information gathering.
- Trust and social cohesion decline.
- Crime rate, disorder, inequity, poverty and development of an underclass, and consumption.

Some of these trends have been reversed for short periods of time, in various places by different cultures, but the overall trend has been negative.

1.2.1. Growth & Bigness

Early in our history, when the very success of the species was in question, we humans learned to reproduce more rapidly than our rates of mortality. To extend our families, we have increased our numbers and our rate of increase exponentially. To ensure the success of our species, we have appropriated the places of other species. Our overpopulation has led to aggression against other cultures and species, then to indifference at their suffering. Even low levels of food and fulfillment at our current size can be maintained only through theft from other species and from future human generations, and through the degradation of billions of humans as well as the ecosystems on which they depend.

To provide for the needs of many and for the extravagant luxuries of some, we have produced waste and pollution on a geological scale, from islands of garbage to skies of acid rain. Manufacturing processes result in the production of new dangers, such as recombined genes, and new substances, which are not easily incorporated into natural cycles. The overuse of ecosystems results in deforestation, devegetation, and desertification, then in depletion of raw materials and depletion of agricultural land. Economic and political pressures, derived ultimately from population pressures, force farmers to intensify their efforts to increase crop production, instigating a dismal cycle of population expansion, environmental deterioration, and poverty.

To provide for our needs efficiently, we have increased the scale of our activities. But we have decreased the diversity of habitats by filling in wetlands, felling forests, plowing grasslands, and irrigating deserts. Agribusiness has caused widespread landlessness; people who try to grow their own food are forced onto marginal lands or off the land. Acquiring fossil fuels also creates landlessness; coal mining in the Black Mesa mountains of the United States, for instance, may force the resettlement of twenty thousand Hopi and Navajo people. Without land, and the economic independence it allows, cultures are more likely to disintegrate.

Our local communities are proud to attract more people and larger industries, but do so thoughtlessly, without regard for the limits of population size or the rate of energy use, without sufficient consideration of the effects on the quality of our lives or on the quality of the environment. Although we make plans for people and their activities, the plans are usually reactions to growth and change. The formal development from planning results in a complex of problems, from pollution to ugliness.

Our societies are big. Our corporations are big. Our impacts are big. This creates discontent because people feel powerless. They feel powerless because they feel that democracy is not working. The country is run by the rich—rich corporations, rich people, rich politicians—and they secure their needs for more money first. In fact the decline in earnings, relative to costs of goods, forces people to struggle with jobs and increased conflict everywhere. Now, at the perceived "end of history" and the "victory of democracy," it is difficult to imagine a better future, at least without questioning the rich, the ideals of democracy, and the corporate good will to society.

We have economic growth; we can see the numbers. But, the growth is premised on saving costs by forcing down wages, or by reducing the number of workers in the name of efficiency, and forcing overqualified workers into service jobs. The growth promotes inequality, improvement for a few and impoverishment for most. It is the growth of a tumor, issuing a healthy glow from a fever and the false image of health. Profits go up, but public services decline for lack of funds. There is no money for schools, none for libraries or parks, little for private institutions, and little for national, state or local governments. Where did it go? Profits? Profits for individual corporations, profits for individuals? Could we find them, can we track the money? We should be able to, since the management revolution has made paper trails everywhere. Perhaps the trails are too complex.

Bigness overwhelms the ideals of cultures, which is why large nations such as China or the United States cut their forests, regardless of respectful religions or special cultural values regarding nature, regardless of the desires of local communities. The nations are willing to sell the wealth of the provinces, even though the provinces want to conserve them.

Something is wrong. But who is to blame? Where is the target? People rail against liberals or conservatives, against corporations or protesters, against big government, or big corporations, big permissiveness, big violence, the lack of faith or lack of prayer, the failure of responsibility or the failure of nerve, against guns, leniency, illegitimacy, bad rock, bad lyrics, bad welfare, bad politicians, bad people, and bad police. But, the real enemy is unseen. Who can argue against democracy or corporate wealth or the general vague feeling that things have improved? Against a reasonable system? Against the bigness of the system?

The course is downward. How can it be turned? How can we diagnose the problems? How can we suggest a path to health? Charles Reich says that we need a science of social change. Ecology is science-based. Conservation is science-based. Even management is science-based. Now economics and politics needs to be science-based, instead of dominated by an old ideology and weak mythology. Reich suggests that between citizens and government is a third entity, economic government, to which has been ceded power to determine the direction and type of economy. The only knowledge we get is knowledge from the economic government, and the numbers look good. We have no other knowledge, except for a weak self-knowledge and vague social knowledge, which tells us something is wrong.

Leopold Kohr identifies the basic conflict between man and mass, citizen and state, large and small communities, as a result of bigness. Kohr's theory of size states that the cause of most forms of social misery is bigness. We have always tried to exceed the physical and biological limits of places rather than recognize them and be guided by them. Every advanced country is now over-technologized. Past a certain point the quality of life diminishes, not improves, with each advance. Big science serves big technology, which supports and is supported by big government. And there is no science like big science, and no administration like big administration. But this enthusiasm is misdirected. Scientific advances and technological changes result in unforeseen consequences, good or bad. They cannot be controlled or legislated against before the fact. But the investment seems too big to abandon.

The planet, including human society, is threatened by the bigness of things. Although nature is big, it has evolved slowly; human size is new and sudden. A snail's pace is good enough for nature most of the time, but with our brief life span, we argue that we need quick changes. The technological advances have not been paid for yet, although the cost in pain and death is incalculable. We will be paying for hundreds of years for those past advances. The economic style is too great, and reckless for ecological systems to absorb its impacts. The scale of things is an independent problem, which can ruin the best intentions of policy. A bigger system to control systems that are now too big might be a mistake.

But some solutions are even bigger. Buckminster Fuller, Alvin Toffler, and the Club of Rome favor a supertechnocracy. Science fiction visions predominate: Gerard O'Neill's orbiting cylinders or Simon Calder's floating domes. R.A. Smith, in "Unibutz," claims that we could achieve a pantheistic-humanistic-cosmic awareness, in achieving technology without materialism, plenty without selfishness, and community without tribalism. His Unibutz is a global goal for leaving the earth and reaching the stars. The voyage would help shape new world structures and give a purpose to humanity. But to what end? Bigness and wealth elsewhere?

Perhaps big science and big technology have too much momentum. Theodore Roszak acknowledges its schizoid attraction and repulsion, with the twin promises of glorious accomplishment and hideous death. Who could escape being torn between yes and no, if even our end would shine with radioactive, Promethean grandeur? Our image of big science—the scientist as tragic hero, isolated in chaotic nature, but strong in his proud individuality, perhaps driven to research by hubris and madness—is a barrier to any new vision, especially a small vision.

1.2.2. Speed & Momentum

The speed of our economies might not be optimal, either. Alvin Toffler has described the fast economies that are forming and concludes that slow economies will have to speed up their responses or risk becoming uncoupled from the fast lane. Yet, it might be good for countries to be uncoupled. Uncoupling economically might be a sound option for traditional societies unwilling to make the same mistakes as industrial ones. Local communities are based on traditional cultures, which have long-term lasting power. Traditional cultures often have wealth-leveling properties, absolute property ceilings, fixed wants, and production coupled with need—all of which results in a stable economy. Then, efficiency and productivity are less important than use and appropriateness.

Furthermore, Toffler says that the nonindustrial countries are faced with a shortage of economically relevant knowledge. Are they? What kind? The knowledge of how to find or grow edible and medicinal plants? The knowledge of how to make appropriate houses and cooking utensils? Toffler touts knowledge-based agriculture as a cutting edge of economic advance; how knowledgeable can it be, if it ignores the erosion of soil and the destruction of beneficial insects? Traditional communities have lost more knowledge than we will have in the near future. What happened to our rich biological knowledge of animals and plants, to our rich mythical knowledge of them?

The path to economic power is through the application of the human mind, according to Toffler, and he urges that "revolutionary" forms of education are necessary. What is more revolutionary than traditional education? Learning about plants, animals, families, and cultures is more relevant than theoretical knowledge; computers and economics can be learned after adolescence. We have more than enough information and secondary knowledge.

Economic success is secondary, as is money, the accumulation of goods, and prestige. We are accomplished in the secondary meanings of life. The satisfactions from being in a culture in place, from planting trees, growing apples, watching birds, playing with children, and making love are primary meanings. And, they are not speed-dependent. Some things have proper speeds. Music is not made more efficient or better by increasing the revolutions of a disk. Food or relaxation requires a human speed. We lack the wisdom to act as if we believed this. Is fast technology a necessary part of happiness? Those who are uncomfortable with primary meanings tend to become addicted to power, speed, and possession, as a frantic way to avoid awareness, silence, or responsibility, as a replacement for being grounded in nature.

Nature provides the source, of wonder, of the sacred, of otherness, and of the wild. By submitting ourselves to positive accelerating feedback loops in economics, we distance ourselves from such primary meanings. Nature possesses power that is not speed dependent. Human consciousness has already had a "revolution"—from the wild to the tame—and many of us regret it; a further revolution to remote secondary meanings sounds more depressing. Animals used to be directly experienced; now, they are humanized and domesticated. Humanizing the world has made it tedious, uniform, and dull. Economics is dull! Toffler's assumptions are dull! The needs he describes are transitive wants, and their only measurement is quantitative. For fertile nature, we have substituted a sterile model of production and economy. The model is reductive: Trees become resources, and people become labor. More is more, faster is better. Although speed is our normal response to dullness, the celebration of speed for itself is ultimately unsatisfying.

What is the result of our fascination with speed in everything? Dismissing nature in disgust, we attempt transcendence through speed. We speed away from nature, from our own bodies, and base our civilization on that momentum, praying, requiring, that it never stops. People's souls die, but secure in their power, they manage the things of civilization and inhabit the treeless flatscapes of the malls of commerce, comforted by the banishment of wilderness and the capture of animals in zoos and of free people in reservations, satisfied that their young are mercilessly tied to televisions and computers, acquiring information without touch and speed without grace.

Nations and communities do not all have to follow the same path and the same rules at the same time and at the same rate. Cultural success is not the "survival of the fastest" any more than it is of the biggest or shallowest or newest. Perhaps if we remain unconscious, there will be a power shift to the fastest that will homogenize and level all human cultures. But, we can consciously imagine alternatives and work to preserve cultural and natural diversity and the richness of existence.

We have the knowledge to save cultures, to restore places, to participate in the cycles of the earth, but extra speed and power are not required. The pace of nature is generally balanced and well established; we violate it at our risk. If we adjust to the pace of the growth of trees and to the movements of animals, we would not be risking catastrophic extinctions and famines, shortages of water and fuel wood, and the death of humaneness.

We do not need to give our power to faster economies. We need to shift power to local communities through self-reliance and participation. A community protects individual freedoms, guards regional culture (values and identity), and holds groups accountable for their use of power. In communities, people can decide to be conservatively sustainable or to grow and gamble on innovation. Communities can have different economic attitudes, paces, and goals. A community that is balanced and flexible, in tune with natural cycles, based on traditional values—in which industrial production is limited to appropriate goods—can absorb the shocks of change far better than an immensely big, powerful, accelerating, postindustrial, momentous, national vehicle.

Others have recognized the momentum of short-term self-interest, self-deception, perceptual limits, overconsumption, polarization, and destabilization. Perhaps big science and big technology have too much momentum. Theodore Roszak acknowledges its schizoid attraction and repulsion, with the twin promises of glorious accomplishment and hideous death. Who could escape being torn between yes and no, if even our end would shine with radioactive, Promethean grandeur? Our image of big science—the scientist as tragic hero, isolated in chaotic nature, but strong in his proud individuality, perhaps driven to research by hubris and madness—is a barrier to any new vision, especially a small vision.

Maybe the failure of our modern civilization is a failure of imagination compounded with a failure of nerve. We cannot imagine an alternative to war, and we cannot act beyond immediate emotion. We cannot imagine beauty in the old and messy nature, and we are afraid to try to do without luxuries or to sacrifice anything to try to change the momentum of industrial civilization.

Scenarios have to consider all the factors determining the future, including change (the speed and rate of change), the momentum of the present (masses of people, habits and investments), and conscious adjustments to environment and society. Scenarios have to recognize the complexity of civilization and technology, as well as the increasing costs of the maintenance of the complexity. Scenarios have to address risks from external environments well as from technological change. They have to anticipate surprises from trends and catastrophes. These factors can be ameliorated by design. Some can be avoided by design.

1.2.3. *Positive trends*
None of these negative gigatrends can be really reversed until human neutrality and remoteness is reeducated into participation and attentiveness. There are already a few trends flowing against the tide. Some positive gigatrends include:
- Adaptation of human cultures and ecosystems over time in Asia, Europe, and parts of Africa, resulting in stable domesticated landscapes.
- Setting aside of areas, such as preservation of ecosystem processes, reservation of archaic cultures, and conservation lands, from industrial interference.
- An increase in the scope of ethics, from family, tribe, nation, humanity, to include reverence for all living beings, first identified recently by Albert Schweitzer.
- An increase in the scope of ethics to include land and forests, identified by Aldo Leopold, and later by Ernst Laszlo to include all systems.
- An increase in the scope of law to include legal rights for ecosystems, such as forests, identified

by Christopher Stone.
- Restoration of forests from abandoned fields, anthropogenic deserts, and ruined ecosystems.
- Practice of comprehensive approaches, such as ecological forestry and permaculture.
- The number of people investing in small businesses in forest products, businesses that are labor-intensive and practice rather than profit-oriented.

Combined with other new trends in housing—such as arcologies (Paolo Soleri) and bioshelters (John and Nancy Todd), and agriculture—agroforestry, permaculture (Bill Mollison), and tree crops (Russell Smith), these trends counter many of the negative ones.

The intent of describing large-scale trends or patterns is to have human patterns fit with observed patterns in nature; patterns have a form, sometimes repetition, and sometimes regularity, but each of these is caused by some limiting factor. Fitting the pattern can lead to both continuity and predictability, and both of these are needed to adapt human activities to natural limits.

Thinking we have conquered nature and are omnipotent, we have quit thinking. Satisfied with our comforts, we do not ask enough of ourselves. With these gigatrends possibly ending in tragedy for humanity, we must continue to ask questions. What kind of planet do we want? Wild or domestic? Managed or unmanaged? How shall we use the resources of nature? For products? To protect watersheds and maintain global biogeochemical processes? As a home for other beings? For recreation? As some kind of balance? How many different places, different ecosystems, or other cultures, do we need? What kinds, in what forms? How many should be wild? These questions lead to new strategies for living with the forests and wild ecosystems, strategies that we can test with thought experiments.

1.3. *Examining Possibilities of Governance with Thought Experiments*

Humanity is already engaged in a great experiment with the planet. We are replacing large, old, complex ecosystems with young, simple fragments, in which fires are suppressed, large predators are removed, large herbivore populations are encouraged, exotic species are introduced, soil is compacted, and excessive biomass is removed—all for the purposes of increasing the amount that can be harvested for human use. Our actions are experiments, whether we want them to be or not. Unfortunately the experiment is not only bad science—there is no control planet—it is ill considered. This experimental course, which may be global and irreversible, cannot be unmade, not by planning or science, much less by our standard methods of ignorance, cupidity, or denial.

There must be a way to refine the experiments, to minimize our impacts, to be less reckless, and to anticipate the outcome of our experiments before we finish performing them. Not all experiments must be physically implemented. Albert Einstein and Leopold Infield suggest that knowledge of laws can be gained through the contemplation of idealized experiments created by thought, Gedanke-Experiment. For example, to address the equality of inertial and gravitational masses, that is, how the problem of general relativity is connected with gravitation, Einstein imagined an elevator at the top of an incredibly high building, and then imagined what research could be done in this local environment. Such experiments might seem "fantastic" in his words, but they might help us understand the universe.

Although ecosystems and political orders are orders of magnitude more complex than physical systems, perhaps we could imagine and use such experiments to help us understand what is happening with our complex planet that is composed of many interlocking ecological systems. One of the more comprehensive thought experiments conducted is "Daisy World" by James Lovelock, to show how the evolution of species would lead to the self-regulation of climate on an earth-like world. Freeman Dyson offers another example of a thought experiment from Isaac Asimov: Saturn's satellite Enceladus could be used to provide water and warmth to Mars; a rocket could be sent to the satellite, carrying self-reproducing automatons, which could make miniature solar sailboats to carry small blocks of ice from it— there would be enough ice to keep the Martian climate warm and wet for about 10,000 years.

Thought experiments can give us clues about what can happen and what is the likelihood of that happening. "And then what?" asks Garrett Hardin again. Unlike medical doctors or scientists, we cannot either wait or directly experiment within a realistic time frame or scale. We cannot experiment at all in a traditional sense, where we hold most variables fixed, while changing one or two variables in experimental runs. Ecosystems operate over very long time spans; furthermore, their historical nature means that they cannot be restarted for tests.

Large-scale, long-term experiments are expensive and relatively few. Most experiments are short-range, small-scale, isolated, and detail dense. Most experiments do not present the hypotheses required for the management of ecosystems. Ecosystem management, because of uncertainties, lack of controls, age, and uniqueness, is an uncontrolled, large-scale experiment. Thought experiments can refine the design of our larger experiments by suggesting better hypotheses and behaviors.

Thought experiments can help us avoid being overwhelmed by details. Thought experiments can help formulate goals and interpret information appropriate to scale. The idea of science is to manage our experiences with generalities. Once the thought experiments are started they can be refined with conceptual or mathematical models, which can simulate the changes and historical development of changes. Computer-based models can permit complex explorations, as well as suggest new patterns and further hypotheses. Through thought experiments, many of the dangers and expenses of our activities can be avoided.

Thought experiments are vital to understanding the complexity of ecosystems. In practice, erring on the side of preservation—the prudent and conservative course—means minimizing the influence of human activities on the land. It means experimenting cautiously with new approaches to ecosystem management and being properly skeptical about any claims for sustainability. It means drastically reducing our demand for natural products, through conservation, reuse, recycling, and human population control, so that the greatest possible numbers of ecosystems are left wild and degraded lands can restore themselves.

Thought experiments can also be used to examine possible scenarios of the future based on our actions. For example, if we continue the current trend of inequity, how might things play out? For example if the rich keep getting richer, how will they have to protect their wealth from the poor? Will laws be enough? Will they need ever-larger armies of security personnel? With already four times the number of civic police, will they need even more? Will corporate police protect the wealth of their stockholders after the civic police give up? Will the poor collapse leaving rich enclaves that have to grow their own food? At what point will the gap be wide enough that the poor have to harvest the wealth of the rich by force? At what number of poor? Will the poor prey on each other first? At what point will the environment be used entirely for a few more years of life for rich or poor humans? At what point might the environment collapse?

Will regional groups, such as the northern hemisphere, form alliances to keep going, after writing off other regions or the southern hemisphere? Will this block be able to defend its resources? Will that extend the time of any collapse? Or accelerate it?

Will the United Nations be able to coordinate some kind of peaceful reorganization? Can a revitalized UN guarantee a rational economic and political strategy for all nations? Should this UN be dominated by a China or a United States, so that it may operate without as much discussion? Is it utopian to think of such reorganization or redistribution for equity? Is this less naïve than allowing the market to sort out entire cultures and regions and consign them to poverty and violence?

The thought experiment presented in this book is incomplete, but suggestive of the kinds that we could be creating and manipulating to guide our plans and models.

A thought experiment can be considered as a personal communication: Intention to intention, or as a simple correspondence. Communication is presentation of one's self, of one's life, that may evoke correspondence in others (similar to entrainment). The activities of two communicators combine to make the universe of the observer more ordered and redundant. The nature of meaning depends on the frame of the observer. Communication is a presentation of one's self to another, through a conversation, in a back and forth process. The word conversation is derived from the French word meaning 'to live with,' from the Latin, meaning 'to turn with.' Since all things are in some sense subjective and unique, the term conversation is appropriate. Conversation creates a domain, which is the appropriate frame of reference. The domain is the environment of a conversation. The conversation is a minimal situation for observing the psychological events of which the participants are conscious. Understanding between participants is pivotal. The conversation is relativistic and reflexive.

The biologist Francisco Varela uses conversation as a paradigm for interactions among autonomous systems. Conversation is direct. Each side has a perspective, the heart of the process. When conversation is considered as a totality, there is no distinction about what is contributed by whom. The process is a coherent event shared by the participants, not a simple information exchange.

1.4. *Other Tools for Addressing Governance*

There are many other tools that can be used to address governing, from Analysis and synthesis to questioning.

1.4.1. *Systems Analysis*

To understand the workings of complex ecological or cultural systems, one could use systems thinking, with its concepts of feedback and emergence. Complex adaptive systems display emergent behavior. As an example of emergence, slime molds can form a community without a pacemaker cell that determines when the cells need to combine. It seems that self-organization is bottoms-up. Emergent systems are rule-governed, though; slime molds explore by adhering to low level rules. Individuals coordinate work, even if they cannot assess the global situation. Emergent systems are local; individual molds "think" locally and act locally. Random action serves to explore local space. Individuals pay attention to their neighbors, and patterns emerge from local activity. Simple behavior seems to work, with local feedback, and more sophisticated behavior "trickles up" to approximate a global perception.

A system is a way to explain part of the universe and to deal with complex behavior. Mario Bunge defines a system as a complex object, every part of which is connected with other parts of the object in such a way that the whole possesses emergent properties that the parts lack. A concrete system is composed of concrete things linked together by real physical, chemical, biological ties. Cells, wolf packs, and nongovernmental organizations (NGOs) are concrete systems. Conceptual systems can be linked by logical relations.

Many concrete systems are open and self-regulated. Many are closed and artificial. Bunge makes a strict dichotomy between formal and concrete systems (conceptual-material). He denies the possibility of mixed systems, but allows real ones to transmit information. He says sets and relations are abstract objects, not identical to concrete objects like molecules. Yet, if the relations are real, are they not concrete in a way? Intrasystem bonds are stronger that intersystem bonds; if not, the system would fall apart.

Social systems have all sizes and degrees of complexity. Governments are more complex than families. Systems can also be constituents of systems, like United Nations (UN). Every concrete thing has properties. Some properties can be known easily; others can be revealed by research. A list of known properties describes the state of the system with finite quantities.

1.4.2. *Synthesis*

Analytic science has reached its limits. Data and information developed by hard studies have undercut the paradigms that guided their investigation. The compartmentalization of scientific fields has exposed the complex connections of the subjects. Science does not need to be based on logical positivism and reductionism, though these have allowed great, although insensitive, changes. A. N. Whitehead thought that what had been missing during the formation of science was a sense of relatedness. Early science saw the world as mechanism; modern biology is seeing it as resembling an organism. Organismic trends can be seen in sciences, from relativity to ecology.

Ecology deals with the relationships of organisms to environments. It is not a reductive discipline, and not readily amenable to quantification. Even scientific ecology is an integrative discipline that extends beyond the bounds of science. In a way, ecology is an amphibious discipline, with the authority of science and the force of moral knowledge. Ecology, studied through its components and relations, is a perspective, a way of "seeing," according to Paul Shepard. It is a perspective of the human situation in its interconnection. For Paul Sears, ecology is a "subversive subject." Ecology is nonreductive, integrative, and amphibious, having the authority of science and the force of morals. It is normative and sensible. Ecology also offers a "sacramental vision" of nature. Ecology is radical— from the Latin word meaning "rooted"—and forms part of a new metaphor that is more appropriate to the unity and interrelatedness of the earth. Ecology is part of a movement of consciousness, concerned with equality, diversity, health, with humane methods, and with a holopoetic cosmology, and ecology affects them simultaneously. Radical ecology offers a new perspective of humanity in the total field of nature and defines balanced relationships with ultrahuman beings and species. Radical ecology addresses the determination of separate wilderness areas necessary for a healthy ecosphere, and an optimum human population, based on net ecosystem productivities and modified by appropriate technologies within ecological and cultural restraints. It urges local, self-reliant cultures with adaptive cosmologies and natural values in wild ecosystems.

An ecosystem is a complex system that interacts with four large global fields— atmosphere, lithosphere, hydrosphere, and biosphere—and their cycles. The properties and behavior of a complex system are determined by its internal organization as well as its relations with environment. There are two fundamental modes of behavior: (1) Maintenance, based on negative feedback loops and characterized by stability, and (2) Change, based on positive feedback loops and characterized by growth or decline. The two modes can create a typical series of behavioral patterns, from stagnation to rhythmic regulation.

Any large system, such as ecosystem or city, is a high-order, multiple-loop, nonlinear feedback system. In the system feedback loops are the basic structural elements. Each loop is a circular path of interaction between several elements. Ecological analysis forces us to look at the obvious— generating nonmarketable use values occupies the occupies the center of every culture because it provides a satisfactory life to its members.

1.4.3. Questioning Things

Questioning has a long history in human experience. The Greek philosopher Socrates was one of the more renowned questioners. He approached teaching through a disciplined, rigorous dialogue with people he met on the street, sometimes by accident or often by design. Socrates tried to get others to recognize the contradictions in their ideas; he assumed that incomplete or inaccurate ideas would be corrected during the process of questioning, and hence would lead to progressively greater truths. He never seemed to reach an end to questioning, however, perhaps because there was no end, that is, the process of questioning could refine any kind of knowledge or ignorance, indefinitely, or perhaps because by itself questioning could only do so much with definitions and concepts. His method was a common search, through conversation, for the goal of truth.

1.4.3.1. The Socratic Method

Socrates asked questions as part of a conversation with others. He seemed concerned with discovering what the opinions of others were based on, an invisible truth that could be made visible with questioning. The questioning forced the other participants in the conversation to try to agree on the truths beneath the opinions. Socrates professed ignorance of the truth himself, in fact or in pretense, ignorance being the first step in the pursuit of knowledge. He expressed skepticism that the other conversationalists actually had real knowledge. The process of questioning subjected opinions to real examples from real experiences—an empirical method—leading to a more general concept—this is the process of induction used in a scientific, homogenistic logic—and then the consequences of the definition were drawn out, through deduction. These definitions were refined by further questioning until all members of the conversation had a better grasp of the concepts. Through thorough questioning Socrates demonstrated that knowledge was quite often uncertain. There was no absolutely certain knowledge. Questions were also meant to examine life as well as belief and truth, and to show that often people were ignorant of their ignorance. Socrates held that disciplined questioning enabled the other to examine ideas logically and to be able to determine the validity of those ideas.

1.4.3.2. The Hardin Extension

For Socrates the goal of knowledge was the acquisition of concepts, such as justice, courage or wisdom. He thought that the truth could be contained in a correct definition. And, he was groping for more abstract definitions. This became a problem, as abstraction became removed from the specifics of living. Socrates was most concerned with examining concepts, but concepts are a small part of reality. Of course, constant questioning of concepts can expose the psychological basis of concepts, and perhaps that is what Socrates meant to do. But, questioning concepts often reaches limits fairly quickly. Socrates never offered any answers, although he assumed that an absolute certain knowledge was possible to become established eventually.

The ecologist Garrett Hardin used questioning to illuminate partial knowledge and to track connections between things. Questions establish the limits of assumptions and perspectives. They can clarify the focus of a problem and test evidence related to any problem. Questioning can be used as a device to focus on a specific problem, not only the extent of the problem, but its aspects. Questioning can also be used to explore specific aspects of the dimensions of thought. Of course, questions can refine the process of critical thinking and can allow refocusing in a wider or narrower context. This type of questioning arrives at answers as workable hypotheses or guidelines for making decisions about operating in the world. Without certain knowledge, however, we can make adaptive decisions, based on partial knowledge. His questioning took on the form of asking what happened then, after an answer was arrived at. "And then what?" Hardin asks. Questioning works in a conversational way by weaving ideas. Konrad Lorenz decided that humanity would indeed have destroyed itself by its first inventions, were it not for the very wonderful fact that inventions and responsibility are both the achievements of the same specifically human faculty of asking questions.

More than an annoying part of a conversation, questions are legitimate ways to approach a known or unknown situation. More than just a way to turn around a conversation, questions are tools that allow you to surround a topic and define it more completely. More than simply an admission of ignorance, questions can form a phenomenological spiral that allows you to return to a subject from different perspectives with different levels of understanding.

1.4.3.3. The Maslow Questioning of the Norms of a Global Government

Questioning can be applied to any human construct, including society and government. The psychologist Abraham Maslow suggested a series of normative questions to be asked before we can even consider designing a good society, much less a global government. His questions have been slightly modified before being answered and extended briefly and tentatively, although they will be revisited regularly.

First, is the norm to be universal, national, subcultural, familial, or individual? The norm could have universal elements, not only for humans but also for all species impacted by humans. Maslow assumes that different norms must be on different levels, depending on the context. For example, there would be some universal human behavioral standards, but special local expectations, to conform to various cultures. For a society and government to include all the beings and systems in the planet, some norms have to be universal

Should government be selective or unselective? Certainly, at the global level, it should be unselected. It must account for all human variability; and accept it when possible and treat it when necessary. It would have to account for prisoners and misfits. The society should be pluralistic, and accept and use individual differences in constitution and character. Humans are not interchangeable or disposable; the insane and aged must be considered. It must integrate all people into a society or work in that direction. Society also has to account for all other living beings that fir into local and global patterns, whether pets and body parasites or tropical fish and trees, which are all part of a dynamic global balance.

Should government be pro-something or anti-something else? Government could be pro-industrial and pro-scientific, for instance, within the set limits of the society and the planet—but, industry must be properly scaled; and science must be cautious. It could also be anti-waste or anti-growth. The size of community cultures could be limited by function.

Should it be centralized or decentralized? The global unit could be centralized, electronically, at least, and socially planned; but individual cultures could be autarchistic, based on self-reliance and interdependence. Both should be flexible. Regions could be centralized for some functions.

Should government be tolerant? Government must tolerate all cultures and nations. Each culture would determine styles and complexity for its individuals. It could aim for taoistic noninterference, but be available for help. Tolerance, however, might be limited by the health of the entire system, so that some traditions and practices might have to be adjusted or forbidden (e.g., genocide or biocide).

What should be done about injustices? Biological injustices exist and can be ameliorated. Historical imbalances, luck, surprise, and catastrophes are always part of chaotic natural systems, but their effects can be smoothed. Social injustices can be rectified, but the government would have to be willing to respond and to have an effective apparatus in place.

Should government determine family attitudes? Family or sexual attitudes have be institutionalized by most cultures. All group adaptations would be determined by culture. At the global level, government would be most concerned with reducing the negative interactions between cultures, which may require adjustments, compromises, and various degrees of isolation.

Should government be open to more than one religion? Government can tolerate any institutionalized religion, so long as it does not impinge on other groups. The spiritual life is a necessary part of a society.

How should leaders be chosen? Leaders within a culture could be chosen by traditional means, within the limits of local laws and customs, even if that included royalty, dictators or anarchy. Leaders of the international framework could be chosen by global referendum from the ranks of cultural or national leaders. The leaders would determine the rough outlines of the relationships of people to each other and nature

For what is an individual responsible? The individual is responsible for the style and simplicity of their life and for its effects on nature and society. The individual is responsible for being tolerant of others, and is free to make many kinds of choices.

How these questions, and many others, are answered partly determines the shape and extent of this project.

1.4.3.4. Questioning Ourselves
Things seem so confusing and contradictory, we have to keep asking questions about how things are done, for instance about old standards for the sizes of pipes or the lifetime of a tool. We have to question lifeboat politics, with its implications of gender, class and race values and inequities. What are the full effects of plastic wastes in the ocean or on ocean species? Behavior is determined by immediate personal consequences (short-term egoism), regardless of long-term consequences in modern and ecological systems. How stable is poverty in the midst of wealth? Why are we not trying radical designs like arcologies? Some of these questions can be answered by further questions. Will the technology harm the environment? Will the process waste energy? Does it use exotic, composite, dangerous materials? Does it really contribute to our welfare?

How can land and people be used well, or what is a good use? What is good knowledge of good work? How can one be honorably native to one place? When will we learn that neither art nor science that can be neutral? What are the risks of consuming now? Losing self-respect, seeing the collapse happen? There is an implicit larger question, once asked by Arne Naess: What is the role of humanity in the destiny of the planet? Then again, what are the risks of acting in unpopular ways? Being ignored? Losing status or being assassinated?

One serious question is what to do with those nonindustrial cultures that choose to continue to be nonindustrial. Should we make a park for them? Should we isolate them in some way or have some kind of boundaries that sort the technology that they can use? Maybe the word 'Park' is not the best way or the best word, since they are not zoological specimens and maybe we cannot save them that way, but what we could do is allow them to create the boundaries they want.

Urban intensification leads to the question: Is there a limit to human numbers? Perhaps space, but is there a psychological limit? People in cities seem to do well with high-contact, high-proximity living. What happens when people are crowded or feel crowded? Physical complaints, emotional complaints, sexual dysfunction, or feelings of fear, seem to be expressed often. There may be limits of crowding. Are there social limits, in terms of the number of people one can tolerate? We may have a requirements for personal space, home space, and wild space.

So one question is why do we consume so much? Why do we consume some things and not others? Overconsumption is a very destructive pattern, and the pattern is defined by deception and lies. Our entire society now focuses on spending, for psychological reasons as well as economic ones. The banks do not help with their campaigns to push second mortgages at higher interest rates. Tim O'Reilly suggests that more than a real estate bubble we need concern for the reality bubble.

As J.G. Speth notes, the fundamental question is how can the operating instructions for the modern world economy be changed so that economic activity protects and restores the natural world. He uses modern capitalism in the broad sense as the actual existing system of political economy as it stands, not as an idealized model.

Maybe, we need a big, formal program for questioning. T.H. Clarke suggests that we parallel David Hilbert's program for advancement and mathematics—the list of 23 problems to be solved by the mathematics community. We should have our own Hilbertian program for the Earth system. This includes analytical questions, normative questions, operational questions, and strategic questions. For example, a first analytical question is: what are the vital organs of the ecosphere? Another analytical question is: what are the characteristic regimes and timescales of dietary variability?

A normative question would be: What are the general criteria for distinguishing nonsustainable paths? Or, what kind of nature to modern societies want? An operational question is: What is the optimal mix of adaptation and mitigation measures to respond to global change? A strategic question is: What are the optimal goals for dividing the planetary surface into natural reserves and managed areas? What might be the most effective global strategy for generating and integrating and data sets? A final example of a strategic question is: What is the structure of an effective and efficient system of global development institutions?

We want the conventional system, with its 'humans first!' motto to lose its hold on our minds. To get to the heart of it, to weaken its grip, we have to attack the weakest point. And that is the question of meaning and value. How meaningful is it to shop? Where is the value in eating Kobe beef? Is this radical enough? Ecological enough? Perhaps we have become trapped by too much cheap energy to question things. We have benefited too much from cheap materials and cheap labor. We have benefited too much from too cheap food. This lets us break our faith with places. So how do we establish standards for places? Instead of profitability we should have health; instead of professional excellence we might have the durability of the community. Along with Wes Jackson, the idea of homecoming must include homemaking, especially now, dealing with remnants in ruins.

Can we design our way out? How can we act if we are ignorant? So far, we have not reduced problems and dangers by gathering more data, creating more theories, or by being cautious about industrial production. Ignorance is a problem. Another is that we cannot live without acting. We have to act on the basis of what we know, which is incomplete. So the question of how to act in ignorance is very important. We can act on the basis of incomplete knowledge when our culture has an effective way of telling us that the knowledge is incomplete and how we should act in the state of ignorance. Unfortunately it is also possible for incomplete knowledge to become the basis of arrogant behavior and dangerous actions. The standards of our behavior should be derived from understanding of our place and communities before incomplete technological knowledge. One conclusion we could make especially regarding uncertainty is that we could reduce the number of problems if we simply live that levels slightly below the lowest level of uncertainty, or the lowest absolute level productivity, of ecosystems.

Design cannot be separated from social and political questions. Designs, as Winston Churchill recognized, especially buildings, steer our experiences and actions. According to Langdon Winner, design includes the deliberately chosen, enduring forms of both material and intangible entities that affect human relations. Ecological design is a field that aims to recalibrate what humans do in the world according to how the world works as a biophysical system and a cultural entity. Design is a large concept having to do as much with politics and ethics as with buildings and technology. Design has to deal with systems in context, then pose questions: Does society have to be organized differently to be capable of doing ecological design? What would this society look like? Do we need to did redesign institutions to be capable of doing ecological design?

Perhaps there is a model of questioning that could serve a large movement. In terms of procedures for management, the U.S. Navy has a workable program for questioning. Because the officers and enlisted men are in for a very limited time, the Navy system seems to be chaotic, but it's been tested and it has evolved over generations the system manufactures safety and efficiency even though there are numerous mistakes under new circumstances and there is a wide range of skills among the crew. Having a crew participate in question the actions of officers serve several purposes. One of them is to keep everyone in touch with the activity, providing redundant checks on actions. This increases safety, so that errors can get detected before they become much larger. But newer crew have a lot to learn in these discussions and criticisms of service training exercises. New crew also do not have the experience of older ones. They are not a sufficient and they're not always knowledgeable about what to do they need guidance. This process is quite sensible. It minimizes accidents. Considering that the Navy operations are dangerous he often at a fast pace and under high stress there are relatively few fatal errors. If the Navy were to follow formal procedure in a strict hierarchy that accident rate would probably rise. One of the problems is that were not taught this in normal situations and so in normal situations we seem to feel that we can make errors in the end they will not do have a high price.

Some people will want to decide boundaries through culture, watershed, or political power. These questions can be answered in meetings. This outline seeks to improve people's circumstances by enlisting them to save their own environment and their own way of life. Democracy itself is kind of like a thought experiment, where questioning and conversing about disagreements and disasters allows us to experiment with them, and our responses to them, before there is real conflict and real suffering. Even if the real disasters are not prevented at least they have been addressed. Dissent occurs within the context of loyalty. Freedom is expressed within a context of law that limits it and protects it. The democratic system avoids runaway feedback. Anthony Barnett suggests that there is a fourth kind of democracy now, a reflexive democracy, direct and large scale, due to rapid news and easy communication.

Questions can widen a narrow field. Hardin points out that concerns about narrow issues, such as pollution, can cause a deep examination of the process, such as distribution theory, that cause or contribute to the issue. Human activity simply produces things that we want and things that we do not want, such as pollution. As we ask questions about who pays and who benefits, we are able to think or rethink about these things.

Questioning can get to the basis of any conversation. But, questioning can also frame and direct the conversation. Questioning also provides feedback for any answers. Therefore, questions will be a critical part of the approach to design. In terms of stimulating learning and creativity, questions are sometimes more powerful than answers.

1.4.4. *Other Considerations: Scales & Limits*
Certain themes operate throughout any questioning or discussion of human places, cultures and their environments. These themes can be used to compare the treatment and development of different places, cultures and environments.

1.4.4.1. Scale in Economics
Size is that quality of a thing that determines how much space it occupies. The word is derived from a French word for court sessions that determined official standards for measurement. There are barriers to the size of nuclear matter, of stars, and as well as of planets. Things divide naturally. They

make barriers or walls. Walls allow cells to live. The proper size of things depends on their function, according to D'Arcy Thompson. The scale of a thing depends on its place in nature. Kohr states the principle that stability and soundness adhere to bodies that are relatively small—this is his theory of small cell architecture. Dynamic balance is self-regulatory, Kohr states, because of "the coexistence of countless mobile little parts of which no one is ever allowed to accumulate enough mass to disturb the harmony of the whole."

Places also reflect changes in scale. Each place has a temporal/spatial order, with a typical physical size and rhythm. Small-scale cultures were egalitarian. But, there is a qualitative change when scale increases. The villages became ranked. The shift in size to cities changed the scale of food collection and trade. For instance, time is perceived at a faster rate in cities than in rural settings.

Economic systems all seem to work on a small scale, and work less well on larger scales, when the market and production become too large. The problems increase and more investment is taken up by the problems. Many kinds of products do not add to the wealth of people. Kohr identifies three kinds of such products related specifically to growth: (1) Power commodities, enhance the standard of society without contributing to material welfare of the members of society; these include tanks, bombs, and government services. (2) Growth products of a second category, density commodities, are necessary due to the increase in population, but do not add to individual happiness. These are traffic lights, hospitals, and fire losses. Growth requires growth products to address this. (3) Growth products of a third category, progress commodities, are improvements made necessary by previous improvements (anti-aircraft guns need better ammunition) or unwanted tie-in products such as license plates or television repair.

Kohr's principle argument against large-scale economies is the law of diminishing productivity. Variables added to fixed units eventually add less to total product than a preceding one. Increase in size or power does not produce an increase in satisfaction or productivity. Kohr points out that Marx failed to link misery to the scale of economics rather than to the style of the system. The problem rests with overgrowth more than style, which is why socialism based on overgrowth looks the same as overgrown capitalism. Small-cell theory, Kohr says, is a fundamental principle of health. We are happiest in smallest units, such as a family or county. The pattern has to be small cells under a federal unit larger than the largest state or community cell. That allows harmony and manageability by ensuring a physical and numerical balance. Then, any kind of central authority can be weak.

1.4.4.2. Political Limits & Security

Politics is the art and science of human government. Politics is the interactive means of providing the basic food and necessities of a community, that is, it maintains the affairs of a community.

Human institutions are also subject to effects of scale. At the level of families and bands, which are often extended families, behavior is understood and exchange is reciprocal. The politics of community is generally small-scale and local. Moral consensus is applied to daily operations. Robert Bellah and associates make three distinctions of politics, of which politics of the community is the first. This is followed by politics of interest, where different interests are pursued, according to agreed-upon, neutral rules; conflict tends to overwhelm consensus in any size community. Finally, the politics of the nation addresses the "higher" affairs of the nation. This level is more concerned with leadership than citizenship. Like the politics of interest, it accepts the status quo of relations of power or distribution of inequality. Symbolism becomes more important (perhaps when a citizen diminishes in importance and the symbolism includes them minimally). Governing nations seems to require a charismatic official, elected leader of professionals groupings; larger and more abstract religions can include a larger variety of people.

Nations have advantages over smaller groups because of specialization (especially of soldiers), technology (especially of weapons) and population size. Nations arose in Mesopotamia, China, Nile, Indus, Mexico, Andes, and West Africa. Larger amalgamated nations only arise through conquest or from duress for protection against other nations. What leads to this complexity? Population growth and attendant processes, including intensive food production and resource use, resulting in public works programs, long distance trade, and specialization.

Government in nations has become subservient to economic actors, according to John B. Cobb, Jr., partly because the ideology of economics is so positive. It proclaims that continued growth will solve most of the problems of modern civilization, from poverty to conflict, although the promise has not been fulfilled. The problems have increased: From food shortages, housing shortages, and energy shortages, to unemployment, inequality of opportunity or goods, environmental deterioration, increase in weapons, and insecurity.

These problems continue due to the limits of politics. For example, the size of society is a real limit; if there are too many people, within a limited territory or limited system, politics cannot provide them with a shared identity or control them. Size limits the distribution of food, housing, jobs, and wealth, also. The time frame of the political society is also a limit; short-range visions of national interest are often inimical to the long-range ecological requirements of the support system. Another limit is the participation of the members of a society. Communities have always had face-to-face limits, in terms of numbers of face-to-face encounters, and, in terms of distance. At a certain size, perhaps 300 people, representation and rules have to supplement direct contact.

Leadership is another limit; the pool of applicants is usually relatively narrow, and dominated by certain kinds of personalities, which may not be suitable for promoting fairness and consensus. The use of power is a limit.

Security is a problem for local communities and national governments. It becomes more difficult to protect against most any kind of weapons. Perhaps the solution is a global one, with the coordinated change in national policies and worldwide distribution of excess wealth.

1.4.4.3. The Necessity of Limits

Limits define locality, local spaces and local systems, from the global. Limits are not only important for life, but also are implicated in diversity and maturity, of organisms and cultures. But, even these limits are based on physical limits.

Although physical and chemical limits are real limits, they are modified by psychological limits, which are compounded by socio-cultural limits, which are further expanded or contracted by political limits. Each 'higher,' more complex level makes other levels more vulnerable to change. The attempt to exceed limits becomes less efficient. One of the most important psychological limits is our ability to process data and to draw conclusions from it. We are so ignorant of the complexities of ecosystems that it is suicidal to pretend to 'maximize' their use for resources. A free market civilization has to be limited by conservative calculations of ecological balance. It is almost impossible to estimate the economic value of this natural balance.

Discussing limits to growth, or any limits, is regarded by many people as a defeatism, as pessimistic, and a blow to human growth. Unseen limits have as real effects as those seen. A community is forced to accept an upper limit, beyond which it cannot grow any further. This is related to the carrying capacity. Denying limits does not make them go away. Furthermore, as William Catton has pointed out, there is a difference between raising the limits of carrying capacity or simply permitting greater overshoot of the limits for as long as possible, with the threat of a greater and more catastrophic collapse later.

2.0. Experimental Images of Government—Utopias

Earlier, simpler, or foreign images of the world are dismissed as being outmoded, useless, or unrealistic. Utopias have been offered as ideal schemes for social and political development, and sometimes utopias offer memorable images. But, most utopias are rejected as irrelevant dreams and self-indulgent imaginings. Yet, as Pierre Dansereau has said, the failures of pollution, poverty, and urban decay are failures of the imagination. Rejecting the solutions of imagination, therefore, can only make the suite of human crises worse.

While utopian ideas might be stimulating, other traditional or accidental ideas might be applied more rapidly. Political realism dismisses utopian ideas as naïve and impractical. People are afraid that such ideas would destroy their investments in power and in collections of wealth.

Political realism, however, is deficient in imagination and results, as well as deficient in courage and imagination. Despite great revolutions in technology and intensification, most people are still poor and threatened with displacement. Despite great revolutions in technology and living conditions over the past several thousand years, people are still very much shaped by unique cultures and small groups. These traditional institutions work very well on a local scale in a specific place. The information is available, but there is no framework to make it work, yet.

The word 'utopia' was meant to be ambiguous, either no-place (outopia) or good-place (eutopia). Perhaps the ideas of no-places have less relevance. The images of good places, however, might be worth considering. Buckminster Fuller was one of the first to consider this second meaning. In the 1920s, Buckminster Fuller began work on an Air-Ocean World Map, as an alternative eutopia that sought to define civic and ecological order through maps of known areas. In 1927, Fuller sketched the World Town Plan, a map that preceded and directly influenced subsequent maps. A 1943 issue of Life published one of Fuller's maps that could be cut up into fourteen pieces and reassembled in the form of a Dymaxion globe. Fuller saw his map as a populist construct to be used as an operational tool by the members of the global citizenry.

In 1954, Buckminster Fuller published the Raleigh edition of his project on the Dymaxion Air-Ocean World Map. In the dymaxion series of maps, Fuller superimposed a spherical icosahedron grid onto the earth's surface to limit the distortion of the relative size and shape of its components. The projection of Fuller's map represents all areas with equal weight. In Fuller's map, the North Pole is the neutral center around which land mass and ocean unfold. Fuller's town plan map, in its projection method and form, highlights the connectivity of his "one world island."

One of Fuller's objectives was to establish a map that does not prioritize cardinal direction, political entities, or hemispheric organization. Instead, the Dymaxion map provides a base for presenting global themes such as human migration, natural resources, and population distribution. Temperature replaces politics as the organizing map feature. In this map, world climate is shown in a range of coloration from warm reds to cool greens and blues. Even though highlighting a specific theme, Fuller's map emphasizes wholeness across the global surface.

A complete eutopian structure would start from such an image of wholeness. A eutopian structure, one that is unambiguously good, could be designed and described. It would outline a science and politics adequate to deal with the creation of good places on earth, where all beings are equal within a framework of high human culture within nature. It would propose an adaptive cosmology to place human values within a global ecology and to balance human development and the preservation of wild places. The framework could protect the integrity of culturally based nations and to address global issues. Global and local issues would be differentiated; the myths of global communities and one-world people would be explained and discarded. Pretending to be world people is a mistake based on a misunderstanding of human limits. People are the products of places and cultures, of land and nations.

Unlike either the political realism of nations or the ideal designs of utopias, a eutopian plan would be based on traditional human and cultural realities and would propose only modest and reasonable changes at local and international levels. For example, there are 500 million indigenous peoples in fifteen thousand distinct groups, such as the Uighur in China or the Kuna in Panama; and, there are over two billion people in hidden nations within massive political structures, such as the Azerbaijanis in the Soviet Union, the Kurds in Turkey and Iraq, or the Tibetans in China. Furthermore, there are regions in some countries, such as the Pacific Northwest in the United States or Wales in Britain, which may prefer independence to forced membership in a confederation. A Eutopian plan could allow any indigenous people with a traditional culture to become an independent nation without fear of conquest or compromise by existing political states. The benefits would outnumber those of a global monoculture and the negative aspects would be more manageable.

Such a eutopian process would solve many problems, from problems of scale to political inappropriateness. Not only would more nations exist in the framework, but alliances and networks would form and reform, as they do now. How would it work? A political framework, based on traditional cultures, coordinated by a global 'regulating' body, based on a modified United Nations, would be possible and desirable. The holistic framework would protect the creation of thousands of good places, or eutopias, based on human cultural realities and on the ecological limitations of places, that is, on homelands. These models already exist—they just need to be better defined and then protected from misguided ideas of growth and progress, as well as from the dominant, consuming industrial culture. This framework would also reconcile the well being of society with the health and continuity of living ecosystems. The international framework would provide paths for policing, international education, and other national needs. This plan would provide a path to independence and formal interdependence.

Before trying to build this framework, however, we first need to understand the history of human cultures, as well as ideal fictions and images.

Figure 20-1. Illustration from Thomas More's Island *Utopia*

2.1. *History of Human Cultures*

All that has been said or written is an interim report on the history of the idea of nature. G.W.F. Hegel stated: "That is as far as consciousness has reached." The study of nature is not a thing that exists on its own. Natural science is a form of thought that depends on the existence of some other form of thought, which is history. Natural science consists of facts and theories. A scientific fact is a class of historical and psychological facts. One cannot understand the first without understanding the second. No one can answer the question about nature (or human nature) unless she knows what history is.

The historian sees civilizations of the past like pieces of petrified wood; the activity has moved on and only a form of waste remains. At the highest level of description, as in H.G. Wells' The Outline of History, most details of the lower levels are lost. Humans have concentrated on the study of human history, to the exclusion of natural history. We have ignored the deepest kind of history—that which arises from broad economic or demographic pressures, that which alters whole habitats and systems. A cultural ecologist looks for the general topography, and wonders about the direction of slopes. But a cultural ecologist rarely recognizes individuals. Surface events reflect the underlying forces that determine livelihood, population, technology—anything that changes the relations between culture and environment.

At first humans were considered special because of their divine spark. Then, they were special because they are disconnected from nature by culture, a magical reification of the opposite of nature, a culture that we can produce at will to overcome the constraints of nature. It has been argued that culture let us push out of the constraints that limit simians and other mammals. Culture was once considered an attribute exclusively in the human domain.

If one defines, as Kinji Imanishi does, culture generally as a form of behavioral transmission that does not rely on genetics, then animals, birds, fish, and perhaps some insects can be said to have cultures. This definition is not limited by the kinds of mechanisms, such as copying or imitation, and it also includes the continuum from guppies and apes to rich human culture, which need not be devalued by being part of the continuum with animals. Value systems and technical achievements are sometimes the results.

2.1.1. *Copying & Animal Culture*
Can culture be defined as any kind of imitative behavior in animals? Culture can be defined as the transmission of information through behavior; imitation is one behavior, teaching is another. Culture, with its new way of transmitting information, involves a mix of: (1) trial and error learning, (2) social learning through observation and imitation, and finally (3) teaching. Culture is one way of transmitting information. Other ways are genetic coding and individual learning, although individual learning is difficult and easily lost without a context.

Some birds learn through imitation. For the bowerbird, the bower is an extension of its plumage and size, for courtship displays, but the extension changes faster than the biology. Evolution speeds up. When the environment supplies tools, new interactions and transactions occur. It is like an external bundle of secondary characteristics according to Edward Hall, quoting E. Thomas Gillard. Bowerbirds no longer pair off to mate nest and raise young. Males gather in clans and get ranked hierarchically. In spring, clans form around arenas for display. Each display court is called a lek. Females mate with the dominant males, those with the most baubles. How does female mate choice change over time?

2.1.2. Imitation & Human Culture

Human culture, and human behavior, need to be defined against a long evolutionary backdrop of deep history, the common ground we share with other animals. Perhaps culture is transmitted through imitation.

2.1.2.1. What is Culture?

What is the world like? How did the world get the way it is? And what is the role of humanity in the world? All cultures ask and answer these questions. Some of the questions could not be answered from direct observation. And, many of the answers are not limited to observable events. Ideas concerning humanity and the nature of the universe tend to form a coherent system in which ideas are integrated or rejected over days or centuries. Culture includes all of the expectations, understandings, beliefs, and commitments that influence the behavior of human groups.

Culture exists in minds, signs, and things, but most importantly in places. The word culture, from the Middle English, meant 'place tilled,' from the Latin *colere* meaning to 'till, care for, inhabit, worship.' For the Romans and English, to have a culture was to inhabit a place and cultivate it, and to be responsible for it.

2.1.2.2. Definitions of Culture

The classical definition was put forward by Sir E.B. Tylor (1871): "Culture ... is that complex whole which includes knowledge, belief, art, morals, law, custom, and any other capabilities and habits acquired by man as a member of society." Although the definition seemed to limit culture to 'man' alone, it definitely restricted it to human behaviors and artifacts. Others, including Claude Levi-Strauss and Leslie White argued that culture required imitation, teaching, and language, and therefore the concept could not apply to other species. In 1952, A. L. Kroeber and Clyde Kluckhohn identified 164 definitions of culture. Most of these definitions are refinements of Tylor. Robert Boyd and Peter Richardson defined culture as 'information capable of affecting an individual's own traits; they acquire the information from other individuals through imitation.' Information is a broad enough concept to include behaviors and artifacts, and the vehicle is identified as imitation.

Peter Berger defines culture as the totality of human products. Culture is everything created as a group, tribe or nation, physical or ideal, in the past or present. This embraces cookware, arrows, steam engines; artworks, books, legal codes; symbols, values, social structures. A cultural system surrounds the network of human interactions with raw materials and forms of life.

A general definition of culture identifies it as the ensemble of values, worldview, aspirations, customs, technologies, techniques and physical artifacts that characterize a people and distinguish them from others. Mary Douglas refined the definition by studying the culture of everyday life, from food and dirt to jokes, bodies, and speech. Dirt, which is a form of pollution, reveals a lot about the system and rules of classification. Understanding what permits things to be called dirty or clean reveals the moral order itself. To see how individuals are controlled by society, Douglas creates two distinctions, group and grid, which she uses to categorize cultures. Group is the outer boundary between people and the world. Grid is the set of social distinctions and delegation of authority that limits how people behave towards each other. This creates a table relating the strengths and weaknesses of cultures. For instance, traditional societies have strong group, strong grid. Some modern cultures have a weal group but a strong grid.

2.1.2.2.1. Metaphors of Culture

The use of metaphors might contribute something to the understanding of culture. Culture is an 'organism' that grows and matures, that is, it is organic and whole, with a finite life span. It processes energy and matter to survive. But, it does not have a skin or genetic limits—nor does it have a genetic way of passing on its characteristics, although it has the memory of its members, and they can communicate.

Perhaps, culture is an 'ecosystem' that is self-maintaining, stable and changing. But, that neglects an ideational component, as did 'organism.' Like general systems, cultures develop over time; they are capable of evolving. There are similarities in their evolution: Similar dynamics and machinery, and a direction towards complexification. Evolution, biological or cultural, depends on two things: The rate at which useful changes arise and the rate that they spread in the communities. But, this neglects internal states and forms of ideas.

It could be said that culture is a 'city,' converting nature into artifact, expanding into new areas, such as suburbs, park zones, and industries, as the physical extension and expression of human intentions. But, the metaphor still does not encompass ideas.

Culture is a 'process.' A nation is a process. Culture is slower than ideology or policy, which may be one reason why we have larger nations. Culture is slower than economic conditions or environmental changes. It is possible that urbanization distorts the activities of a culture.

For individuals, culture is a pair of 'glasses' that allow us to see some details or patterns; that is, it is an add-on to the human animal that focuses and shades perception to permit survival (yet perhaps blind us to slow change and possible catastrophes). This metaphor implies that many do not need culture or that culture can be removed or replaced at will. Feral children, beings without culture, have difficulty surviving; removing culture, even if possible, would reduce people to a feral level. Another culture can be grafted onto a first culture, as people immigrate into a second culture, although that can be a long, incomplete process.

Culture is also a 'hologram.' It is a whole that arises when the reference beam of nature shines through the mental patterns of a human group. This metaphor could capture the interior and exterior aspects of culture. The reference beam colors and shapes the culture differently. The culture could develop, however, only with decay over time, not through a transformation. These metaphors, although interesting, have limitations. A broader attempt at definition might be more fruitful.

2.1.2.2.2. Synthetic Definition of Culture
Culture stretches vertically to include the physical, economic and political. It stretches horizontally to include society as a whole. In fact, culture is concerned with all things and beings. It is organic, like Aristotle considered a work of art, and whole. So everything in it is interrelated in some degree. Many relationships are encompassed by the holistic perspective of culture: The relation of people to themselves, to each other, to objects they create, and to their natural environment, and to their cultural environment. These bear on psychological well being, social bonds, material legacy, and on the association with other forms of life.

These many definitions overlap and can be combined in to a synthetic definition, with common properties: Culture is a system of shared beliefs, values, customs, behaviors, and artifacts that members of society use to adapt to the environment and to adjust to each other, and that is transmitted to succeeding generations through learning behavior and language, so that culture and the environment constrain and construct each other over time. This definition might be refined later. As in any system, a culture can be described by its basic properties (Table 21222-1 contrasts the properties of six relevant systems).

Table 21222-1. Contrasted Properties of 6 Defined Systems

Fields	Places	Ecosystems
Process	Dynamic Change	Course
Autopoesis	Self-making Wholeness	Identity
Differentiation	Differentiation	Openness Diversity
Integration	Integration	Coconstrained Construction
Constancy	Constancy	Stability
Metalysis	Renewal	Productivity
Cultures	Good Places	Good Societies
Conduct	Action	Method
Wholeness	Individuality	Self-extension
Flexibility	Richness	Variety
Adaptation	Conviviality	Cooperation
Constancy	Consistency	Loyalty
Vitality	Health	Harmony

Each of these systems has six similar properties. A field is a conceptual device used to describe aspects of the universe and to unify theories of light, magnetism, electricity, particles, and gravity. A place is a field that has been differentiated by a history or by actions of living organisms. An ecosystem is a place that has a unique combination of physical properties, organisms and cycles in a typical pattern. A culture is an emergent pattern from an ecosystem, created by a species to adapt to systemic changes. A good place is a culturally modified system that extends long-term harmony and sustainable development. And, a good society is social system that enhances the health and development of individuals, the ecological base and the society itself.

2.1.2.3. Properties of Culture
Culture is imbibed through a process of social interaction. People acquire culture unconsciously through social interaction, as well as consciously, through apprenticeship or formal learning. The young, or new members of a culture, observe others and imitate that behavior. Cultural models are internalized by individuals, so that part of culture resides in the mental sphere of people. Beliefs and knowledge are not shared equally by all individuals, thus culture is shared differentially.

Humans use conceptual devices, such as symbols, to communicate abstract ideas about nature or society to one another. Through our linguistic capacity, we can use symbols as meaningful representations of reality. Public shared meanings provide a set of designs that allow an educated individual to survive nature and society. The understanding and practice of culture is shared in a culture.

2.1.2.4.1. Conduct as a Property of Culture
Conduct is the course of cultural behaviors through a behavioral landscape or field. New mathematical treatments of fields tend to be three-dimensional. Rene Thom's catastrophe theory and Conrad Waddington's epigenetic landscape are two such theories. The epigenetic landscape field can be used to explain why chickens on one side of a fence cannot get to the food on the other side, even though they could walk two meters to get around the edge of the fence. The chicken's need path or chreod is deeper than the path of a cognitive chreod around the fence. So, the chicken can only go toward

the food. If the need chreod is too deep, the chicken cannot explore with a cognitive chreod, although a less hungry chickens might be able to.

In humans, this explains why necessity cannot be the mother of invention; the necessity path, starvation for instance, is too deep to allow exploration of a shallower path of daydreaming or design. The broader landscape of leisure is needed. Conduct can be described as the stable path of culture through a landscape of possibilities. Once the course has been set, it is most likely to channel subsequent behavior, unless some event triggers a deeper course.

2.1.2.4.2. Wholeness as a Property of Culture

Culture provides an identity for its members. It tells them who they are, where they came from, and why they are special. Identity is basic to human existence. People are identified by their roles. A person is an incarnation of his and her group—even in industrial culture, one is identified as an astronomer or farmer.

Identity is that persistent quality that serves nothing; it is. Identity can be described apart from its performance in interactions, but not isolated. The relationship between identity and wholeness is a rhythm, with unique patterns. In fact, culture is concerned with all things and beings in a whole.

2.1.2.4.3. Flexibility as a Property of Culture

To paraphrase Arthur Koestler, culture is a holon, a stable subwhole in a hierarchy that displays structural gestalt constancy and rule-governed behavior. The rules lend order and stability to the whole, as well as flexibility. Flexibility means not being over connected, or not being too rigid or efficient. Than means that culture is able to slough off people or community structures and to incorporate new people and structures. Culture is able to keep some options and unused connections open. Some of the flexibility comes from different ways of establishing connections in specific places.

Culture is bounded, but open to flows of energy and materials. In fact, it requires a steady input and output exchange flow. It requires order, but not too much order. It is a loose-fitting patchwork of ideas, relationships and things. It is tolerant of discontinuities and contradictions, and this gives it flexibility. Humans can tolerate inconsistency and operate with contradictory beliefs: Soldiers fight for peace; ministers save the unborn for starvation. If the contradictions become too great and maladaptive, however, then the culture can collapse. Cultures that become too isolated often stagnate, then collapse, even if they do reconnect with other cultures.

2.1.2.4.4. Adaptation as a Property of Culture

The patchiness of culture is parallel to the co-constrained construction of a species and its environment. Culture has to balance between embracing change and resisting change. People show a desire for new things, but often fear and resist change. According to most theories of cultural adaptation (or integration or evolution), resistance to change is normal as a cultural process. Groups like the pygmies have specialized to fit the requirements of the environment, successfully. This makes it difficult to adopt other cultural arrangements. On the other hand, resistance to change itself is an adaptive mechanism. According to Betty Meggers, it works as a successful "cultural isolating mechanism." Isolation remember is what allows a culture to develop in the first place. But, then can it force a culture to become stagnant?

A primary culture is adaptive because it aids survival in the ultrahuman world. Its ways of living are sophisticated survival mechanisms. Each way of life is a set of adaptations to the limits of the environment. Primary thought patterns are highly disciplined intellectual structures that make the world coherent and meaningful. Many rituals of the tropical American Indian tribes are concerned with ecological balance, though not necessarily self-consciously. Co-constrained construction enforces coevolution, the emergence of a highly ordered complexity to full structuration. Polyandry in Tibet may be an adaptation to limited resources. With monogamy and every woman married, there would be more children to strain the resources available.

2.1.2.4.5. Constancy as a Property of Culture

The cultural system is stable and persistent in time. It is a general property of some systems that acquired information is used to close the door to further inflow. A mature culture needs less information, since it works toward preservation, and closes itself off to information that does not fit the shape of the culture. The effect of maturity is to allow a maximum variability between systems with slight external differences, such as place or initial conditions.

Stability is a Property of cultures. This can even be stated in Newtonian terms: A culture at rest tends to remain at rest. According to T.G. Harding (1960), when forced to act on changes, a culture will only accommodate those changes that preserve its fundamental character. Stability is the ability to maintain identity under the flow of external forces and disturbances. A culture has to be able to resist disturbances that are too disruptive. Resistance is a positive act for a self-reliant culture. Culture also has to be resilient enough to recover from intermediate and small disturbances. It has to accommodate changes that contribute to its identity.

Stability can also be related to compartmentalization, communications, richness of interactions, and connections. With order and integration come stability and security, without which no one can survive. When human societies were small, the amount of control and security required was small. Although societies have grown, human security has not. Primordial security comes from a physical, knowledgeable relationship with nature.

2.1.2.4.6. Vitality as a Property of Culture

To be constant and stable, a culture has to be vital; it has to be productive, to be able to convert energy and materials into foods and structures for survival. The system is self-creating. It renews itself as its contents change, as disturbances change the parameters of the system. What barriers are there to cultural renewal? How can they be overcome?

2.1.2.4.7. Properties Related to Principles

Knowledge of properties is useful to understanding a complex system, but interacting in the system requires other tools. In order to make sense of the sheer multiplicity and complexity of their environments, human beings create abstractions. An abstraction is an idea created to refer to all objects that have certain properties or characteristics in common, e.g., all birds. Abstractions can be generalized, e.g., all things that fly, but at each outer level the objects have less in common; thus flying things include insects, mammals, reptiles, seeds, and spores.

What makes something valuable is not in its own properties alone, but also in its relation to the ecosystem as a whole. The "usefulness" of a thing or species does not rest solely in its appearance as an individual entity, but rather in its existence in a web of relationships. What and how it 'is' essentially involves a complex series of relationships between the various events that are going on inside and outside its boundaries over large and small spatial and temporal scales. To understand the physiology of an ecosystem requires that all viewpoints be considered together (top-down, bottom-up, or across the landscape). Human health, and the health of its domestic and artificial systems, depends on the health of the supporting ecosystems.

Within topics of history, ecology and global government, a number of properties, principles, standards, and practices will be presented suggest ways to formally address every situation (to some extent). Properties (or characteristics) are qualities that distinguish unique individuals, systems, or patterns; Gregory Bateson calls them differences that make a difference. Principles are fundamental rules or laws that we can use to create models of the propertied systems. Standards are examples of quality or value established by authority or consent, which can then be repeated as procedures to be applied in practice.

For instance, maturity is a general property of some ecosystems, where acquired information is used to limit further inflow of new information. A mature system needs less information, since it works toward preservation rather than growth. The limit of maturity allows variability between systems with slight external differences, such as temperature. Diversity is also an emergent property of ecosystems, arising from the activities of multitudinous beings learning to use the productivity of the system to thrive and reproduce. The ecosystem is self-organizing, but diversity is not a goal of the system.

Principles of ecology, as well as of government, can be based on the properties of systems; they can also be adopted from a number of fundamental philosophical, historical, scientific, and cosmological principles that were first presented in other contexts by thinkers such as Whitehead and Einstein. Very few of these principles are absolute or universal; in fact the further one gets from physical or chemical principles, the more likely there are significant variations or exceptions. Nevertheless, they are essential to the understanding of ecosystems and quite useful in applications in managing the environment. Principles, combined with common sense and good judgment, are necessary as guides in the absence of definite knowledge. They give us a broad predictive ability. For each principle, we have to ask, how will it affect our objectives for that ecosystem or community?

Most of the principles stated so far have been global principles; some principles may apply to a particular region; others may exist at a very local scale. This is even truer for standards. Will standards vary with different principles? Then, how would our operations vary? The global provides the framework for the regional, which provides the framework for the local—the level of detail and participation. Standards are very important for forest practices or certification, to provide consistency of judgment regardless of the owner or certifier; they also form the basis for any appeal of judgments. They should be clear, unbiased, and applicable.

For any application there have to be short-run and long-run decisions. The decision to shift from an industrial model of forestry towards an ecoforestry model, for example, calls for an integrated planning approach and support from a number of areas. There are certain general standards that can be identified: Do not clearcut in most cases; only take less than the annual growth rate, from those trees in abundance; use natural regeneration with good diversity and distribution of parent seed trees to protect native gene pools; do not bring in fertilizer, herbicides, pesticides, or any toxic pollutants; use the lowest impact removal methods possible, combining sustainable selection with careful directional falling, and a low impact access system that insures all features of a fully functioning forest ecosystem are left intact; and restore, maintain and or keep all values associated with fully functioning ecosystems, intact.

Once properties have been identified, principles have been distilled, and standards have been set, practices can be put in operation. Many specific changes would occur in the human use of other species and ecosystems. These would allow us to: Recognize individuality in trees and other beings; recognize the feelings and emotions of animals and the sensitivity of plants; promote a noncommodity approach to forestry; minimize the devastation of wild forests and wild ecosystems; and, emphasize habitat loss as a human ethical issue.

Applying ecological practices to our cultural patterns, in the near and far future, we could try ways that biosphere cultures can be converted to ecosystem cultures (after Ray Dasmann), characterized by wonder and wildness. We could identify and promote ecosystem lifestyles, characterized by frugality and joy. We develop a basis for management techniques for finite ecosystems, especially wild forests, which would link ecological sustainability with the richness and diversity of ecosystems, as well as with human pleasure. Starting in this way, we could work for immediate solutions to inequity and destruction under worsening and thankless conditions.

Properties, principles, standards, and practices can be combined to be useful political and scientific guides (see the lists in the *Ecodex* 9.0). For another forestry example, one property of a mature forest is its wildness. The corresponding principle is that a forest ecosystem is self-making and self-ordering without human control and management. Our objective for this forest is to allow the foresting process to continue, whether we take resources from the forest or not (since forests can be influenced or interfered with by acid rain, pollution, and other industrial effects). We can set standards that are likely to keep mature forests wild, such as: Limit biomass removal to 2 percent of the total forest; use appropriate techniques, e.g., single tree selection, horse skidding; retain mature structure in the forest, e.g., 19 snags per hectare and 23 nurse logs per hectare (in mature Ponderosa pine for instance); preserve surrounding landscape patterns. Practices are the physical implementation of strategies. It is the course of action that shapes the developing systems according to the standards set and mindful of the properties and principles. We could present the combination in a series of scenarios or thought experiments. This would modify our world images and resulting behaviors to bring them into harmony with established processes.

This four-fold approach makes it easier to identify and deal with unformed ideas, some outdated traditions and bad practices. Bad practices can destroy ecosystems and leave wastelands. Industrial practices are sold as producing 'better quality' and more volume. Its myth is 'bigger is better.' They have to be integrated solidly into operating ecological systems. Even good practices that seem workable in the short-term have to be fit in a long-term perspective. Farming and irrigation practices can make small changes to soil moisture and salt content, which can affect productivity and soil stability. Grazing practices can cause small changes in vegetation populations and lead to small changes in climate and sometimes to desertification. Humanity has changed the environment enough to influence its own health. Bad practices can lead to ecological errors that lead to deterioration. Having excess energy available in fossil fuels has allowed us to ignore inefficient or damaging processes of exploitation. Industrial fishing takes over 12 times as much energy to catch fish as the fish provide in food energy. With excess energy, we can burn our other wastes rather than avoid them or recycle them.

Good practices can use ecological design to consider and shape the health of the whole system. Many traditional practices in place-based cultures are already adapted to the limits and constraints of the ecosystems, and many times have increased their diversity and stability. Good practices can conserve crucial aspects of systems. Many established cultural practices, such as taboos and hunting restrictions, have ecological value in protecting sensitive populations. Improved practices could reduce the land area being converted and simplified, by integrating it with cities and roads, and make things more efficient. Limit use of wild populations and reshape domestication from slavery.

We have to recognize that ecosystems are not perfect and certain; they can only be changed or improved within limits. We have to accept change, uncertainty and surprises, although we can anticipate and direct them to some extent. Ecosystems are the result of historical processes that are mathematically atypical. Furthermore, they are not randomly structured. A system drives to a nonequilibrium state as a mature ecosystem. The adaptively reorganized system is not necessarily more stable, but it is optimally resistant to the outside conditions that elicited the self-organization, a natural normalization process.

At the government level, the practices of environmental conservation must be complemented by careful policies. Societies have images of the future that influence their policies, and those images can be shaped by knowledge and persuasion. Human beings can and have created new ecological values by collaborating with, or following the laws of, nature. Governments need to setup up circumstances that encourage feedback at every level to avoid the errors of detachment or scale. Without feedback, too many poor decisions about crops and cities are made. At the global level larger scales of feedback with a much-longer time line are necessary, but this could be a major push for a global government and its member cultures and commonwealths.

2.1.2.5. Functions of Culture

Culture has to deal with the facts of life, from change to death, so that people can survive in their communities in their places. Freeman Dyson distinguishes three crucial biological inventions in the transition from unicelled organisms to multicelled: Death, which allowed differentiation of the future from the past; Sex, which enabled the characteristics to be shared and mixed; and Speciation, which increased diversity through separation and genetic barriers. Life can experiment with the diversity of forms and functions.

Dyson notes that each biological invention has its analog as a cultural invention inhuman societies: For death it is tragedy; the fact of death is made a theme in ritual and drama. Great cultures have distilled great works from the fact of death. For sex, it is romance, where sex is turned into a thing of mystery and beauty, in dance and poetry. Speciation has been transformed into cultures and languages at the human level. The flexibility of social institutions grew out of differences and places.

2.1.2.5.1. Culture Grounds

A culture orders a whole cosmos by selecting what is important from the undifferentiated phenomena of nature and presenting it in a basic image to be learned in myths and stories. People in a primary culture share a common image of their world (from the German word meaning 'man-image'). The image is a construct of human knowledge that reflects human awareness of a local environment. The image is constructed metaphorically, but treated 'as if' it were true. A traditional way of living evolves with people's experience and knowledge. The image then 'grounds' and guides their behavior.

Grounding is more than the expression of a local place through culture. It is also the expression of individual behaviors through culture. Culture can be observed through individual actions, but culture exists as a pattern that allows that emergence. Individual and collective entities have to be understood and balanced. Both are important parts of a whole system. Culture limits and constrains individual behavior with its conventions, but individual behavior extends culture, by acting and communicating.

2.1.2.5.2. Culture Orders

A culture orders a whole cosmos (from the Greek word meaning 'to set in order,' which was applied to the human face as well as to all of nature, and what was beautiful was also morally admirable). What is important is often beautiful. Every culture strives for beauty that goes beyond utilitarian values. People structure their worlds with their own group at the center.

Cultures occupy a particular territory. This is especially true of the Campa, in a tropical forest in Peru, and the Ituri pygmy, in a tropical rainforest in Africa. The features of their cultures are unique to their places. They literally could not live with images of desert or ocean, like the Taureg of the Sahara or Samoans of the Pacific. Regardless of the features of a place, myths are created to give it special significance in the order of things; giving mythical significance to a place strengthens a people's identification with it. People identify with their place and often equate their own characteristics with it; the Ituri consider themselves as bountiful as their forest, while the Mongols are as undeniable as the wind from their plateau.

2.1.2.5.3. Culture Explains

Culture explains the universe. It also explains the behavior of its adherents. By explaining reality, culture binds the human and ambihuman, and the past and the present, into a meaningful whole. Culture explains why traditions are necessary. It explains why things are as they are, and how they came to be that way. It can do this in stories, and sometimes stories need a special language to explain, such as Wataluma or Latin. In modern culture, a scientific theory is a statement that explains some aspect of the world. It allows one to ask certain kinds of questions.

Knowledge and understanding allow survival in fragile habitats. The !Kung San of the Kalahari desert exist in small communities that enable them to continue traditional hunting and gathering without depleting their resources; they hunt eighty types of animals. The Hanunoo of the Philippines distinguish 1600 plant species, where scientists only know of 1200 in the same area.

2.1.2.5.4. Culture Integrates

Culture provides a filter between humans and environments (and in a way culture serves as another evolutionary filter). It designates what we attend to or ignore. It has to screen less valuable information to avoid information overload, even in archaic times. Culture acts like a trigger. It allows less information to activate the system. And this is the only way to increase information handling, when the system is larger and more complex—of course, this is what stereotypes and metaphors do. Culture programs the individual or institution.

Culture provides an identity for its members. It tells them who they are, where they came from, and why they are special. Identity is basic to human existence. People are identified by their roles. A person is an incarnation of his and her group—even in industrial culture, one is identified as an astronomer or farmer. Jurgen Habermas identifies culture as a set of subjective meanings held by individuals about themselves and their world.

2.1.2.5.5. Culture Justifies

Another function of a culture is to justify human activities, in order to have those activities continue. Unless an activity satisfies a basic human need, it may not be repeated. The needs may be physical, psychological, or social, such as acquiring status. In ancient China, people found justification of their world view in the matrix of nature—perceived cruelty in nature justified real cruelty to and by human beings.

A common culture provides an ideal framework for public and private decision making. The Sami in northern Scandinavia have institutionalized ways of avoiding conflict, for instance, by shaming those who try to impose their will. People in a culture may enlist religion to justify transfer of wealth to the rich and the leader. The shared religion also makes strangers act more peacefully without kinship; it gives people a (nongenetic) reason to sacrifice their lives for an institution.

2.1.2.5.6. Culture Controls

Some human behavior is controlled and population regulated through the use of space. Most foraging populations, furthermore, regulate their density well below the limits of the food supply. Culture controls many behaviors, from hunting to birthing. Women control sex, birth, weaning, and often population size. For Australian aborigines, women are regarded as controlling social harmony, health and connections to land, while men, with more time and strength, tend to control creative activities and hunting for prestige foods.

Cultures have been self sufficient for thousands of years. Although some of them fail, others last for quite a long time. The Desana, for example, have existed in the Amazon for over four thousand years by maintaining an equilibrium with the environment. Ecosystems are local, not global. Although we regard communities as being tied together globally, each community is alone. Each culture has to be responsible for its own welfare. Preserving the local environment is one requirement. A culture is a way of doing things by a unique people with an identity, with a history, in an environment, communicating in unique ways, and using materials in unique ways.

2.1.3. *Effectiveness of Culture*
There are similarities of concepts between culture and ecosystem. Culture is a sloppy concept, like an ecosystem. Culture is also scalable, like an ecosystem, and can be nested within larger systems. The properties of a culture resemble those of any system, such as an ecosystem. They include: Identity, openness, productivity, co-constrained construction, and vitality.

Like an organism or ecosystem, a culture has needs for it to continue. It needs: To be grounded in place, to be secure or partly isolated; to have a dynamic order, promoting health; to be complex and sophisticated, with checks and balances; to be comprehensive, to allow change and diversity; and, to have and manage adequate resources.

Like an organism in an environment, a culture engages in activities and interrelations, such as change and development. It can compete with or take-over other cultures. It can cooperate and trade. There will always be some clash or misunderstanding, from having different images and metaphors, limits and rules of behavior. The strengths of a culture may allow it to persist for a long time; its weaknesses, though, ensure that it will eventually fall apart.

2.1.3.1. Strengths of Culture
A culture has social and ecological functions. These things are the strengths of culture, when they work. The image a people have of their world makes sense of the overwhelming confusion of nature; it gives people a unique identity and justifies their behavior. Culture ties them to a place, whose qualities are known and preserved.

A culture is adaptive because it aids survival in the ultrahuman world. Its ways of living are sophisticated survival mechanisms. Each way of life is a set of adaptations to the limits of the local environment. Primary thought patterns are highly disciplined intellectual structures that make the world coherent and meaningful. Many rituals of the tropical American Indian tribes are concerned with ecological balance, at low levels of exploitation and trade (though not necessarily self-consciously, according to Gerardo Reichel-Dolmatoff).

2.1.3.2. Weaknesses of Culture
Culture does not fit together into a perfectly integrated whole. A culture is a loose-fitting patchwork of ideas, relationships, and things. There are discontinuities and contradictions. The balance of freedom and necessity ensures that no culture will ever fit its environment or its members perfectly. Humans can tolerate inconsistency and operate with contradictory beliefs: Soldiers fight for peace or ministers save the unborn that they may starve. If the contradictions become too great and maladaptive, however, then the culture dies. No culture has developed a perfect balance of human and situational needs. Some do better than others. But, all cultures change and age. As a culture ages, it may become indifferent, self-centered, and forgetful, suffering rigidity and cultural amnesia.

2.1.3.2.1. Holding Arbitrary ideas

People sometimes construct their worlds from preconceived notions. Success in one area may become associated with a chance happening, an event that is repeated as superstitious behavior to continue the success. In this way, a maladaptive image of nature can be built. Some primary traditions may work against the conservation of a place; for instance, the Algonquian notion that game animals spontaneously regenerate after death means that there is no reason not to overhunt. Modern ideologies have even been shaped by the principle of endless wealth; the economist Adam Smith believed that the real price of anything was just the toil spent acquiring it.

2.1.3.2.2. Remaining Indifferent

Industrial cultures desacralize nature. Since the advent of the machine image, the concept of the sacred has been reversed. In the primary view, the familiar was sacred. When modern cultures made the familiar trivial, it became profane. The quality of sacredness was bestowed on the unknown, on wilderness or children. In industrial culture, all aspects of life become interchangeable artificial units, including soil, water, and land. This view impoverishes humans by claiming all consciousness for humanity. Detachment leads to a loss of the sacred. Many different peoples have deforested their lands and poisoned their waters, regardless of their religious ideals as Buddhists, Taoists, Moslems, or Christians. Industrial cultures are indifferent to the limits of a natural carrying capacity.

2.1.3.2.3. Overexploiting Nature

All peoples want some power over the natural order. Primary peoples rely on ritual acts instead of machinery. As technology supplies power to primary peoples, rituals decline. Power increases exploitation, disturbance and interference. Exploitation can become pathological, when it interferes with the natural processes that maintain an ecosystem. The intrinsic worth of beings can become supplanted by monetary value. For example, some North American Indians were seduced into the fur trade by the lure of manufactured materials. The spread of power has two other effects. The natural order becomes simplified, the human world becomes increasingly complex—and both orders become unstable. Applying culture beyond a small scale gives rise to behaviors that are nonecological and unsustainable.

2.1.3.2.4. Being Incomplete

The very circumstance that makes each culture unique—being in a unique place—ensures that each culture is limited. All cultures produce destruction and waste; all of them produce at least some of the opposite of the good intended. A culture rarely meshes perfectly with the natural order or even its own social order. Cultures rarely have long-range plans; they do not concern themselves with global problems. They rarely consider any cultures other than their immediate neighbors; they do not have policies to help them. They are rarely conscious of the long-range effects of their activities.

2.1.3.2.5. Staying Inflexible

It was thought that cultures could vary infinitely and change rapidly. This is an exaggeration. Change is not always easy or adaptive. The inertia of cultural practices makes change painful. People may become fixed in permanent roles and personalities. Even if cultural attitudes are appropriate, they can trap a people if there are no longer functional reasons for the practices. The Nembi of Papua New Guinea may be trapped in their system; making stone axes is difficult, when thousands of steel ones are available, although the ritual of making axes can bond people. Cultures can determine inappropriate attitudes towards nature. The English treated tropical lands as enemies to be defeated, then enslaved them in plantations. Their cultural attitude as conqueror of nature led them to treat biogeochemical cycles and soil requirements as temporary obstacles in a world where everything had its price.

2.1.3.2.6. Keeping Exclusive

When the largest social unit was the tribe or nation, it was possible for the local mythology to represent other people outside its bounds as inferior, and the local inflection of human mythology as the one true mythology. The young were trained to respond positively to tribal members, to love their home, and to project hatred outward. But, there is no longer an outward. Cultures need to recognize other cultures right to existence, as valuable adaptive patterns (although some degree of isolation may be needed, especially for archaic cultures).

2.1.3.2.7. Being Aggressive

Are humans innately aggressive, or does the nature of the culture of civilizations promote aggression? Cultures allow more aggression against people outside the home culture. The size of a local population increased the likelihood of its success. For cultures, size was important. More important cultures were larger and more aggressive. Aggression may be encourage to protect a culture trapped in low food outputs or scarce resources. Aggression would be important to protect a culture, but it can become a prime way of relating to other cultures, especially very different culture, or neighboring cultures that may hinder the expansion of the home culture. Cultures need not be limited to aggression. They can also divert aggression from violence and war into propaganda and art.

2.1.3.2.8. Ignoring Limits of Culture

A culture will often develop without concern for limits of complexity or scale. How large or small can a culture be? How simple or complex? There are human cultural limits in numbers. For instance, a minima might be genetic, at only 2000 people; but for ideomass, the minimum might be one million. A maximum, based on wilderness, might be ten million, or there might be a social maximum of forty million. Each limit must be worked out, depending on place and the structure of the culture, but they should not be ignored.

2.1.4. *Diversity & Universals of Cultures*

The functional requirements of culture are rather minimal for humans, being only food, clothing, shelter, and reproduction. Throughout their history, humans have been able to convert animal and vegetable resources into all their needs for food, shelter, and clothing. Differences in environments were reflected in the styles of these things. Other requirements, such as respect, comfort, and self-fulfillment, depend on cultural systems, and the differences in local environments and cultures ensures a diversity of those things.

The origin of clothing, for warmth or prestige produced ecological changes in local animals. According to Mark Stoneking, body lice may have evolved from head lice after a new ecological niche, clothing in this case, opened for them. Using a molecular clock, he calculates that clothing appeared about 75,000 years ago in Africa. Perhaps clothing appeared first as a symbol of status, but clothing allowed the move to colder climates. Much of the diversity of human clothing has to do with the diversity of localities. And, much has to do with the aesthetic sense and human invention. Clothing is often the first thing noticed when cultures meet. In the eyes of another culture, clothing differences are often exaggerated. For instance, Westerners seeing Africans or Polynesians for the first time focused on the absence of clothing or on body adornment. Naturally, Africans seeing Westerners for the first time emphasized the elaborate clothing and facial hair.

Behavioral difference may be noticed after a longer acquaintance. Behaviors and symbols may take decades to understand. Many gross operations of a culture seem familiar and may be comforting in their familiarity. All cultures seem to have certain things in common. Of course, many of these are referred to as soft universals, since everyone needs shelter. Other differences may be the result of contacts between cultures, because cultures are mimetic, that is, they copy one another. This may be the secret behind agriculture, cities, and industrialization.

Perhaps cultures seem to have universal characteristics because humans are of the same species, have similar requirements and similar bodies. All people live in groups, have some form of shelter, and have an incest taboo. Even though a process may be universal, the implementation and symbolization of it may be quite different and unique. Some scholars have argued that these universals could allow a global human culture. That may be true, although the relationship of a local culture to a global culture may also be problematic.

Cultural Universals (expanded after G. P. Murdock 1945) could include: age grading, faith healing, joking, population policy, athletics, family living, postnatal care, feasting, kin groups, pregnancy usages, body adornment, fire-use, property rites, folklore, propitiation ceremonies, calendar, food taboos, language, puberty customs, community organization, funeral rites, cooking, magic, religious rituals, cooperative labor, games, marriage, residence rules, cosmology, gestures, mealtimes, courtship, gift-giving, medicines, sexual restrictions, greetings, modesty, soul conception, dancing, mourning, status differentiation, decorative art, hair styles, murder taboos, division of labor, hospitality, music / singing, tool-making, home/housing, mythology, trade, education, hunting taboos, numerals, ethics, hygiene, visiting, ethnobotany, obstetrics, war / conflict rules, etiquette, incest taboos, weaning, inheritance rules, personal names, and weather control.

2.1.5. Changes & Cultural Transformations
Cultures emerge from groups of human beings living in places. The variables of the environment influence cultures in a number of ways. For instance, a high Net Community Productivity (NCP) of an ecosystem can allow larger annual crops, or, a low number of sunny days can contribute to psychological depression. Cultures have been unique programs, using local materials and ingenuity, for satisfying basic human material and spiritual needs. Cultures develop over time as the groups change and always seem to grow larger. Cultures are influenced by climate, resources, and of course by human ideas about their places and themselves.

There may also be larger patterns of human culture. For instance, reproductive success and overshoot of resources may always occur in the development of a culture. The asymmetry of sex and violence, ecosystem conversion, and limited time horizons are also things that seem to develop.

As place changes, a culture changes. As people change, under the influence of each other and other cultures, a culture changes. Culture does not fit together into a perfectly integrated whole. A culture is a loose-fitting patchwork of ideas, relationships and things. In that sense it is parallel to species adaptation to an environment. There are discontinuities and contradictions.

William Thompson identifies six major shifts in the transformation of human cultures. The first he calls the feminization of primates; females abandoned estrus and became open sexually (200,000 YBP). In observing synchronicity between bodies and nature, women established system of symbols and notation (art 50,000 YBP). Then women discovered that they could collect enough cereals in three weeks to last the entire year, more than a hunter could kill; but it required storage. Agriculture gave a surplus; that and crop failure and excess property led to excitement of war (Agriculture 9000 YBP). Civilization became the domestication of women, according to Thompson. This emphasized a patriarchal structure (Civilization 5500 YBP). Industrialization (200 YBP) is really an intensification of civilization, still an ektropic process. In each case of cultural absorption, there was an attendant process of miniaturization. The forest was miniaturized in clumps of trees; animals were miniaturized in artistic image; time on a lunar tally stick; plants in a garden; women in a household; nature by culture in 1800 (206 YBP) under the glass roof of the Crystal Palace; and now by the new consciousness surrounding the old. Planetization, along with miniaturization (48 YBP), contributed to the idea that the planet was an organism, that it could maintain itself in the environment of the solar system, and that it could balance its atmosphere with living communities. The first photograph of the earth in space became the symbol of the change in consciousness.

2.1.6. *Is there a Global Culture?*
Human societies have tended to grow larger over time. With the change in scale of populations, other changes have occurred in the structure of settlements, fields, governments and religion. These changes may foreshadow some kind of global culture.

2.1.6.1. The Growth of Megacultures
Some cultures grow, and in growing, decide that growth is a good thing to have without limits. Many lucky accidents, such as the rediscovery of the American continents, gave some European cultures an impetus to keep growing. Other developments, such as science and industry, followed the conditions created by plagues and environmental restraints. The Chinese became a megaculture by incorporating other cultures into an empire. The Spanish became a megaculture after benefiting from their exploration and exploitation of the Americas and western Pacific. The English became a megaculture after establishing an empire from North America and the Caribbean to Africa and Asia. North America became a megaculture in the Twentieth-Century. Each megaculture was able to dominate part of the planet with its influence and to see some of its products or rules become ubiquitous.

Global capitalism undermined many traditional cultures by offering consumerism in the place of traditional cultural guides for behavior. Social roles seemed irrelevant by comparison, if the good life could be bought without effort. Yet, it did not seem to work in Europe and the U.S. Instead of being free from economic want to develop their potential as creative human beings, people became trapped in a consumer cycle. Self-actualization was postponed for self-gratification. Democracy seemed to be good for balancing a middle class in some cultures, but it ignored other cultures and economies.

By virtue of its demomass and political system, China is becoming a megaculture. Chinese products are dominating the economies of other nations.

2.1.6.2. Emergence of a Simple Global Culture
Trade and exchanges by various cultures extend to distant lands. Over time, a global system starts to develop, with newer connections and technologies, which draw the cultures and civilizations, of all ages, into a tighter pattern. Some global civilization may result, but what effect will it have on the earlier patterns? So much is lost, in terms of ways of being and acting in a more natural, less technological environment. The world has acquired a global economic structure.

A global political system is emerging, as there is increased vertical differentiation, evolving from nations and regions, which leads to differentiation into political groups and economic interests. The world does not function well politically at a global level. It could be made better. It functions in the absence of a common culture or language. There is no world law, but there is a set of rules regulating international behavior; these are generally observed and understood. There is a small homogenous subculture, which belongs to the rich elites of every nation. This serves to integrate to some extent.

The modern world has become a very interactive system, especially with computer and communication technologies, which can lead to totally integrated mass communication and the extreme compression space and acceleration of time. It is said that the global system has no center. That is a good thing. But, it is expanding without limits and that is not a good thing. It could cause the disintegration of natural systems that are interlinked with our economic exploitation.

Perhaps this emergence can be linked with the major cultural revolution identified by W.I. Thompson, Planetization, as there is absorption of a new consciousness surrounding the old. Other earlier revolutions resulted had a similar attendant process of miniaturization. The forest was miniaturized in clumps of trees; animals were miniaturized in artistic image; time on a lunar tally stick; plants in a garden; women in a household; and, nature by culture in 1800 (under the glass roof of the Crystal Palace). The question is whether consciousness can create a global culture.

2.1.6.3. Is Global Culture Possible?

Is there such a thing as a global culture? In his Notes Towards a Definition of Culture, published in 1949, T. S. Eliot suggested that a "world culture which was simply a uniform culture would be no culture at all" and that humanity would be de-humanized in a miserable nightmare. But, since we could not give up the idea of a world culture, knowing that we could not imagine it, and conceiving it only as a logic logical term of relations between cultures: "We must aspire to a common world culture, which will yet not diminish the particularity of the constituent parts."

The local and the particular are required parts of culture, so global culture has a contradiction. Eliot noted that difficulty in a national culture of Britain: "We have not given enough attention to the ecology of cultures. It is probable, I think, that complete uniformity of culture throughout these islands would bring about a lower degree of culture altogether." He concluded that a national culture should be a constellation of to benefit each other and the whole to flourish.

The disappearance of peripheral cultures, in Britain and elsewhere, might be a calamity, but, modernity, in the predominant versions of liberalism and Marxism, sees the goal of history in a universal world culture. Alas, one wonders if a global culture would be worse than the national cultures that are so irreverent with their peripheral cultures. In destroying world peripheral cultures, there might not be any culture left to be global.

The 'McDonaldization' of the world is about economic dominance, the homogenization of trade networks and consumer rituals. This may undermine the identity of other cultures, but does not make a global culture, the idea of which has become a consumer object as much as burgers, fries and coke. Other local phenomena, such a Hollywood movies or Chinese slippers, that extend around the planet are local things that have been globalized. Cosmopolitan travel has the same flavor. Some cultures have more power because of these competitive advantages.

Although modern communications technology could work the same everywhere, it also may allow cultural differences and complexity to remain. The center seems to yield to the periphery, as other cultures all have hotel rooms, burgers, slippers and things. People can react by emphasizing the uniqueness of their ethnicity. No real globalism can exist until cultures and nations create a framework for the use of and protection of the capital of the planet, or until cultures enter into dialogues about a common global culture.

2.1.6.3.1. Upside of Global Culture

A global culture, which could emerge from the interactions of local cultures, could allow for more rapid exchange of ideas and things between individual cultures. It could provide the opportunity for trade in special goods, which have the potential to benefit every culture. It could provide paths for communication that might stimulate cultures. Cultures could learn from one another. A global culture could present a global morality, built on universal human tendencies, that would not be prescriptive of our private and public behaviors, but it would be proscriptive of damaging behaviors from murder to obsessive greed. Global functions and problems, such a atmospheric warming, would be easier to address. New global economic or political structures would also be easier to address, as would global problems, such as the overconnection of markets.

2.1.6.3.2. Downside of Global Culture
According to most theories of cultural adaptation (or integration or evolution), resistance to change is normal as a cultural process. Groups like the pygmies have specialized to fit the requirements of their environment, successfully. This makes it difficult for them to adopt other cultural arrangements formed in different environments.

Nature makes divisions and diversity. We need no more a unity of all people any more than of all wolves or fleas. Is it wise to have a single world? A single market in a single culture with a single control? It might create a suite of disastrous problems.

Hyperadaptivity is a serious condition that allows humans to adapt to poverty, bad diets, crowding, stress, suffering and immense natural loss. Of course, we are unconscious of many of these problems. Capitalism does not seem to be adequate as the only global economic strategy. It breaks down useful limits and boundaries. The homogeneity of forms promoted by a global communications and advertising campaigns leads to loss of diversity. A severely limited number of ways leads to a lack of flexibility (stagnation). Then, we have the hyperpersistence of error, in the forms of stupidity and violence, which forms a positive feedback loop. And, interactions are accelerating.

2.1.6.4. Considering a Global Frame for Small & Large Cultures
The desire to refine the focus has allowed the frame of reference to be neglected. An adaptive holoculture could place the human values of all cultures into a global framework. A new world order is a cultural problem more than an ecological or economic one. A global culture could incorporate the positive features of traditional civilizations: Personal security, respect for the individual, responsibility for actions (self-discipline), social integration, concern for others, and reverence for nature.

Such a global framework for culture would also consider important principles drawn from ecology. The proper attitude of an ecological global culture would be care (in Heidegger's word), a positive spontaneity, but also a "letting be," a reverence toward the wild alienness of nature, a willingness to comply with the limitations of natural systems, and a willingness to reduce the dominance of natural systems and to set aside wild areas. In addition, a global perspective might define: An authentic concept of humanity, rational economic development, a holistic education beyond that of a native culture, the responsibilities of societies to themselves, others, and the earth, and respect for all cultures.

The truth of human cultures and wild ecosystems is apprehended through myth. Cultures, through myth, need to fit our growing knowledge of the geology and biology of the earth into our hearts. Mythology is constructed as a poetic system. Campbell states that "Mythology—and therefore civilization—is a poetic, supernormal image." Mythologies and religions are great poems. When recognized as such, they point through things and events to the ubiquity of a presence that is whole in each.

2.2. Designing Ideal Cultures: Utopias

The City, Amanote, speaks these lines in Thomas More's 1516 fantasy, Utopia, about a perfect commonwealth, a society without the problems and poverty of a young English capitalism.

Felicity's Children
Wherefore not Utopie, but rather fitly
My name is Eutopie, a place of felicity

While relating his story in Latin, More made puns on the Greek names he used: The name of the city, Amanote, means "dream town;" the name of the traveler himself, Hythlodae, means "dispenser of nonsense." The title is also a word play; to the Greek word meaning place (topia), could be added a prefix meaning no (ou), or good (eu). He used 'u' as an ambiguous prefix; no place sounded like good place.

Utopias are fictions by definition. More had said that it was a fiction whereby the truth might "slide into men's minds." More invented and named the modern utopia. Unlike the earlier Republic, which Plato presented as an aristocratic ideal to be contemplated, More's utopia is meant to be a description of an achieved egalitarian society.

The citizens in More's utopia were uniform and regimented: Everyone had the same clothing, housing, and work schedule. Strong peer pressure existed for people to use their leisure time constructively for the public good or to improve their personal virtues. The electoral unit, the family, was autocratically ruled by the patriarch and a hierarchy of princes. Decisions were made by councils elected from public officials, who met regularly with these princes. The utopians solved the problem of population growth by setting up external colonies, where it was considered unjust for natives to hold onto land that they were not 'using'—much in the way the Spanish and English approached colonization in the Americas during the same century.

In Utopia, Thomas More comments on why there is less need for work or long working days: "for where money is the only standard of value, there are bound to be dozens of unnecessary trades carried on, which merely supply luxury goods or entertainment. Why, even if the existing labor force were distributed among the few trades really needed to make life reasonably comfortable, there'd be so much overproduction that prices would fall too low for workers to earn a living."

The basic argument, that a few hours of labor a day for everyone would be sufficient to supply all the necessities and comforts of life, is a good one (previously achieved in many archaic hunting and gathering cultures). The residents of Utopia reject beautiful clothing. More used a monastic metaphor, associated with strictness and deprivation. But, More neglects the importance of aesthetic needs. Having everyone have one simple garment would not be acceptable. People like to improve their things. Clothing, for instance, can reflect differences in taste or status, and people will devote much time and money to clothing.

In Utopia, money is eliminated, and therefore many crimes no longer exist. But, More does not adequately consider the human need for prestige and honor. People kill and cheat for prestige and honor as often as for any gold or symbols.

For More, Nature deserves respect, if for no other reason than she is capable of turning against us, and must be treated with care. But, nature is regard as endless and can be converted to cities and fields with each new utopian colony.

More expected that part of the meaning of *Utopia* would be carried in the dialogues inspired by the book. Chronologically, More created a good place first, and a society constructed from the moral and rational ideals of More himself second. As More wrote, he realized that humans could make any good place less good, that they can seek less than the optimum, or reinvent original sin. Human nature creates conditions that reverse its good. Absurdities are invented, toyed with, and embraced. It is human nature, to attempt to escape all control, or to express the desire to be wicked. More's vision had an immediate effect on the growth and development of his country.

Utopias as visions of ideal societies can be found in almost every culture: In prophecies, visions, dreams, myths, and ideologies. George Orwell suggests that the utopian vision has been consistent since Plato, with its dream of justice through reason, through the elevation of public life, and through the regulation of private life, community property, and good breeding. Utopias are not just visions of noplace, but of otherness.

The ideas of a golden age and an ideal city were combined in modern western utopias. The discovery of new continents opened new possibilities for utopias. Utopias have always been placed in distant lands, populated by people with strange customs. Plato envisioned a perfect model for the Athenian form of social organization; his Republic was located on an island in his present (2500 years before our present). In response to Plato, Aristotle suggested that it is impossible to say which model for a society is best. No organization can be ideal under all conditions and at all times. The organization depends on many factors, from social organization and size to the state of relations between neighboring states.

Christian utopias, such as Augustine's City of God, began with inward change, but led to heaven. These first utopias were idyllic; they described the good life, either material or spiritual, as tranquil and unchanging, but located in other places. In these utopias, liberty was less important than happiness or goodness. Many utopias try to control society through the state—as in Plato, More, Fourier—to ensure safety and peace. Other utopian writers, such as Morris, Kropotkin, and Bookchin, suggest abolishing the state entirely. Another distinction in subsequent utopias is between private or collective ownership, with the degree of openness, or with the level of technological solutions.

In many utopias, nature, rather than be protected or preserved, is deliberately transformed, according to geometric and scientific models. Francis Bacon, in The New Atlantis, writes: "the fathers of Salomon's House summon natural phenomena and create new species to dominate and transform nature, even to the point of eliminating it and making it superfluous." The goal of Bacon's utopia is the inflation of human power over the universe, to create human ease and human happiness. The simplicity of earlier visions was due to the assumed scarcity of goods.

With the exploration of all the continents and oceans, utopias began to be located in other times, the past or the future. For Saint-Simon, Fourier, Comte, and Marx, the good times were in process, and the goals for the future were fixed and codified. The predicted Utopia would be achieved eventually, given institutional and technological propensities. Morris and Howard rely on the garden metaphor. This requires complete design and control in some instances. The garden is dominated by external design without internal human changes.

Later utopian thought put less emphasis on individual and social content. Theilhard de Chardin regarded man as the spirit of the earth, part of a process leading to the "hominization" of the earth and the spiritualization of humanity. The present is also rife with unanticipated developments, such as population growth, blossoming energy use, and waste that follows use everywhere. Other thinkers, including Skinner and Maslow, emphasized the psychological dimension of utopias, recommending personal changes.

In the past century, the concept of place began to be combined with different prefixes to indicate wrongness (dys) or badness (kako), as in dystopias or kakotopias. Among others, Huxley and Orwell traced paths of visions gone awry. Huxley relies on a wilderness metaphor, with a simple natural lifestyle, characterized by a hands-off approach. But, is there recognition of the human contribution to the goodness of place? Is there enough respect for the power of nature? We recognize that nature may treat us well; we should recognize that nature will provide opportunities for us, but also that it may remove them through the occasional violence of its chaotic systems.

As the visions became less positive, utopias became less adequate and less desirable. Few utopias, although Ernest Callenbach's Ecotopia is an important exception, have been created since the 1940s. Callenbach and Bookchin suggest alignment with natural cycles, preventing disruption by eliminating pesticides and using only renewable energy. Marius de Greus suggests that this model is the most neutral and has the fewest weaknesses. Even ecological utopias can be static, however. Callenbach, for instance, offers a static model in the Pacific Northwest. Most utopias still tend to be isolated, since they could not compete with the expanding industrial system. Modern utopias present a very limited set of lifestyles, usually revolving around the simple good of a frugal lifestyle.

Utopian thought has a reputation for being unrealistic. This thought is considered to be the dangerous dreams of unreal fantasies. Many commentators, such as Frank and Fritzie Manuel, conclude that utopia is dead. Perhaps this conclusion is just the recognition that reason is not enough, and that human technological power over nature has a higher price than we thought we would have to pay. Perhaps it is the conclusion of people without a strong system of spiritual beliefs.

Utopian thinkers, in questioning the whole of society, often urge its total reconstruction. Utopias have had a great influence on modern industrial society, with their ideal visions of society and their promotion of the benefits of scientific technology. Ironically, these tendencies, especially detachment and nuclear weapons, have the possibility of making real kinds of utopias, literally 'no-places,' on earth.

Traditional utopias look towards a past of ideal peace or a future of ideal postindustrial technological harmony. They do not look enough into the present, into other cultures. In present cultures, however, lie suggestions of the size of society, limits to growth, and appropriate technology.

The value of utopian thought is in questioning all the presuppositions of today. The question: To what extent are problems inherent in the existing social economic or political order? Or rather, in the scale of that order? People want to break from the problems of the past and yet keep the positive aspects of it. They want to have dreams and create their societies in the images of those dreams.

2.2.1. Images Cast Shadows

Our dream of civilization and nature in modern industrial culture is the dream of order and beauty, but as Aldous Huxley notes, the dream of order begets growth and tyranny, and the dream of beauty ends in monsters and violence. Striving for the good life for many has left us with crowded roads and regimented jobs; trying to build beautiful cities has given us gigantic boxes and neighborhood violence. Trying to fulfill our dreams of comfort and security has provoked global threats and local nightmares. The dream is a nightmare that reflects an unbalanced and immature image of the earth.

The collective image that people make of their place on earth is a world (derived from the German word for 'man-image'). The image is constructed metaphorically, but considered 'as if' it were true. Each world is based on a root metaphor, according to Stephen Pepper, which is a good device to discuss them. Root metaphors are comprehensive and dominate our attitudes towards things. If the image is incomplete or does not fit environmental conditions, it may fail. People who constructed their worlds from preconceived notions sometimes did not survive. The Aztecs, for example, based their cosmology on the belief that the sun needed human blood to survive, and so they sacrificed great numbers of lives to ensure the sun's life. Their political policy was based on raids for victims, and this policy contributed to their overthrow and decline with the arrival of the Spanish.

The use of flawed images can destroy the environments of cultures as well as the cultures themselves. When Easter Island was settled by Polynesians around 1500 BP, it was fertile and uninhabited. Despite their technological and food-producing skills, ideas on how to deal with surface stones to increase productivity seems to have precipitated genocidal warfare between two groups of believers, those who wanted to keep the stones and those who wanted to throw them into the sea, although stresses from deforestation, erosion, and limited kinds of crops, as well as from cold winds and drought, likely contributed to the violence. By the time of the island's rediscovery by Europeans in 1722, mortality from social chaos had reduced the population to about 1100, significantly less than the approximate high of 8,000 (estimates have ranged as high as 20,000 or 30,000). The population dropped to 155 by 1886, although at an increase of 3% per year since then, the population is now over 2000 and supported by tourist trade.

Table 221-1. Root Metaphors. By contrasting the views of metaphor enumerated by Max Black with Pepper's four root hypotheses, a rough correlation emerges. Two other hypotheses can be added to the schema: Animism, which Pepper rejected as inadequate, and holocosmology, which considers all views valid within limits.

Root Metaphor	Context	Dynamic
Animism (Mythology)	Identity	Identity
Formism (Rationalism)	Substitution	Similarity
Mechanism	Decoration	Similarity
Contextualism	Utility	Congruity
Organicism	Wholeness	Interaction
Holocosmology	Frame	Star

Modern industrial cultures also have defective images. Our root metaphor of the machine extends down through all levels of society to the economic and the personal. An image of a culture can be stated as a series of principles, such as: "the universe is mechanical; humanity is master of the universe; and all persons are equal." These metaphors have allowed inhabitants of some nations to treat people, plants, animals, and nature as robots that can be modified or replaced. The cost of that image has been the diminishment and destruction of lives and environments. Metaphors can limit cultural possibilities. For example, the metaphor "labor is a resource" implies that, like any common resource defined by industrial society, labor is cheap and can be used up. Modern economies, embracing another metaphor "nature is capital," draw on the accumulated "capital" of ecosystems for production. By ignoring the real cost of the capital, as well as the costs of natural services, such as nutrient recycling, soil building, and atmospheric renewal, these economics create a temporary wealth that will disappear when the capital is exhausted or the society collapses. Decisions regarding resources are made on short-term economic grounds and lead to material shortages and environmental degradation.

Powerful images can influence cultures over centuries. The principle of plenitude, restated in Christian terms, presents that an intelligible creator gave an earth of unlimited bounty to humanity for its use. This principle seemed to be confirmed in the Renaissance with the discovery of the richness of heaven, microscopic life, and unexplored continents. Many modern political ideologies and economic systems have been shaped by the principle of endless wealth. Adam Smith calculated that the real price of anything was just the toil acquiring it.

These ideas are parallel to the idea of unlimited good, where anything, even virtue, can be multiplied indefinitely. The invalidity of this principle comes with the recognition of limits. Without limits any good becomes devalued and is wasted. Limits contribute to value. The universe is limited; the earth is limited; individuals have limits. These modern metaphors are defective because they do not fit our surroundings. The crises of cultural images have tremendous physical consequences. For most of human history, the habitable earth has been a mosaic of separate territories and peoples. Different groups developed distinctive ways of dealing with their nonhuman surroundings. Each way of dealing can be referred to as a culture, a pattern of behavior based on shared beliefs adapted to the local environment. Culture can be expressed as a symbolic language. The particular symbols concerned with cultural institutions as manipulative objects are political symbols. Politics deals with words, which are arbitrary symbols for events or things. The wrong relationship of things and symbols can result in misguided politics and violence. Political decisions are made on narrow political and economic grounds. The gradual narrowing of the focus has resulted in a citizenship in industrial cultures that is the abandonment of responsibility on the assumption that others know how to manage things; government itself is the assumption of responsibility, without sufficient knowledge that result in a suite of problems.

Wrong decisions and wrong relationships have resulted in creating places that are nowhere. To create our noplaces, we have accepted the gifts of bigness, speed, and uniformity and allowed the thefts of life, intelligence identity, and choice to negate any gain from them. Combined with our own failures of charity, imagination, will, and courage, using piecemeal knowledge and unrelated ideals without regard to traditional knowledge and practical experience, we have created common faceless cultures to sit on our flat, placeless utopias.

2.2.2. *One World Through Reason* (The Formation of the United Nations)
After the end of the war in 1918, there was a popular vision of one world, without walls or barriers. The most desirable way of creating the "one world," as Wendell Willkie called it, was through reason, although reason has not been used historically to consolidate or shape nations—France, Germany, the U.S., and Italy, among others, were united by force. The notion of a world government seems to satisfy a basic human craving for unity and order, but, at the current stage of international relations, there seemed to be no agreeable path toward a single benevolent world order.

The partial adaptation of international institutions is insufficient for a world order, especially if these bodies are only advisory. The United Nations (UN) is the only body with the machinery for constructing a world system; the beginnings of ecological politics can be found in the special services of the UN—UNESCO, FAO, WHO, and the various technical aid services. As long as ecological and political problems are addressed in a framework of nationalism and military power, however, these organizations are treated as peripheral and relatively impotent.

Despite its good-hearted programs on disease and education, the UN cannot deal with widespread starvation, or acid rain or the whole complex of global problems. The UN does not seem to have a good grasp on global problems either. The 6th and 7th special sessions recommended financial aid, annual transfers of resources to poor nations, and a charter of economic rights. It is unlikely that this will happen. There are too many vested interests.

It has been said the UN has no use beyond recommending the avoidance of violent conflict. As it is, the UN has found many uses in setting standards for human health and education, as well as with human rights. It has not been as effective recently at stopping genocidal behavior in some countries.

As it is structured, the UN is not capable of handling the responsibility for international order. Despite its emphasis on peace and international security, the UN has been able to mount only a relatively few peace operations—perhaps only one every two years for its sixty year history. Although many of these have been successful, they have had to be approved by the Security Council and to be run understaffed and underfunded. The peacekeeping efforts in Bosnia were not effective.

Not in Somalia either. The attempt to guarantee democracy in Cambodia was not effective.

Milton Eisenhower had said at the UNESCO conference in 1949 that for the UN to be effective, it would have to have a police force stronger than any nation's armed forces. While that could work, few nations would permit an international superpower. Most nations would also consider it to be an intolerable burden and worry that it would control the world in a unity that would have no liberty for any nation.

Is the UN due to be a monster world-state? Perhaps healthy small states could be united into healthier larger organisms. But, the UN cannot survive on good will. As it is now the UN is a union of some large powers and many small ones. The UN functions only with the consent of the reluctant four or five biggest states. Their veto power is a reflection of their power and might.

It has been said that there are no fundamental disagreements in the UN, now. But, then, this is a limited UN, not much trusted or invested in. It has also been said that there are no universal agreed-on truths of social organization. This is not a problem, because cultures organize, then societies. All an enhanced UN would do is keep standards and coordinate cultural organizations.

It has been said that the UN is a forum for the same power politics in disguise. That has been a problem with the original establishment of the UN and its reflection in the Security Council. The universal values of the UN Charter come from the victors of the world war in 1945. The UN was never meant to be for free nations. The Security Council was the preserve of great powers, with the undemocratic veto power. Restricting membership in the Security Council to great powers, and its use of the veto principle, indicate that the UN is imprisoned by the status quo. The values and memberships simply need to be modified and enlarged. Should the UN get rid of all veto power in Councils and return to persuasion?

It has been said that the UN bureaucracy worships consensus, otherwise called the "handmaiden of evil" by autocratic states. But, consensus is what allowed human societies for millennia to reach decisions. It has been said that there is a danger in having a strong Secretary General powerful enough to prevent war. No Secretary General has had the power to prevent wars. Is preventing war less dangerous than allowing uncontrolled conflicts?

It has been said that public discourse would be suffocated in a peaceful world. That is always possible, but we know that it is suffocated in a warring world, even if it is a multitude of small, undeclared wars. Discourse is considered unpatriotic for criticizing bad decisions made in wars or in 'undeclared conflicts,' the current political euphemism for wars, but discourse should not be suffocated by unevenly applied ideas of patriotism. It has been said that a vision of world peace is unrealistic; leaders would have no tragic memory of the latest conflict and little earned wisdom in dealing with conflict. It is argued that these "shallow, callow, child-like leaders and their advisors" would commit some grievous miscalculation leading to a holocaust or war. One answer? Three words: George Double-U Bush. For the most part, the current leaders have power expressly due to their skills of manipulation, not due to experiences of tragedy. Furthermore, peace would not be the end to struggle or conflict. Natural limits, human conflicts, and the long adjustments to peace and equity would provide many large challenges.

It has been said that the UN dominates the world, that it is inflexible and unaccountable. But, it is no less accountable than any elected body. Officials and programs can be changed or removed.

It has been said that international goals are best realized through national self-interest. This must be the old wisdom. It might have been true, if nations were perfectly rational and knowledgeable; they do not seem to be. Nations now seem to be the handmaidens of corporations, whose interest is only in profits for shareholders. The views of shareholders are notoriously short-sighted. The UN is limited by images and ideals of progress. The UN's solution to economic problems is "sustainable development"—that is, "growth that respects environmental constraints," as if growth respects any constraints. The Bruntland Report indicates a five to ten-fold increase in world industrial output within the next hundred years before population stabilization occurs. While the appeal of growth is unarguable, it is really not likely to be sustainable in any meaning of that word, since sustainable growth does not recognize known ecological limits. Furthermore, the UN has no power to coerce its members when it does make good recommendations.

Our attempts at social improvements have proceeded without order, without sufficient insight and perspective, without sufficient confidence, without a comprehensive plan, and without a great dream. Our politics has been corrupted by special interests. The structure of our civilization comes from anonymous builders and mediocre designers, minimal engineers and rapacious financiers. We work within the rules as they have been for decades, rejecting any alternatives as too utopian. The rules themselves have been shaped by centuries of social metaphors and utopian ideals. The rules within which we have been operating for the last sixty years, or even since the Treaty of Versailles, are inadequate. It is not a matter of what is the best thing to do within the rules as they are at the moment, it is a matter of changing the rules.

2.2.3. *Ending Up Nowhere* (History of Competition & Conflict)
Most humans are dominated by the idea of competition: It is us against the environment, us against others, and us against ourselves. Everywhere antagonism pervades our society—college presidents lead their groups into battle for bestness; political parties blame each other for one hundred years of bad planning; we compete for jobs, status, dollars, and mates. Conventional violence—war, murder—captures news headlines, but structural violence—mining, schooling, hospitals—pervades society unacknowledged. Most relationships seem violent in a competitive society.

Many human societies advanced by fighting and expanding. Fighting is a common form of human behavior, occurring in children, as a ritual limited by pain, and in adults, as failure of communication or understanding. The growth of the brain and its capacity for abstract thought seems to have bypassed the ritualization of social conflicts common to other mammals. Human fighting is not as formalized; and, this is what permits humans to slaughter one another. Most tribes followed two standards of morality: One for insiders and one for outsiders. Most aggression was directed outwards and the losers were often exterminated.

Many tribal groups federated into national units. A nation, by definition, has a single, central government representing people who occupy contingent lands and are consciousness of a common identity. The professional ruling class is divorced from kinship bonds; structure is stratified and internally diversified. Almost the whole land surface of the globe is divided into centrally governed states. Human affairs are managed within the framework of these autonomous units. Decisions are made on narrow political and economic grounds, rather than on environmentally sound principles.

2.2.3.1. Trapped in Images: Myths & Peace
The two great myths, progress and nationalism, arose with the industrial cosmology. The author Aldous Huxley described progress as the theory that one can get something for nothing, that the gain in one field is not even paid for in another. Progress assumed that all consequences could be foreseen, and that the ideal ends in the future justified the most abominable means: Robbery, murder, or cheating. Progress was considered good, and primitive groups only obstructed the civilized nations' march toward paradise.

According to Huxley, nationalism was the theory that the state was the only true god; all others, especially other states, were false. Conflicts over prestige or power were crusades for progress and nationalism, for the Good and the True. Lord Acton observed that nationalism aims solely at making a nation, the abstract idea of the political state, and not at liberty or prosperity for people. He also predicted that the result would be moral and material ruin. Nations are basically exploitative of other nations and smaller cultural groups, which may not be considered nations because they lack a permanent military: The United States concentrates on Latin America; Europe on Africa; Japan over Southeast Asia; Russia over Eastern Europe; and China over Tibet. The reasons for this continued behavior include: The rapaciousness of society; the acceptance of war; and the economic advantages of large-scale operations. The cultures of industrial nations are based on unethical accumulations of materials. Inequality is maintained by power, not persuasion, and also by the assumption that solutions are extrinsic and external and have to be found by spreading out rather than intensifying efforts to find solutions at home.

National powers work, through progress, to maintain the good life for their leaders and followers (although differentially). Major powers deal formally and informally with each other on survival problems, such as nuclear crisis or ecological crisis, but compete on other issues. Politicians should think about the hunger and squalor of billions of human beings and the destruction of habitats with billions of ambihuman lives, before dedicating themselves to their personal fortunes and the missiles needed to protect them. The system of management, like all paradigms, slowly becomes a means of excluding experience foreign to the notation. It becomes a form of authoritarian control. Programs become responsible for dimensions of misery beyond any considered.

Our politics will improve when we realize that we are the biggest ecological problem. Ecology studies the details of the binding of all beings in the earth into a whole. Ecology, like god, is not to be mocked, as Gregory Bateson said. There are no such things as little sins. Even human plans are now part of the ecology. Bateson warns that all ad hoc measures leave the deeper causes of problems uncorrected, or worse, permit the causes to be compounded.

2.2.3.2. Committed to War
Those who believe in the theology of nationalism are committed to fight. War is a way of conquering or creating new nations. It is a nonprogressive way of promoting progress, especially innovations in certain kinds of technology. What have been the causes of war? We know some causes from hunting societies or chiefdoms: Insults or broken agreements, or competition for resources, from food to land. Nations created new causes: To unify other cultures and resources, or to deunify the enemy and to unify the aggressor.

The war ethos has been expanded and reduced to absurdity. War has become so big that there can be no victories or victors, and possibly no survivors. The only remaining purpose can be the total destruction of the combatants, as nations, as well as natural habitats. Sadly, the only people who do not know this, or admit it, are those in decision-making positions, who are compelled to prepare for what they subconsciously know would be a terrible disaster. Their power has trapped them in the momentum of their nation, afraid to be caught in any criticism. Yet, they direct the money, skill, and knowledge of their citizens into projects that lead to misery, servitude and hideous death, and not to life, liberty, and happiness.

The intellectual rationalization for the continual preparation for war is the old Roman adage: "If you want peace, prepare for war." This adage has been so completely taken into the modern heart that most of the larger nations have spent over half of every century in war, according to Pitirim Sorokin. Preparation for war has always led to war. There seems to be no reason that the present arms race will lead anywhere else, even in times of relative peace.

Power politics makes problems that cannot be solved except by war. Questions about defining the best nation or the best religion lead to organized slaughter as the answer. "War is not merely a political act," said Clausewitz, "but also a political instrument, a continuation of political relationships …" As long as human institutions were large and brittle, war was an effective way of disassembling them. This form of social renewal, however, was very expensive. Marx may have been partly right when he said war was necessary under certain conditions, as a last resort. But, those conditions no longer exist. His observation may have been true from the 1830s to the 1940s, but it has been rendered false by modern weaponry. Nuclear war can destroy the parts as well as the connections, cultures and ecosystems, as well as senile political structures. It may not be able to discriminate.

War has become an integral part of the modern economy. The war industry, as measured by expenditures, is on the order of $200 billion a year. Defense problems in the U.S. are perceived as problems of hard technology; psychological and social research is considered irrelevant. Security is analyzed in terms of Newtonian physics: Blocks, actions and vacuums.

There are other dangers and benefits to war. There are, of course, benefits to war. It equalizes opportunities for some. It foments change, any kind of change. It gives a sense of the past, if the past needs to be measured by conflicts and victories. It leads to more advanced technologies and to faster social responses.

The economic rationalization is even more crucial for nations. Armament piling has become a vital part of the U.S., Russian, Iranian, and North Korean economies, among others. The recovery from the U.S. depressions in the 1930s was not complete until the rearmament surge to combat the Axis powers. The Korean and Vietnamese wars also spurred the U.S. economy. U.S. prosperity has its basis in the preparation for death. The fear of Russian competition (in 1970) ensured government expenditures of billions of dollars for 'deterrence.' The vested interests in this system are almost insurmountable. The concrete companies and bomb makers put up their own puppet politicians to guarantee their part of the spoils.

The dangers include the fact that war has been regarded as meaningful struggles against people who would kill or enslave others. The 'side-effects' are rarely considered or counted. War also leads to an overweening respect for large government. The cost of war excludes the social distribution of wealth. Consider the plight of the Russian or the U.S. poor. The situation is much worse in disadvantaged countries. The war industry, as measured by expenditures, is on the order of $200 billion a year. Kenneth Boulding says that it is an unrecognized paradox that the cost of maintaining the war industry is greater than any possible damage that could be inflicted by an enemy. Furthermore, war intensifies the depletion of resources; therefore, it is counterproductive to fight to steal another nation's resources. For centuries, warfare has resulted in incredible wastes of resources. The latest multinational conflict, which began in 1914, and has been hot and cold during this time, has been the most wasteful.

The winners of a large war will need to be pitiless, according to Kurt Vonnegut, for pity will be suicidal when resources become exhausted. War is considered to breed strength and nobility. The values of strength, nobility and bravery were suitable for certain hunting societies. But, even the weak and lazy can get food and shelter in this world without plundering. Humanity is clever at taking more than what it needs from nature. Evolution is thought of as the survival of the fitter. Nobility and cleverness may not best fit a species for survival, if they require competition and war. Perhaps mankind will perish for its nobility— but is it noble to be extinct?

Perhaps it is the fate of humanity to die a radiant death, taking most other living beings with them. Who could resist the glory of complete annihilation? Perhaps that is the fate of humanity. But what is fate? The hand of God, or the idea of Tolstoy—that historical events are determined by the summation of innumerable decisions by the anonymous masses of humans that add up to a tendency. In particular terms, the small decisions to buy automobiles, poison coyotes, plant trees, or live simply, add up to fate. Fate certainly concentrates power in corporate, military and political hands, which still belong to human beings, who cannot find consolation in mega-deaths.

Nuclear war is unthinkable. Limited disarmament is unworkable. Human and environmental degradation are unconscionable. Is anything thinkable or workable without being hopelessly utopian? The problems of aggression, nationalism, war, and peace are problems of human nature, symbol, culture, politics, ecology, and size. They are not simple problems and not easily solved. They are interrelated as human groups are technologically, economically, ecologically, and politically interdependent. Human interactions have been dominated by symbols. The most powerful set, embodied as nationalism, has a direct relationship to war. Large-scale war can create utopias, places that are nowhere, on earth.

The United Nations made war illegal; one nation cannot attack another. But, that has not made a lot of difference. Cultures try to destroy other cultures. Big nations try to absorb or punish small nations. The aggression by the United States against Iraq is a crime against humanity according to the Nuremberg principles established by the victors of the conflict in the 1940s. Those principles were enforced by hangings at that time. The war was sold to the U.S. Congress with lies and propaganda, but even exposure was not enough to reverse the decision to stay the 'course.' Perhaps U.S. citizens are naïve about their role in making peace or securing its need for oil. Perhaps that naiveté has to do with the luck of never having been invaded, flattened or destroyed by another nation.

2.2.3.3. Fear of Peace

What is peace? The absence of war? The absence of large-scale organized conflict? Peace means, in the original Latin, 'confirming to an agreement.' An agreement is part of a conversation between two or more people, which usually results from an effort to avoid some kind of conflict. Peace requires conversation, the exchange of opinions, wants, and problems within the context of meeting.

Robert Kaplan states that tragedy "requires a sense of history," implying that war is tragedy and peace is timeless. He suggests that peace leads to a 'preoccupation with presentness, the loss of the past and a consequent disregard of the future.' He continues arguing that because peace is pleasurable and pleasure is a momentary satisfaction, therefore pleasure, as well as peace, is inseparable from convenience, a temporary, timeless, uniform satisfaction. Should we not outlaw love-making and eating as well? Or all momentary pleasures? These are strange arguments: People in war time damning peace, as if it were the worst threat to the planet. Have we ever had such a dull time of peace? And, did the people who experienced the satisfaction of peace complain and lust for the tragedy of war?

Why is universal peace something to be feared? Would it lead to great dullness or great evil? Tragedy does require history, for it cannot operate without it. Peace requires history and tragedy as well.

Is peace without a sense of history? Peace seems unchanging and historyless, with fewer dramatic changes, but people seem to want to sacrifice anything for it. The common, written history of reference is the usually the history of the victor, with great leaders and great changes, but that itself is a small limited mythical history. Real history includes all kinds of changes, from geological ones to the development of cities. Perhaps people mistake peace for a static vacuum.

How did we get this way? Bad genes? Bad images? People have images of nature as violent or of humans as naturally violent, which contrast with other images of nature as cooperative and humans as peaceful. Some of the logics of our cultures promote a dualism where either one is true, but not both. The logic of opposites creates a false dilemma, a fallacy, where there has to be a winner and a loser, where opponents have to fight over one thing or one way. This logic has the advantage of simplifying complex situations into one adversarial relationship, which can only be decided by conflict. But switching logics, or expanding the logic that dominates global conversations, can allow seemingly contradictory ideas to exist together, such as simplicity and wealth, or peace and artistic creation.

Overwhelming desires? In Buddhism in general, desire is an obstacle to peace. Suffering can be reduced only by following certain practices. There is conflict between desires and suffering, between needs and wants, between ideals and actions, between expectations and real events. Neither desire nor suffering can be totally eliminated by behavior patterns, which will always cause more desire or suffering by the very nature of human wants. Peace for Baruch de Spinoza is a virtue that springs from force of character. It exists with other virtues, such as self-control or self-regulation. Some desire and suffering can be reduced through education. Art educates and liberates the individuals of society in a gradual and peaceful process. In spite of the cultural forces dominant at any moment, an individual has the potential to determine a different course. Art can reduce or rechannel desire, and thus reduce the suffering that comes from maximized desires.

Runaway scale? As long as there is no limit on violence, wars can continue to engage plants, animals, even entire habitats and civilian populations, as often as soldiers and weapons. Conflict has to be descaled. It could be limited to a small number of representatives from each culture or group, so that the scale of peace would always be larger than the scale of conflict.

So, if we made an agreement to limit conflict to certain arenas and to certain sizes, that could be a form of peace. Peace could be a process of resolving conflicts between cultures. Some conflict is unavoidable, due to human nature and ideas of honor and possession, due to different images and beliefs about how the universe operates, and due to misunderstandings and accidents. Much conflict is related to fear, fear of loss, loss of security, loss of effort and opportunity. However, as long as violence is an accepted response to conflict, events will continue to be violent. The proper response has to be self-restraint and mutual constraint. Conflict has to be delinked with violence. All conflict is not bad. It is a challenge and stimulant to an individual and a culture. But, it has to be responded to in such as way that people think and develop, and create a considered response. Limited peace would to match the limits of conflict.

Peace is also a freedom from public disorder. Disorder is also unavoidable. But, it has to be kept below a cultural ceiling where it could destabilize the culture. That requires the agreement of a culture and inhabitants. Like conflict, disorder is a challenge that requires a creative response, rather than attempt to destroy disorder.

Is peace just nonviolence? Nonviolence is a psychological choice by an individual; it may be a cultural rule if enough people practice it. It is a way to resolve conflict through nonresistant awareness, which includes witnessing and understanding, conversation and mutual constraint. Conversation, remember, involves listening as well as speaking, in responding to another person. It exposes common themes and builds trust. So, nonviolence, or peace, is not a passive, head-hanging response to dominance. Bearing witness to injustice, that is to the results of dominance and violence, of inequity and prejudice, is a form of action that requires courage and persistence, and results in knowledge and the spread of awareness. The Quaker tradition of bearing witness is a turning towards events, and participation in those events. There are degrees of witnessing from observing to communicating, such as writing letters or making telephone calls, to acting nonviolently and negotiating for changes in events. Nonviolent action can neutralize aggression by refusing to offer positive feedback, that is, more violence in response.

Is peace just cooperation? Conflict is the result of differences in perception or needs. But differences can be resolved without conflict, without automatically assuming an adversarial stance. The subject of the conflict can be recognized as a common challenge—more than a problem that requires a solution, or a final, one-time fix, challenges are opportunities for change and development.

When conflict was thought to be the primary mode of operation in nature, it justified human conflict and violence, not just to fellow humans, but to animals and all of nature. With the scientific understanding that cooperation is much more prevalent in building guilds among animals and stable habitats, the operation of nature becomes more understandable. Cooperation builds partnerships and mutually beneficial relationships between individuals, species, and communities. Cooperation is more than the avoidance of conflict. It is the recognition of emergent benefits. It is finding security in sharing, or in new ways of being, rather than by eliminating competitors.

Cooperation is one aspect of peace. Ways of cooperating include communicating needs and negotiating for redistribution of resources. As it goes along it may be necessary to mediate two desires, or to arbitrate a decision. But, this is done though sharing in a conversation, by building consensus through common themes and conversation, by identifying shared goals and needs, in an atmosphere of trust, where feelings and ideas are shared, taking as much time as necessary, with as little outside agenda as possible, to be committed to the benefit of both groups in the process.

Is peace just harmony? Peace can also mean harmony or concord. But, harmony can contain discordant notes and themes and weave them into a rhythm. Harmonious action can change patterns of domination of cultures and individuals. Harmony has to include conversation with other species, and trust in nature as a generally beneficent system, our mother system and home. Although humans cooperate with each other, cooperation with other species is best characterized by allowing them opportunities for living, despite a measured exploitation.

Peace is unknown territory, terra incognita. We have not been there often, except by accident. The path to conflict is easier to define—it results from fear, from the desire to defend and to be violent. The new path requires as much bravery as violence does; it requires patience, it requires effort to find out why and what is needed.

There are, of course, numerous ways to achieve peace, such as requiring everyone to belong to the same religion or social class. This tactic has been tried; it did not work. Perhaps we could limit conflict in new ways, such as personal conflict between leaders or their champions. Or, assign all power to an Global Union. Or change the focus of war to nonhuman astronomical events, such as meteors.

Figure 2233-1. Plowshare as a Symbol of Peace (Evgeny Buchetich)

2.3. The Potential of Good (Eutopias)

Most Utopian discussions have to do with places as literature or as literary alternatives to real world ecological and political situations. Marx and Engels criticize utopian thinkers for lacking a thorough analysis of power relations within a society, as well as of economic developments that bring about changes. Karl Popper criticizes utopian engineering for expecting to make massive changes that would affect the entire human society. He says, correctly, that our knowledge and experience are too limited to expect that such changes would benefit society and people. It is too limited; there are far too many uncertainties and risks.

Nevertheless, utopias serve a vital human need. One important and valuable aspect of utopias is their play with new ideas or combinations of ideas. Another aspect is as thought experiments that let us work out limitations and goals.

The other sense of utopia, that of good places, should not remain silent. We need utopias to define visions for the future, but we need a different kind now, not the visions of no-places or of the wrong-places, but of good places—Eutopias.

Before trying to build a framework for good places, we first need to understand what makes good places, and then how we encultured human beings can make good places, whether with centralized planning and global prescriptions or with ecological plans and local control. And we need to ask more questions: Are good persons, institutions or societies enough? Are good ideas, images or dreams enough? Are good, coordinated efforts enough? Perhaps these questions can be answered with wild ideas and thought experiments. Dreams and imagination are needed to describe desirable futures, to support plans, and to outline goals.

In that sense, eutopias fits in the tradition of thought. The approach is both descriptive and prescriptive in novels, which allows readers to interiorize the system and appreciate the details of the life within. Eutopias is a thought experiment to apply real alternatives, derived from the baseline of cultural experiences, to the problem-ridden monolithic applications of industrial civilizations, to try to diversify and fit it into a regenerative pattern.

Utopias may be impossible, but good places are possible. Good places already exist everywhere. There is a place in Africa, by the northern Abderes in Kenya, where a stream winds its way through gardens and orchards, by low houses, and crowned cranes stalk between rows of vegetables; flocks and herds graze on fenced pastures, and wild animals fed nearby. Such places can be found in every place of the world. Perhaps by logically working out the limits and adaptability of humanity, good places can be created for almost everyone.

In totalitarian utopias, people must be controlled, the threat being that, without discipline there would be immediate disorder and the utopia would collapse. As we know, it is impossible to avoid disorder, which is a necessary part of any physical and social system. A system with flexibility, such as a eutopian system, could incorporate disorder without being destroyed.

Taking it cue from utopian writings, eutopias asks the broadest questions about society and the environment. Where would you like to live, in urban or rural or mixed? How close to nearest large store? How often should your neighbors visit unannounced? Once a week, a month, always, never? What should your neighbors do? Be artists, scientists, laborers, game players, or be multi-faceted?

Rather than a single nonnegotiable truth, as would be imposed in Plato's *Republic*, the inhabitants of eutopias would "play" with truth. In fact, their education, taking cues from Schiller, would encourage play at all levels.

Culturally-based nations can provide a greater spectrum of intricate descriptions and possible relations than any one single thought experiment. That is why they need to be the basis of good-places-in-the-making. The framework is enriched by the ideals and visions of nations. This is consistent with the intuitive knowledge that many styles of life are sustainable.

This is where eutopias would work effectively: Accepting the unpredictable nature of natural and social processes, yet managing adaptively on a micro-planning level. Eutopias would incorporate tradition and working past elements, rather than breaking with them. As Edmund Burke, reflecting on the French Revolution, noted that society had gone through a natural process of development, forming traditions and institutions that provided rules of behavior known to the people. We tend to forget how much discipline already exists in every society. People abide by most rules, from driving on one side of the road to preserving their children from molestation.

In eutopias, it is important to work with what exists, with what has already worked in place, with history and culture. Eutopias can start in California, Sri Lanka or any place that can support a nationhood aligned with a cultural history, without having a standard army or special currency.

The eutopian vision would start with immediate needs for everyone, but then allow people to be as extravagant as they want within the general social limits. Most people like the place they live, and they like their culture, so it is not necessary to force them to stay in place or be what they are. That does not mean that they do not want to live better, just that they do not all want to be Swiss or U.S. citizens.

Despite the eloquent pleas of Wendell Berry and Gary Snyder, that people ought to stay put and put down roots in a home place, we may not want to base the frame of eutopias on that idea. People have been nomads for a longer time than farmers or city dwellers. It might be better to accept that movement and dislocation is part of the harmony of life and try to minimize the negative effects, especially combined with consumerism and energy waste. The civilization of cultures is not a steady state, but it can be accommodated in a flexible framework. Flexibility is an important eutopian characteristics, along with resilience, adaptivity, and surprise—that is danger—Callenbach recognized that in his Ecotopia; places need to offer excitement and danger.

A new model may solve some problems but will definitely create new problems; Niccolo Machiavelli reasoned that this would always happen. This is a good argument for eutopias, since changes would occur mostly on a small scale, easily correctable. That is why eutopias can be a framework, by limiting human evil and good to small places, with minimal control or competition.

There is no single model of government that will fit all cultures, all traditions, all needs or all nations. But, governments can be held to common standards through an international body. Eutopias tries to structure the global commonwealth of nations by proposing specific common goals, regarding weapons disbursement and population limits. It offers a consideration of distributive justice among nations and between the generations of every nation. It offers visions of culturally-based nations in equilibrium with nature, using ideas from ecological design and conservation biology.

The eutopian framework is more than a simple perspective; it is a design for a self-renewing process using proven cultural methods to improve human situations and environments. The frame is not a final goal, but a way to allow the many small useful, culturally determined (or limited) changes that we need for our survival on the planet as we like it.

Eutopias is a cheap solution because it uses the parts already in place. It is within reach of any people in any culture, regardless of how fast or technological. And also, because it limits the ways of big, expensive solutions.

Eutopias is not a big law; but, it is a big story, large enough to allow all other stories. It is changing and open-ended. It is conservative, but that becomes an instrument to create peace and justice everywhere. It keeps human rights connected with species rights and land rights.

Eutopias is a framework that holds all the other pieces of solutions and makes them part of a whole thing. It helps us to understand the whole thing, the whole set of relations with people, land, and other beings, with other cultures and the ranges of technology. Eutopias is a framework that holds many centers, beginning with the centers of different human cultures and including the centers of nonhuman communities and guilds.

Eutopias addresses the whole, because the health of the whole depends on the health of the wholes that make it up—the health of wildernesses, the health of civilizations, and the health of ecosystems, that is, inhabited places that are made through living.

Figure 230-1. World Government Arcology in Antarctica (proposed)

3.0. Recognizing Challenges & Problems for Government

Leadership and later governing, were effective ways to adapt to the vicissitudes of every environment. People who were the best hunters, builders or healers were followed by others; their expertise and duties were limited to the realm of their experience. These people belonged to various types of kinship groups: The nuclear family, the expanded family, and various types of descent groups, such as lineages or clans, where people claim common ancestry. Each type can be characterized by its size, formal political system, marriage forms, and leaders. Nuclear families last only as long as parents and children live together; descent groups are permanent units that continue to exist even though their membership changes with births and deaths.

Other groups, such as tribes and states, are not based on kinship, although some groups may be. A tribe is a group of independent communities occupying a specific region, sharing a common language and culture, which are integrated by some unifying factor. A chiefdom is a regional unit in which two or more local groups are organized under a single chief, who heads a ranked hierarchy of people. Individual status is determined by closeness relationship to the chief. When the cooperation within or between larger groups became more difficult, leadership became more formal. Leaders became necessary with conflicts between cultures as well as new problems from settlements and styles of getting food. As cultures joined, or were forced into, civilizations, leadership became more hierarchical and complex.

The state or nation is the most formal of political organizations with political power centralized in a government that can legitimately use force to regulate the affairs of its citizens, as well as its relations with other states. States maintain civil and economic order through a central government with specialized subsystems. The populations are divided into at least two socioeconomic classes, including the masses the fewest opportunities, privileges, rights, and obligations. The major concerns of government officials are to defend hierarchy, property, and the power of the law.

As the patterns of leadership and government became more complex, the structure became more hierarchical and detached from immediate results. The costs of maintaining government became less cost-effective. In addition to the original problems of leading, interacting, and sharing, new problems emerged as a result of scale and style. The unwieldiness of the government added problems.

The original problems became more complex, none more so than now, when human interference has converted most wild habitats and has started to effect the climate. These environmental challenges are putting stresses on local and national governments, which did not develop to handle large-scale challenges. And, there is no global government to address everything as a whole.

3.1. *Environmental Challenges*

The solar system is isolated from many of the powerful effects of the galaxy, such as black holes, exploding stars and other violent phenomena. The sun keeps its planets in regular orbits, although their elliptical shape and wobble alters their solar input. The sun varies the kinds and intensities of radiation, but it is rather constant. The earth is located in a beneficent zone for all three states of water. The moon keeps the earth at a relatively constant tilt and adds energy to the system through its gravitational attraction. The dynamics of the sun, as well as the systems and cycles on the planet, provide the resources and constraints that living forms use to create ecosystems for living.

Ecosystems themselves, as a result of historical changes and development, make stresses and challenges to participants. Normal things like floods or diseases, add challenges. In addition to physical challenges are perceptual limits in terms of size and time. The effects of historical changes by human influences can result in significant changes, losses and catastrophes. Human behavior, stupidity, violence and poor distributions can add to challenges.

A challenge is a calling into question or a demanding task (a challenge is defined as 'a call to take part in'). It is about consciously choosing to see what can be done, rather than dismissing a conflict as terrible and unsolvable. We tend to think of problems as unwanted 'side-effects' of the wanted main-effects, but all effects are equal, as Fuller noted, and must be addressed as equal. A problem (from the Greek words 'to throw forward,' which is what we tend to do with them) can be considered as a question proposed for solution. Problems could be considered also as challenges that we must respond to continuously, in the process of living, not as puzzles that have to be solved once for all time. Addressing a problem often has to do with a power struggle, which becomes part of the problem. If problems are regarded as challenges that require a social response, then some conflict can be avoided. The problems of cultures, and of natural ecosystems, can be identified and understood if we understand the properties and operations of ecosystems.

Table 311-1. Contrasted Properties of 6 Defined Systems

Fields	*Places*	*Ecosystems*
Process	Dynamic Change	Course
Autopoesis	Self-making Wholeness	Identity
Differentiation	Differentiation	Openness/Diversity
Integration	Integration	Coconstrained Construction
Constancy	Constancy	Stability
Metalysis	Renewal	Productivity
Cultures	*Good Places*	*Good Societies*
Conduct	Action	Method
Wholeness	Individuality	Self-extension
Flexibility	Richness	Variety
Adaptation	Conviviality	Cooperation
Constancy	Consistency	Loyalty
Vitality	Health	Harmony

3.1.1. *Properties of Ecosystems*

A system is a way to explain part of the universe and to deal with complex behavior. An ecosystem is a complex unit whose components keep its structure and function stable, despite changes and disturbances in its surroundings. An ecosystem is a material thing. Unlike an animal, which is a tangible thing, an ecosystem is an imperceptible thing, like an electron. Real things are changeable objects. The ecosystem pattern has a structure that includes organisms and abiotic substances. It has a function of taking a flow of energy and cycling material substances. History, structure and stability are emergent properties of an ecosystem. There is play in an ecosystem between adaptation and nonadaptation, or between co-constrained construction and deconstruction; completeness of either process would result in collapse of system.

Good places are set in ecosystems. To understand place, we must discuss the properties of working ecosystems. Ecosystems develop as information accumulates; information is generated by participating species and their physical structures, such as burrows or paths. The general properties, the inherent things, of an ecosystem include: Course, Identity, Openness, Coconstruction, Stability, and Productivity (see Table 311-1).

3.1.1.1. Course as a Property of an Ecosystem

The field provides the order required for producing individual organisms. The coming-to-be of organisms, that is process, is a fundamental feature of reality. The organism is what it does. The process of nature is not merely rhythmic change, it is a creative advance, producing new forms everywhere. The organism undergoes a process of evolution in which it produces new forms in itself. The process creates a course of motion.

The course may be stabilized in time (Conrad Waddington's idea of homeorhesis). The changes in an ecosystem are symbolized by trajectories in multidimensional phase space; orderliness can be described in terms of constraints on trajectory courses, and these constraints can be visualized as attractor surfaces. The name for a Property of an attractor surface in multidimensional space is a chreod (also a Waddington term meaning 'fated path'), rather than a valley. Chreods have various shapes and slopes of varying steepness. These paths can be fixed, but are probabilistic.

3.1.1.2. Identity as a Property of an Ecosystem

An ecosystem is a whole. The ontology of any living system is the history of the maintenance of its identity as a whole through continuous self-making, or autopoesis. If there were no identity, there would be no differences and so no relationships. Without relationships, there would be no things, no events, and no universe. Objects precipitate out of relationships and are defined by them.

For the universe to show stability and persistence, different entities must have stability and persistence. Identity is that persistent quality. Identity serves nothing; it is. The relationship between identity and wholeness is a rhythm, forming unique patterns. George Leonard identifies it as the silent pulse at heart of our experience that is always there. A system's identity can be described apart from its performance in interactions, but not isolated from it.

Ecosystems are part of an unending, imperfect process, without any final state. Furthermore, the human attempt at perfectibility through self-improvement causes disharmony, which is part of the same imperfect process. Each system is a practical application to place. Unknown factors determine a large part of the operation of any system. Furthermore, there is chaos in every system; there are plagues and random frenzies.

Dependent on a constant flow of solar energy, the system is self-making and whole, but bounded in definite shapes and sizes. The system is limited by a complex of conditions. The health of the system occurs within those limits.

3.1.1.3. Openness as a Property of an Ecosystem

The ecosystem has to be open to flows of energy and materials. Closure, e.g., well-defined boundaries, with steady input output flow rate, is not a contradiction. The boundaries are permeable, allowing exchanges of energy and matter. Too much openness would allow the system to be overwhelmed by the environment. Too little openness would cut the system off from the environment and it would run down, in terms of energy. The system is a local system, with specific structures and functions.

Random order is open; it has degrees of freedom. Differences can be related to degrees of freedom. An order with more differences has more degrees of freedom. The macro-order limits degrees of freedom. Movement could not occur without a free order or disorder.

The vast number of interrelationships between systems keeps them open. For example, grassland is affected by climates, soil conditions, fires, surrounding communities, and human agents. Ecotones between systems are usually shifting.

A partial process requires cuts in the whole, boundaries. Identifiable components organized internally with structural boundaries, creating a definite structure with specific functions.

The environment has been constant enough for organic evolution, but variable enough for natural selection to be challenged. Variability challenges organisms to adjust and thrive. Variability, even in small ways, leads to diversity. Diversity, as a measure of genetic variability in ecosystem, enlarges information in a system. A mature system needs less information, since it works toward preservation. The limit of maturity allows maximum variability between systems with slight external differences, like temperature. The variation of climate, for instance, an external disturbance, can change the physical and chemical parameters of an ecosystem. Acid rain causes biochemical and soil chemical reactions, which in turn provide in-form-ation to other organisms, which use it to regulate their physiological processes which can effect the entire system, e.g., insect damage changes the level of seasonal growth of trees.

3.1.1.4. Co-constrained Construction as a Property of an Ecosystem
The organism and environment are co-implicative, co-defining, and co-constructing. They engage in a process of self-assembly, where the complete self is the organism-environment system. Construction requires participation, complexity, and development. The process of construction involves a self-presentation offering new symbiotic relations and novelty.

Novelty always enters with environmental change, which serves to maintain the openness of the system. Novelty enters with fluctuations. The "strategy" of ecosystem development is increased control of, or homeorhesis with, the physical environment and novelty—probably to protect itself from perturbations. There is a fundamental shift in energy flows, as increasing amounts of energy are used for maintenance. As more and more energy is used for maintenance, the net community production (NCP) approaches zero. The mature system becomes more efficient, as it supports a larger biomass with the same amount of energy. The food chains become more weblike, dominated by detritus chains as opposed to linear grazing.

Construction depends on diversity for the reciprocal constraint. Local context allows for more rapid construction. The constraint forces species to change. As they participated in the arrangement of a system, complexity emerges from the interpenetration of processes of differentiation and integration, processes running simultaneously from top and bottom and shaping the hierarchy from both sides.

The ecosystem 'learns' the changes, e.g., seasons, of the environment. Any system formed by reproducing and interacting organisms must develop an assemblage in which production of entropy per unit of information is minimized. It is a general property of some systems that acquired information is used to close the door to further inflow.

A mature system needs less information, since it works toward preservation. The limit of maturity allows maximum variability between systems with slight external differences, like temperature. As a mature system, it continues to move to a point of high maturity, recovering from disturbance to its original trajectory, where productivity declines and stability increases. "Nature tends to become baroque in situations permitting high maturity, with little energy left for large changes," according to Ramon Margalef (1968).

3.1.1.5. Stability as a Property of an Ecosystem
Stability is the ability to maintain the identity of a system under the flow of external forces and disturbances. Stability can be refined through the specifics of persistence, resistance, resilience, and accommodation. Persistence means stability or continuity, in general, or the state of being in a continuous flow or coherent whole for a duration; specifically, it can mean a lack of change in a system parameter, like number of species. Resistance is the ability to withstand disturbance to a system and to continue. Resilience is the ability to recover from stress following a disturbance. Consilience is the ability to absorb change and still maintain the system identity. The system adapts to and accommodates disturbances.

Stability can be related to ideas of compartmentalization, communications, richness of interactions, and connections. Stability is a complex topic. Ulanowicz suggests that stability might be explained by diversity flow topologies, where flow topology is a descriptor of how ecosystems develop. The homeostasis of the ecosystems, that is, stability, as originally proposed by Eugene Odum, becomes the result of regular flows of energy and materials. Growth and development are characterized by a qualitative formalism of increasing ascendancy, which explains the drive towards coherence, efficiency, specialization, and self-containment.

3.1.1.6. Productivity as a Property of an Ecosystem
Productivity is the ability to convert energy into living forms and the ability to incorporate materials into living forms. Productivity, in general, depends on the vigor, or strength or vitality, of the system. Health is the overall ability of a system to maintain itself under a normal range of environmental conditions (which may include hurricanes, volcanic eruptions, or fires). Obviously, a pioneer community may change the conditions to favor a new level of the system with new components. Health is a dynamic measure of ecosystem organization, vigor, and resilience. Organization is described by diversity and connectivity; vigor is related to the amount and speed of productivity; and resilience is a measure of reaction to stress. Too much stress, for example, leads to unsustainable patterns of behavior; continuous stress leads to a breakdown of processes that becomes irreversible—the system dies. Health is a dynamic quality of the whole, the result of a harmonious interaction of all the analyzable parts that comprise the whole forest with the surrounding larger environment.

Adaptive ecosystems are not static orders; they are flexible, as well as historical and irreversible. Ecosystems develop knowledge-bases that reflect knowledge of themselves and their environment. The strengths of local systems lay in the diversity of values and in their fitness to particular places. A flexible, organic network holding all beings and natural groups.

3.1.2. *Changes in Ecosystems*
Everything moved, the planet changes, ecosystems are dynamic. The planet is relatively old and large, with a unique history and many dynamic ecosystems. As conditions change and individuals change, the pattern of an ecosystem changes. Change causes extinctions, death, suffering, destruction, life, accomplishment, beauty, and joy. Nature, for A. N. Whitehead, consists of patterns whose movement is essential to their being. These patterns are analyzed into events or occasions. Process is dynamic change in an unfolding flow. Process is the fundamental feature of nature. In a process view, organisms are dynamic structures that are immanent and simultaneous with the process, rather than a consequence of natural selection of past random mutations.

Ecosystems, the essential unit of ecology, must be seen in dynamic and historical terms. The vast number of interrelationships between systems keeps them open. For example, grassland is affected by climates, soil conditions, fires, surrounding communities, and human agents. Ecotones between systems are usually shifting. Each ecosystem is unique and original. Ecosystems change over time. This historical component allows them to build to maturity or to adjust to disturbances by becoming simpler.

Relatively constant flows of energy and matter allow ecosystems to appear stable. Persistence means continuity or the state of being in a continuous flow or coherent whole for a duration. The system is constant if it stays relatively unchanged in form or composition. This means a lack of change in a system parameter, like number of species. The system is persistent in time if it is self-maintaining, mature, and hysteretic (historical). The system changes and develops. It loses and gains species over time, but is still recognizable as a short-grass prairie, for instance. The integrity of its functions has not been greatly affected by changes in species. The system can have degrees of difference, malleability, and still be the named system. The system may have different states that oscillate. It may also have a trajectory to a mature state. Resistance is the ability to withstand disturbance to a system and to continue. This is Robert Macarthur's meaning of stability, from his analysis of food web structure; it is similar to Holling's concept of 'resilience.' McArthur's stability is less predictable, and it is more expensive to maintain. Resilience is the ability to recover from stress. The ecosystem can be thought of as elastic. The elasticity refers to the time required to recover its initial structure and function after some kind of damage; it is the speed that a system returns to former state following a disturbance (as a measure in the community matrix). Finally, consilience is the ability to absorb change and still maintain the system identity. The system adapts to disturbance. It accommodates disturbances. It incorporates new things, such as new organisms. It tolerates new levels of things, such as increased heat. It fits the changes within the structure and function of the system. Amplitude is a measure of the maximum amount of damage a system can sustain and still recover.

Wild landscapes are affected by climate, soils, interactions, and disturbances. Domestic landscape is affected by land use as well. The greatest changes have been brought about by the destruction and creation of forests. With the predominance of artificial or managed forests, it is important to consider the qualities of naturalness in the landscape. Forests are expected to meet the needs of society by producing timber, creating wildlife habitats, and providing recreational opportunities for people.

The water cycle is linked to other cycles, especially the carbon and oxygen cycles. When the water cycle changes, as a result of naturogenic or anthropogenic actions, the other cycles change also. The interaction of cycles means that if one cycle is disturbed or interfered with by human activities, other cycles will also change.

The atmosphere is the place of gaseous cycles, such as water vapor, oxygen, and nitrogen. Changes in the atmosphere is driven by solar energy. This is one reason why the atmosphere is so dynamic; The distribution of heat drives very rapid circulation patterns, much faster than oceanic or terrestrial changes.

Ecosystems are what they are as the result of the diversity of life—all forms of life contribute some value to the system as a whole. The whole system is already self-ordering and self-renewing. Any ecosystem not subjected to outside disturbance changes in an orderly and directional way: The complexity of structure increases and the energy flow per unit biomass decreases. The physical environment limits the type of change. Homeostatic (or homeorhetic) mechanisms protect the system from many disruptions. Thus, maturity is self-preserving. When conditions change, the system may go to a state of lower or higher diversity.

3.1.3. Ecosystem Problems: Drought

One major ecosystem change is the change in the moisture in a system. Changes in plate tectonics, as well as orbit can influence ecosystems. Changes in ocean current patterns and wind patterns can shift moisture flows away from a system. In short time spans this can create stresses in a system, creating floods or droughts; in the long-term it can simply shift entire ecosystems.

Human cultures tend to fill all available space, carrying capacity space, even though some of the spaces are occupied by other species or other cultures. This makes them prone to crash when the climate changes, especially over longer time spans (either longer spans or longer patterns). They have adapted to marginal environments with behavior and technology, such as that for water storage and grain storage, to buffer themselves against the known changes of the environment, but when an unknown change happens, such as a nine-year drought, they fall apart. Few people have the luxury of moving to an open area. Smaller populations can adapt faster to smaller resources.

The trouble with complex, self-regulating systems is that very small changes have large consequences—Reid Bryson points out that shifted rainfall patterns caused whole cultures to disappear. In some cases, where conditions, like drought, are cyclic, in the Sahelia region of Africa, humans expand during the good times, only to perish when the drought returns. In other cases, human activities, such as deforestation or overgrazing of herds, can cause weather changes. We tend to approach the limits of use of some environments. We also tend to overdependence on modern high-energy methods of agriculture and on some key resources, like water.

Drought was a major consideration for the Mayans, who had built so far from water. Maybe the southern centers were sited for water. Much of the culture was devoted to collecting and distributing water. The water lily had iconographic significance because it was indicated good water quality. Between 810 and 910, Mayans had three droughts of three, six, and nine years, in 810, 860, and 910. They entered the drought with a maximum population and limited flexibility.

Drought is blamed for arid land problems in Australia, but drought is inevitable. Aridity is determined by air currents and topography. Rainless episodes are normal in regions of erratic rainfall. Sensitive pastures may be overgrazed in good years, but the damage is not apparent until a drought. Sheep during the Australian Gascoyne droughts starve; there is enough water for thirst, but not enough for plant growth for food. Survey teams in the Gascoyne region recommended the most ecological strategy was to temporarily abandon the affected sections. The recommendation also was made to graze only half as many sheep. These recommendations were ignored by grazers, who needed the income immediately.

Drought, or access to water in general, may seem to be an insurmountable problem. Water has been a problem in many civilizations, from Mesopotamian and Indian to Chinese and American. The changes in wind and rainfall patterns or river beds have resulted in drought. In Mesopotamia, for instance, cities compensated for declining rainfall by irrigating wheat and barley with canals. But that lead to salt retention in the soils. By 3500 BCE wheat and barley crops were equal. Wheat can tolerate salt at only 0.5% in the soil, but barley can take twice that. By 2500 BCE wheat had fallen to 15% of the crop, although overall crop yields were still high, then to less than 2% by 2100 BCE. By 1700 BCE no wheat at all was grown. Overall yields fell 42% between 2400 and 2100 BCE, and by 65% by 1700 BCE. It was written that the earth was white with salt. After much intensification, the land collapsed. Many of these things are long-term problems and do not become evident for several generations. They are also very difficult to reverse. For a society that needs surpluses to continue, with growing dependents and growing people, there is little flexibility to change. The only way to avoid the problems was to let the land be fallow for long periods until the water table fell. This alternative was impossible due to food demands.

When cities started to fail, as a result of attacks or droughts, people were able to emigrate.

Many returned to herding, or when possible, hunting and gathering. For thousands of years, starting possibly 11,000 years before the present, people participated in a cycle of emigration to rural areas when time were bad and immigration back into cities when the ecosystems recovered and could be made productive again.

In complex, self-regulating systems very small changes have large consequences. In some cases, where conditions like drought, are cyclic, in the Sahelia region of Africa, humans expand during the good times, only to perish when the drought returns. In other cases, human activities, such as deforestation or overgrazing of herds, can cause weather changes. The scale and rate of changes allows people to view the situation as natural, but once these catastrophes pass a threshold, the people and their cultures have been trapped by their demands, and only severe reduction or collapse can allow the system to regenerate.

Drought has been a major urban or rural problem. Even cities that have been located on rivers have been destroyed by long droughts (usually over ten years). Fresh water has become an intractable problem in the past 50 years, as more aquifers have been drained and more water sources are used for industrial purposes, such as cooling or washing away wastes. Areas of the Americas and Asia still rely on irrigation, and people steadfastly ignore the warning signs of drought and collapse.

3.2. The Challenge of Population

Populations of living organisms tend to grow until they are limited by physical or biological factors. The maximum number of individuals that an environment can support is its carrying capacity, which fluctuates with various factors. Physical limits may be absolute or flexible. Population control can either be accomplished through crowding, by the food supply, or by natural resources.

Although early human populations increased or decreased, the overall human population started slowly increasing at the end of the Ice Age. With agriculture, fertility increased (although sickness and mortality also increased).

3.2.1. Population Growth
What is the reason for the rapid population increase? Biologically, when a pine tree starts to die, it puts immense effort into its seed crop—is there a human analogy? Did the activity of hunter women decrease fertility that increased when they stayed in place? Did hunter women control fertility by prolonged breast feeding or sexual abstinence? Did being in place remove that control?

Agriculture, growing crops and raising animals, provided more food, but it was less nutritious and less palatable. By increasing the population, agriculture increased widespread hunger. The reduction in biodiversity, by monocropping, undermined biodiversity and caused some ecological crises, that resulted in periodic and devastating famines.

Agricultural populations increased and spread, bringing their crops with them, pushing hunters into the periphery where crops could not grow. Once the initial agricultural startup costs were paid, such as truncated diversity and nutrition, and the decrease in human size and health, other advantages accrued, such as specialization, creating a different form of political control, which allowed armies. Agricultural society now had a massive advantage over foraging societies.

Despite famines that caused hundreds of nations to wobble or collapse, the overall human population kept increasing. The world population is increasing at an alarming rate. By 1900, the rate started to increase steeply. At a rate of increase of two per cent per year— that is below the current rate—the earth's human population will reach 50 billion by 2100. By 2280 it would be 1.2 trillion. That is 300 years from now (1980, the year of this sentence); 300 years ago John Milton's *Paradise*

Lost was popular reading.

Nations that seem to have adequate resources, may be growing too fast. Even the Union of Soviet Socialist Republics, with all its potential agricultural land, and its uncertainties of drought and frost, Canada and Australia, may be increasing their population too fast. Population growth can become a political weapon, in a democracy, when two groups coexist, with neither ecological differentiation nor geological separation, and only breeding control for coexistence. For instance, in Sri Lanka, the Sinhalese and the minority Tamils, breed for political control, ignoring population control. Voluntary controls fail; the population increases by almost two and a half percent per year. The problem of population control is a tribal problem, not a racial or economic one. It is a local problem, more than a global one. Even with trade and charity, in most areas population is limited by local resources and local limits; only in a few cases, such as the Netherlands and Hong Kong, can a population be supported by massive ghost acreage elsewhere.

Sir Charles Darwin's view of humanity was that it was not domesticated. Humans were still wild. Unmastered, they have no breeding control; therefore, they will eat to the limits of the natural food supply and press against social and biological limits. The global population explosion, an example of autocatalytic nonlinearity, is not considered a problem for many thinkers, such as Eric Jantsch, who believe that this growth constitutes an essential factor in the creative act of gestalt formation. Growth does lead to intensity at some stages of development in the life of a species, but growth can stop, and development can also lead to the kind of creative intensity identified by Jantsch and others with mindless growth.

Population growth cannot continue indefinitely. Population is intrinsically inseparable from the question of access to resources. The time has gone when one nation can unload its population problems on another; and this applies to all countries.

The principles of ecology can offer information on human societies. For instance, the principle of competitive exclusion states that two dissimilar races cannot occupy the same niche in the habitat. If humanity is wild, this may help explain war and racism. Territoriality is no longer a rule in human ecology, though the instincts may still be operative. Human ecology defies maintaining its population at an optimum level. The young are overproduced and protected; the least fit are not eliminated. Medical science has also increased the number of old and maladapted dependents of society. Problems with populations bristle with social and political implications.

A balance in birth and death rates is necessary for ecological stability. We have controlled epidemic death and infant death diseases. We need to correct the overbalance in births, or risk having nature do it. Toughness and ingenuity might be required.

3.2.2. *Population Size*

Populations are still growing exponentially. The world population is almost five billion people (1980). It is over six billion (2001). Current technology allows a large population to live at the cost of the depletion of resources, thereby reducing the potential for future life. From linear thinking, a population of up to 40 billion can be projected; but at what level, for how long? Darin-Drabkin and Lichfield claimed that with efficient use of land resources, the population could be 50 billion; that we have the technological power to fulfill these estimates, but need organizational changes and proper planning to allow it. It is unlikely that humanity would be ten times happier or more creative. History and tradition are difficult to change. What would happen to forests and animals?

Leopold Kohr has a velocity theory of population, in which aggregates of humans (or atoms) increase mass by addition and through an increase in speed. Population density multiplied by energy use creates pressure on environment; mass times speed equals pressure ($MV=P$); The answer is not in search for new sources of fuel, but search for means of production and decelerated way of life using less energy. Not necessary to lower standards of living. We must either introduce voluntary pressures now, or let the system introduce them later by its own dynamic. There are ways for voluntary reduction, however. There could be tax incentives for those families who control their size.

When power density reaches carrying capacity, a system is considered developed; when it exceeds capacity, it is overdeveloped. The maximum number of individuals that an environment can support is its carrying capacity, which fluctuates with various factors. The greatest number of people over time implies that the living population be limited to biological carrying capacity. Any permanent destruction of carrying capacity to allow a larger living population implies a future reduction in population indefinitely, or until ecosystem restoration (if possible). Those who favor negative population growth may maximize the number of lives total, at a sufficient level of wealth.

Physical limits may be absolute or flexible. Population control can either be accomplished through crowding, by the food supply, or by natural resources. There tend to be as many people as there are utilized natural resources for and unpolluted room and food for.

Numbers of a country should not exceed the scarcest of commodities. A values boundary would be implemented in industrial countries. As vital systems are used for nonessential purposes, like using water to wash a private automobile, the population must be reduced.

3.2.3. *Cultural Status*

Perhaps related to population growth and size, have come changes in cultural status, especially related to equity, distribution, and dominance. Status has to do with standing in society, and with appearance and ownership. Status may come from longevity, of the self or ancestors, as well as from the results of good decisions, from hunting for example, or from owning more than others, or just more things or more people. Status is a powerful human need, and may drive the growth of goods or populations.

As distribution becomes more unequal and as conflict occur more between groups, dominance and slavery appear, and are both related to status.

Darwin has been criticized by Malthus for extending the popular theory of economics to the natural world. It is true that the biological considerations of economics inspired an economic description of a biological law, but Darwin enlarged and supported the metaphor. He retained the idea of hierarchy, but status became a form of fitness, specifically in birds and mammals. It can be argued that status has fitness values in human groups also. For instance, a woman is more likely to mate with a man who has higher status in the community.

Status is a social need, which is justified in the culture. Status levels in traditional society included: Nobles, commoners, and slaves. Slaves were captured or purchased. In earlier days, people were sometimes captured by enemy tribes. The return home of the captives, either through payment of ransom or owing to a retaliatory raid, was called u'mista—that is, a special return. Like other property slaves were given away as gifts. Occasionally, they were killed and eaten during the cannibal dance. A commoner was simply anyone without a chief's position, potlatch position, seat, or standing place. They are not a class with a function. At times, nobles may retire from potlatch positions and become commoners. Kinship was the main determinant of status. For the Kwakiutl, the display of status validated the social system. The redistribution of food validated the cultural status of the leader.

By 2400 YBP in Mesopotamia, there was status differentiation, as evident in the sizes of homes. Oddly associated with permanent settlements were inequalities of status and wealth. Furthermore, other social things developed such as complex division of labor, with castes and slave labor. Trade increased and competition increased. This may have had to do with resources that were abundant and could be stored, and transformed into political prestige and power. Agriculture provides more status, more wives, more things. It allows armed struggle also. Art, in addition to luxuries and profits, was tied to status.

3.2.4. *Equity & Distribution*

In almost every size of human groups status is divided unequally. In hunting groups, better hunters become the hunting leaders. The success of a hunter allows the hunter to distribute the cuts of the game between others, often according to an understood set of rules. In larger groups, with a surplus of materials, the materials are distributed according to status. People have equal access to status positions in society. The number of positions of prestige is adjusted to the qualified candidates. Status is separate from wealth. An animal divided up according to ratios regardless of who kills it.

J. S. Mill narrowed the scope of economics to production and the scarcity of means; he considered distribution to be a political process, since it depended on laws and customs that varied widely in different cultures and ages. One function of culture is to distribute material goods or energy. Economic culture defines the means of production and livelihood, techniques of distribution, and values and norms underlying economic behavior (can be more closely related to kinship. Order is a cultural problem. Order provides stability and security. Cultural order is necessary to deal with the redistribution of wealth and power.

With the creation of more wealth or new wealth, the distribution becomes skewed. Accumulation increases. More kinds of wealth become invented, dangerous, and useless, and more skewed. But, as long as an economy does not reach the limits of wealth, it can keep growing; these new kinds of wealth allow that. Cultures encourage the unequal distribution of resources.

Wealth is based on production in capitalist countries. The production of wealth from growth depends on technology. The technological perspective is oriented toward materials and not humans or forest processes. Nature is considered to be a resource to be exploited. The immediate objective of technology is to create wealth through knowledge. Technological activities are justified on humanitarian grounds, scientific discovery increases the well-being of human society, yet the social consequences of scientific activity are ignored; short-term suffering will be offset by long-term benefits, it is claimed. But because the long-term view is not taken, long-term benefits will be worse.

Economic growth can produce great wealth for some. Fortunes await those who can increase the demand for unnecessary items, such as electric swizzle sticks or pet rocks. Free enterprise provides initiative to any willing to show a profit without regard for the immediate consequences. The economist Paul Samuelson illustrated the skewed distribution of wealth with an income pyramid made out of children's blocks: if each layer represented $1000.00, the peak would be as high as the Eiffel tower, and most of us would be within a meter of the ground.

Inequality is more the result of differential development than of exploitation. According to Boulding, the greatest source of the differential is different rates of accumulation of knowledge, capital and organization; the rates are essentially internal properties of cultures. Although a minor element in terms of transfers, it is a large psychological perception, which may need to be compensated for in a global community.

Most of the wealth used by modern economies is nonrenewable. These resources are limited, interrelated and distributed unevenly. Forests are a special problem; although trees can grow to a good size in 30-40 years, forest ecosystems may take 300-600 years to develop and then last for thousands of years. Oil, coal, peat, and some woods are functionally nonrenewable. Geological time periods are required to produce them.

The distribution of symbolic and real wealth is very inequitable as the result of historical trends, old economic rules, and cultural confusion. Karl Marx considered that misery is caused by class conflict about distribution of material things. Some of the problems of distribution have to do with the size of society and the scale of its operations. For instance, in Hutterite communities, usually less than 150 people, the distribution of goods rarely failed; people got their share, rarely less or more. With a larger group of Hutterites, the distribution started to fail, and the group divided.

The modern market distributes some benefits to all, but its scale allows unfairness. Economics are the harmonious distribution of wealth among people. But, problems outside small-cell scales. Kohr points out that Marx failed to link misery to the scale of economics rather than the system. The problem is with overgrowth more than style, which is why socialism based on overgrowth looks the same as capitalism overgrown. The change in scale drove the changes, from the transition of states, from surplus distributors, to tribute-driven to commercial exchanges. There were political transitions from leaders, to chiefs, to tribute systems, and to economic and political trade systems.

3.3. *The Problem of Cultural Dominance*

Strength or status can give rise to dominance. A dominant is an animal or person with greater influence in the community. Dominant behavior may be biologically-based or cultural. Dominance gives priority of access to food, sex, or space. In a majority of primates, males are not dominant over females, except where there is a large size difference. Where sizes are roughly the same and where female coalitions occur, there is not much sexual dominance. In some human groups, males may attempt to dominate females with the threat of physical violence, for instance, among the Yanomamo. Among other Amazon peoples, such as Mundurucu, it may be due to control of ritual objects and rituals, for dominating ceremonial life. In spite of the cultural forces dominant at any moment, an individual has the potential to determine a different course of action.

3.3.1. *The Use of Slavery*

To be enslaved means to be owned as property and divested of freedom and rights, or it means to be completely dominated. The word 'slave' comes from the old Slavic word for the Slavic people, who were among the first slaves to be held in Europe.

Slavery is the idea that people can be held in bondage to perform work. The Greeks thought that freedom depended on some slavery. Some societies thought that their economies depended on slavery. It was actually thought that slavery improved the lives of slaves, since they were often considered to be from subhuman groups. It was also thought that it was a personal decision or personal right, although the slave might feel differently. There are of course, different kinds of slavery now. For humans, there are living slaves, but future generations might become enslaved to the decisions of their parents, especially as regards losses and debts. Animals have been enslaved. Machine slaves were the next economic boost. Finally, industrial societies have energy slaves, ten to twenty for each person. Slavery is based on a number of assumptions, such as contempt for the enslaved, or denial that there is wrong doing.

Kinds of slavery can be distinguished: Opportunistic, Institutional, Or Comprehensive. Opportunistic slavery was the result or raids or conflicts with other bands. Institutional slavery included labor force collection, as practiced in Egypt in 4500 YBP, or economic slavery, as run by the British 300 years ago. Comprehensive slavery refers to the use of wage earners, animals, and energy.

3.3.1.1. Opportunistic Slavery

Many archaic cultures had slaves, who were usually the victims of conflicts between bands. In Nez Perce gatherings and celebrations, slaves were exchanged, with furs, roots, berries, and fish. Slaves could often intermarry with their captors and acquire status; their children were almost always free. Slaves became a separate social class in some archaic societies. By 5000 YBP a stratified class society had developed—slaves at the bottom, then peasant farmers, craftsmen, then the elites of administrators, religious and military. In Assyria, slaves could not wear veils. Slaves worked everywhere in Assyrian society, even running businesses. Some people entered slavery voluntarily to pay off a debt.

3.3.1.2. Institutional Slavery (Economic Labor Collection)

For the Tukano of Peru, the Maku group was a slave class, that is, a source of slaves. The Kwakiutl also had slaves, who were captured or purchased. Like other property, slaves were given away as gifts. Usually, they were captives kept near the door to guard the house. Occasionally, they were killed and eaten during the cannibal dance. Viking raiders and colonists owned their own land and used Irish slaves for work and for wives specifically (based on genetic evidence). As the number of slaves diminished through death or marriage, some farmers lost their land to absentee landlords, who, without ecological or personal feedback, would make poor decisions about crops and practices.

Economic slavery occurred in Mesopotamia, Slaves worked in all levels. Many were prisoners of war; some were criminals being punished; some entered slavery to pay off a debt. But, slaves could also own a business. If a slave married a free person, their children would be free. Slavery became specialized with agriculture, in China and Egypt.

In China, by 1615, slavery was hereditary, for agricultural or household slaves. Slaves reflected the stratification of society as it became more complex. Slaves in the Americas were needed because the amount of acreage increased with the discovery of new lands; the acreage and the slaves were considered necessary to develop more wealth. Slavery kept labor artificially cheap. This dampened the incentive to develop new technologies, but, new technologies eventually surfaced because they proved to be cheaper than slaves.

The appearance of mechanical devices such as the sugar mill and Eli Whitney's cotton gin helped to support the system of large plantations based on a single crop. The Industrial Revolution after the late eighteenth century swelled the population of towns and cities and increasingly forced agriculture into greater integration with general economic and financial patterns.

Internal slavery was a feature of Europe from the Romans to Middle Ages, but disappeared when feudalism disappeared, and labor was no longer the scarce factor in production. With the opening of America, however, land opened up—or rather was claimed and conquered—faster than it could be filled with European people. Therefore, colonists tried to force native Americans into labor. Native Americans, however, were still dying from European diseases, which made them unsatisfactory as slaves. Europeans looked to another tropical continent, Africa, where the people were resistant to old World diseases. Less than thirteen years after Columbus, in 1505, African slaves were introduced into Haiti. Over 350 years, ten million more were brought over, in a large trans-Atlantic trading circuit that involved rum, sugar, cloth, and timber as well.

In the American colonies, the independent, more or less self-sufficient family farm became the norm in the North, while the plantation, using slave labor, was dominant, although not universal, in the South. With the British, Americans, Africans, and Spanish, slaves became a commodity in a trading empire.

3.3.1.3. Comprehensive Slavery

After the enslavement of peoples, some dominant cultures turned to the enslavement of nature and then of energy. The English treated tropical lands as enemies to be defeated, then enslaved them in plantations. Their cultural attitude as conqueror of nature led them to treat biogeochemical cycles and soil requirements as temporary obstacles in a world where everything had its price.

The new economics of the industrial age depends on wage slaves, that is, people who need jobs to get necessities in urban areas. An overeducated labor pool led to secretaries and then managers, and to the fulfillment of the managerial revolution. Now, industrial society is able to use energy slaves to accomplish work. Energy, in human work equivalents, from animals, natural and fossil fuels, that is used to perform work. The institutions of slavery raise questions about our relations to each other and to nature. What is our human relation to reality, slave, master, participant, or partner? Cosmology describes the place of a culture in reality. Cultures can determine inappropriate attitudes towards nature and that can result in ruin for the air and land. Although slavery is officially condemned in virtually every nation, the inappropriate use of people, animals, machines and energy continues, as a necessary part of the agricultural and industrial economies.

3.3.2. *Colonialization*

What is colonialism? Who does it, who benefits? The history of colonialism starts with one culture dominating another. The Phoenicians sent out colonists to found Carthage. Settlers from Carthage founded Barcelona. The Greeks made colonies in Italy, Sicily, Turkey, Libya, and Spain. Norway sent people to Iceland and Greenland, France, and Ireland. India sent colonists to Sumatra, Borneo and Java. The Inca moved villagers to Ecuador from Bolivia. Southern Indians called Tamils, crossed over to Ceylon, which was occupied by the Sinhalese. And, of course the Europeans tried to control all of their global trading by controlling the people and the resources in Africa, the Americas, Asia and the pacific.

Colonial countries introduced new ethnic rivalries wherever they took over. English imported Indian people from India to work sugarcane fields. By 1970, half the Fijans were Indians. Fijans tended to eat strangers and castaways, sometimes enemies from raids (and some recipes were the same as for pigs). But, only men could eat human flesh because of the strong manna.

In Tasmania, aboriginal people had woolly hair rather than curly, were shorter, had brown skin rather than the matte-black of the continental Aborigines. In technology, they had digging sticks and spears, but not boomerangs or woomera (*atlatl*). They understood curating fire, but could not start it. Their 12,000 year separation for any other people or culture is the longest for any people, even Rapa Nui. The English wanted to create or recreate a European world, without savages. The native peoples did not fit. All of Tasmania was first made into a prison; all the native people killed off. The culture was destroyed. The environment was destroyed. The English were not tolerant of dissent, variety or diversity. Neither seems to be the modern civilization.

The Kuna women of the San Blas islands, north of Panama, wear clothing with appliquéed materials in geometric designs with real and mythical beasts and random words or letters copied from travelers. Now popular with tourists, the Kuna, who were never conquered or subdued, and the only people still living on their islands, even now must require ships to pay homage to the chief, aboard the ship, in terms of meal or gifts. The Kuna build simple, large houses and cultivate bananas, breadfruit and calabash trees. All other Caribbean people were displaced or killed.

Colonial administration required central government and strong armies. The Ottoman expansion into Europe annexed one food-producing region after another. Sustainable intensive farming was abandoned as colonialism gained. There is a direct connection between colonialism and the abandonment of land, having to do with urban immigration or slavery.

3.3.3. *Humanity as Pandominant Agent*

The forces of history include geological processes, as well as solar system effects, such as the output of the sun or meteorites. Certainly, they include the environment, such as climate and the distribution of resources. Especially important are human impacts on ecosystems, such as deforestation, identified by John Perlin as perhaps the reason for the decline of many civilizations, from the Hittites and Babylonians to the Romans and English. Another impact is desertification, according to Uwe George and others. Disease patterns, according to W. H. McNeill, are crucial. To disease, Jared Diamond adds steel and guns as forces that have shaped human history and societies. Then, there is simply luck, the position of a culture in the stochastic chaos of nature. By their activities, human beings change the places they live. Much of the change is easily incorporated in the cycles of renewability of the ecosystems. However, humans often change the directions of such systems by simplifying or degrading the systems.

In this case humans act as agents of interference. Human exploitation at the tremendous physical scale that occurs in industrial states is different from exploitation by other species, because it results in the destruction of the entire system, the very basis for renewal of a system that human beings, as well as other species, need for life. Human actions are damaging global biogeochemical cycles, such as the carbon or nitrogen cycle. For instance, deforestation, burning, wetland loss, and industrial processes are releasing massive quantities of carbon dioxide into the atmosphere, which disrupts the carbon cycle. Although the destruction of large species, from whales to frogs, has a dramatic effect on ecosystems, the destruction of microbes, which generate oxygen and recycle nutrients, has a critical impact on the entire food web. These actions are global, like a large volcanic eruption, but, unlike a volcanic eruption, they are constant and hourly.

Humanity is acting as a biological agent. Humans have had a great impact on nature, and should be considered themselves as a force of nature or as special agents of change. One analogy of humans as special agents is as a parasite: A consumer feeding on another living organism, usually inside, drawing nourishment and weakening the host. States acted like macroparasites, according to William McNeill, but becoming less violent or unpredictable over time, as they adjusted to their host populations.

Humanity becomes an autoparasite, a new pseudospecies. Technology enlarges the number of niches for us; tools fit humans to different habitats, displacing other species. We steal from animals and plants, from the earth, and from our own descendants. Hobbes foresaw this war of each against all. The systematic destruction of human beings and animals is not an isolated peculiarity. A fat parasite often kills it host and then dies itself. Perhaps, humanity is an agent of a different sort, a systems agent that encourages only positive feedback.

Perhaps human expansion is like a cancer. Alan Gregg (1955) compared the world to a living organism and the explosion in human numbers to the proliferation of cancer cells. He sketched other parallels between cancer in humans and humans' cancer-like impact on the world. Cancer cells proliferate rapidly and uncontrollably in the body; humans continue to proliferate rapidly and uncontrollably in the world. Crowded cancer cells harden into tumors; humans crowd into hardened cities. Cancer cells infiltrate and destroy adjacent normal tissues; urban sprawl devours normal open land. Malignant tumors shed cells that migrate to distant parts of the body and set up secondary tumors; humans have colonized just about every habitable part of the globe. Cancer cells lose their natural appearance and distinctive functions; humans homogenize diverse natural ecosystems into artificial monocultures.

Malignant tumors excrete enzymes and other chemicals that adversely affect remote parts of the body; humans' motor vehicles, power plants, factories and farms emit toxins that pollute environments far from the point of origin. It is not in a tumor's self-interest to steal nutrients to the point where the host starves to death, for this kills the tumor as well. Yet, tumors commonly continue growing while the victim wastes away. A malignant tumor usually goes undetected until the number of cells in it has doubled at least thirty times from a single cell. The number of humans on Earth has already doubled thirty two times, reaching that mark in 1978 when world population passed 4.3 billion. It is over seven billion now. After thirty-seven to forty doublings, at which point a tumor weighs about one kilogram, the condition is usually fatal—that would be the population equivalent of 5.4 billion people. We have exceeded that; the question is whether it has been fatal—large complex systems may take a long time to collapse—or if the system has more flexibility than an organic body.

The metaphor of cancer may be more appropriate than a footprint. After all, a footprint can stimulate some kinds of ecosystems, such as short grass prairie. What humanity does is transform the ground under the footprint into a cancerous new human system.

Humanity is acting as an ecological agent. Every species exploits its environment to the extent that it can, with no regard to consequences. Usually, each species is checked by another, because there are so many competing for the same food, and equilibrium is maintained. Partial knowledge and isolated technology have allowed us to exploit our environment beyond what is desirable for us or for other species. While continued, moderate exploitation is necessary to live, massive, unbalanced exploitation is unwise. Wise use of resources would not make the world less habitable. We are part of the system and must protect its health.

By distorting the equilibrium, we have destroyed whole species and favored many others, many wild as well as domesticated. Rats and mice have been carried to all parts of the world and live in direct competition with humanity, invading our buildings for food and shelter. Crows and coyotes have also profited from their human association.

Humanity is acting as a geological or climactic force. No single change is exclusive to humans as a species, but they are excessive, rapid, compounded, and large-scale. For instance, there is movement of soil, but also massive erosion. There is movement of minerals, but also disruption of mineral cycles. There is the addition of novel elements into the atmosphere, but there is also a massive release of carbon and plastics. When people use more of the earth's supplies in a certain period than can be replenished in the same period by the sun, they are eating into the natural capital. Humans have caused the extinction of hundreds of species. Getting timber for fuel and construction, and clearing land for agriculture, have destroyed whole habitats. Demand for timber has been insatiable, for houses, ships, newspaper, and fuel. Trees have been cut from vulnerable watershed sites, with resulting floods, erosion, and diminution of rainfall and water table.

Vegetation holds soil in place, reduces wind speed at the soil surface, and improves water absorption and transport in the soil. Erosion destroys soil and makes it difficult for plants to be reestablished. Recovery, if it occurs, may take decades. Erosion is an ecological catastrophe on a planetary scale, causing thousands of higher plant and animal species, and countless lower species, to be lost forever. This is what is planned in Brazil and South America. It is not known how massive deforestation through overgrazing, firewood collection, and timber exploitation will affect terrestrial and atmospheric systems. Perhaps we should just accept erosion. Erosion is picturesque. Cezanne's paintings of France are striking. The abstract terrain of Greece is pleasing to many.

Only in the nineteenth century beginning with G. P. Marsh, did people start to realize that humanity has done as much to change the environment as the environment has done to mold human history. Many people did not change their behavior in time to solve the problems. Worse, the current civilization is global, not local, so, there will not be a migration to new lands. Humanity is dominating every ecosystem and bioregion.

3.4. Problems: Challenges & Traps

Sometimes, rearrangement leads to a position of not being able to rearrange further. In many cases it is hard to tell if the destructive use of land preceded ecological problems or followed from efforts to maintain production after an ecological challenge. Cause and effect are hard to separate. The same environment that challenges a culture with some kind of change, also offers opportunities with the change. New resources can stimulate economic activity and increase the level of living.

Cycles that do not operate with the right kind of feedback function as traps. Thus, on an elemental level, phosphorus becomes trapped in an ocean sink, and can only be recycled by long geological processes or by specific harvests through human activity.

Karl Marx contended that humans live in cages, partly natural and partly of their own making. However, human actions can modify the situation. The word 'cage' is a metaphor; it implies being trapped. It is however, a metaphor that can be expanded with a description of space as a four-dimensional box. Perhaps the trap is a better metaphor, since we depend on nature and society as a foundation for life.

Traps function in different ways. The use of resources by a people, where the replenishment rate is constant and the rate of use exceeds it, is a serial trap. This trap results in ecosystem degradation that is less reversible. The industrial age mistakes the rate of discovery for the rate of recovery.

Agriculture is an energy trap, because it allows a higher concentration of energy, that is, higher yields, but then it requires more energy be put into the system to maintain it. The system has to produce more energy than it uses to be sustainable, with a surplus for trade.

Sedentism is a trap. As the population of sedentary communities increased, the wildlife numbers decreased. The productivity and narrowness of food increased. Thus, there was less possibility of returning to the foraging lifestyle. People became committed to the new lifestyle. Intensity was no longer an option either; it had to be pursued. Habits were set. One problem of sedentism is that the individual cannot simply move away to avoid conflict. People are tied to a particular place and have to communicate to adjust to sharing places.

The city is a different kind of trap, that offers intensity and opportunity, but requires massive imports of supplies to survive. The size and scale of cities create the dual centers of attraction and despair.

The cultural trap is that: One cannot transcend culture unless one knows the hidden structure, axioms and unstated assumptions about how life is lived, viewed, analyzed or changed. Cultures are systematic wholes composed of dynamic interrelated wholes. They are more easily described from outside with comparison to another culture, although transmitting culture to youth and watching the culture collapse expose hidden structures.

Language and art are also traps. Language because one is limited by words. Art because one is limited by styles or demand. Even if cultural attitudes are appropriate, they can trap a people if there are no longer functional reasons for the practices. The Nembi of Papua New Guinea may be trapped in their system, making stone axes with difficulty when thousands of tradable steel ones are available.

Global capitalism can lead to a consumption trap. Capitalism claims to serve the wants of the people, but it spends half its income creating more wants in people. Not many of those wants are real, or as real as cereal and roofs. Few of the soft services satisfy real psychological needs. Markets advance individual desires and not social goals, by offering running shoes, not inner city restoration. Instead of being free from economic want to develop their potential as creative human beings, people are trapped in a consumer cycle. Self-actualization is postponed for self-gratification.

Furthermore, capitalism can undermine traditional cultures by offering consumerism in the place of guides for behavior. Social roles seem irrelevant by comparison, if the good life can be bought without effort.

Being in a trap means much-reduced flexibility and fewer choices. Climate can drown whatever is in the trap. That is, being in a trap makes one vulnerable to many other changes that could be avoided if you were not in a trap. When the weather got colder, then hunters and gatherers could move south. Cities could not. Civilizations are more fragile and more vulnerable to smaller climactic changes.

Addictions. Such as those to foods or oil or money, make it difficult to escape from a trap, a trap being a kind of energy well or gravity well. Addictions can amplify some emotions, such as fear or hate, especially as they relate to the possible end of the addiction or the threat of that end. Addictions can justify illegal behavior, especially those that seem necessary to continue the addiction. Of course, many cultures are addicted to the illusion of control and power. The U.S. is trapped in the belief that only it, among nations, can bring prosperity and peace to other nations, with trade or violence. Eventually the trap is escaped, or more likely destroyed or collapses with its victims.

3.5. *Problems: Conflict & Collapse*

Collapse is often part of physical, biological and cultural cycles. Collapse can happen when a culture is too static in a changing environment. It can happen a culture selects growth to try to overcome certain environmental obstacles.

The Lowland Maya formed around 1100 BC. By 200 BC the massive public architecture was rising. Temples and palaces were built. Vast public works, such as aqueducts, were undertaken. The arts flourished. The entire landscape was modified for planting. The zenith of organization and population was between 700 and 900 AD. Perhaps 75 percent of the region was cleared for agriculture at that time. The Maya had a high density, stressed population, with intensive agriculture, complex hydraulic systems, in large centers, with an elite class, calendars and rituals. Population growth triggered competition and conflict, which led to positive feedback of the thing that caused the stress.

Drought was a major consideration for the Mayans, who had built so far from water. Maybe the southern centers were sited for water. Much of the culture was devoted to collecting and distributing water. The water lily had iconographic significance because it was indicated good water quality. Between 810 and 910, Mayans had three droughts of three, six, and nine years, in 810, 860, and 910. They entered the drought with a maximum population and limited flexibility.

People suffered from the stress. Analysis of skeletons shows that in the Late Classic they became more fragile. Although people became 7 centimeters taller by the Early Classic, by the Late Classic stature of men had declined markedly; also degenerative bone conditions, bad teeth, scurvy and other pathologies. There was a collapse and depopulation, from 3,000,000 to 450,000, which has never recovered. The current population is 1,250,000.

Collapse probably improved things for the peasants, without the burden of rulers, elite, priests, and artists. In the long run even the peasants were decimated, perhaps due to environmental deterioration, stress, and in-fighting. By the time of the Spanish, the area seemed to be unbroken forest. The Spanish introduced malaria and hookworm, which made the forest worse to live in. In some cases, such as Maya, environmental degradation did play a role in collapse of the civilization, either as a cause or effect. Complex societies put harsher demands on local environments. Political regimes set production demands too high.

Elman Service uses a biological analogy, where social organizations are modeled as plant or animal species that are initially successful because adapted to niche, but later become overadapted and less general. In this model collapse is part of an unalterable natural cycle. Adaptation denotes a systemic homeostasis in which a range of variability is activated in response to various environmental and social perturbations. Service believed that complex systems were maladaptive since responses to stress were less flexible.

Table 350-1. Kinds of Collapse

Reason	Main factor	Related factors	Examples
Resource depletion	Salinization	Political instability	Mesopotamia
	Soil nutrient depletion	Erosion, malaria, political competition	Mayan lowland, Easter Island
	Water table drop from tectonic shift	Revolt	Chimu, Peru
	Climate change, drought	Salinization	Hohokam
	Climate change		Hopewell
	Exhaustion of game, timber, soil	Competing centers	Cahokia
	Nile flood failure	Destruction, parasites, over-taxation, over-elites	Egypt
	Flooding	Collapse of trade	Harappan, Indus
	Climate, drought	Famine, migration	Mycenaean
Resource change	Climate change	Deforestation, erosion, invasion	Roman
	Preferred resource Bison increase	Moisture, Grassland increase	Pecos, NM
	Introduction of iron	Conflict	Hittite
Catastrophe	Maize mosaic virus	Overpopulation Lack of flexibility	Maya lowlands
	Earthquakes, plagues		Teotihuacan
	Malaria	Lead poisoning, exhaustion, political corruption	Roman state

This is not good argument, because it does not consider weed species or the maturity of the system. In a systems model, collapse is part of stochastic process, which implies that civilizations will die, but not necessarily within a definite time frame. In the general system model, complex systems are hierarchically composed of many stable lower and intermediate orders, strongly connected horizontally, but less so vertically. The problem may be more one of size than complexity.

Human cultures tend to fill all available space, especially carrying capacity space, even though some of the spaces are occupied by other species or other cultures. This makes them prone to crash if climate changes. They have adapted to marginal environments with behavior and technology, such as that for water storage and grain storage, to buffer themselves against the know changes of the environment, but when an unknown change happens, such as a nine-year drought, they fall apart. Few people have the luxury of moving to an open area. Smaller populations can adapt faster to smaller resources.

Perhaps one reason for collapse is due to overconnections, just like in ecosystems. This is a problem with modern globalization, in the 1990s, as well as with simpler globalization connections, such as in the 1300s.

Table 350-2. Further Kinds of Collapse

Reason	Main factor	Related factors	Examples
Invasion	Invading Aryans	Effete society	Harappan, Indus
	Invading Mycenaeans	Thera eruption, earthquakes	Minoan Crete
	Invading Dorian Greeks	Climate change, drought	Mycenaean
Social dysfunction	Class conflict	Militarism, over-taxation, degradation	Mayan lowland
	Peasant revolt		Huari, Peru
	Group Conflict	Agricultural collapse deforestation	Easter Island
Economic inefficiency	By-passed trade routes. Agrosystem unproductive	Spanish gold ruined economy. Expansion of government/army	Ottoman 1500s
	Increase scale for control	No support for surplus population Contrast with rulers	Chinese dynasties
Political dysfunction	Loss of provinces	Increased taxation	Babylon
	No inheritance from old rulers	Continued conquest to enrich new ruler	Inca
	Bad management	Lack of economic development	Spain 1700s
Bad luck, or chance events	Weak Emperors	Mismanagement of Huns and Visigoths	Rome
	Loss of agricultural land	Unsuccessful competition with Venice	Byzantium
	Loss of territory	Switch to farming	Ik
Other factors	Mystical	Loss of virtue, exhaustion of energy	Rome
	Spiritual exhaustion	Bad luck, invasion	Rome?

Collapse is the rapid significant loss of an established level of sociopolitical complexity. Various kinds of actions can lead to cultural collapse:

1. A breakdown of central authority. Provincial provinces may break away. Revenues to government decline. There may be foreign challenges. People become disaffected. Military may be ineffective.
2. Central direction is not possible. The center loses power. Distribution of goods may suffer. Trade declines. It may be ransacked and abandoned. Small states start to emerge in the same territory.
3. No law and protection for people. Public art and monument construction cease. Literacy may be lost.
4. Remaining urban populations reuse the architecture. Spaces are subdivided.
5. Palaces and storage facilities may be abandoned. Technology reverts to simpler forms. There may be a reduction in population size and density.
6. Peripheral ecosystems and animals may recover or may not.

Furthermore, collapse can be put into a matrix that includes the primary factor and related factors, which may be necessary but insufficient by themselves.

Of course, some of culture does not collapse. The ideas produced by a culture may spread and reproduce. The culture of ideas continues through people leaping to other places. Again, some parts of a culture may collapse, such as the Southern lowland Maya, while the Northern upland culture continues to survive. Again, lower levels may survive with many of the ideas of the larger complex. So, the Roman Empire collapsed but not Britain or France. The Germans went back to chiefdoms.

Sometimes the collapse is thought to be the result of internal moral or technological failings, as well as conquest or some other external influence. Cultures are adaptive systems that have to integrate a number of challenges, opportunities and pressures, from drought to invasion, and then reconciles them to changing economic and political situations. Collapse can happen by luck, chance that is, or just a coincidence of bad leadership, bad images, cultural problems, external social pressures, and environmental degradation.

3.5.1. Intensification & Civilization

Farming allows intense food production in a minimum area. Farming increases carrying capacity. But, many regions are best suited for pastoral nomadism or wild gardening or foraging or fishing, rather than farming.

The successful cultivation then intensified trading of cultivars and resources between groups. Village specialization may have been the best adaptation. Then the economy of redistribution created regional temple and market towns that regulated the trading in goods. Cities are an intensification of trade and agriculture, and the things that surround them.

Gravity a fruitful metaphor for intensification, for desire or crowding. Gravity is a universal long range force. It is like centripetal, where the center of gravity is the center of the city. For the earth, the center is the sun. But, the sun is part of another gravitational sphere, spheres within spheres like soap bubble in foam. As a metaphor gravity might explain why people are attracted to and move to cities: Intensity. Opportunity may increase due to the concentration of people. The number of links dramatically improves the possibility of better or more communications. Although gravity may explain the intensity of compression or miniaturization, it has trouble explaining the intensity of expansion. The metaphor raises some questions: How is danger related to intensity? Is it being exhilarated by the closeness of death? If the populations increased, would intensification have been necessary?

Civilization is a term for the combined phenomena in the neolithic revolution, starting with agriculture, which increased biodiversity at first, then led to ecosystem take-over. Agriculture required a new technology for tools, such as hoes and plows. It also required the engineering of fields. Land ownership was invented to protect the heavy investments in labor and invention. The subsequent trade in foods required better paths and transportation. Food storage and trade become concentrated in cities.

Record-keeping, in the form of tablets and then writing, became necessary to keep track of stores and trades. Further engineering was required for large stores, as well as standardized pottery. This required specializations in new trades, from potters to smiths and artists. Managers were required for recruit labor for fields and hydraulic engineering.

Concentration in cities permitted and promoted these changes. Permanent settlements contained working houses. Supplies and control required a new infrastructure of massive buildings, better roads, and fortifications.

This paralleled the rise of a religious elite to control the unknowns of weather and crops. And, this was followed by a military elite, which took over protection and combined it with universal gods, which led to the rise of royalty and kings. Heroic buildings increased to provide palaces for royalty. Warfare was necessary to procure foods in times of famine or to protect the stores from less fortunate cities.

The increase in personal property, combined with the redistribution of wealth, led to social hierarchies and classes. Public ideologies were developed to attune the people.

Civilization provided immediate advantages, including supplemental animal labor, more property for everyone, especially the opportunity to have luxury items, the use of records instead of memory, which allowed verification and less misunderstanding, some leisure time for doing nothing, and the production of ale, as a mind-altering substance. Unfortunately, there were disadvantages, such as an increase in the amount of work, not only for production, but also for public projects. Leisure was reduced overall. Living required more work and materials for records, as well as trade and trust with a larger group of people. Personal property had to be stored and protected.

Industrialization is really an intensification of civilization, which is still an ektropic process. In each case of cultural absorption, there was an attendant process of miniaturization. The forest was miniaturized in clumps of trees; animals were miniaturized in artistic image; time on a lunar tally stick; plants in a garden; women in a household; nature by culture in 1800, under the glass roof of the Crystal Palace; and now by the new consciousness surrounding the old. What is intensity?

Intensification brings cultures together faster. Conversion increases, technology and industrialization increase. Intensification is a gigatrend that could lead to violence. For instance, intensification leads to urban living, which increases creativity, as well as some kinds of illness, which leads to physical weakness, which leads to changes in population, which leads to intensification of resource use, which leads to the potential for conflict, which can lead to dislocation and violence.

3.5.2. Patterns & Renewal

Nature consists of moving patterns whose movement is essential to their being. As a rope makes the knot visible, so the body is a pattern made visible. The body is a movement that maintains a topologically stable pattern; it is a vortex but not the water. The thing, the pattern, is a cross section cut through the movement. The mind is an invisible knot that is capable of recognizing both visible and invisible patterns, that is to say, a rope is not always necessary for the demonstration of a knot. Culture is also this kind of pattern. Culture can be analyzed into smaller blocks; the pattern of the whole organization is reflected at every division in differences of organization on either side of boundary. The wholeness of the character of a culture is reflected at every level. Patterning relates symbolic meanings in the context of a cultural system as a whole. The patterns form another level of meaning that has to be addressed in understanding a culture.

There are patterns of interactions of cultures, which arise out of several possibilities: Indifference, trade, competition, cooperation, conquest, or respect. Some archaic cultures seemed to be limited to indifference, that is, they ignored one another, and to trade. Competition and conquest may have accelerated with the acquisition of territory for agriculture. Cooperation and respect seem to have occurred under some circumstances of trade or unification.

The mode of operation of nature consists of a rhythm of dissolution and reformation. Perhaps this process applies to cultures. Often the elements of a culture will simply be rearranged by a succeeding culture. A new culture can only be made from the heritage of the old. The International Workers of the World urged its members to make the new world in shell of old one (in a way similar to genetic recombination perhaps). Our survival depends on the capacity to remake the image of the world from within, phoenix-like.

3.6. Habit & Hope

Are we doomed by our failures to live in nowheres and noplaces, to have the same jobs and the same common rewards? Is being placeless hopeless? Is hope what we should depend on?

In his writings, H. G. Wells prophesied the collapse of civilization and the reversion to barbarism, with the eventual rescue by a race of supermen. Human nature desires a grand explanation to place its daily doldrums into a grand frame. We must abandon the Nineteenth-century grand design approach, however, with its attractive simplicity, and substitute an awareness of humanity as participants in nature, within natural laws. The complexity and fluidity of problems exclude simple, rational argument. Until recently, attempts to resolve contradictions created by urbanization, centralization and bureaucratic growth were viewed as a counterdrift to progress. Any critic was a treated as a discounted outcast.

There is a conflict between economic growth and the preservation of the environment. Economic growth usually triumphs, but it upsets natural rhythms. The devastation of the biosphere is the greatest threat to the survival of humanity. It may not be perceived as such by most people or their governments because of more immediate concerns, such as war, poverty, epidemics, energy, inflation, and unemployment. Nevertheless, the failure of conservation is a direct cause of the worsening of these problems. Society may hinder human understanding with a burden of distractions, injustice, and inferior loyalties.

Most of us will occupy ourselves with externalities, and hope, in the traditional sense, that our children will be wiser—but how can they ever be with no one wise to teach them? Children are cultivated as the leaders of the future— they expected to solve the problems that adults failed to solve. This future is the keystone of the salvation-through-schooling mystique—if it was true once, there is now too great a lag time between taking a civics course in junior high school and using it as adult forty years later. These things need to be taught to adults or especially to the old, who are traditionally leaders. The dying and the old hardly matter to the young and ambitious; their feelings lie as lightly on the scale as their own future. The old themselves default in their responsibility and the young in theirs. Responsibilities are passed down through generations without ever being taken.

Any mind, even most ingenious and fertile, may fall back on habits of its cultural inheritance; humans are social animals with cultural heritages. The outlook of merely a secure and satisfying life, without great ease and rich comfort, may be threatening to many consumers. The contest is not between us and them, but between the reasoning mind and biological limitations. Can there be a leveling up, now, or is there only the possibility of leveling down? The crisis emerges from our state of consciousness. It may be infinitely more difficult to transform human sensibility than to pass laws. We are isolated from the past and future by a disease.

3.6.1. Hope & Science

Technology offers human beings a vision of a world with a stable population, freed from poverty to live in peace, sharing the world's resources. Industrialism, more than that, promises humanity a paradise on earth, after displacing the promise of paradise in heaven. Now, psychology promises its own myth of paradise through self-knowledge and medical improvement.

Science holds great promise for improving the human condition, through understanding the climate and ecology, improvement of agriculture, and the development of soft energy sources, but the lead time for research is long and unpredictable. Interest in ecology has inspired a number of plans and models of the world. The worst are disoriented, useless and uninspiring. The best are notable by their criticisms of the former.

Most popular plans are based on thoroughly terrifying assumptions: Continued, accelerated economic growth, as well as population growth; further industrialization; less distribution of wealth; continued inflation; continued centralization; and complicated technological solutions. Many of these plans rely heavily on scientific studies (MIT SCEP), computer models (Forrester and Meadows), or even science fiction (Kahn). We hope that we can avoid the worst of those assumptions. However, as Ben Franklin noted, those who live exclusively on hope may die fasting.

The present causes of the ecological crisis lie in the combined action of technological advance, population increase, and conventional, erroneous ideas of the nature of humanity and the environment. Garrett Hardin asserts that the problems of the ecological crisis are direct results of the tragedy of the commons reproduced on a global scale. Therefore, overpopulation, pollution and resource depletion can have no technical solutions; they can only be ameliorated through political reform, which can only result from changes in perception.

3.6.2. Implications of Good & Evil

The public gets used to messages of doom, but there are evils that survive identification in the light, and yet go on, like the reification of money or deification of war. Simple codes divide the world into good and evil too neatly, whether in the Christian bible or Reagonomic policy. The world is not simple, alas, and goodness does not grow like tomatoes. By trying to focus on either extreme, of pure goodness or pure evil, we miss the ambiguity and uncertainty of situations, most of which occur in a mixture. Our ethics and ideologics are not composed to help us live in a mixture, with the inevitability of uncertainty, or with the possibility of enantiodromia (a thing turning into its opposite).

Humans usually distinguish unambiguously between good and bad; most ethics intend to further the good and suppress evil. We search for essential difference between good and evil in vain, because the constituents are the same. The distinction lies in the way the pieces are assembled, the structure. The universe is comprised of good and evil, that is, it is agathokakological. Everything seems to work by complementary opposites. Not all good things go together in the same category, exclusive of all evil things. The attempt to isolate the good accelerates enantiodromia and can actually create evil.

Good can be defined as intention and action in the context of the rules of a culture, using ambiguous signs creatively. A sign is anything that signifies something other than itself. Signs are arbitrary, according to Ferdinand de Saussure, that is to say, they have no necessary connection to things. When we set goals, as for the goodness of our forestry practices or charitable institutions, we base those on the meaning of the symbols, which can have many more than one meaning.

Signs make many connections to physical events, thus intensifying them as well as miniaturizing the events in the signs. Signs become dense with meaning. Patterns are available to the mind, and the reality of patterns emerges from events and becomes as real. But, also a reality that can be extended. The play of signs results in good or evil; that is to say, the manipulation of signs, in a field of surprise, due to other levels of meaning, can be interpreted as good or evil.

Culture provides rules that limit play, so that it stops short of death or destruction. Games have rules. All cultures work that way. Ethics and economics are rules of behavior; politics is the practice of changing the rules as society changes. Politics, however, is changed by scale from good to evil; there are too many of us in each system to share discourse. This is much more so on an international level.

The rules of a culture can be expressed in signs or words in the context of the culture. A shift in context can change the meaning of a word. We do not think of physical events, such as gravity or fusion, as good or bad; they simply are. A physical movement is turned into action in the human realm by human intention, which is open to interpretation and ambiguity. Signal play without cultural structures can result in evil.

Words have meaning because of their shared history and context, by their place in a whole language, which adds to meaning of the word. The combination of words in a conversation, with body language and intent, are more important than individual words. The dialogue process helps get past dualities such as good or evil. Metaphor and humor lend new clarity.

In having good as a goal, we cannot calculate the result. Good is a feature of the path of actions, as is evil. We cannot aim at it and shoot, or even stare at it. We must approach sideways, through a field of good and evil. This is one thing a conversation can do, or a poetic series of statements: Let us approach sideways.

3.7. The Possibility of Good

Good is an interesting word, with a long history. The current version is derived from the old English word, *god*, meaning suitable or fitting, similar to the words meaning a 'suitable time' and to be 'pleasing.'

Humans cannot know, or even think of anything, according to Robert Zajonc, without some involvement of emotion, that is, at least a vague feeling of good or bad. Good is problematic. The search for good is measured by personal criteria, personal judgment, and personal reflection. On the other hand, there are questions of what one ought to do, that is, morality. Good and bad mean different things to different people. Your standards or codes might be different from mine. Therefore the meanings of the words will be different. Furthermore, doing bad to one person sometimes results in good for others, or vice versa. Sometimes, just to feel good, people destroy the works of others, or living beings, or an entire ecosystem.

In the long run, as John Fowles suggests, maybe all our judgments of good and bad are meaningless. All actions, good or bad, interweave so extensively as time passes that their individual goodness or badness disappears. Each becomes lost in the other. One should do good for one's health, for instance, or the health of the forest community, not because the action is an action or for the sake of doing something good. In doing, we choose between good and bad actions; the judgment makes us human and susceptible to error. We just have to be aware that choosing good can result sometimes in its opposite, through enantiodromia.

3.7.1. The Necessity of Evil

Evil is a disintegration, a juxtaposition of opposites, with some parts striving to suppress others. Good is the synthesis and reconciliation of the same parts. In ancient Hebrew, good and evil is a single word meaning 'everything.' Everything is disintegrating and synthesizing all the time. Disintegration is necessary to the process. We are aware of values as conflicts tear us; we can reconcile values in just proportions to resurrect whole body.

3.7.1.1. Size & Evil

Humans became more and more prone to alter the earth, because of an increase in the human population and in the means of destruction, not necessarily because of a change in attitude. Both American Plains Indians and Africans exhibited this change in their situations. Indians, for example, used the newly acquired horse and gun to become more efficient, and careless, hunters. Although our behavior may not be qualitatively different from our remote ancestors and the worst pathologies of wild animals, which usually result from miscommunications under certain circumstances, it is quantitatively different. More and more activities affect larger and larger parts of the planet; many problems have global effects now.

In tropical areas in the past, people practiced land use that permitted the vegetation to maintain itself despite human exploitation and the constraints of soil and climate. With population and production pressures, tropical areas everywhere are rapidly being exploited. The consequences may be disastrous.

Size is almost always the greatest threat. In spite of the fact that many Buddhists planted trees regularly, the Buddhist traditions of wooden temples and funeral fires contributed to the denuding of large areas of forest. It is our misfortune to live at a time when the accumulated effects of the conversion of nature for human ends are becoming obvious and cutting into the survival potentials of many other species.

3.7.1.2. Separation & Evil
From medieval times, scientists found that glass could separate materials and distill liquids. Astronomers and microscopes found that glass could be shaped to focus light waves to reveal the very small and the very distant. Portions of the universe were placed behind glass in a laboratory world. Glass was very useful. Scientists came to rely on its advantages, but they were unconsciously imprisoned by its limits.

As science cut the connection to direct observation, it became as blind as mathematics to the 'outer' world. The formality of science made statements about the outer world tautological. This proved to be a problem with quanta, species fitness, and psychological needs. Scientific hypotheses form filters like glasses. They cannot be shed entirely, but their effects can be understood.

Glass has advanced our civilizations by permitting the easy separation of fluids and reactions. But, it leads to an objective attitude towards living beings and nature. Being "behind glass" has become the metaphor, first for a scientific approach to knowledge, then for a utilitarian ethics and a teleological ethics.

Scientists have experimented with biological processes behind glass (*in vitro*) in the laboratory. The primary commandment of Jacques Monod's ethic of objectivity is observers should not participate in the workings of the world. But, detachment from nature is detachment from the basis of knowledge. We distance ourselves behind glass. This detachment is the greatest threat to the welfare of nature. It permits the vivisection of the "voices of existence," as Neil Evernden warns. Only recently, in theoretical physics and in ecology, has it been realized that there can be no perfect detachment and objectivity. There can be no perfect insulation from the object of study.

We have created a hard glass between the mind projecting and the object receding. Sometimes we doubt if there is anything on the other side that can be seen. Glass also forms a window for consciousness, which swamps the mind with the 'error of the eye,' in Marshall McLuhan's phrase. Vision, whose mode is successive and not simultaneous, is emphasized and split away from the total sensorium. After human consciousness places the glass, human needs shape and tint the glass. Utilitarianism casts a thick, convex glass, to focus on the individual. Romantics use a tinted, concave glass, the better to see the whole.

The evolution of human mentality has put us all behind glass. We use glass to protect ourselves from the ambiguity and messiness of nature. We have made an experiment of ourselves; our mentality has evolved behind glass. We have isolated ourselves by technology. We have seen more on television, but are moved to do less. C.P. Snow has commented that watching deaths by starvation in Africa on television screens could mark the end of any moral community of humanity.

We are behind glass and fear it will break. Augustine remarked to the Romans: "What glory is there in the largeness of empire, bright and brittle like glass, and forever in fear of breaking." Reason alone cannot cure what it caused. Glass cannot divide humanity and nature; nor can we humanize the planet without dehumanizing ourselves. We can put things and beings behind glass, but we lose them. Relationships are so strange and complex that they cannot be understood behind glass. The glass creates an illusion of objectivity. Being behind glass allows us to pretend that we are separate; this pretense allows evil. We need to break the glass. We need a sanctified vision of life from a deep participation.

3.7.1.3. Freedom & Evil

Freedom is a description of possibilities. Freedom allows many values and behaviors, but not necessarily all. Freedom is considered the opposite of determination. Most theorists are worried that freedom would be denied in any modern utopia or dystopia. Both Fritz Schumacher and Eugene Odum refute this in numerous arguments. Some freedom is needed to realize human potential. A right amount is needed; and this amount can be determined ecologically and ethically.

But, in addition, one must understand that existence is already half determined; freedom and necessity must be balanced at about fifty percent (compare with the fifty percent redundancy requirement in information theory). Too much freedom, the refusal to acknowledge what is determined, would inflict the self-determination of each on the self determination of the many, resulting in social chaos, and reducing other freedoms. Too little freedom, the refusal to acknowledge what can be done, results in stagnation. Recognition of the laws of nature is what allows the only real freedom within them. We do not eat poisonous plants, or breath water, for instance, although both can be done with adequate preparations.

3.7.1.4. Knowledge & Evil

Knowledge increases our opportunities, that is, our freedom; we pay for freedom with the risks of mistakes. Knowledge is power and power can possess its owner. Humans have the power to alter vast processes in nature, and not enough care to refrain from trying. Even if we know better, we must care to act with concern for others.

Once we become aware that the unintended byproducts of industry are harmful to a species population, then the destruction of that species becomes an intention if we do not alter our behavior. Destruction is then a matter of choice and responsibility rather than ignorance.

3.7.2. *Intention & Evil*

The first act of a utopia must be to come to terms with the evil seeds of good intentions. Evil can arise because of the contradictory nature of reality, the nature in which all institutions subvert the values for which they are founded; all values seem to be achieved in conflict with opposites. Does evil come out of our efforts to do good? Developed nations are in a double bind in dealing with famines: If we do not feed starving people, they will die; but, if we do feed them, more will die later, unless they have renewed their crops or reduced their populations.

The process by which a movement turns into its exact opposite has been identified as a swing of reversal; romanticism rejected industrialization, but became mechanized. The German attempt to unite Europe left it divided. The line curves upon itself. The rise of ecological consciousness is an offshoot of the space program's view of the planet. Values too strenuously proclaimed often go to their opposite.

Aid is an illustrative example of this kind of swing. Basing foreign aid on a belief in spurring industrial development is a tragedy. The second outcome of a massive distribution of food to poorer countries is often a depression of local agriculture. Common-sense solutions to some problems just worsen the problem. Michael Gordon illustrates the pitfall of halfhearted help. Aid can be the prime cause of suffering that it is intended to relieve, increasing the sum of human misery. Medicine and infant care can be cruel, if the infants are neglected later. Aid humiliates the receiving country, Gordon says, and corrupts or angers the donor country. But the innocent suffer with the guilty. The alternative can be greater starvation a few years later. Aid as a program for action is incomplete and too simplistic. Schumacher stipulates that the best aid that could be offered is intellectual.

The editors of The Ecologist are even more radical in their recommendation: In view of the psychological and material debacles thus far, no aid at all is best. Even intellectual aid is questionable; our ideas and inventions may not even be applicable. Now, with our proliferation of information, especially concerning products like cars, vacuums, clothes, and grooming devices, we raise people's aspirations without satisfying any of them.

The author H.G. Wells invented the idea of futurism, predicting and planning a culture for future global development. "The future cannot be predicted, but can be invented," according to Dennis Gabor. The first step in inventing is to learn everything possible about the past and the present and then try to identify those possibilities that may be realized and then to choose from among those possibilities to invent a desirable future.

Karl Marx realized that ideas become a material force when they take hold of minds of people. But, first the ideas must be formed. We may remake our part of the earth, which is part of a solar system, which is part of a galaxy of over 100 billion stars in an archipelago of galaxies. If we are unable to create a place here, the fault will probably be, to paraphrase Shakespeare through Cassius, in ourselves, and not in the stars.

We are behind glass and fear it will break. Augustine remarked to the Romans: "What glory is there in the largeness of empire, bright and brittle like glass, and forever in fear of breaking."

Figure 360-1. Possible Independent Regions in North America. Many of these areas overlap with folk cultures (African-American-Atlantic), with New Age designations (Ecotopia-Cascadian), or with new territories (Nunavut).

4.0. Reviewing Cultural Adaptations to Challenges & Problems

Human cultures have adapted to different environmental conditions over tens of thousands of years. The vernacular designs of many cultures are superb adaptations to their local environments. Many tools and buildings were planned and built as a response to difficult conditions, and are models of beauty and efficiency. These cultures need to operate within local and global processes, as well as within human structures. Cultures become critical design factors since their adaptive patterns, such as agriculture and technology, create opportunities and problems on local, regional and global levels. Human populations have a significant impact on the planet, especially through conversion of ecosystems and the addition of exotic elements.

4.1. *Agriculture Cities & Civilization*

Humans adapted to the uniqueness of their places, communicating the uniqueness with their innate abilities with gestures, words and languages, creating a body of knowledge about places, and then creating traditions and practices.

As the climate changed at the end of the last ice age, conditions changed radically as the atmosphere warmed and wind and moisture patterns shifted. The loss of large prey species, and the drying out of northern forests, combined with thick stands of new grasses, forced changes in diets, as well as in hunting and gathering styles. And, these resulted in changes in settlements and technology.

4.1.1. *Adopting an Agricultural Style*

Agriculture is a system of plant use that people developed towards the end of the ice age, when the weather and other conditions became much more variable. Changing climate after the last ice age forced many animals and plants to migrate or adjust. It is possible to look at agriculture as an adaptation to those conditions, which included drought, species shifts and extinctions. Changes in wind patterns brought more moisture to some areas and new populations of plants. Growing plants allowed people to survive longer droughts and the disappearance of large game animals. Of course, it is also possible that after 40,000 years of gradual but constant population growth, people had filled all the available open niches for hunting. In that case agriculture was an adaptation to the shrinking availability of land for hunting and gathering.

4.1.1.1. Historical Pattern of Agriculture

Agriculture is the use of plants in a place. Human groups came to understand details of plants as they collected them for use. With changes in the distributions of plants and animals after the end of the last ice age, some groups settled near lush concentrations of plants, such as wheat grasses. These groups gradually started selecting and replanting some varieties. As they traded surplus grains with other groups (for minerals, plants or animal products), the other groups planted their grains in areas where they did not normally grow, often dry areas with poor soils. The plants required care, in the form of water, fertilizer or protection. The large pattern of agriculture has been the selection of a few plants, an increase in the scale of planting and the assumption of control of all phases of the plant life.

4.1.1.2. Advantages of Agriculture

Agriculture offered many advantages. The source of food was more stable and more reliable. The plants could be isolated in fields or behind walls. Travel was reduced, since the plants would be brought to people, instead of people traveling to select plants when they were ripe. The select plants would have increased food value and decreased toxicity. There would be a surplus that would allow people to live in one place, where more people could be supported on a smaller area of land. The surplus would also allow intoxication to be domesticated and expanded. Humans learned to cultivate soil, plant seeds and wait until crops grew. A hunter needed 10 square kilometers per person for nourishment; intensive agriculture lowered this to 1 hectare (1/100 a square kilometer). Agriculture could be 1000 times as efficient in terms of area.

4.1.1.3. Ecological Changes from Agriculture

Agriculture is an integral part of the environment in which it is practiced. Agricultural systems are distinctive types of human-modified ecosystems. An agroecosystem is a natural ecosystem that has been modified, or arrested at an early stage of succession, an immature stage. This is a form of disturbance by humans.

In an ecosystem, humans are just one more group exploiting the system. But, in agroecosystems, humans are manipulating the entire system, that is, they are modifying the system and isolating from neighboring systems. They do this in many ways, by: Simplifying the system by removals; managing the system with domestics; and harvesting the bulk of productivity. Each of these has effects on the system. Simplifying the system, or lowering diversity, allows fewer species in the system. Not just the crop species, but pest species. Crops are analogous to early colonizing plants, that is weeds, which exploit ephemeral resources following disturbance and maximize their seed output. Plowing favors crops that grow rapidly.

How did agriculture affect culture in early Mesopotamia, for instance? Just as a result of irrigation? From changes in religion, from otherworldly gods to specialist gods? There are many general associated changes from shift to agriculture; they can be considered cascading effects from positive feedback loops. For instance, clearing larger areas of land and irrigating to transfer water to land lead to technological improvements in the channeling and manipulation of water. New tools extended efficiency. More crops required new ideas of storing foods. There were more innovations in general. Domestic animals were used to haul loads and then work in the fields for preparation or harvests. This required new kinds of digging sticks and new kinds of harnesses. The kilns for ceramics required more wood, which often came from newly cleared fields or transport from remote forests.

The creation of more kinds of material goods led to the accumulation of more material goods, that is, more things. Things had to be measured and tracked, and that required counting and sorting. Books had to be kept. A currency of exchange had to be invented to allow things to travel less and be more still, in place (see Table 4113-1).

There was an increase in the size of labor input into agriculture. There were specialized occupations related to tools, specialized occupations related to trade, and specialized occupations related to conflict, protection, control, and project management. There were changes in distribution of food substances and things. Not only things, but people concentrated into villages and towns. Luxury goods and wealth accumulated. Society may have stratified first by specialization, some of which had more prestige, then later by prestige itself. To protect things and places, new specialists in protection were developed. Control and conflict increased. At some point control of social activity lead to control of the poor, control of women, of animals, and control of wild areas and animals.

Table 4113-1. Agricultural Summary of Effects

Agricultural Change	Economic change	Social/political change
Seeds/resources	Trade	Standard value, writing
Manipulation	Increase size	Domestication dependence
Personal fields	Ownership, limits	Conflict, Protection / taxes
Working	Increase in hours	Changes in status
Water needs	Canals	Cooperation
Timing	Calendars	Schedules
Tools	Technology	Specialists
Specialization	Specialists	Pay, records
Distribution of crop	Pottery	Standard sizes, records
Surplus accumulation	Storage places	Protection, buildings
Sedentary Life Styles	Field exhaustion	Field expansion
Permanent fields	Settlement	Mobility decrease, Growth
Permanent settlement	Cities	Concentration, critical mass
Distribution of crop	Pottery	Standard sizes, records
Surplus accumulation	Storage places	Protection, buildings
Property accumulation	Larger homes	Protection

Commercial farmers have to cope with a constant parade of new crop varieties as varietal replacement due to biotic stresses and market changes has accelerated to unprecedented levels. A cultivar with improved disease or insect resistance makes a debut, performs well for a few years, typically five to nine years, and is then succeeded by another variety when yields begin to slip, productivity is threatened, or a more promising cultivar becomes available. A variety's trajectory is characterized by a take-off phase when it is adopted by farmers, a middle stage when the planted area stabilizes and finally a retraction of its acreage. Thus, stability in modern agriculture hinges on a continuous supply of new cultivars rather than a patchwork quilt of many different varieties planted on the same farm. The need to subsidize monocultures requires increases in the use of pesticides and fertilizers, but the efficiency of use of applied inputs is decreasing and crop yields in most key crops are leveling off. In some places, yields are actually in decline. There may be several underlying causes of this phenomenon. Yields may be leveling off because the maximum yield potential of current varieties is being approached, and therefore genetic engineering must be applied to the task of redesigning crop. On the other hand, the leveling off may be because of the steady erosion of the productive base of agriculture through unsustainable practices.

Cultural differences between ecology and agroecology include: Different perspectives, for instance, human-managed systems rather than openness; different goals, such as productivity and efficiency instead of survival; and, different principles, like subsidization more than wildness. Crop ecology for agriculture is limited by intense labor. Special cultural practices are developed to engage the work and celebrate its successful completion. There are many personal and social consequences from the adaptation of agriculture (see Table 4113-2).

Table 4113-2. Other Consequences of Agriculture

Psychological consequences	Increase in compliance and obedience
	Stress due to uncertainty of yield
	Increase in hard work
	Reduced food choices, malnutrition
Sociological Consequences	Sedentarization of people
	Altered relations, status competition
	Change in world views
	Increase in movement of goods
	Rise in central authority, hierarchy
	Use of irrigation to increase yields

4.1.1.4. Agriculture & Population

Agriculture did produce one unexpected change. Initially, farming peoples suffered from increased sickness and mortality. But, they also saw greatly increased fertility. Populations in Europe increased one-hundred-fold. Of course, agriculture allowed people, by virtue of remaining in one place, to have more children than they could previously, in hunting bands, carry or travel with. So, the sedentism of agriculture allowed larger populations to exist in place. Furthermore, the nature of work in agriculture meant that more children were useful for labor.

Population increased rapidly, despite nutritional problems. Perhaps the fertility of women increased when they stayed in place. Being in place may have removed those controls from prolonged breast-feeding or sexual abstinence. Agricultural populations increased and spread, bringing their crops with them, pushing hunters into the periphery where crops could not grow. Once the initial agricultural startup costs were paid, such as truncated diversity and nutrition, as well as decrease in human size and health, other advantages accrued, such as specialization, creating a different form of political control, which allowed armies. Agricultural society now had a massive social advantage over foraging societies.

Perhaps related to population growth and size, have come changes in cultural status, especially related to equity, distribution, and dominance. Status has to do with standing in society, and with appearance and ownership. Status may come from longevity, of the self or ancestors, as well as from the results of good decisions, from hunting for example, or from owning more than others, or just more things or more people. Status is a powerful human need, and may drive the growth of goods or populations. As distribution becomes more unequal and as conflict occur more between groups, dominance and slavery appear, and are both related to status.

4.1.1.5. Population Size after Agriculture

The maximum number of individuals that an environment can support is its carrying capacity, which fluctuates with various factors. Physical limits may be absolute or flexible. Population control can either be accomplished through crowding, by the food supply, or by natural resources. There tend to be as many people as there are utilized natural resources for, and unpolluted room and food for. The greatest number of people over time implies that the living population be limited to biological carrying capacity. Any permanent destruction of carrying capacity to allow a larger living population implies a future reduction in population indefinitely, or until ecosystem restoration (if possible).

4.1.1.6. Property Increase after Agriculture

Agriculture, by creating permanent places, allowed people to accumulate far more property than they could carry or put on a horse or buffalo—or move. This new property allowed people to have things that were luxuries rather than needs. It let them collect things that might normally be given away or reworked. Agriculture set in motion many kinds of physical and technical changes, that resulted in further social, economic and political changes. Many of these are intricately related and developed out of previous changes. Trade, for instance, expanded from a few necessities, such as seeds or ochre, to many forms of tools and luxuries.

4.1.1.7. Disadvantages of Agriculture

Disadvantages of agriculture include a dramatic increase in work hours, especially during harvest time. All the work that was previously covered by natural processes, from propagating to irrigating, was now accomplished with human labor. In addition to that were requirements for tools and storage devices. Despite this, there was a decrease in nutrition, as the overall diet was less diverse and less complete. There was an increase in fertility and a population increase, perhaps at a rate thirty times as fast within generations.

The form of agriculture, from simplification of the system to an increase in scale of the system, not to mention intensity of energy and use, resulted in the degradation of ecosystems, including erosion, siltation, salinization, and an explosion of pests. Modern agriculture replaces the biota, or transforms the ecosystem into an artificial system. Furthermore, with fertilizers robbing foods of nutritional values, more of each food is required to meet nutritional needs; for instance, the nutritional value of broccoli has declined almost 500% in 50 years, which means we have to eat 5 times as much as our grandparents.

Highly specialized systems are accelerating the change from 'palaeotechnic' to 'neotechnic' agriculture. This change minimizes costs and maximizes profits, but it also narrows the ecological basis of world food production and decreases human livelihood. Life on the planet cannot afford the continuous genetic narrowing generated by agriculture. The application of modern agricultural techniques in tropical areas disregards the local realities, and is socially and ecologically disastrous. Traditional ways have operated successfully for thousands of years, although not without serious problems of their own. But, these problems may be overcome, unlike industrial problems, which have fundamental flaws and cause rapid conversion.

4.1.2. *Concentrating in Cities*

A city is a place where a large number of people live permanently. The polis, the classical city-state, was a place where the citizens depended on and maintained the whole, which cared for and outlasted the individual. The Stoics declared the cosmos to be the great city "of gods and men." The citizen became related to the cosmos as a whole, in the same way. For those in Mesopotamia, the whole city, and not just the temple, was conceived as an earthly imitation of the cosmic order, a sociological middle cosmos, established between the macrocosm of the universe and the microcosm of the individual. Through the priesthood, the one essential form of all was made visible. The early Sumerian temple tower, with a hieratically organized city surrounding it, became the model for the Hindu world mountain Sumeru, for the Greek Olympus, for Aztec temples, and even for Dante's Purgatory. The Sumerian city was organized in the design of a quartered circle. This design has been a favorite for cities and utopias, as well as for many cosmologies.

The whole city, and not just the temple, was conceived as an earthly imitation of the cosmic order, a sociological middle cosmos, established between the macrocosm of the universe and the microcosm of the individual. Through the priesthood, the one essential form of all was made visible. The ideal landscape became the middle region, the garden between the complete order of the city and the complete chaos of the wilderness. The garden is cultivated from the wilderness as a middle landscape. The garden is a human order, but not usually sacred.

Cityscapes still contain gardens. Gardens and parks have been designed to express an idealized view of natural and agricultural scenes, since Sumerian times, at least, over 5000 years. Many names for the landscape—grove, lawn—are drawn from the imagery of the garden. The complementary aspects of landscape planning are the invariants of a given area and the artistic imagination of a planner. Conrad Aiken recognized that "The language and the landscape are the same, for we ourselves are the landscape and are the land." The city expands at the expense of gardens, fields, and then wilderness.

Many other cities were placed at the intersection of rivers or trade routes. Cities have distinguishing characteristics, such as permanent buildings, specialized buildings, monumental buildings, and large populations, which have increased over the millennia, from 2000 people to 50,000 or millions of people. Another characteristic is the density of the population, as a result of the shape, size and number of buildings. Cities in general are not self-sufficient; they rely on outlying areas for food and resources. Cities are places with surpluses that can be traded for things from other groups or cities; cities become central places in an area that provide services for outlying areas. The specialization of occupations in a city promotes trade of special goods. Specialization and unequal distribution allows people to become stratified in distinct classes, based on specialization and differential rewards. A city is also a place characterized by organizational complexity, with universal rules and central institutions.

As people are attracted by the advantages and excitements of cities, the size and number of cities increases. The spread of cities increases. Their areas are added to that of the vast agricultural lands, which together make up the physical impact of human habitation on the surface of the planet. The characteristics of cities change also, as their sizes and shapes are formed by desire and consumption. They become more "ideal" and more uniform, and with less and less to make them different and unique, they start to resemble ideal noplaces.

4.1.2.1. City Patterns
The earliest villages and possibly the first cities were established near water, near hunting and gathering grounds. In general, cities formed in areas where there was surplus and where larger groups of people were needed to deal with surpluses. Many of the first larger cities (500 or more) were located on waterways needed to irrigate crops. Permanent special buildings were needed to store surplus. Permanent buildings were built as homes, since people were living in one place all the time. Buildings began to increase in size to express faith in the place and the gods of the place, but also to express new differences in status or wealth as the labor system became more hierarchical.

Some cities were built as farming storage complexes, others as religious centers, others on trade routes to facilitate trading. Some cities built walls to protect their surpluses, wealth or people. Soldiering became a specialty. Cities came to resemble artificial land forms, such as mountains or canyons. Only certain plants or animals were kept in the cities. Almost the entire land surface was covered with buildings, paths or roads.

4.1.2.2. The City as an Ecosystem
The city was an adaptive exploitation of shifting environments. It was an adaptation to an ecological niche and a cultural niche. At first cities allowed for the coexistence of hunters and herders with the local farmers and residents of the city. The city is exploitation of a geographic site, which has a

multilevel history from geology to plants and humans. The structure of a city might be like a cell, a specialized structure with a transmissible memory in the nucleus. Or like a sponge; the city cannot use sun to get energy but must use surrounding environment (plants) and other organisms in the water. Sponges must circulate food brought in, using energy from that food. A city has own metabolism, that is a network of circulatory structures used for exchanges. Water and wood (energy) are carried by channels to cells of organism (homes in this case). Channels also carry wastes.

As an ecosystem, a city has fewer plant and animal species. Many factors influence its balance with its environment. Water flow is a factor affecting the landscape. Household wastes are another factor. A network of corridors perforate the landscape; the number of small patches increases, and there is a reduction in other kinds of patches and corridors. Flows include energy, information, people, materials, and pollution. The net productivity of the city ecosystem is negative, due to massive imports of food and energy.

The size of a city grows, apparently without limit. During the mass migration from 1800 to 1991, urban population in developed countries rose from five percent to seventy-three percent. A mass migration in less-developed countries, from 1940 to 2004, the city population rose from three percent to over fifty percent. As cities increase in size, there is less flexibility for change. Land use planning and design becomes more important.

This size expansion has caused problems, effects, and side effects—that is, main effects that are unwanted or unanticipated. Villages lower connectivity to the landscape by increasing patches and corridors. Agriculture gets more homogenous, decreases fallow areas. Stream corridors are destroyed by environmental degradation. Connectivity is lowered, the matrix is minimalized. The nutrient mineral cycles are disturbed. The atmosphere is disrupted, resulting in drought and storms. Microclimates change, with heat islands and dust domes. There is lower photosynthesis and productivity, with lower diversity leading to homogenization (with cosmopolitan species) and inefficiency of use of energy and materials, and decaying infrastructure (roads, sewers, buildings, houses).

Urban ecosystems and agroecosystems, however, are less resilient than natural ones, due to the constant expenditure of human and fossil energy to maintain them. Cities need the environment for resources, food and water. People in cities tend to organize the environment by controlling markets and transportation on which the agricultural systems depend. Cities also produce large quantities of waste that have to be absorbed. Cities pollute air and modify climate. They are heat traps by absorption of solar and the production of heat.

4.1.2.3. Changes from City Living

The city is a consolidated area, a permanent part of the landscape, with stable home sites and larger, permanent houses. There are impressive public buildings and monuments that can lead to civic pride and use. The city offered opportunities for specialization, for choosing a mate from a wider pool of candidates, for excitement and stimulation, and for wealth. The city has a critical mass for inspiration and invention (in art and science). Of course, the city offered better protection from invading groups and it offered a more stable food supply

Living in a city also had disadvantages. It meant one had a smaller living space, lower standards of living, and a less varied diet. There was a greater chance of disease, nutritional deficiencies, and crime. The larger population meant an increase in competition and possibly a decrease in personal rewards. Public art styles could be limited. Due to the large populations, cities tended to ecologically degrade the surrounding areas. Although cities were fine adaptations to the climatic and environmental changes as the ice age was ending, they were vulnerable to larger groups of enemies and to longer environmental problems such as long droughts, over ten years, or series of changes.

A society based on cities, with a complex social organization, engages in a whole series of changes. Rather than reciprocity, economies are based on a centralized accumulation of materials. Social status is changed through tribute and taxation. Formal records-keeping arises, from knotted strings to cuneiform. A state religion develops, where the leader takes an important role, as for instance as god-king.

Table 4123-1. Urbiculture Summary

Change	Leads to	Which creates	And changes
Permanent crops	Irrigation	Salinization, exhaustion	Kinds of crops
Permanent buildings	Storage, property	Possessions, greed	Movement
Massive monuments	Status	Competition	Relationships
Trade	Common value	Standards	Shortages
Managers	Rise of elite	Taxes, power skew	Hierarchy
Transportation	Roads	Crowding	Perception
Water/Baths	Increased use	New reservoirs	Shortages
Walls	Protection	Separation	Inside/outside
Centralization	Concentration	Intensification	Obedience
Culture mixes	Violence	Laws	Behavior
Ecosystem replacement	Degradation	Protection	Invasions, disease
Unsustainable use of water and wood	Distribution	Drawdown, money	Money
Specialists: Artists, clothiers masons	Luxuries	Redistribution	Production patterns
Crowding density	Disease	Immunities	Health

This table (4123-1) is not able to show multiple causal chains or how changes lead to or influence other changes.

4.1.2.4. Intensification

Cities are an intensification of trade and agriculture, and the things that surround them. Gravity a fruitful metaphor for intensification, for desire or crowding. Gravity is a universal long-range force. It is like centripetal, where the center of gravity is the center of the city. For the earth, the center is the sun. But, the sun is part of another gravitational sphere. As a metaphor gravity might explain why people are attracted to and move to cities: Intensity. Opportunity may increase due to the concentration of people. The number of links dramatically improves the possibility of better or more communications. Although gravity may explain the intensity of compression or miniaturization, it has trouble explaining the intensity of expansion. The metaphor raises some questions: How is danger related to intensity? Is it being exhilarated by the closeness of death? If the populations increased, would intensification have been necessary?

Cities are where most people live, where most resources and energy are consumed, and where most wastes are produced. The city becomes a center for intensification and excitement, but it also causes environmental challenges to appear faster and larger. A city changes the local environment around it, pulling in medium size cities, as it did in Mesopotamia, and reducing the number of small satellite cities, which are made continuous with the influence and attraction of the center city.

Urbanization was the result of permanent settlement and population growth. The growth of the settlement and intensification followed. There was specialization and engineering of a more complex infrastructure, with canals, larger buildings and massive monuments, and fortifications. Religion and trade enlarged in scale. Specialization As result of surplus food and larger population, special people can create a flow of specialized objects. The population has to be large enough to support a market.

Jane Jacobs asserts that cities are at the root of all economic growth, from agricultural, manufacturing, and technology growth to the information explosion, and therefore import replacement is the cause to all economic growth. This idea challenges one of the fundamental assumptions of Classical and Neoclassical economists, who consider the nation-state to be the main player in macro-economics. Jacobs argues that it is not the nation-state, but the city that is true player of this world-wide game. She speculates on the further ramifications of considering the city first and the nation second, or not at all.

The advantages of urbanization included consolidated area and stable home sites, with larger, permanent houses. Public buildings and monuments became more impressive. This formed a critical mass for inspiration and invention, including art as well. Measuring and writing, inventories and commercial dealings followed.

The disadvantages, however, included population increase, an increase in diseases and the danger of violence. There was a limit to public styles of art, ecological degradation of surrounding areas, and increased vulnerability to collapse. There seem to be limits to our personal space and levels of tolerance to human intensification, also. Urban intensification leads to the question: Is there a limit to human numbers? Perhaps space, but is there a psychological limit? People in cities seem to do well with high-contact, high-proximity living. What happens when people are crowded or feel crowded? Physical complaints, emotional complaints, sexual dysfunction, or feelings of fear, seem to be expressed often. There may be limits of crowding. Are there social limits, in terms of the number of people one can tolerate? We may have requirements for personal space, home space, and wild space. Psychological limits may be the basis for some of the great failures of human life, for instance, the "failure of perception." We cannot see slow change or anticipate it. No one really sees the incredible interdependence of humanity and nature, of diversity and success. We do not seem to be able to see others as feeling human beings.

4.1.2.5. Discussion of Cities: Ideal or Trap
Is the city a human ideal? An environmental ideal? It can offer ideal environments, as well as different kinds of physical environments, from streets, and squares, to religious monuments and parks. What is it about a city that commands awe? Increasing populations can lead to intensification of production, through labor or mechanization. Is the city a trigger for intensification? Interdependence becomes overconnected and then a trap. First cities were of bricks and concrete. John Thackera thinks that cities are held together now by human attention spans, which may be more gaslike than solid. The technology that dominates attention spans, such as the wireless infrastructure, just adds a new layer, as people still live in brickworks. Certainly, the city has always been an incubator of new forms and ideas. And, the medium for cultural transmission has been ideas, more than genes or bodies. And, there may even be standard units of cultural transmission by imitation, such as memes (Richard Dawkin's phrase for the unit of transmission; see later for a more detailed discussion), of which cities, agriculture, and fashions are examples.

How did cities start? Was a town formed by neighboring villages? Thucydides used the word *synoecismus* to refer to the union of several towns and villages under one capital city. Was the city a result of technology—The wheel, cart, or metallurgy? According to Rod Brooks, cities started from a subsumption architecture of organization, where higher levels of behavior subsume the roles of lower levels to take control (also called bottom-up organization). So, people start with villages, and get the kinks worked out; who lives where? Who does what? This fits with the idea that cities were adaptations to permanent siting, slow overpopulation, and changing environmental conditions.

When the villages are working, you can make a few towns. Coordinate the logistics of streets, sewers, water, lights, and law. When the towns are successful and reliable, you can make a capital city, adding a layer of law, taxes, schools, maybe trading and heroic institutions. The cities can be combined into a state or empire, which has new responsibilities, such as taxes and international affairs and defense. The empire subsumes the other levels, but lets them operate independently. Of course, there are advantages in the group. And there are further emergent structures. Especially international trade and forms of education. Of course, at some point, the cities are no longer adaptive to the environment.

How do cities end? Abandonment? Collapse? If the top level collapses, the others can continue to function. This is what happens with certain kinds of collapse. How does civilization steer? Does it push or pull? Pushing can result in a backlash or revolt. What is best for the individual is not always best for the species. What is best for the person is not always best for society.

Is it possible to have cities without states or vice versa? A city is an adaptation to keep economic surplus in one place. A state is a political unit governed by a central authority. Like a city, a state has to delineate rights and responsibilities for citizens, regulate social relations, e.g., marriage and family, support a religion or ideology, integrate networks of communication and transportation, control redistribution, control punishment, and have a monopoly of military forces and weapons.

How is size important? Is it centrality important? Ancient big cities included Uruk (10,000 to 40,000) and Harappa (20,000-25,000). Mohenjo-daro of the Indus Valley Civilization was one of the largest, with an estimated population of 41,250. Later, Nineveh and Carthage each had 700,000. Alexandria was large (~400,000 by 32 PE). Rome had an estimated population of 1 million by 5 BPE. Baghdad exceeded a population of one million by the 8th century PE. The largest cities now include Tokyo, Japan (28,025,000), Mexico City, Mexico (18,131,000), Mumbai, India (18,042,000), São Paulo, Brazil (17, 711,000), New York City, USA (16,626,000), Shanghai, China (14,173,000), and Lagos, Nigeria (13,488,000).

The best cities are no longer the largest. The best are considered Vancouver, Copenhagen, Zurich, which are usually less than 2 million. For a long time cities required larger numbers of people to be intense enough for stimulation and creativity. But, now new technology provides the stimulation and could allow cities to be significantly smaller, perhaps 10 or 20 thousand. A growing population creates environmental resistance to itself, in the form of reduction in the reproduction rate as the population approaches carrying capacity. Due to various time lags, e.g., to increase when conditions favor or to react to unfavorable crowding, the density can overshoot the capacity. Human population is controlled to some extent by self-crowding. The overshoot has to be on a local scale, never on a global scale. The Russian geochemist S. Vernadsky concluded that the property of maximum expansion is inherent in living matter as it is for gas expansion or heat distribution (and ideas in cities?). The pressure of life can be measured in terms of velocity. For cities, immigration can increase fast and cause overshoot and subsequent oscillations. What would happen if all cities overshot simultaneously?

Is there a trend to larger cities? Should it be continued? Should arcologies replace unplanned cities? What about limits or nesting into optimum size groups? The degree of aggregation, as well as overall density, which results in optimum population growth and survival, varies with species and conditions (this is Allee's Principle); undercrowding, as well as overcrowding may be limiting. Aggregation can enhance group survival. Fish in a school may tolerate higher doses of poison than individuals. Bees can create more heat to survive than individuals. Applied to humans in cities, aggregation is beneficial, up to a point. But, bee or termite colonies can get too big.

How important is connectivity? Cities are unavoidably entangled in global nets, now. Cities used to be limited by the local carrying capacity. With global nets, self-correcting feedback can take too long. Localization makes feedback visible and more immediate. It makes more self-reliant cities.

How can we look at humanity? First we were wolves, catching animals and eating them. For thirty thousand years. Then we were cows, standing in places eating grasses, for ten thousand years. Now we are termites, swarming over everything in furious dances of labor and status, for the past five thousand years.

Are we urban by nature? Have we changed from hunting to urbaning? Of course, we may be preadapted for cities. We are clever social animals. We prefer edge habitat so as to move between other habitats. Urbanization is a characteristic of an edge species. Civilization produces edges that people like. Wilderness is fragmented into islands and patches. So, there is no more deepness, no more interior to wilderness. What are other edge species? Raccoons, coyotes, crows, and rats.

We are foragers and predators. What are the needs in human nature that a city answers? Perhaps the city is what wilderness was, according to Eisenberg, a place of passage, a place to be brave and test yourself. Humans have always worked to abstract their specialness. The city seems to be another myth of separateness and independence from nature. The city is the laboratory of human creativity, kept apart from the mother of nature. Lewis Mumford saw city life as a compromise between the hunting stage and the farming stage. The female principle of home is wed to the male principle of predation. Perhaps the city is a throwback to hunting. People are more likely to wander, and are less attached to a place?

Are cities unnatural? Is urban living a preadaptation? We are of course social animals. We prefer edge habitat. We are hunters and foragers. Why is the city growing everywhere? Especially Africa, South America and Asia. Parts of Manchester and Detroit are being abandoned.

Are cities declining? Certainly, there has been a decline in the quality of living spaces, irrespective of energy or resource use. Some cities have declined in population as areas of a city are deserted. The decline of cities due to the replacement of creative architecture by architecture that lacks organic order and connection, may be due to a declining interest in planning, as a result of economic values, suggests Eliel Saarinen.

Are cities the ultimate creation of civilization where people can enjoy culture free from want or physical extremes? Or, are cities a gross alteration of nature that destroys human life and dignity—a gross ecological error. As long as cities grow without negative feedback, the second will occur. When ecology helps the city ecosystem fit in the surrounding ones, then the achievement is worthwhile. The city depends on its environment.

4.1.3. *The Complex of Civilization (or Neolithic Revolution)*

Many phenomena interacted during the Neolithic revolution. Not simply agriculture or urbanization, but profound economic and social shifts occurred. Agriculture, by taking over an ecosystem, allowed a short-term increase in biodiversity followed by a long-term decrease. To increase control, new tools such as hoes and plows were developed; the fields themselves were engineered with added irrigation systems. Gradually other ecosystems were taken over. Land use became a formal ownership to reflect the investment in all of the above. Land ownership was a logical step with permanence, as individuals dedicated themselves to a relatively small area. The technology of tools advanced, as did the engineering of fields and water systems.

Permanent settlement resulted in more permanent buildings, as well as in massive buildings and monuments, fortifications and religious centers. This led to an increased infrastructure to supply water, access, transportation and waste. Sedentation and surplus allowed larger populations and increased fertility. The subsequent trade in foods required better paths and transportation. Food storage and trade become concentrated in cities.

There were dramatic economic shifts that included trade, craft specialization, professional art, record-keeping, writing, direct engineering (pottery), and standardization. Personal property increased dramatically; one no longer needed to carry everything one owned. Records were needed to supplement the memories of individuals, since many individuals were required to keep track of stores, trade and rations. This required specializations in new trades, from potters to smiths and artists. Managers were required for recruit labor for fields and hydraulic engineering. Labor shortages on public projects required recruitment of labor from within the city or from outlying areas. Animal labor was applied to some activities.

This lead to many personal advantages. People had more property. It was not necessary to make everything for one's self, or know how to. One could trade for needs or luxury items. There was a new kind of leisure time, for doing nothing, as opposed to joining societies and telling stories. Ale was on tap for the entire year, to permit voluntary dizziness as a recreation; one no longer had to wait for trees to provide fermenting berries.

Unfortunately, the advantages lead to disadvantages. For instance, more work was required, especially to contribute to public projects and taxes. There was less overall leisure time. Trade for things required trust, which was a more difficult commodity between strangers. Records had to be kept of all the new kinds of transactions. Extra property had to be stored somewhere and protected. The distribution of luxuries and necessities was skewed, so some people had much more than others, in terms of things and respect.

Social and political changes were equally dramatic. With the distribution of power and materials, a political religious elite arose. And, to protect that, there was a rise of military organization, which allowed royalty and kings to replace or diminish religious leaders. Public ideologies replaced tribal or personal beliefs. Social hierarchies became more pronounced, and wealth was redistributed according to rank in them. Warfare became necessary for protection, or to acquire needed resources, or to control the social hierarchy.

There were advantages to these changes as well. People could expect uniform laws and protection from theft or violence. The stratification provided stability and identity with place or specializations. There was a greater diversity of jobs and places than ever before.

And, these advantages lead to disadvantages. A worker could be conscripted to work on public projects or to serve in the army. Workers had to pay taxes in the form of percentages of food or wealth. Social stratification could deny one access to luxuries and other things, and the stratification was not always fair. Bureaucrats, as well as medical workers or farmers, might have higher or lower status at different times. Power was also distributed differentially in society. In the larger population of the city, people were more vulnerable to violence.

Labor shortages to harvest crops lead to recruitment and some specialization, especially with tools and irrigation (engineering). The surplus of crops, with its necessity for allocation and storage lead to record-keeping and perhaps writing. With labor specialization and records came further specialization, especially with crafts (art) to make standard containers for distribution and professional art to provide necessary images, decoration and luxuries. Economic interaction shifted from reciprocity to formal exchanges. Trade expanded to include special products, tools and artworks.

Concentration in cities permitted and promoted these changes. Permanent settlements contained working houses. Supplies and control required a new infrastructure of massive buildings, better roads, and fortifications. This paralleled the rise of a religious elite to control the unknowns of weather and crops. And, this was followed by a military elite, which took over protection and combined it with universal gods, which lead to the rise of royalty and kings. Heroic buildings increased to provide palaces for royalty. Warfare was necessary to procure foods in times of famine or to protect the stores from less fortunate cities.

The increase in personal property, combined with the redistribution of wealth, lead to social hierarchies and classes. Public ideologies were developed to attune the people. Civilization provided immediate advantages, including supplemental animal labor, more property for everyone, especially the opportunity to have luxury items, the use of records instead of memory, which allowed verification and less misunderstanding, some leisure time for doing nothing, and the production of ale, as a mind-altering substance. Unfortunately, there were disadvantages, such as an increase in the amount of work, not only for production, but also for public projects. Leisure was reduced overall. Living required more work and materials for records, as well as trade and trust with a larger group of people. Personal property had to be stored and protected.

Social political changes include the rise of political religious elite, then the rise of military organization, then the rise of royalty and kings. Public ideologies followed, as did social hierarchies and warfare. Increases in personal property paralleled rationing and the redistribution of wealth.

4.2. Using the Environment: Economics

The formal study of how people use their surroundings is economics (from the Greek words meaning 'law of the house'—house is used as a metaphor for human society and nature). The word has come to mean the management of resources to supply human needs. It is basically concerned with sharing resources to meet physical needs of a people.

Although economics is a social science that studies human behavior, it considers itself a positive science. As a social science, economics addresses human problems. The acknowledged fundamental problem of economics is the contradiction between scarce resources and unlimited human wants. The kinds of resources and the possibilities of using them in production are considered in the scope of economics, as are the role of the government, business cycles, monetary details and policy, stabilization and growth, international trade, consumer behavior, production costs, pricing, and resource markets.

4.2.1. Traditional Economics
Natural economies are based on solar energy and plant productivity, as well as geological heat and energy. Ambihuman systems (those surrounding the human) operate under natural limitations; they are empirical assemblages whose properties have been shaped by chance, filtering, and selection over millions of years. They stress adaptation to the environment and the survival of a breeding society.

Traditional human economies, although basically dependent on the same energy and production, reverse the priorities. Human concern is for individual survival by modifying and managing the environment. Over the past 40,000 years humans have used many economic systems, which can be characterized by reciprocity, distribution, and redistribution. Variants of the last system have included tribute economies, command economies, and market economies, all of which are forms of redistribution.

4.2.1.1. Reciprocity
Foraging bands divided their labor by sex; this seems to be a cultural universal and a natural division. Ostensibly it was done to allow people to use their unique strengths. Men fished and hunted,

while women gathered marine animals, worked in gardens, and women with children gathered plants and insects. Later, labor was divided by age (age grades) and class (social division by prestige and religious rights). The fruits of their labor were divided reciprocally, to family, friends, and all other members of the band.

Foraging bands in general moved their camps regularly, from three times per year to once every three years. There were some instances of permanent settlements. Soon associated with permanent settlements were inequalities of status and wealth. Furthermore, other social things developed such as complex divisions of labor, with castes and slave labor. Trade and competition increased. This may have had to do with resources that were abundant and could be stored, and thus transformed into political prestige and power.

Traditional reciprocal, or subsistence, economies are dismissed as providing only a slim margin between life and death, which Marshall Sahlins exposes in his book, *Stone Age Economics*. If we think about it, there are numerous advantages in the way of life of archaic peoples: Fewer working hours, perhaps three or four per day; more leisure to talk, sleep, engage in rituals, and make love; a diverse and healthy diet; deliberate underproduction, usually well below the maximum levels; deliberate control of population growth below maximum levels; and, deliberate under-use of resources, resulting in a small ratio of people to resources. Subsistence economics means simply that surpluses are not accumulated. This might make them more vulnerable to food shortages, although the low ratio reduces the possibility.

These economies still occur in many places in the world, although they are under pressure to adopt the form of capitalism used by the nation in which they operate. The mark of these economies can still be seen underlying capitalism; many people in capitalist countries volunteer for their community, swap, trade and give away many different products, as well as hours of labor, which are not accounted for by most forms of capitalism.

4.2.1.2. Distribution

The basic change in economics is from equal sharing to a form of collection and redistribution, which allowed for specialization. Big men distribute the products of their own activities. Headmen are more informal, in bands of 50 or villages of 150. Every one knows and understands others; reciprocity is the bank. Headmen are leaders without power. Big men give away extra wealth. Chiefs accumulate it.

This form of economics seems to be rare now in the Pacific areas, where it was practiced. Perhaps it is shadowed in certain kinds of industrial exchanges, for example, between bosses and underlings or laborers.

4.2.1.3. Redistribution

Redistribution involves a different kind of step in exchange. Things are given to a chief and then redistributed to whomever is favored by the chief. Almost every kind of subsequent form of economics involves some form of personal or abstract redistribution.

4.2.1.3.1. Chiefdoms and Redistribution

Traditionally Chiefs redistribute the fruits of other's labor. That is to say, production is kin-oriented and reciprocal. Tribute, in the form of food or luxury wealth, is mostly redistributed by a chief (as a kind of informal taxes). The family is still the unit of production. In general, supplies are not accumulated. The institution of bridewealth serves to redistribute wealth from the bridegroom's family to the bride's family.

4.2.1.3.2. Command Economies

Command economies try to control the entire economy. The state owns the basic means of production, as a historical response to capitalism and inequalities. The communist model provided many things for many people, while maintaining a large war and research establishment. The philosopher Karl Marx thought that socialism was inevitable, that public ownership of the means of production would provide equality and social security for all people. But, in practice the distribution of wealth was very inequitable, as a result of historical trends, old economic rules, and cultural confusion. Therefore, some people were treated as more equal than others. As a result of central planning, the patterns of life under the communist model were pressured to be uniform and efficient.

Command economies, such as Marxism and Socialism, are underrated as having free market functions in some areas. Yet, the strengths of this kind of economy—especially the planning of production and the control of resources—are not admitted. Instead, the military competition that ruined many command economies is left out of the equation, and thus this form of economics becomes a distant also-ran. The collapse of Marxism and Communism was the end of one kind of history, the belief in salvation by society, and a secular religion foreseen by Rousseau. Peter Drucker says a new post-capitalist society will use the free market as a proven mechanism of economic integration—although it is not free! Market economies have begun exploiting the resources, such as the forests of Siberia, while at the same time trying to rehabilitate other resources, such as the forests of East Germany and Poland. This contradictory behavior is due to a combination of economic myths and practices.

4.2.1.3.2.1. *Tributary Economies*. Certain chiefdoms use command economies. Chiefs distribute the fruits of others labors, sometimes according to social need, but sometimes for the prestige of peers or nobles. Early Chinese empires up to the 1400s were tributary economies. In fact the Chinese explorations in the 1420s were by fleets prepared to accept tributes from other peoples.

4.2.1.3.2.2. *Social Economies*. Socialism is where the state owns the basic means of production; this was sometimes a historical response to capitalism and inequalities. Hybrid systems have existed, such as a tributary system in medieval China, or do exist, such as Democratic socialism in England.

4.2.1.3.2.3. *Market Economies*. Market economics exhibits the same symptoms as traditional and command economies. For instance, industrial cultures have far higher incidences of starvation—50 million children starved to death in countries with market and command economies in 1978—than archaic cultures with traditional economies, perhaps because of indifference or tolerance for suffering. Our industrial culture is approaching a form of subsistence now, in the sense of a minimum of necessities—but we will not be able to leave after we have eroded the soil. Perhaps we will be less tempted to exploit the land for short-term profit, since we have to remain after the profit leaves. Market economics avoided the same fate as command economies by having a larger store of trust and credit. But, they exhibit some of the same shortcomings, such as gross inequity from the leaders to the followers. Military expenditures may still ruin some market economies.

Modern market economics privatizes profits and commonizes costs. One consequence of this is the decline of common or private lands resulting in environmental degradation. The value of goods in monetary value is determined by supply and demand. At the very beginning of the Industrial revolution, the English encouraged trade to increase wealth, which led to Mercantilism, the government regulation of the economy to ensure growth by granting monopolies, which could be said to be the start of global unity. This led to an accumulation of capital from mercantilism. Capital required more energy and new technologies and thus led to capital production, where goods are privately owned, yet there is a separation of people from land and resources. Eventually, there was a shift to assembly-line factories using fossil fuels. Capitalism is disruptive of resources and culture; plus unequal exchange leads to accumulation. Thus Corporations as large individuals lead to monopoly capitalism.

Considered as the only factor, the invisible hand is a failure. Combined with strict and fair regulations in some nations, it has allowed a more chaotic capitalism. Modern market economics has proven to be more slippery at avoiding any kind of regulations created and imposed by the populace or representatives.

4.2.2. Modern Economics

Modern economics is defined, by Roger Chisholm and Marilu McCarty, as "the way people make their living." Economics attempts to address the 18th-century concerns of Adam Smith by using a scientific method to collect and interpret information—in fact, economics considers itself a science like physics, chemistry, or biology. Smith had noticed the trend in England away from mercantilism (where the central government regulated the output of goods for trade for gold) towards a free-choice economy, where people would decide what to make and how much to sell it for. Smith thought that a free market of independent buyers and sellers would let the entire community prosper as if an "invisible hand" were guiding it. That is, competition would increase public well-being, or to say it in a different way, self-interest is linked with common interest (or "What's good for General Motors is good for the USA"). Many countries in the 18th and 19th-century, including the United States and Canada, adopted the free market system, and their citizens did acquire more symbolic wealth.

Economics considers itself a positive science, that examines "what is" with theories, as opposed to a normative science, which addresses "what ought to be." Oddly though, Chisholm and McCarty establish a list of goals (thoughts) for an economic system that includes: Productivity and growth—growth is necessary for living standards to rise, and individual self-interest has proved to be a stronger motivation than patriotism, altruism, or recognition; stability and security—stability in the form of full employment and set prices; security as providing the material necessities to the elderly and poor; efficiency—where the maximum amount of needed or wanted goods is produced from scarce resources with minimum waste; and, personal freedom and equality—by enhancing the personal dignity of everyone with maximum freedom, that is, the elimination of discrimination and limitations on opportunity.

The focus of economics, however, is rather narrow, in that the concept of resources is very limited and the unlimited wants are not much discussed. There is no psychology or ethics; there is no ecology or aesthetics. There is no concern with the triviality of the free choice of a worthless doodad. There is no thought for beauty. There is no concern with the welfare of the other beings that share the ecological community. Like the old discarded physics, economics applies a rigid standard of objectivity to its analysis.

4.2.2.1. The Modern Model: Abstraction & Accumulation

The metaphor for the economy used to be a simple mechanical model for turning resources into products. To be successful, the economy had to grow and turn a profit continually. Unfortunately, the assumptions of the model were also simple and failed to consider human needs and natural cycles, causing great suffering and great disruption. The old analogy of the economy as a machine leads to bad assumptions: That everything is a resource; That resources are unlimited; That production must continue endlessly; That the economy has to keep growing to survive; That the purpose of the state was to legitimize exploitation; That the purpose of humanity was to multiply, produce, and consume; and That the purpose of the universe was to supply human needs.

The bad assumptions of the machine analogy lead to false economic beliefs: That mass production is most efficient; That obsolescence is necessary for successful growth; That people's needs and wants are fulfilled by advertised products; and, That quality does not matter very much. These bad assumptions and false beliefs lead to problems in the economy as a whole. These colossal problems include: Overgrowth, with an increase in complexity and costs (many of them social); Economic and ecological instability; Social burdens (from pressures on families from relocation and powerlessness); Misdirected efforts on ill-conceived, low-quality products; and, Slack consumer attitudes and employee performances.

Economics has not been unsuccessful with its models, for instance the model on buying behavior, but it has become a highly abstract academic discipline. All its abstractions are applied to the real world without acknowledgment of the high degree of abstraction involved. The philosopher A. N. Whitehead warned that the economic method would triumph if the abstractions were judicious, but even judicious abstractions had limits, and the neglect of those limits lead to disastrous oversights. Considering a fictitious human nature under imaginary circumstances and thinking it is real is the fallacy of "misplaced concreteness" according to Whitehead. Daly and Cobb suggest that the classic instance of the fallacy in economics is "money fetishism," where the characteristics of an abstract symbol, such as limitless growth, are applied to real commodities and values.

As an aside, Daly and Cobb point out that modern economics might better be called chrematistics, after the distinction made by Aristotle between chrematistics and economics; the former related to the manipulation of property and wealth to maximize the short-term abstract money value to the owner, whereas economics was the management of the household (community) to increase the concrete value for everyone in the community over the long-term.

Business as usual, with its inertial model of growth, could end in catastrophe for humanity and its environments. Industrial cultures, with their characteristics of simplification, naiveté, homogeneity, and incompleteness, turn wild landscapes into "flatscapes," where variety disappears and significance is ignored for the comfortable standards of meaningless continuity. Rapid growth might precipitate a catastrophe sooner, while modest efforts at environmental protection and increased efficiency may only postpone catastrophe a few years.

4.2.2.2. The Wealth of Nations
J. S. Mill and Jeremy Bentham used the Associationism of D. Hartley to develop a Felicific calculus in which individuals were social atoms (another ghost of the old physics) seeking pleasure and avoiding pain—and benevolently controllable through arithmetic. Since then, economics has become more scientific and mathematical. Economic "man" (used as the traditional term for Homo economicus) is still considered a kind of cash-register, however. There is also a strong relationship between Protestant religion and economic development (just the opposite of Marx, who regarded religion as a superstitious atavism).

The sociologist Pitirim Sorokin indicated that the wealth of an area was a function of its physical attributes and its culture. In fact, the attributes are only possibilities until appropriate perceptions and technologies exist (due to culture). Economics has always been concerned with measuring wealth. The basis of wealth has been variously described as labor, resources, production, net plant production, and information. Yet, no single basis is adequate. Perhaps wealth is just as simple as what we value. The basis for Smith was a basic resources considered by economics: Labor.

4.2.3. Holeconomics

John Stuart Mill wrote that beyond the progressive state lies the stationary state; each advance is to approach it. A stationary economy is not synonymous with a stagnant economy; there is always room for developing and increasing the scope of economic culture. It could be highly sophisticated, dynamic, and imaginative. Mill said: "It is scarcely necessary to remark that a stationary condition of capital and population implies no stationary state of human improvement. There would be as much scope as ever for all kinds of mental culture and moral and social progress; as much room for improving the art of living and more likelihood of its being improved." Mill's vision of a stable state was a response to the goal of an industrial society. Technological progress would abridge labor, not necessarily increase production. In a state of equity, persons would have room for solitude and leisure development. But Mill's idea was anthropocentric—"man" was not bound to protect nature.

Herman Daly concludes that the steady state economy is both necessary and desirable. He notes that in the definition of economics, as the study of the allocation of scarce means among competing ends, the entire ends-means spectrum is not considered. Only intermediate ends or means are considered, not ultimate ones. He anchors the ultimate means in physics and ultimate ends in religion. Economics falsely concludes that the middle ranges represent the entire spectrum. In another computer model, Ervin Laszlo calls for an across board reduction in population, investment, and resource usage, to create a steady state with the present disparities maintained.

Some theorists, like Samuelson, have concluded that growth is necessary to rid the economy of disparities. But, development instead of growth would equalize wealth more efficiently—after all, economies have been growing for at least 400 years and the disparities have increased. There is no necessary association between development and growth, as Daly and others have shown. Development means the introduction of an innovation. Economic development will require technology. Ecologically sound technologies will minimize stress to the environment. Economies could be modeled after climax vegetation and not successional vegetation, where diversity in scale is greater. A community is forced to accept an upper limit, beyond which it cannot grow any further. Further growth results in destruction or disruption of itself and nature. This is the law of the maximum. Production could be stabilized in a steady state economy, a mature economy, like a climax system, where processes and cycles are constant. A steady state economy must be based on natural laws and ethical principles. Natural laws include thermodynamics and ecological theories. Rules of economics, laws of nature, and ethical principles must be related.

There is another distinction between growth and development. The ecological social approach (or a redistributive environmental strategy) to development makes it irrelevant to discuss global limits to growth. Local limits are far more significant to the majority of population. Regardless of how much food exists, people will starve unless they can get it. Redistribution of resources and improvement of environmental quality (home environment) are more important than increased production by sophisticated technology. The natural capacity of regional photosynthesis must be the limiting factor in development, especially in tropical and subtropical areas.

Development calls for a social and educational organization, more than technological style. Styles of technology must be determined by culture and context. Such development requires a local authority working with suitable economic and ecological conditions. No authority can be affective without the participation of the populace. To stop growth, a strict regulation of the productive system is needed. States should be able to control which products are made, and with which technology. Practical implications of the steady state are that nonrenewable resources will be conserved as much as possible, by recycling, while erosion, depletion and pollution are minimized; energy sources may be greatly decentralized and diverse. Using a field concept for development emphasizes the dynamic transformation of the domain, rather than its structure as an individual. Selective advantage or cost benefit become adjectives or afterthoughts to the domain.

Jane Jacobs, in *The Nature of Economies*, argued that the same principles underlie both ecosystems and economies: "development and co-development through differentiations and their combinations; expansion through diverse, multiple uses of energy; and self-maintenance through self-refueling." The Nature of Economies, also in Platonic dialogue form, is based on the premise that "human beings exist wholly within nature as part of the natural order in every respect." Jacobs' characters then discuss the four methods by which "dynamically stable systems" may evade collapse: Bifurcations; positive-feedback loops; negative-feedback controls; and emergency adaptations. Their conversations also cover the "double nature of fitness for survival," traits to avoid destroying one's own habitat as well as success in competition to feed and breed, and unpredictability, including the butterfly effect characterized in terms of multiplicity of variables as well as disproportionally of response to cause, and self-organization where "a system can be making itself up as it goes along."

4.2.3.1. Holeconomic Wealth

Economists try to bronze the economy in its current structure, but it is a changing system. Since it is changing, strategies that are appropriate at one stage are totally inappropriate at another. This is the remorseless working of tragedy. Any lasting economy must have a dynamic approach. Wealth must be renewable.

Rich sensory experiences can be derived from direct contact with nature, but economists and planners rarely mention these values. Light, wind, dirt, plants, and birds, all perform during a walk, but not with the same meaning as crops or dogs, which is for their utility—they just are. People do not live without these things. All values are based on a healthy ecology. It must be kept healthy; arable land must be limited, and mineral exploitation must be limited.

There are two roads to wealth: producing a bigger pie (supply) or reducing each portion (demand). This assumes that wealth is defined as supply divided as demand. If supply is limited then wealth can still be increased two ways: reduce expectations of individuals or reduce the number of individuals. Supply may be mostly material things, but not status, for instance; demand has the more psychological dimension. Therefore, wealth will always have a psychological dimension.

For this reason, Gregory Bateson thought that economics may be founded on a fallacy. Economists cannot account for intransitive preference: where a is preferable to b, b to c, but c is preferable to a; as in Money being preferable to resources and resources being preferable to wilderness but wilderness is preferable to money. Preference curves in economics should not intersect.

An individual's perception of environment is a semantic map that forms the context for decision making by delimiting possible acts. People respond to felt needs; economic growth occurs when these psychological needs are stimulated and satisfied. As soon as people think that they need clean air, like snowmobiles, these demands can be met somehow.

Values are based on knowledge, which is measured partly in terms of information, where information can be considered a source of wealth. Some business economies are based entirely on providing information. Information is apparently boundless. Yet it can be manipulated. It is information that defines the use of resources by people. For example, hydrogen is worthless unless technologies exist to transmute it to helium and manage the released energy. What is not limited is our use of information. A sophisticated technology needs fewer resources. The natural productivity of ecosystems is less important if food can be grown intensively in tanks using solar energy.

The Gross National Product (GNP) is the money value of the final goods and services produced by the economy. It includes all the goods and the bads. That is, it is a measure of throughput, the flows rather than the capital stock of wealth. Meadows suggest that capital stock could be maintained with the lowest possible throughput. That would require redoing the economy and its technologies and making them more efficient. The trap is seeking the wrong goal. The way out of the trap is identifying goals that reflect the real wealth, then focusing on result not effort.

4.2.3.2. Limits of Economics Revisited

Both ecology and economics attempt to understand and predict the behavior of complex, interconnected systems where individual behavior and flows of energy and material are important. There are many other common or similar processes: resource allocation, optimal behavior, and adaptation. For each ecosystem, and at each level of technology and kind of social structure, there is an optimum size of population that offers a high quality standard of living. The optimum size in this sense is a working one based on our knowledge of all of the factors—and we cannot know everything. No one has complete information about the current environment or the results of their actions. Complete knowledge is not necessary, however—only the knowledge of a law of the minimum. For humans, trade can ease the law, but not repeal it. Rachel Carson demonstrated that we lived in a world of limits.

Resources may not be absolutely limited, in the sense that history shows that advances in technology can expand the availability of resources; less is needed to produce more. But, the same history also shows that humans reproduce up to the new limit of misery allowed by the new technology. New advances are used to increase the size of humanity, not its happiness or wealth. Society is growing at the same time as needs are growing, resulting in lessening of natural systems.

The redefinition of wealth in an ecological framework would tie it to limits, which might increase human enrichment and natural preservation. Diversity is a form of wealth. Differences do not necessarily cause conflicts because each can fill the needs of others. Since nature is a non-zero-sum game, many groups can gain at the same time, ambihuman and human.

4.2.3.3. Poverty of Humanity & the Earth

In general, poverty is a lack of things that others have, especially necessary things. There are different forms of poverty. For instance, one form is the lack of needs, such as food or money. Another is the lack of natural or public services that would provide food and shelter. On the other hand, what is the use-value of feet in Los Angeles? The lack of potential is harder to define, but it means that people who suffer that poverty cannot improve him or herself, or change, or develop. Finally, the lack of luxuries has become a form of poverty. The idea of affluence in a global village creates a new modern kind of poverty, the potential poverty of not having what is possible somewhere in New York or Paris. Modernizing needs creates a new dimension of poverty. This adds a new discrimination by a violent cargo cult that seizes traditional cultures.

Industrial society is constantly mobilized for emergencies with, in the battles against non-education, poverty, diseases, and terrorism. Industrial development has never been nonviolent or respectful to people or nature. Some human poverties are poverties of the local ecosystems. Loss of entitlement to a natural resource base needed for foraging or agriculture is a political poverty. Interference with or destruction of the processes of ecological balance and renewal, the loss of diversity, the loss of capacity for the renewal of ecological systems, are ecological poverties.

4.3. *Playing with Possibilities: Politics of Cities & Nations*

For Aristotle, politics was the science of the possible. The city, or polis, was a human artifact whose structure could be modified by reason; it was potentially a work of art in which only the capability of the artist limited the expression. The polis was made for the amateur; and it produced more complete men (women were erroneously considered lesser beings at the time). As a science, politics, or ecocybernetics (a neologism meaning governing the house) was concerned with two things basically, a way of distributing power and luxuries, and a way of surviving contact with others.

Archaic nations governed their areas independently. Their political principles were similar: all land is communally owned by the tribe, although household goods may be personally held; all decisions were made by consensus in which everyone participated; chiefs were not coercive rulers, but teachers and leaders with specific duties limited to their realm— medicine, war, or ceremonies for example.

When the Europeans or Chinese settled many areas, they brought their centralized governments. The original goal of the U.S. republic, according to Jefferson, was to make each person a participator in the everyday affairs of government. But the government (state or federal) has become gigantic, managing the area from remote locations of power, and participation has dwindled. Despite a recent emphasis on personal responsibility and international cooperation, our political institutions have not responded.

Central politics overwhelms local politics. It dominates the process of decision-making. Politics deals with words, which are arbitrary symbols for events or things. The wrong relationship of things and symbols can result in misguided politics and violence. Decisions are made on narrow political grounds. Citizenship in industrial cultures is the abandonment of responsibility on the assumption that others know how to manage things; government is the assumption of responsibility, without knowledge, that leads to immense and interrelated problems.

Government promises to judge disputes in values and protect its citizens from external attack. Modern government, however, is the abandonment of responsibility on the assumption that others know how to manage things.

Politics occurs, it is now recognized, in an ecological context. There can be no separation of politics and ecology. Every political act has ecological consequences and every ecological decision is a political demand for control over use of the environment. Herb Hammond describes the kind of control that occurs in British Columbia.

Ecological, economic, social, and religious phenomena are part of the broad definition of politics. The basic goal of politics is the "survival of the community" as William Ophuls identifies it. Politics is the interactive means of providing the basic food and necessities of a community. As survival is survival within nature, politics rests on an ecological foundation. The organization of a community must be in accord with natural laws. Political participation depends on information, much of which can be provided by ecologists.

Ecological consciousness must be identified with political consciousness. Politicians need to think about the hunger and squalor of billions of human beings and the destruction of habitats with billions of ambihuman lives, before concentrating on missiles and private fortunes. As Bateson has said, 'Ecology, like God, is not to be mocked.'

For Aristotle, politics was the science of the possible. The city, or polis, was a human artifact whose structure could be modified by reason; it was potentially a work of art in which only the capability of the artist limited the expression. The polis was made for the amateur; and it produced more complete men (women were erroneously considered lesser beings at the time).

The purpose of politics, which is the activity of governing. Politics depends on common rights, trust, information, and consciousness.

Politics is the science of government; it has to do with the regulation and government of a nation or state, the preservation of its safety, peace, and prosperity, the defense of its existence and rights against foreign control or conquest, the augmentation of its strength and resources, and the protection of its citizens in their rights, with the preservation and improvement of their morals.

The function of politics is to ensure that decisions are taken at the right level. A state protects individual freedoms, guards national culture (values and identity), and holds groups accountable for use of power. Procrustean politics, as in China and other countries, fits the guest to the bed. It brings survivors of the revolution into line and exiles or destroys the rest; it is inefficient.

Democracy is a more flexible strategy, but it is size specific; as size increases, more hierarchical structure is needed. Majority rule transfers functions to an impersonal system. The logic of individualism creates conditions that require constraints. Politics has to make them palatable. Although we realize that nothing in nature is without some limit or cost, we may dislike giving up what we now consider (wrongly) as rights. Humans may have to expect much less than they want, even though many expectations are rising.

Ultimately, politics is about the definition of reality itself. Social reality is created. Different societies have had different realities. The Athenians despised the merely wealthy, for instance, and respected community service. North Americans, on the other hand, revere wealth; community service is romanticized on television but hideously underpaid. Politics is also the art of creating new possibilities for human progress. The current system is defective, however. Although it is admirable to work within the system to prevent further environmental degradation, it might be necessary to produce a change in consciousness that would lead to a new political paradigm.

Besides size and power, there are other things that make governing difficult: Division of labor (are there professional citizens?), centralization, and technology. The interrelations of these things necessitates discussing them at the same time. Political institutions are not givens or timeless. Taking from the strengths of earlier forms, it might be possible to modify government to be more effective. The first step would be to form an independent government for each ecosystem.

An ecosystem is a good candidate to be an independent political unit. It is a governable size. It has clearly defined boundaries, as an ecosystem, that is the ecological community including humans, and not a state or county whose boundaries have been determined by rectangular grids at human whim. The kind of government, with more clearly defined, might look different.

4.3.1. *Forms of Governing & Leading*

There are only a limited number of behaviors that people can take to interact with others in their culture or nation: They can ignore the others as too different or due to internal conflicts of their own. They can trade with them. They can fight them, or, they can cooperate with them. Some of these behaviors do not benefit others, but people can be lead or persuaded to better behaviors.

There are many ways of leading people. Some ways offer models to follow; others represent people in group decision making; and, a few make all decisions themselves. There are formal and informal ways. Almost every way, however, involves more prestige or status for the leader. Sometimes that translates into more meat, more goods or more wealth.

Leadership is the process of leading, that is, providing direction to others. Political leadership, the sense used here, is often formal and refers to a person in a position of authority, as a result of possessing skills at directing. The number and kinds of leaders are compared in Table 431-1.

Leaders, or headmen, help others by choice. Big men distribute the products of their own activities. Chiefs redistribute the fruits of other's labor. Kings take a percentage of resources from the peasants and give it to retainers or use it for public or religious displays. Emperors often represent on a larger scale by far.

Dictatorships need great leaders, or at least powerful ones, to be successful. A dictator may be self-appointed or backer or appointed by a military force. Idi Amin in Uganda, is an example. In some states, the dictator is described as a president; Fidel Castro in Cuba was also the head of the Communist party. Kim Jong-il in North Korea seems to have complete power and refers to himself with numerous titles.

Rome once had a ruling triumvirate. Bosnia and Herzegovina has a three-member Presidency, each of which are elected by a different constituent nation. The position of the President of the Presidency rotates between the members. Modern Switzerland invests leadership collectively in seven-member Swiss Federal Council. The President is a member of the Federal Council elected by the Swiss Federal Assembly for a year and is merely *primus inter pares* (first among equals).

Some states have a Parliamentary system of government, in which the President is the head of state, sometimes with only ceremonial duties, depending on the constitution, and the Prime Minister is the head of government. Countries with this system include Germany, India, Ireland, Italy and Singapore.

In nations with a Presidential system of government, the President is the head of government and the head of state. The United States and Venezuela have this system, where the President is more powerful. Democracies need effective and educated citizens. Democracy is the work of the people (remember the Negro spiritual: "We are the ones we've been waiting for").

Table 431-1. Political Systems (after Aristotle)

Number of Rulers	Kind of Ruler	Ruling in Interest of	Chosen by
One	Leader (headman)	Band	Consensus
	Big man	Tribe	Consensus
	Chief	Chief Nobles	Ancestry Gods
	King	Monarchy City-State	Self Parent
	Emperor	Tyranny of Few	Self
	Dictator	Self/Power structure	Military
Few Collective	Triumvirate Co-ruler	Aristocracy Oligarchy	Citizens of State Few (Rich)
Many	Prime Minister President	Polity Voters Democracy Ochlocracy	Voters People or College Poor People
All	People Anarchy	Self-All Community anarchy Direct democracy	All People

Leaders themselves may be influenced by choosers or controllers. Controlling groups such as the military, political parties, ruling elites, or religious elites sometimes place higher expectations on the leader, such as transformational change. The leaders may encourage their followers and believers to worship leadership. The followers may become uncritically obedient.

In the United States, the President is elected by the Electoral College, which is made up of electors chosen by voters in the presidential election. Each elector is committed to voting for a specified candidate determined by the popular vote in each state. However, due to skewed representation, it is possible for the candidate with fewer national votes to win the electoral votes in the Electoral College and get the presidency, as happened in 1888 (and again in 2000).

Leaders, with choosers and controllers, are part of the governing process. The forms of government range from tribal leaders and chiefs to anarchy and direct democracy. These forms work best with small populations where everyone is known, even if they do not share the same culture. Other forms of government, such as authoritarian dictatorships, monarchies, and republics, have worked with larger populations. At the largest sizes, the bureaucracies and infrastructures have more in common, regardless if the government is socialist, parliamentary, or democratic.

Larger nations require larger governments, to make laws to accommodate differences in cultures. Specialists are required to resolve conflicts. The specialists often have a monopoly on weapons and the spectrum of information.

Table 431-2. Kinds of Governments

Leadership/ Decisions	Egalitarian Leader	"Big man"	Chief Hereditary	King Hereditary	Representative
Bureaucracy	None	None	None Crony level	Many levels	More levels
Monopoly of Force & Info	No	No	Yes	Yes	Immense
Resolution Of conflict	Informal	Informal	Central	Laws, judges	Laws, judges specialists

4.3.1.1. Traditional Small-scale (Elders, Chiefs, Kings)
The Coeur d'Alene people had strong leaders. Each village had a council with male and female members. A large village had a headman or woman who regulated economic and religious affairs. Their only real power was their persuasive abilities and the public esteem they built up. Chiefs were elected or deposed by the council. The band chief regulated basic resources. Next in authority were a war leader, hunting leader, and shaman, chosen for their respective skills

Marvin Harris shows how headmen are associated with hunting societies, big men with horticultural societies that are larger, and chiefs, still larger, and starting to accumulate goods. Headmen are more informal, in bands of 50 or villages of 150. Every one knows and understands others; reciprocity is the bank. Headmen are leaders without power. Big men give away extra wealth. Chiefs accumulate it.

Chiefs have proven ways to keep the underlings happy or at least resigned. They arm the elite and disarm the public, that is, monopolize force. They use the monopoly of force to maintain order and reduce violence. They redistribute some of the wealth in public displays and games, a kind of informal tax refunds. Chiefdoms were successful in Kwakiutl, Rome and Hawaii.

Kings enlisted ideology or religion to justify the transfer of wealth to the king and rich retainers. The shared religion also makes strangers act more peacefully without kinship. It gives people a reason to sacrifice their lives for an institution, nongenetic. The king was the central human representative of power. The Mayan king gave blood, with other nobles and prisoners. Blood is the home of the soul; it is valuable and the most powerful gift.

Mesopotamian cities had councils of elders to make decisions. They would appoint a leader to lead in war or trade. The word for this leader, lugal, eventually came to mean king; after 4800 YBP, also gods changed from natural forces to war gods. Agriculture gave a surplus; that and property led to excitement of war. In China, in the Warring States period, the nature of war changed: from an Aristocratic monopoly of soldiers to one with standing armies, professional leaders and peasant soldiers. China. New towns were planned and built by ranked lords at the edges of the state. The king gave land, title, ritual things, and a clan name. The King served as his own priest because he could contact his ancestors.

4.3.1.2. Modern Large-scale Government

As leaders had more followers or constituents, they needed help addressing problems of income and payout. They needed a large bureaucracy to maintain records and make local decisions. For example, large-scale irrigation appears in Egypt first in 7100 YBP. In Mesopotamia, complex systems could have been managed locally by farmers, although there may have been conflict with upstream users. But, cooperation is necessary, especially in villages and between villages later. As a result large-scale water systems were first managed by religious leaders, then later by secular leaders. As problems developed, temporary military leaders became permanent hereditary kings. Palaces were built and staffs numbered thousands.

Power became centralized in the king. As the populations became larger, the king had to have representatives. Centralization and representation became necessary properties of large-scale government.

4.3.1.2.1. Monarchies

A monarchy is the rule of one person, who inherits power from gods or from ancestors. All great monarchies had their state religion, in the case of pharaohs and some emperors this could even lead to a religion where the monarch (or his dynasty) was endowed with a godlike status. On a different scale kingdoms can be entangled in a specific flavor of religion: Catholicism in Belgium, Church of England in the United Kingdom

4.3.1.2.2. Empires

Emperors tended to lead large-scale societies (50,000-200,000), state societies that had literacy and public art. Until 1912, China was just a succession of dynasties where government was the same whether times were bad or good. There was an emperor, bureaucracy, system of laws and a political ideology. Their country was the "Middle Kingdom" superior to all other cultures. Han emperors had created a civil service, a bureaucracy where officials were hired based on examinations rather than birth. There was no difference between social classes in education, in theory.

In Japan, warring clans, led by chiefs, fought until about 500 AD. Then, the Yamato clan was supreme. Prince Shotoku Taishi established law and order in the region and tried to establish diplomatic relations with China. Empress Suiko urged the people to accept Chinese political ideas, notably the system of Imperial rule, which would increase her own power. The Confucian values of orderly society with its emphasis on obedience to authority and value of harmony, as related to civic opposition, were adopted. The introduction of the Chinese style also led to a bureaucracy to carry out government duties, a central tax system and land distribution. The provincial government was run by officials reporting to the emperor.

Under the domination of powerful families, the emperor and court had less political authority and devoted themselves to ceremonies and arts. The shoguns, head of clans, had the political power. It was the Shoguns who divided the people into four classes: warriors, artisans, merchants and peasants, all of which were now hereditary.

4.3.1.2.3. Republics

Traditionally, a Republic was a form of government where a sovereign leader held authority that was granted by the people. The sovereign ruled according to law. Rome was this kind of republic.

Often the leader took power militarily and then accepted the authority of the people afterwards.

In the U.S. republic, the power is also derived from the people, who agree to be ruled by law, but the leader is elected indirectly. The citizens, who may be a smaller group than all the people, vote for representatives to be responsible to them.

In general a republic is a state whose head is usually elected rather than hereditary. Autonomy and the rule of law are the basic requirements for a republic. The term republic is applied to a state where political power of the government rests on the consent of the people governed. Republics had been formed specifically to be independent of a state religion. It ids an appropriate choice of government where there are many religions in the nation, such as the United States. Other monarchies, from the Soviet Republics to North Korea, are antireligious. Other modern republics, such as Iran or Israel, offer a state religion.

The word republic comes from the Latin words, meaning "thing of the people." So, there is a verbal association with democracy, which means, in Latin different words, "rule of the people." Many historical forms of republicanism shared beliefs in the self-determination of a people and in basic human dignity, but the disagreed on the means of achieving those believes. The word republic became ambiguous regarding elected or hereditary rules and about how economic liberties would be regulated.

There are many kinds of republics—it is a popular word, like democracy. There are: Basic republics like France, federal republics such as India, which has a representative democracy of states, and confederations like Switzerland. The Islamic republic of Iran is governed in accordance with Islamic law. The People's Republic of (North) Korea is governed in the name of the people by the strongest leader.

Republics can be oligarchic, that is, ruled by the strongest leader, or dictator, who has no formal hereditary right to rule. Republics can be headed by a monarch, a constitutional monarch, where most real power resides in democratic institutions. The essential characteristic, more than title as king or president or supreme leader, is the exercise of power in a nonautocratic way.

4.3.1.2.4. Democracy

Direct democracy got a bad reputation starting with Greek city-states. In fact Athenian democracy was so limited that it more resembled an oligarchy. The fear of Greek statesmen was that stupid people might vote and make things worse. Direct democracy is a rule by the will of the majority, although there are no checks or balances under law in a direct democracy.

Representation itself developed from the medieval institution of government by monarchy, then later from aristocratic government. The combination of monarchy and aristocracy has shown itself to be very elastic and adaptive, ending up quite similar to democracies.

When the Europeans settled North America, they brought their centralized, representational government. Madison recognized that there were local limits to direct democracy. A republic, however, where citizens assemble and administer it by representatives, could be extended over a larger region.

John Adams and the creators of the U.S. Constitution and representative democracy, sought to avoid the rule of the mob, which they thought might be possible with Thomas Paine's idea of having sovereign power rest in a single body—even of the people, thought at the time to be ignorant (news traveled slowly), avaricious (less than now), and fickle (subject to trends as they still are). The original goal of the U.S. republic, according to Thomas Jefferson, was to make each person a participator in the everyday affairs of government.

Abraham Lincoln though that the Declaration of Independence established norms for equality that were inadequately developed by the Constitution. He thought the authors intended that it apply to all people, but did not mean that all people were equal in all respects. The Declaration provided the legal basis for the Union. Webster, echoed by Lincoln, thought that the people made the government.

4.3.1.2.4.1. *Ideas Goals & Characteristics of Democracy*. What democracy always requires is informed opinion, community support, imagination, and constrained conflict, which can refine ideas and programs. Ideas need to be argued through. Openness, relaxation, trust, and flexibility are needed. Good opinions result from education and thought. Better opinions are formed during the deliberative process.

One goal of democratic government is to represent all people. Another is to allow for change of government without violence. In a representational democracy the government operates on consent. The people retain the right to demand change. The general characteristics of representational democracy are: The direct rule of the many by the few; and citizens share in government, but the law is supreme over them.

4.3.1.2.4.2. *Changes to Democracy*. After all, representative democracy was created from above, by its rich, powerful architects. There was no promise of direct democracy. But, the weakest want to see an effect of their vote. Traditionally democracy has defines the people, as land-owning men, or old, educated white men, or educated middle-class people of any color or religion, or all people who can learn to register.

The scale has changed. The government (state or federal) has become gigantic, managing the area from remote locations of power, and participation has dwindled. Despite recent emphasis on personal responsibility and international cooperation, our political institutions have not responded. Big government is elephantine, controlling, paternalistic, offering a bureaucratic welfare state that has to know everything about its constituents; private markets are solipsistic, anarchic profit mongers that influence private decisions with false advertising and lies.

Karl Marx criticized bourgeois democracy for its false promise, hypocrisy, and inability to deliver on its promises. But, democracy fostered many civic groups that helped to fulfill functions. The civil society includes clubs and associations, charities and religious groups, environmental groups, educational groups, the neighborhood watch, volunteer fire departments, in fact any nongovernmental, nonprofitable public activity, for any purpose, except voting.

Corporations started to supplant voluntary organizations as nongovernment actors. And, many civic groups have become like corporations; many churches, schools, and foundations are also just special interest groups. Even environmental groups have been polarized, despite their public agenda of public and environmental good.

Compare democracy, which exists to serve the people, to businesses, which exist to make a profit. Which is more responsive, regardless of reasons? Which is directly dependent on its customers for funding? Who asks: What do customers want? This problem illuminates some of the structural flaws of modern democracies: The indifference to responsibility for voting, not including the withdrawal of survivalists, separatist religions and others; the disenfranchise of communities; overspending on elections by candidates; the nonefficacy of some kinds of laws, especially drug laws that fill the prison system; the role of money that eclipses the role of voters, e.g., spending is insane and special corporate interests are given first consideration, e.g. NAFTA; the role of media conglomerates shifting consciousness towards what they want to be more profitable, e.g., they buy news and politicians; the role of communications and computing technologies in shifting consciousness, or suppressing it. Television and computers may suppress social interactions, which may result in psychological changes, such as withdrawal and cynicism. Of course, computing and television could contribute to education and direct interaction and interactive communication; and finally, the encouragement of pressure groups that shift policy to some interests. These are small knots of interest representation that wield power and influence far beyond their numbers. Yet, for citizens this can be a more direct effective use of their money. Lobbying can be directed by the rich or any group that has interests.

4.3.1.2.4.3. *Dissatisfactions with Democracy*. As Plato recognized, democracy has a tendency to transform into its opposite—tyranny. Freedom can turn to slavery; we can even get enslaved to the pursuit of freedom in everything.

Democracy tends to resemble oligarchies of Athens and Sparta. The same that were rejected by Franklin and Washington as being based on virtue, in favor of utilitarian regime that channeled selfishness towards kinder ends. The founders also felt it necessary to filter the whims of the masses through an elected body, and disperse power by dividing the government into three branches.

People are dissatisfied with democracy. Why? Is it incomplete, biased, or big, inefficient, or indifferent? U.S. democracy is becoming oligarchic; it is allowing the domination by single persons or single elite groups. There has always been a tension between democracy and oligarchy, between freedom and security. Is the budgeting process democratic enough? Transparent enough? The reality of short-term elections tends to suppress the unpleasantries of long-term problems, such as the warming planet.

At what point does the democracy not function as a government of, by for the people? At a certain percentage of confidence? What happens when an elected official is mocked or not trusted, yet not recalled or revolted against. The whole dance becomes a nonzero sum game, where justice cannot be won without diminishing liberty, where free-market freedom cannot be supported without diminishing equality. Free markets get surrounded with a miasma of solitary greed. As rights increase, on every dimension, limits to action also increase.

Participation needs to increase. Business need to recognize their ecological and political obligations. Scientists, engineers, and teachers, also need to recognize their ecological and political dimensions that they automatically participate in. Our political problems are global problems caused by our species. Our ecological problems are caused by the scale and type of our impacts on the planetary system. We still have the traditional problems of growing food, building houses, creating jobs, and being secure, and creating art. As well as avoiding natural catastrophes from meteors, floods, fires, and insects. But the new dimensions introduce a greater risk to our survival.

4.3.1.2.4.4. *Reinventing Democracy*. Richard Barber listed three general challenges to reinventing democracy: The struggle of indigenous people; the problems of civil society, and global capitalism.

With the friction between the welfare state and free markets, the civic society, which spawned them both, has withered away. Like the government, civil society has a high regard for public good, but it was not a coercive monopoly. It was a public ground of thousands of religious, social, groups in a voluntary private realm. Like the private markets, it provides material needs to its members, but unlike them, no monetary exchange is necessary, no profits need to be made and taken—it was concerned with helping without remuneration, but with the expectation of complementary behavior. Civil society can mediate between the extremes, and in fact pick up needs, such as housing or the environment, that are often missed by the government or economy. A civil society could keep politicians true amateurs rather than professionals. It could teach markets how to respect character and not let it be consumed.

Civil societies are different in each nation. Democracy tends to be distinctive in each nation, perhaps as a result of the unique culture, land, and history. This political diversity is unavoidable, but it should be desirable. In Switzerland, communal rights are considered more important than individual rights. Great Britain does not have a separation of powers. Ireland does not force the state to be separate from the church. Ethiopia's Constitution tries to address the tribalism that characterizes groups there. France is a centralist nation. Germany is federalist. Russia, as does the Basque part of Spain, has the idea of cooperatives. Most democracies are centered on nations. A shared identity on a shared territory. National consciousness has contributed to democratic consciousness. Yet consciousness of nationalism seems less important than constitutional or international consciousness.

The differences in civic society are a basis for experimentation with democratic forms. Thomas Jefferson suggested little revolutions, every couple of decades to make the experiment fresh, as well as break up unproductive hierarchies of power. We could start these revolutions in numerous ways, or example, by requiring politicians to give away their wealth before entering office and by forbidding them to earn more than their government salary after holding and leaving office, or, putting real ecological limits on the activities of corporations.

Democracy itself is kind of like a thought experiment, where questioning and conversing about disagreements and disasters allows us to experiment with them, and our responses to them, before there is real conflict and real suffering. Even if the real disasters are not prevented at least they have been addressed. Dissent occurs within the context of loyalty. Freedom is expressed within a context of law that limits it and protects it. The democratic system avoids runaway feedback.

Anthony Barnett suggests a reflexive democracy. Barnett asks if there is a fourth kind of democracy now, direct and large scale, made so by rapid news and easy communication.

A modern of, by and for the people. If democracy can be made adaptive, and if it can be based on ecological perspectives, then it would be reflexive. The government of the people, by the people, for the people. Was good enough when most of the people were not part of the democracy. Things have changed. Not only all people depend on government, but also all of nature depends on it. People have become conscious of the ecosystem services that support them and the plants and animals who also require those services. Yet, all living beings are affected by what a rapidly changing, large-scale species does. We have come far enough to understand that these beings and systems need to be considered with any political decisions

An ecological democracy has the form that of the people includes the extension of self to the larger Self that extends through local animals and plants and supporting ecosystems. A government by the people is the goal of direct democracy, but it can be expressed in a representative democracy as government by fair representation of the people and all beings that have a vested interest in the territories claimed by the government, which forces representatives to have to consider the health of the ecosystem and then the people before their personal economic interests. Governing for the people can be expanded to include for all residents of the territory of supporting ecosystems, including people, domestic plants and animals, wild associations, and even plants and animals that can not live well with people, such as large carnivores. The human component means all of the people, not just the majority, or the friends and families of the representatives. All people have to represented according to minimum standards. People do have shared common interests, including a healthy environment, meaningful employment, education, security, and health standards, but they also have personal interests, such as roads or factories, that may not be shared by a minority or majority.

4.3.1.2.5. Communism
Communism is a theoretical system of social organization. It is also a political movement based on common ownership of the means of production. As a political movement, communism seeks establish a classless society, either through reformation or revolution, especially the overthrow capitalism through a workers' revolution. Large-scale communism is associated with The Communist Manifesto of Karl Marx and Friedrich Engels, which predicts that communist society will replace capitalist society. Communism has more generally come to refer to the political, economic, and social theory

of Marxist thinkers, as well as life under Communist party rule. A revolutionary form of government and stage of socialism that emphasizes the requirements of the state before the individual, and which is characterized by the equal distribution of economic goods in a classless society.

Marxist theories motivated socialist parties across Europe, although the Russian Social Democratic Workers' Party, the Bolshevik branch headed by Vladimir Lenin, succeeded in taking control of the country in 1917. After the success of the Russian Revolution, many socialist parties in European countries became communist parties. After World War II, other communist regimes took power in Eastern Europe. Shortly afterwards, the Communists in China, led by Mao Zedong, came to power and established the People's Republic of China. Among the other countries that adopted a Communist form of government were Cuba, North Korea, Vietnam, Angola, and Mozambique.

The communist model provided many things for many the people, while maintaining a large war and research establishment. The philosopher Karl Marx thought that socialism was inevitable, that public ownership of the means of production would provide equality and social security for all people. But, in practice the distribution of wealth was very inequitable, as the result of historical trends, old economic rules, and cultural confusion. Some people were treated as more equal than others.

As a result of central planning, the patterns of life under the communist model were pressured to be uniform and efficient. Yet, the strengths of this kind of economy—especially the planning of production and the control of resources—were not admitted. Instead, military competition ruined these command economies and socialism is considered a failure.

All of these forms of government have flaws. Almost all are guilty of human rights violations, although some dictatorships or communist states may be guilty of more violations. All forms have problems with economic inequity. Every form has a problem with the applications of technology. Every form tends to overwhelm its environment by scale of operations.

4.3.1.3. Myths of Politics
Political myths can distort the work of politics. These myths have developed over the past hundred years, as the beneficiaries to growing inequity justify that inequity. The greater the investment of a people in a system, the greater the number of myths and the harder it becomes to argue against the myths. Political myths, like any cultural myth, meet a human need.

Myth: Democracy is the best system for everyone, even if it has to be forced on them with violence and nondemocratic methods. Answer: Democracy allows people to work together. But, people can work together without being in a formal democracy. They can still make decisions about their daily lives, from food to education.

Myth: Globalism is the solution. Answer: Joseph Campbell noted that when the tribe was the relevant social unit, it was possible for mythology to represent all those beyond its bounds as inferior. The young were trained to respond positively to tribal members to love their home and project hatred outward. The concept of tribe and state is expanding toward an ecumene, an inhabited earth. Today, there is no outward on earth. Our mythology has to grow also, to include the whole planet. There is no practical elsewhere anymore. A global mythology cannot afford to teach of elsewheres. It must teach of a multiplicity of cosmologies.

Myth: Global warming is a myth generated by scientists in the pay of the environmental lobby; the extreme predictions obstruct development and growth, and they will not come true anyway. Answer: Global climate change has been established by scientists as a real threat to human health and safety. Natural factors, such as the eruption of Mt. Pinatubo, may temporarily mask the effect of global warming. If warming continues, global climate change could convert croplands to deserts; sea-level changes would flood low-lying areas; and shifting rainfall patterns would affect crops and fisheries.

Myth: Human supremacy. Nature is a hierarchy, and man is at the top of the heap. Science can achieve a balance between the needs of people and the environment, and can even improve on natural systems. Extreme environmentalists stand in the way of human progress and threaten the quality of human life. Answer: The fates of the natural world and survival of humans seem inextricably linked. The environmental movement has worked over the past twenty years to improve the quality of life for people—from improving air and water quality by pressing for the Clean Water and Clean Air Acts, to warning communities about the danger of toxic releases from manufacturers. The naive belief that corporate scientists can replace what nature took billions of years to create will deplete natural resources rapidly.

Myth: Regulations are strangling the business that is the business of the country, resulting in loss of vital production and thousands of jobs in forestry, mining, recreation, and other industries. Answer: The regulations that the few—the rich, the greedy, the destroyers, the anti-environmentalists—seek to eliminate and characterize as "extreme" are the very rules which protect the human rights considered fundamental by all Americans: The right to breathe clean-air, drink clean water, and to protect their homes and property from the greed of people who would profit at any price. Furthermore, environmental protection is a growth industry. Every year, the environmental industry grows by five to six percent; it is projected to rise to a $300 billion dollar a year industry by the end of the decade.

Myth: We do not need to save every endangered species and subspecies, particularly when people's jobs are at stake. Extinction is a natural part of evolution. Using science, we can determine a balanced approach for protecting important species and jobs. Answer: While extinction is a natural part of evolution, human activities have accelerated it 10,000 times. Natural selection is the process for strengthening biodiversity. Furthermore, this diversity provides many solutions to health problems. Many jobs rely on the health of species and ecosystems—from the fishing industry to the pharmaceutical industry. The annual value of drugs derived from plants alone is over $40 billion.

There are other myths, of course. There is the myth of innocence (after Patricia Limerick), or it's not our fault—it's a natural catastrophe, sudden market forces, government trends, or the stars. Give us subsidies or let someone else pay for the damage. Also, there is the law of diminishing accountability, encouraged by strategic games of avoidance, which lets us maintain our innocence.

4.3.1.4. The Importance of Leadership
Leadership can refer both to the process of leading, and to those entities that do the leading. Leadership can have a formal aspect, as in most political or business leadership, or an informal one, as in most friendships. A leader is assumed to have special skills or competencies. Leaders of bands or tribes were often specialized in specific activities such as hunting or social integration. Although leadership can be exhibited by an individual, either a group of people or a heroic character can show leadership.

Leadership is often confused with transformational change, although usually leaders are the last to change. Leadership may also be associated with respect, obedience, or worship of the leader. National leaders may be presidents or queens who make the decisions for their countries. Global leaders, however, will have to address a wider spectrum of needs, and balance them.

Even in representative systems, leaders may have ceremonial or reserved powers. Leaders need to have idea people (like F.D. Roosevelt had), but they also need to have jesters and clowns to mock their mistakes and pride. In most every nation, leaders have too much power, as well as too little information, humility or wisdom.

4.3.2. Functions & Branches of Governments

People have chosen, or allowed, or suffered many kinds of governments and institutions, including rule by king or co-consuls, presidents or oligarchs, communism or democracy, aristocrats or anarchy. Societies are constituted by people and their ideas about government and justice, among other things. Ideas and behavior continue to evolve in a natural and then cultural contexts. The individual human being is a result of a family and local community, but law evolves in a larger culture. Law is now an important part of social structure.

Humans consider themselves to be self-creating and self-ordering. But, that is because they are part of a context of self-ordering processes. Government is part of that self-ordering process, wherein specialists make decisions based on their expertise. Specialization is built on trust. We trust that others will produce enough grain for them if we make a plow for them. Government has to balance giving and receiving of things and services. It preserves the balance of society.

But, governments do not always balance giving and receiving very well. Since they are run by people, and people tend to put their own interests first, governments can be tyrannical about refusing to distribute power and goods. Which tyrannies are acceptable? The abuse of power by kings, or abuse of power by corporations? Unjust executions, or cancer from toxic wastes? Government mismanagement, or the abandonment of communities by capital?

Governments are accountable to the laws that they make. Enforcing the law may keep governments more balanced.

4.3.2.1. Evolution & Law

What is government? Tribal government was based on customs and who was best at certain things, from hunting to resolving conflict. In tribes and empires laws were formed to overcome differences in customs. Government now is based on laws. But, it also needs to be based on information as well as on general common human values (and shared human rights).

4.3.2.2. Separation of Powers & Functions

Aristotle, the Greek philosopher of 2350 years ago, recognized the importance of a "rule of law" for states, as well as a central government with a separation of powers.

The framers of the U.S. Constitution wanted to form a government that did not allow one person to have too much authority or control. While under the rule of the British king they learned that this could be a bad system. Yet government under the Articles of Confederation taught them that there was a need for a strong centralized government.

With this in mind the framers wrote the Constitution to provide for a separation of powers, or three separate branches of government, a legislature, executive, and judicial. Each has its own responsibilities and at the same time they work together to make the country run smoothly and to assure that the rights of citizens are not ignored or disallowed. This is done through checks and balances. A branch may use its powers to check the powers of the other two in order to maintain a balance of power among the three branches of government. The checks and balances, combined with a separation of powers, gives responsibility to each branch to oversee the others, but the branches must be equal. Partly this is done by having overlapping responsibilities.

4.3.2.2.1. Legislative Branch

The legislative branch of government is made up of the Congress and government agencies, such as the Government Printing Office and Library of Congress, that provide assistance to and support services for the Congress. Article I of the Constitution established this branch and gave Congress the power to make laws. Congress has two parts, the House of Representatives and the Senate.

The functions of the legislature are: To make laws, and to check the executive branch by confirming appointments, and investigating executive branch activities.

4.3.2.2.2. Executive Branch

The executive branch of Government makes sure that the laws of the United States are obeyed. The President of the United States is the head of the executive branch of government. This branch is very large so the President gets help from the Vice President, department heads (Cabinet members), and heads of independent agencies. Typically, the President is the Leader of the country and commands the military. The Vice President is President of the Senate and becomes President if the President can no longer do the job. The Department heads advise the President on issues and help carry out policies. Independent Agencies help carry out policy or provide special services.

The executives could include monarch, prime minister or a cabinet. The functions are: To execute laws; To execute policies; To Control policies; To appoint officials; To Command the military; and, to Veto legislation.

The executive branch could be headed by an Executive Council of seven, with these specialties: Internal Coordination, External coordination, Ecological affairs, Cultural Affairs, Religious affairs, Economic Affairs, and Communication. This Council would elect a President for internal affairs and a Prime Minister for external affairs.

4.3.2.2.3. Judicial Branch

The judicial branch of government is made up of the court system. The Supreme Court is the highest court in the land. Article III of the Constitution established this Court and all other Federal courts were created by Congress. Courts decide arguments about the meaning of laws, how they are applied, and whether they break the rules of the Constitution.

The functions of the judicial branch are: To maintain the integrity of the Constitution; to interpret laws; and to check the executive branch by questioning enforcement of those laws?

4.3.2.2.4. Other Branches

Are three enough? Or too many? All three deal with the rule of law, to make, execute, and interpret laws. There is no reason there cannot be a fourth or fifth branch. People have suggested the "people" or the press as a fourth branch. The Philippines have three branches plus three regulatory commissions, on for civil service, one on elections, and one for auditing all accounts. The Netherlands have a Water Authority Board. Iran has an equal religious leader and Board of Guardians, although they may have more power than the traditional three branches. Some countries in Africa recognize the role of tribal leaders in government.

Is the rule of law enough for nations? Should there be rule of information or rule of religious beliefs? The formal power of beliefs might be separated into knowing, expressing and wise application. Are those enough to be separate? Informational power supports law, but it might also be more important than law under some circumstances, and law should be allowed to support information. An informational power might be separated as well, into research, applications for planning and wise assessments.

4.3.3. Functions of Politics

The functions of politics are internal and external. Internal functions are characterized by activities like the fair distribution of food and rewards. External functions are: To coordinate interaction with other nations; and to decide matters of exchange of people through emigration and immigration.

4.3.3.1. Internal Functions

Internal functions include: To promote the survival of the nation and communities; To preserve the balance of society; To maintain the affairs of the nation and communities; To guarantee fair distribution of food, goods, and necessities; To manage the distribution of power; To preserve the safety of the nation with laws and defense; To represent the citizens, to educate them, protect their rights, and remind them of their morals; To resolve conflicts between citizens; To regulate the activities of citizens regarding safety of the environment; To encourage conversation and communication; and To moderate the forces of change (internal and external).

4.3.3.1.1. To Promote Survival of Communities & Nation

Politics has to be successful enough for a new generation to take over ruling the culture and nation. If rulers promote the wrong images, that do not fit the environment, eventually a nation will collapse.

4.3.3.1.1.1. To Preserve the Operation of the Environment. Nations are embedded in places. If the place itself, the environment, fails, then no political assurances will be able to feed hungry people. So, political decisions should not interfere with the operation of global cycles or local renewal.

4.3.3.1.1.2. To Preserve the Balance of Society. Place sustains government. Land sustains government. Land produces food and resources, but the land is not equal or consistent. Poor land does not produce as much as rich land. Agriculture in general does not seem to produce as much wealth as business. Business does not seem to produce as much wealth as artists (symbols and abstractions have fewer limits on productivity). So, government needs to preserve some balance and equality by giving and taking. Individuals are produced by a community. So, the community in place seems to be the source of most of the wealth. Restoring balance in a small community can dislocate people. Leon MacLaren states that balance can be restored by depression, war, or revolution, and it can be painful. Of course, planning and conscious adjustment might be less painful and less risky.

4.3.3.1.1.3. To Encourage Conversation & Communication. We can best understand the social aspect of culture by realizing that the central function of human symbolization is communication and requires adherence to understood conventions. Constant communication allows a culture to be coherent. Lack of communication can lead to unhappiness or violence.

4.3.3.1.1.4. To Manage Individual Civic Relations & Conflicts. Many cultures have built-in limits to local kinds of conflict, but conflict between cultures requires some laws or understandings. Behavior has to be understood in a context as meaningful. Sometimes conflicts are the result of language, behavior patterns or simple geography. There has to a path to resolve conflicts, either consensus, mediation or neutral judgment.

4.3.3.1.1.5. To Decide Limits to Growth Development or Movement. Keynesian economic theory, the predominant theory in industrial countries, holds that the full utilization of resources is necessary to ensure full employment and the maximum social good. This economics depends on economic growth to avoid crisis. The major premises assume that: Population will grow, that social good is related to the equitable distribution of material products, and that if resources are limited, technology can erase the limits. The economist Kenneth Boulding referred to this as a cowboy economy, an economy that has yet to bump against the limits of wealth.

In the U.S., the mentality of the frontier bloomed as the physical frontier was being closed.

This mentality assumed the nature of a myth, that all people would prosper in the frontier way. Even though the 1890 census recognized that the frontier was no more, and warned people to use what they had, the people themselves have sustained the myth of limitlessness. The myth has become stronger than the logic of limits. Corporations and banks have used the myth to offset the dismal flavor of their economics. The victims have been tricked into passionately defending their own exploitation and that of the environment.

Growth is rarely an unlimited process in nature. Unlimited growth is only an economic characteristic if the economy refuses to recognize physical and biological limits. Because people seem to have unlimited wants, some political rules need to be in place to allow equal distribution before some can amass vast fortunes.

One solution is to work within limits of sustainability. Population could be stabilized. Consumption could be stabilized, especially with a shift to recycling and solar energy generation. The technology already exists, but educational and political problems are more difficult.

4.3.3.1.2. To Manage the Affairs of the Communities & Nation

Hutterite communities were able to manage their community as long as it was less than about 150 people, Garrett Hardin noted. With more than that, distribution of goods failed, due to some doing less than their share or getting more. So, the Hutterites split communities into two, when they got too large. The scale of community can make some things work better. The force that keeps individuals from laziness or greed seems to be shame, which seems to work as a force only in smaller communities. In a small community, a person can be shamed into working harder or into being less greedy, but in larger communities shame does not work as well. Maladaptive behavior may be less visible or the malcontents may form a subgroup that justifies their behavior. Hardin suggests that most utopias do not consider such a change in scale.

Many archaic cultures mismanaged their natural resources, but got away with it because their impact was relatively small. Some cultures were not as lucky, the people of Ur, for instance. Luck, as well as size, has a lot to do with the success of some human cultures. Many other cultures mismanaged the affairs of communities, but they were able to survive because of brute control.

The industrial cultures are mismanaging their resources and affairs, but may not be able to control or organize—or luck—their way out of their problems. Modern society has benefited from modern means of management. In fact, management has made industrial operations, from science to agriculture, possible. But, to continue without disaster, it needs to re-empower local voices, especially indigenous peoples, poor, displaced, and women. It needs to encourage unique local management solutions, such as the water management on Bali. It needs to adjust to optimum scales that are more efficient and just.

4.3.3.1.2.1. *To Guarantee Fair Distribution of Food & Necessities.* With the complexities of civilization, with various levels of responsibility and duty, politics has to make sure that necessities are distributed in a timely manner. The infrastructure, that is the bureaucracy, the coordination, storage areas, trucks, and other things, have to be in place and functioning.

4.3.3.1.2.2. *To Guarantee Fair Distribution of Power & Rewards.* Power in physics is the capacity to move. Socially it is the capacity to act. Power is the capability of making things move or happen. Power is not only making things happen, it is a way of controlling which things happen. Having power determines who gets to decide. Power allows dominance. If power is concentrated in one or few people, then there are fewer opportunities to challenge or limit it. Concentrated power can lock or gridlock patterns of movement; this is not always healthy, since many problems need many different solutions. Absolute power is no longer accountable to lesser power.

In archaic societies everyone has some power. Power is given to those who have better abilities, at hunting, healing or coercing. The real power there is the ability to persuade others. First persuasion yielded power, then strength, then knowledge. Power can come from strength or a connection to another form of power, ancestral or holy. Power can be derived from the permission or weakness of others.

The creation of large dense communities required new forms of power, due to size and organizational problems. No matter how big the bureaucracy, for a while it only controlled human muscle power. That limited their reach, regarding armies or builders (of pyramids). Traditional states had trouble controlling regional potentates or their armies completely. New forms of energy expanded human power and control.

Scale of governments or corporations gives them more power. Management techniques, or technology, can augment power. Power allows more waste. But, power diminishes the ability to see or feel, or suffer, the consequences. Power often reduces the perceptions of those who have it, such that they use power to simplify ecosystems rather than imagine working inside the systems. Having rewards gives people more power. Such power can be expressed in buying patterns as well as bribes.

Corporations increase their power temporarily because of our failure to grasp their nature. Misunderstanding of power or nature can allow a temporary expression of power. The competitive way of life, as it dominates, distorts the meaning of power and demand, and causes imbalances of power and demands.

Governments with concentrated power can be tyrannical about redistributing power or rewards. Inequality in rewards is maintained by the concentration of power. Rewards and power are treated as primary needs, which results in imbalances. Power can lead to detachment from primary needs and natural wealth. Rewards give more power, so that the two form a positive feedback loop that sometimes cannot be controlled, by the user or the less powerful. The cycle becomes self-reinforcing.

If power is spread more evenly, through many leaders and many kinds of leaders, then they can check each other and power is balanced. Under many constitutions power is dispersed by dividing into separate branches. Humans are momentarily powerless to replace or transcend the circuitry of natural or cultural systems. People often have the power to deny using the power, especially when it can destroy places or human values.

4.3.3.1.2.3. *To Promote Safety & Security*. Without safety and security of the primary needs of food, clothing, and shelter, there will not be a cultivation of secondary needs that promote higher culture. Ultimately security is the availability of food, materials and energy. There are levels of security, starting with a healthy ecosystem, and the ability to use it, protect it, and restore it. Security also requires that resources be available to be used, conserved and substituted. Socioeconomic security requires a healthy culture that can distribute basic needs equitably and efficiently. For people to be secure, all of their needs, such as self-actualization, have to be encouraged.

Safety is a basic human need, physiological and psychological. Safety is increased when people accept limits on their social behavior, when natural disasters are anticipated, and when technological extremes, such as nuclear accidents and wastes, are safeguarded. Safety does not mean wiping out large predators, such as alligators or sharks, to ensure than no one ever gets bitten or eaten; it means reducing exposure to wild animals, by reducing the overlap or reduction of territories. Animals have to balance their own safety with migration and food-getting. Safety does not mean killing every form of bacteria or virus; it means limiting exposure, being healthy, and preventing the spread of pandemics through accelerated travel and sharing. Ecologically, safety means leaving functioning ecosystems outside the circle of human domination.

Safety is increased with higher standards for sanitation as well as with technology. It means minimizing the potential for harm in a work or play situation. This occurs when governments and corporations take higher risks than the communities and cultures, accept a burden of proof for new developments, and accept higher margins of error and certainty. Safety is increased with laws, such as those concerned with cheating, thieving or killing. Laws that limit dangerous things, such as guns, expand safety.

4.3.3.1.2.4. *To Adapt to Internal Forces of Change.* The principle of change indicates that nature is in flux, culture is in flux. Politics is concerned not only with how power and authority are exercised but with how these relationships get transformed. We are interested in the forces that sustain consensus as well as in the forces that bring about change. Intensive change is the development of consciousness or social sophistication; it is characterized by consciousness, connection, and communication. This should apply to cultures also. Extensive change results in the development of cities and technology; it is characterized by conquest, colonialization and consumption.

As humans stay in place, they tried to extract more resources from the same area. This requires new ideas and technology. Which resulted in denser settlements, which resulted in new technology and new social organization. This is extensification. Innovation is influenced by the growth and intensity of population, by the expanding and intensified activities of states or cities, and increasing trade and commercialization. The ease of communication also increases rates of innovation. Perhaps that is why it went east-west in Europe and Asia and north-south in the Americas. Accidental innovation became a culture of innovation, that is, it was encouraged and used.

Civilization is shaped by extensification and intensification, and complication and complexification, although on a local level there were booms and busts of individual civilizations. Why do countries lag behind in industrialization? Why do they need to join the race? Economists argue that their policies or attitudes are at fault, that their environment might be poor. That they are unorganized. That they are fearful of change or exploration. That does not seem likely though. Often the problem can be resources or domination, but sometimes, it is the social predisposition to change, as a result of historical or cultural factors.

4.3.3.1.3. To Represent Citizens
The early Sumerian temple tower, with a hieratically organized city surrounding it, became the model for the Hindu world mountain Sumeru. The king was the central human representative of power. First there were cities and then empires of cities, with kings to represent citizens. Leaders always try to represent members of a group.

In archaic cultures, when people could not present themselves at every meeting, it was useful for someone to represent them. Some degree of household autonomy is sacrificed to some larger order group in return for greater security against attacks by enemies or from starvation. A government promises to judge disputes in values and to protect its citizens from external attack.

The people of a nation-state were first given full sovereignty officially in 1648, with the Peace of Westphalia. Representative governments still use that sovereignty to claim responsibility for their actions, without recognition of any international body. They also represent citizens in matters of economic opportunities and trade, to attempt to guarantee access and fairness.

4.3.3.1.3.1. *To Educate People Scientifically & Morally.* Thomas Huxley thought that people in nature were Hobbesian, unfit for civilization unless culture educated them. The same essential belief was held by Sigmund Freud. But, the contexts were, and are different. The thought of Huxley was dominated by ideas of competition and fitness, and that of Freud by individuals in society, from hysterical women and conflicted children to selfish businessmen and power-blinded leaders. The context now is drones in an industrial flatscape.

The modern state has an educated bureaucracy to manage information. It requires compulsory education, resulting in mass education and mass literacy. Mass literacy disenchants the cosmos by undermining traditional and magical ways of thinking. Testing traditional knowledge became a habit. Difficulties of dealing with a half-hearted half-educated public, of dealing with a hard-hearted, hard-headed professional elite, only add to the problems of a culture.

Education may be a necessity, but it has to be a freely offered broad education, based on rich philosophies and sciences. It has to be adaptive. Tribes in the Brazilian Amazon, for instance, have stopped using chainsaws and tobacco, to live more traditionally. They also set up educational centers to show others how it is done.

4.3.3.1.3.2. *To Protect Their Rights.* In a traditional English village, inherited bundled rights provided commoners with rights of grazing and gathering fuel wood non-destructively "by hook or by crook," which indicated the way wood was gathered by shepherds. The form "commons" is plural, and refers to the whole group of commons, subject to these effects.

As rights have expanded, they have also been made more explicit in laws and codes. There is a form of an International Bill of Rights, covering human and ambihuman. This would cover workers rights. Residents expect to have equal rights and opportunities.

4.3.3.1.3.3. *To Outline Their Duties.* In addition to having rights, citizens also have responsibilities to participate in government and to live as wisely as possible, to make good places. Often, duties have to be made known through education and communication from the government.

4.3.3.2. External Functions of Politics
External functions are those outside the boundaries of the nation. But, those functions may have dramatic influences on the shape and course of a nation.

4.3.3.2.1. To Coordinate Interaction with Other Nations & Cultures
The possible kinds of interactions of groups or cultures are: To ignore each other; to exist separately with trade or contact; to compete for resources and people; to cooperate with each other; to fight for dominance or territory; or to destroy the other. For interactions leading to violence, a number of trends that can be seen. These are feedback loops that loop around to the beginning, also.

On the other hand, alienation can lead to selfishness, gangs, and anarchy, then neighborhood control by criminals, psychological stress of urban environment, substance abuse, family breakdown, lack of control, and violence. Prejudice can lead to segregation, discrimination against indigenous populations, destruction of cultural heritage, ethnic disintegration, an inadequate sense of identity, psychological alienation, and violence.

Conflict starts with people, but extends to animals, natural events, and nations, leading to the unfortunate metaphor of war. What is a definition of war? Does it have to do with the number of battles or dead? Or with having a professional army? Does it have to have a beginning and an end? Does it have to be a certain scale? Does it have to be agreed on by both sides or all parties? The whole process and its effects are complex. As violence and conflict occurred on larger scales, they were called wars.

4.3.3.2.1.1. *Personal Conflicts.* Individual conflicts often resulted from insults or broken promises. In Mesopotamia, people paid fines for hurting others. For instance, severing the bones of another man with a weapon resulted in a fine of one mina of silver.

When arguments could not be resolved, there was open conflict. Resolution of individual conflicts was usually informal within the confines of the community. For Inupiat and other egalitarian cultures, song duels are a ritual pacific form. The disputants publicly insult one another until the audience laughs down the loser. If individual disputes are not resolved, then they are settled by community consensus.

The predominant value in small cultures, and then large, was harmony. This minimized conflict that might have resulted from inequality. Confucian concepts of ritual and etiquette helped to regulate social conduct and made people feel good about their station. For example: "Inequality is the nature of things" and "seek no happiness that does not pertain to your lot in life."

Table 43321-1. Kinds of Conflicts and Wars

Kind	Reason	Examples
Personal Conflicts	Insults, broken promises	Palouse, Aborigines
Leaders Conflicts Group conflicts	Social insults, food, territory	Uruk
General's wars	Food, Luxuries	Babylon
Psychological wars	Prestige Glory Idealism Patriotism	Greece, Macedonia
Professional Soldiers wars Army wars	Food, territory, unification	China, Rome
Kind	Reason	Examples
Religious wars Royal wars National wars	Territory conversion	France, Britain
Economic trade wars	Control of resources in colonies	Britain, France, Spain, Portugal, Germany
Chemists war, with poison gases and explosives	Territory expansion	First World War
Physicists war, with radar and nuclear weapons	Territory expansion	WW II
Mathematician's wars, with computer-guided missiles.	Resources Potential threats	Iraq Gulf War 1
Electronic wars, to destroy computers and databases.	Destruction of information or economic structure	WW II
Ecological wars	Destruction of land base Against Nature	Vietnam, Iraq Pesticides, Medicines

4.3.3.2.1.2. *Group Conflicts.* In a Tiwi example, a dispute occurred because the elders of one band reneged on their promise to bestow daughters for marriage to the sons of another band—a violation of norm of reciprocal marital exchange. Two war parties of fifteen warriors each met in adjoining territory. They wore white paint symbolizing anger. Both sides exchanged insults the first day. Then agreed to meet the next day for socializing and renewing acquaintances. The third day the duel resumed; words escalated into wild spear throwing that wounded a few spectators and warriors. Then, the fight ended.

Is warfare limited in band societies? Could it be due to a lack of interpersonal competition for status? Are people taught to be restrained? Are conflicts are resolved by ridicule before getting out of hand?

Population density was controlled by the traditional approaches to resources. In archaic societies, cooperation and consensus, as opposed to competition and individual exaltation, permitted planning to remain informal. Population growth triggered competition and conflict, which led to positive feedback of the thing that caused the stress.

In Mesopotamia, complex systems can be managed locally by farmers, although there may be conflict by upstream users. But, cooperation is necessary, especially in villages and between villages later. As a result large-scale water systems were first managed by religious leaders, then later by secular leaders. Usually irrigation is necessary because the rainfall is unpredictable. Wars started from depressions in food production or storage. Mesopotamian cities had councils of elders to make decisions. They would appoint a leader to lead in war or trade. The word for this leader, lugal, eventually came to mean king; after 2800 BC, gods changed from natural forces to war gods. Agriculture gave a surplus; that and property led to excitement of war. In China, in the Warring States period, the nature of war changed: From an Aristocratic monopoly of soldiers to one with permanent standing armies, professional leaders and peasant soldiers. Conflict was resolved centrally by a chief or king, who held a monopoly on power.

Does every society have war? The anthropologist Carol Ember surveyed band societies and found that sixty-four percent waged some kind of war.

4.3.3.2.1.3. *Intercultural Conflict & War*. The reasons for war have gone from insults and personal conflicts having to do with bride exchange, broken rituals and personal honor to group and external reasons, such as territory, resources and patriotism.

The nation states are closely related to large-scale violence, usually having to do with trying to consolidate their power (global war). They then have a monopoly on power(monopoly rents). They specialize on political and economic issues (e.g., the Spanish ransacked the planet for gold). They enlarge and consolidate their territoriality, which gives them increased capacity for marshaling resources (maximum global functions with minimum territorial burden).

Wars, like the recent one in Iraq, are based on weak assumptions: That the war can be waged by blasting away any threats, and that it can be contained by using conventional weapons. But, like most actions, it has affects that can get magnified in the larger system. Furthermore, the war breaks out of the barriers that the participants try to create, destroying properties and civilians—there are no longer any safe buildings or noncombatants, and ruining the social and ecological fabrics.

All wars now are ecological wars that destroy the basis of civilization. There are no non-monotonic effects with war. There are no side effects. There are only effects and they can all be measured. Perhaps the next war will be to directly destroy the ecological basis of a nation, an extreme scorched earth policy by the aggressors. These wars would be social wars that destroy entire generations and traditional social structures. Perhaps, future wars will have less to do with honor and territory and more to do with crises, such as famine, population, and environmental collapse. Perhaps, wars will have to do with symbols and religion, again, as they have in the past.

4.3.3.2.1.3.1. *Advantages & Disadvantages of War*. War has advantages and disadvantages. One of the advantages of war is its long tradition, being simpler to understand than rights, the attendant macroeconomics or the workings of enantiodromia. Another advantage is that war is cheaper than ever before, especially to attack. Of course, war is also stimulating and fun, at least for the victorious survivors, who are bonded by the danger.

It used to be that it cost more to attack than to defend, with preparations and supply lines. Now, It costs more to defend against a bullet than to attack with one. Cheap bullets destabilized the western U.S., but laws and enforcement, also with bullets, restabilized it. Possibly the same thing will happen with cheap cruise missiles. Maybe not, as the cost of attacking will now continue to be less than defending. This means that the world may become more violent and less stable. Can information warfare be cheaper, or less destabilizing? No, because information attacks may be even easier to perform. Unless everyone has the same weapons.

The disadvantages are greater than the sum of all advantages. Ecosystems in disputed and ravaged territories are always disrupted, damaged or destroyed. Human suffering is always made worse than it was before the war. And, war never solves the original problem.

4.3.3.2.1.3.2. *Style & Scale of War.* Politics is the management of people through equitable distribution of resources, and the management of relations with neighbors or trading partners, using negotiation or force, war if necessary. Wars have changed in style and scale. From disagreements, wars have become a centralized state function. From religious reasons, where Gods lived with people, it has gone to the secularization of state concerns.

The essence of war is to defeat or destroy an enemy. Governments are efficient killing machines. On the average in the nineteenth century, states killed 3.7% of their subjects. In the twentieth century they killed 7.3% of the world population.

War as related to growth. Often the same factors that allow unsustainable growth allow unsustainable war. Growth is promoted for its advantages, usually without recognition of its difference from development.

The historical rhythm between war and peace inevitably leads back to peace. When does peace occur, when it is won? Unlike many forms of war, peace is a process with a less rigid beginning. It can never be won or kept permanently. It does not have the prestige or honor of war, and perhaps this is why so much less times and effort is devoted to peace.

Is there a way to limit war, within the context of peace? Is there another way to humiliate or embarrass an enemy, and let some other kind of balance be found? Is there a way to limit violence to heroes or to leaders, as if either would agree to have their individual expertise be responsible for a whole population.

4.3.3.2.2. To Decide Matters of Emigration & Immigration

National governments have the right to determine their own immigration policies, even though the policies are influenced by many other factors, from disasters to invasions, which are outside the control of governments. Governments need to balance emigration and immigration in a context of a satisfactory population suited for its environment, based on their own carrying capacity and principles.

4.3.3.2.3. To Adapt to External Forces of Change

Extensive evolution is the horizontal spread of species. Extensive change is the spread of cultures through many ecosystems. Human migration was a form of extensification. That is, when the size of foraging communities made hunting and living problematical, some humans moved away. Only when they could not or would not move, did it become intensification, which required different strategies to live, such as intensive food-gathering strategies. Exploitation of new areas shows the ecological power of the species. Intensive development of a place shows the creativity of the species.

Politics has to adapt a culture to external forces, from climate change to invasions of exotic plants and animals. A culture cannot escape the rhythms of nature. Some events, such as earthquakes or floods can be anticipated with plans and architectural designs.

4.4. Expanding Ethics to Encompass the Global

Humanity is an integral part of food chains and part of an organic cycle of birth and death. Humans need to recognize that they automatically participate in everything, and that they cannot unparticipate by choice. Participation starts at the quantum level, through the ecological and cultural. Human nature does not find meaning in an absurd world, but discovers its structure through interaction with the ultrahuman order. Human identity exists partly in relation to nature; the destruction of one involves the other.

The word ethics is derived from the Greek word meaning 'custom,' which itself came from the Sanskrit word for one's 'own doing.' Since it was used in the plural, it meant 'doing together.' The word 'morality' comes from the Latin word for will of the people; the singular meant the 'will' of a person. It was probably derived from the verb 'to measure,' as to measure one's way, or to go one's way. Morals means the 'way of going together.' Ethics means 'doing together,' which of course one does in living together. And, in an anthropometric universe, this is entirely appropriate.

Ethics are assembled inductively, from experience in living in places. Because of the uncertainty of human actions, ethics has to encompass the far past and distant future. No one knew that when DDT killed mosquitoes, it would concentrate in the food chain to kill birds. Values are time dependent, and ecological time can be very long indeed. The futures we invent are viable only if they are compatible with constraints imposed by evolutionary past. An ethics that requires a long-range responsibility also requires a new humility, since technological power exceeds the ability to foresee its consequences. An ecological ethic recognizes the moral obligation to leave the world habitable for future generations.

Leopold proposed a conservation ethic, dealing with human relationships to land, plants and animals. The land ethic Leopold had in mind was a sense of ecological community between humanity and other species. "When we see land as community to which we belong, we will use it with love and respect." Such an ethic would change the human role from master of earth to plain member of it. Predators are members of the community; and no special interest group has the right to exterminate them for the sake of benefit for itself. This attitude is important for habitat protection. Leopold describes the extension of ethics as "actually a process in ecological evolution. Its sequences may be described in ecological as well as in philosophical terms. An ethic, ecologically, is a limitation on freedom of action in the struggle for existence. An ethic, philosophically, is a differentiation of social from antisocial conduct. These are two different definitions of one thing. The thing has its origin in the tendency of interdependent individuals or groups to evolve modes of cooperation."

The extension of ethics to animals and land is an ecological necessity. Extended ethics defines a social conduct that is a mode of cooperation and, ultimately, symbiosis. Leopold argued that ethics are voluntary limitations of freedom, necessary in a complex world of which we remain incredibly ignorant. Ethics are developed in response to problems that arise from increasing knowledge. Science has phenomenally increased our knowledge of physical and biological processes. It has now become the basis of our moral code, but it cannot very long be a science divorced from feeling and art if that code is to help us survive. To do this science requires aesthetic perception as well as disciplined thinking and feeling. As there is a rational component to ethical judgments, so there is an intuitive and emotional one, also. An evolutionary ethic suggests that humans avoid tampering with complex evolved systems, not because they are good, but because they are the basis of life at this stage of development. Ecological ethics is situational because ecology is the study of changing systems. The morality of the act is determined by the current state of the system. Adaptive modes should conform to ecological patterns. An ecological ethics is based on attributes of ecosystems and human compliance with ecological laws. The aim of an ethic must be harmonious to the idea of the world's population of living beings.

Ecological ethics is a series of rules for living together. Most sets of ethics make the rules easy to follow. They emphasize the differences (relativism) or similarities (absolutism) of human beings only; or of the individual or the group; or of good feeling, reason, or desire. But ethics has to confront the individual, embedded in a community, located in a bioregion, on earth. And the rules really are not as easy as human systems have presented. Albert Schweitzer made them too difficult, with the need for a constant valuing, but neither are they that difficult. An ontological ethics can be detailed only on a local level—even when it uses a global strategy.

Individualism can be tempered with the concept of common good, the good of the whole. The whole is diminished by individual loss, but the individual is crippled by the loss of the whole; wild children, for example, are never really human. Human good cannot be considered apart from the common good. We are in larger communities like an organ in a body. In The Laws, Plato has the Athenian say to a youth that all things are ordered with a view to the preservation of the whole, each portion contributes to the whole, and every other creature is for the sake of the whole. Ethics has expanded in wholes, from the family, to the human community, and to the ultrahuman community, on which all depend.

Ethics now considers almost every human being and human interaction. The restriction of ethics to exclusively human modes of existence, however, leads to a troublesome isolation. Human beings are not separate from their social and biological communities and these communities are embedded in ecological contexts with biogeochemical processes. Ethics must be extended to the framework and to the nonhuman communities in the framework, without which there would be no human health or wealth. Through science as well as through mysticism, we understand that communities of other beings have their own values and rules for living together. It remains for us to integrate and codify human rules that recognize the values and rights of other beings.

How do we share things, including power? Michael W. Fox proposes a biospiritual ethic as a unifying set of principles, ethics and values that will bring about a nonconflicting state of one earth, one mind. The ethic is based on the biological fact that all humans and living beings are kin and that life is spiritual—love is stronger than violence. It arises from seeing humanity in an ecological perspective.

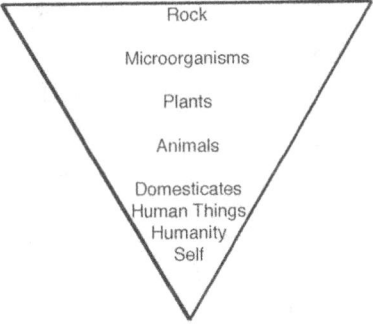

Figure 440-1. The inverted pyramid of ethics (Self includes family and local groups).

5.0. Creating Ecological Patterns for Developing Global Government

Government is part of the pattern of a society. Part of the function of government is to perpetuate the society. Societies also embedded in and depend on the productivity of the supporting ecosystems and the vitality of the member cultures. Neither perfection or survival are guaranteed by the health of the context, however. The properties listed below are somewhat indefinite and incomplete; although understanding them and applying them can improve human situations in a challenging planet, government is needed to apply human activities in ways that are healthy for all levels.

5.1. Making a Good Society

5.1.1. Properties of a Good Society

Because the properties of good societies depend on the properties of good ecosystems and good places, good ecosystems and places have to be preserved. These properties are both nested and dependent (see table 511-1).

Table 511-1. Contrasted Properties of 6 Defined Systems

Fields	*Places*	*Ecosystems*
Process	Dynamic Change	Course
Autopoesis	Self-making Wholeness	Identity
Differentiation	Differentiation	Openness Diversity
Integration	Integration	Coconstrained Construction
Constancy	Constancy	Stability
Metalysis	Renewal	Productivity
Cultures	*Good Places*	*Good Societies*
Conduct	Action	Method
Wholeness	Individuality	Self-extension
Flexibility	Richness	Variety
Adaptation	Conviviality	Cooperation
Constancy	Consistency	Loyalty
Vitality	Health	Harmony

Stable, good societies must pass the social institutions to a new generation, but without sacrificing everything for posterity. The traditional object of economics is the administration of scarce resources; this needs to be extended to an indefinite line of generations. There is the question of the quality of life from one generation to the next; possibly the present should be regarded as the distribution of a dowry to succeeding generations.

5.1.1.1. Method as a Property of a Good Society
Because human beings exist as part of the natural order, the properties and principles that underlie good societies also underlie ecosystems. Method is such a property and it allows the development of society through differentiation and recombination. It allows the development of society through the use of energy and self-maintenance. Growth, for instance, allows society to avoid stagnation or collapse, although only for a time, then it has to split or adjust its size through emergency measures. Feedback, positive or negative, is method for society to adjust to various natural or social limits. Feedback can allow a society to deconstruct or reconstruct itself as it progresses. Society has to weave a course between its successful competition to support and renew itself and its tendency to overdevelop and destroy its habitat and place.

Human societies in place use methods to create their societies and these methods have properties based on the properties of ecosystems and good places, such as process, change, course, conduct, and action. Methods are the motors of change that drive the development of societies. Methods may conflict or fit together but their action causes human bonds to be more flexible. Method addresses the efficacy of society; it is method that can fragment the image of or world or place and reduce fitness. It is method that can work up appropriate beliefs and behaviors. Methods of observation, for instance, can determine what is seen or important. Methods of behavior can lead into the character of the society. The world and society are accessible through methods of describing, analyzing or synthesizing. A poor method can lead to the fragmentizing of society or nature.

A method is a way of doing something or the regularity and orderliness of the actions of doing (from the Greek words for 'pursuing a way'). Goethe said that "the methodology of forms is the methodology of transformations." Goethe attempted to use his method to produce an organic and morphological world-history. This methodology is part of nature. It reflects nature. Rilke wonders whether or not all the dynamics of nature, including those of human society, are hieroglyphics of the methodology of thinking. The scientific method multiplied human dividends with the industrial revolution, but it destroyed the fabric it was examining. New ways of thinking are being developed in terms of instructions and normative modes, and that these are beginning to provide methodologies capable of achieving the necessary, challenging tasks.

5.1.1.2. Self-extension as a Property of a Good Society
The Property of self-extension, and its corollary ideas, uniqueness, design and centering, emerges from the properties of good human places, ecosystems, and the field: Individuality, Self-extension, Ordering, Identity, Boundedness, Autopoesis, Wholeness, Form, and Uniqueness. It is those properties modified by adaptation and ethics.

The individual extends far beyond the skin. Extent can be more than just in space. People extend themselves in time by planning for their heirs. The extensions are connections, not only physical connections but intention as well. Extending the place into other ecosystems allows nature do the work. Whitehead seems to find it necessary to divide the cosmic process into two properties, extensiveness and aim. Extensiveness means that the process is spread through space and goes on in time. In fact, he considers extensiveness more basic than the arbitrary factors of four dimensions or "electromagnetic laws." Extensiveness is the binding of the physical world by relatedness.

5.1.1.3. Variety as a Property of a Good Society
The property of variety, and its corollary ideas, valuation, consciousness, and self-analysis, emerges from the properties of good human places, ecosystems, and the field: Richness, Challenge, Diversity, Openness, Flexibility, Difference, Discretion, and Limit. It is modified by adaptation and ethics.

Flexibility is potential for changer within a system. Variety provides flexibility in systems.

Flexibility is needed to correct our mistaken allegiance to the machine image of life. If we survive then we need to always preserve more flexibility for future mistakes. As we know, it is impossible to avoid disorder, which is a necessary part of any physical and social system. A system with flexibility can incorporate disorder without being destroyed. What barriers are there to renewing institutional flexibility? Or to restoring ecosystem flexibility.

The realization of hard realities does not mean a return to a dark age. We will have more flexibility if we choose our way, and salvage much of the industrial revolution. Natural systems are characterized by resiliency and flexibility, and high productivity, too. We need efficiency, but a higher efficiency—an efficiency in life, not one department of life. There must be a positive flexibility; potentials not used must be preserved for future use to accommodate dead ends, mistakes, or change.

Civilization will have to follow a circuitous route, practicing rigorous self-discipline and economy, more than if we had started earlier. There must be far fewer people than now; the mess and heat generated by vast multitudes will always be ruled out by the natural laws within which all things function.

Zonal diversity can be used to develop different resource production systems in a local area. This increases the likelihood that production will fluctuate nonsynchronously so that support for human populations is constant. Of course, keeping flexibility and reserves could have the same effect. By forming a complex society, the scale of production is raised from a local group in limited territory to a regional population in diverse territories. Even hunter/gatherers engage in similar "energy averaging" systems. A smaller size could mean more flexibility and faster response to local conditions.

Plans can be made within the limits of variables, although it is not safe to be limited by lethal variables, as Gregory Bateson recognized; closeness to limits reduces flexibility, that is, uncommitted potential for change.

5.1.1.4. Cooperation as a Property of a Good Society

The Property of cooperation, and its corollary ideas, awareness, complexity, intensity, and patterning, emerges from the properties of good human places, ecosystems, and the field: Conviviality, Adaptation, Awareness, Intensity, Development, Complexity, Participation, Integration, Connection, and Infolding. It is modified by adaptation and ethics.

Cooperation implies convivial or appropriate technology. The word convivial means social, from the Latin word *convivium*, meaning living together. Ivan Illich, in *Tools for Conviviality*, sketches a meaningful community where workers have control of their tools and their lives.

There would be a selective reduction of industrialism. Large industry might still be needed for certain things, such as televisions or computers, but the technology of the future must be valid for more people under varied conditions. There should be a proper mix of handicraft labor, intermediate technology and heavy industry. Economics would become characterized by friendship and cooperation. The root problem is how to live with technology in a mature manner. We need an ecological awareness at all levels, where humanity is part of system.

5.1.1.5. Loyalty as a Property of a Good Society

The Property of loyalty, and its corollary ideas, equity, attachment, investment, and love, emerges from the properties of good human places, ecosystems, and the field: Consistency, Abiding Restraint, Tension, Stability, Accommodation, Constancy, Investment, Love, and Regularity. It is modified by adaptation and ethics. Loyalty is the constancy of a place modified by attachment to and investment in a place, by the members of a good society.

Loyalty is defined as the faithful adherence to an ideal, cause, duty, nation, or place. It implies an obligation to support or defend those things. People give their loyalties to family, culture and place. Loyalty can form the context for agreement or dissent.

Loyalty can be corrupted or bought, however. Capitalists, for instance, can generate consumer loyalty through a massive scale of gift-giving, which allows the capitalist system to survive for a while longer. Loyalty could increase social stability, whether loyalty to the family, place or political system. As loyalty is transferred, the criterion of rights is transferred from the nature of 'man' to the community of persons; both law and justice, as well as obligations and rights, are reduced to equity issues. Thus, new nations demand to participate in a common justice, as opposed to the extension of natural rights.

5.1.1.6. Harmony as a Property of a Good Society

The Property of harmony, and its corollary ideas, balance, education, care, and acceleration, emerges from the properties of good human places, ecosystems, and the field: Health, Meaning, Vitality, Productivity, Renewal, Cycling, Process, Movement, and Flow. It is modified by adaptation and ethics.

Harmony (from the Greek word *harmos*) means 'fitting.' Extended definitions of harmony include: The combination of parts into a pleasing or orderly whole; or, an agreement in feeling and action. To harmonize means to associate different things in a proportionate arrangement. Proportionate is the due proportion of two things having a reciprocal relationship or an equality in measure. If nations were defined as having an equality of measure, not necessarily size or force, then the harmony of nations could be promoted. In Chinese medical tradition, the highest good is harmony, especially social harmony, or good relations. A good person is one who creates and maintains harmony. And, harmony involves the body and emotions. Perhaps this is the best working definition of health. It is harmony that comes from adaptive history. It is not the musical kind exactly, but more like the mutual restraint of groups of organisms.

Harmony is the agreement of method, extension, variety, cooperation, and loyalty in a social and ecological context of good societies in good places. Harmony in a society is the agreement of actions, feelings, ideas, and interests that results in peaceable relations. Harmony is society can be reduced or destroyed by cheaters, 'free-riders,' or anti-social individuals. But, society itself may select for traits of reciprocal altruism or altruistic punishment in other individuals.

Harmony is mutual constraint within a shared adaptive history. It is constraint that limits the scale of a society. Harmony requires understanding and then planning for adjustments. Harmony requires adequate ecological information and the infusion of its significance in human affairs. And, it requires the time to do this, with the practices of caution and reverence.

5.1.2. Dynamics of a Good Society
  (Being Edited)

5.2. Making Good Places in Ecosystems

Good places can emerge from healthy ecosystems. Because human beings live in ecosystems, the description of good places as healthy ecosystems has a human psychological dimension. Good places at this level are good human places, where human activity has invested place with human meaning while allowing the operations of the field and ecosystem to operate.

5.2.1. Properties of a Good Human Place Emergent from an Ecosystem

These properties are roughly the same as those for ecosystems. What makes the ecosystem "good" is a human judgment about the feel and use of a place, on whether a place provides basic goods, services and amenities. Are there special qualities that make a place good for human habitation? We have to allow the same process that makes healthy ecosystems operate to make good places.

The key to the properties of good human places is the addition of psychological and cultural elements to those of ecological places. Good human places emerge from good places, which depend on healthy ecosystems. Both properties and activities must reflect or allow the functioning of every level below it.

5.2.1.1. Action as a Property of a Good Place

Action emerges from the special properties of fields, places and ecosystems when they are combined with human activities in place. Action is not merely rhythmic change, it is a creative advance, producing new forms everywhere. The organism undergoes a process of evolution in which it produces new forms in itself. In this level, it is human action.

5.2.1.2. Individuality as a Property of a Good Place

Individuality, and the ideas of identity, self-extension and creative ordering, emerge from the special properties of places and ecosystems, identity, boundedness, and whole form. And, these properties emerge from the properties of the field, autopoesis, uniqueness, and wholeness.

The place produces its own individuality. Even with human beings as a component, the place is self-creating. Its wholeness emerges from the interactivity of the components. The place is self-making and self-organizing. It has a characteristic or defining mixture of diversity and complexity.

Just as a place has a unique identity, a human place has a unique identity. The human place has a unique boundary defined by unique physical and or mental limits. The place is a unique local as a host for unique ideas about it. It has a specific size and shape. It has its own integrity, as a whole place

Identity with a place is the extension of Self to Place or the extension of the smaller self with the larger self. Humans identify with places. This identity is a form of rootedness; the place is a center of existence. Identity is the persistent quality of a relationship among things.

Humans and their communities are embedded in places. The Taureg of the Sahara have created an image, a world, that could never be relocated to the rain forest of the Campa in Peru. Place is a platform for ordering a world. The individual image of a place is modified by memory, experience, emotion, imagination, and intention. The social image of a place is influenced by individuals, myths, history, and consensus. The images reinforce each other over time. Each place and culture is unique. It is the place that offers specific images.

Human beings gravitate into groups to live. Every culture needs its own local, sacred center, that cannot be broken if the group is to survive. Communication across the barriers of culture is necessary for a world community, but from firm cultural bases. The complete surrender of cultural identity is as dangerous as too little openness. Home requires rootedness, at-easeness, and regeneration. Von Uexkull describes the importance of rootedness in his concept of lived-world (*umwelt*). Feeling at home is a state of awareness; losing the feeling may cause a crisis of anxiety.

As ecosystems mature, so can human beings. Maturity allows the development of the narrow ego of a child into the comprehensive structure of an adult human being. The capitalized concept refers to the development of a deep identification with all life forms. This concept is known in the history of philosophy under various names: The universal self, the Atman, or the absolute. Maturity is linked to the increase of identification with, and care for, others. Albert Schweitzer noticed the expanding circle of care from family to humanity to animals, although cultures have different emphases.

5.2.1.3. Richness as a Property of a Good Place

Richness, and the ideas of diversity, variance, and challenge, emerge from the properties of places and ecosystems, that is, from openness, diversity and flexibility. And these arise from the properties of the field, from difference, limit, discretion and unfolding.

The boundary of a human place is open to the external supply of energy and materials. It is open to human movement in and out. Its structure, of independent units, allows this. Its functional use and storage of energy allow this. Its typical patterns of connectivity contribute to the whole pattern. As a result of its place in geographic context, it receives challenges in the form of weather and earth movements.

Species richness may stabilize ecosystem properties, such as NPP. Frank and McNaughton (1991) showed that plant community structure (and productivity and biomass) is more stable when a greater richness of species is present.

Reality for an amoeba is less than for a fish and much less than for a human. The richness of experience is in proportion to an organism's capacity to receive and decipher and influence the proximate environment. But the organism receives from reality what it puts in, that is, it enriches reality.

Good places should be in proximity to other systems and paths, other systems for energy and material exchanges, and paths for human goods and the exchange of ideas. Proximity relates to richness and challenge. What is impaired in the absence of a rich ecology is the individual's knowledge, not only as a person, but as a member of a species. Harold Searles' thesis is that the environment constitutes one of the most important ingredients of human psychological existence. There is within the individual a sense of relatedness to the total environment. Searles needs to expand the limit, as Schweitzer does regarding the concern of ethics, to include the wider sphere of all that lives.

5.2.1.4. Conviviality as a Property of a Good Place

Adaptation, and its ideas of completeness, conviviality, and cooperation, emerge from the properties of places and ecosystems, from participation, development, and complexity. And these come from the properties of the field, from registration, integration, connection, and renewal.

A deep relationship with a place is as necessary as one with other humans. Without it, existence loses much of its significance. A range of experiences can spring from a place, from depression to the peak experiences described by Maslow. The opposite feeling is possible where there is no richness of place; in the dullness of place, everything becomes oppressive and life becomes tedious. But, this and the drudgery is part of a commitment to place; it is acceptance of restrictions. The richness of life forms contributes to the realization of human values and are also values in themselves; the Deep Ecology movement emphasizes this, also. Simple species contribute to richness and diversity of life. The history of life presupposes an increase of diversity and richness.

Humans adapt to place as they live, as their communities live, over many generations. They become attached to a place. Attachment to place is a form of deep love, from which many other virtues for living well, such as frugality and humility, spring. Place allows us to rediscover a participating consciousness and a symbiotic connection to the living earth. Participation means living with other species, the literal definition of conviviality. The organization of perception, meaning, and thought is intimately related to specific places. When the symbols of a world lose their meaning, through wrongful application or abstraction, sickness and disintegration result.

The Masai people, for instance have survived many challenges, including drought and disease, years of colonial rule and partition, the intrusion of the free market of modern economics, and political control by new states, Kenya and Tanzania. They demonstrate that a herding society without political leaders and with social autonomy can survive with large-scale social systems. Many other peoples, such as the Aborigine of Australia and the Desana of Peru show developmental responses to environmental, population and social challenges; they have developed adaptive, problem-solving, intensifying social structures of their own.

5.2.1.5. Consistency of a Good Place

Consistency and its related synonyms, abidingness, tension, and restraint emerge from the properties of places and ecosystems, from stability, constancy, resistance, resilience, and accommodation. And, these are based on the properties of the field, constancy, regularity, and endurance.

Stability is the ability to maintain the identity of a system under the flow of external forces and disturbances. Stability can be refined as constancy, resistance, resilience, and accommodation. Stability can be related to ideas of compartmentalization, communications, richness of interactions, and connections. Stability is a complex topic.

Constancy means stability or continuity, in general, or the state of being in a continuous flow or coherent whole for a duration. Resistance is the ability to withstand disturbance to a system. Resilience is the ability to recover from stress. It is similar to elasticity, which refers to the time required to recover initial structure/function after some kind of damage; it is the speed that a system returns to former state following a disturbance (measure in community matrix). Accommodation is the ability to absorb change and still maintain the system identity. The system adapts to disturbance. It incorporates new things. It tolerates new levels of things. It fits the changes within the structure and function of the system.

When humans are part of the mix they may tend to try to preserve short-term stability by reducing the flexibility of the system. This allows more control for minor disturbance but reduces the ability of the system to response to large-scale disturbance or interference. Stability allows security and confidence in knowing, and this allow exploration and play.

5.2.1.6. Health of a Good Place

Health, harmony and vigor are properties of good human places; they emerge from the properties of places and ecosystems, such as vitality, productivity, renewal, and continuity. And these properties can be derived from the properties of the field, from process and flow to unfolding.

Vigor means strength or vitality. Vigor is related to productivity, that is, the ability to convert energy into living forms and the ability to incorporate materials into living forms. Vigor is related to the amount and speed of productivity. Health is a dynamic measure of ecosystem organization, vigor, and resilience. Organization is described by diversity and connectivity; and resilience is a measure of reaction to stress. Too much stress can lead to unsustainable patterns of behavior; continuous stress leads to a breakdown of processes that becomes irreversible—the system dies.

Health is a dynamic quality of the whole, the result of a harmonious interaction of all the analyzable parts that comprise the whole forest with the surrounding larger environment. The addition of humans to the mix does not necessarily make a place less healthy or vital. Especially if human adaptation to place is slow over time, giving other entities time to adjust.

5.2.2. Dynamics

The properties are part of a structure of a good place, but they must be expressed in action, as part of the process of open systems. Many properties can be described, but pieces could be missing. The structure is necessary to contain and fit the properties, regardless of what is missing. Some properties, especially those dynamics underlying ordered behaviors, are lost in the process of analysis and are denoted by symbolic terms such as 'field' or 'persistence.'

The normal operation of our adaptive activities, such as agriculture, urbanization, or industrialization, are resulting in degradation of wild ecosystems and the biocide of entire species. We are facing a massive failure of interspecies dynamics, which will have devastating ecological and psychological effects. Only by creating a new ecological politics, with new regional and global functions, can we restore meaning and health to the large wild systems on which we depend. At a basic level, the integrated dynamics of nature and human nature reflects the methodology of our human thinking. And, this is what needs to be enlarged with new metaphors and perspectives that address the entire planetary system.

5.3. Expanding Possibilities with Ecological Politics

Ecological, economic, social, and religious phenomena are part of the broad definition of politics. The basic goal of such a politics is the "survival of the community" as William Ophuls identifies it. Politics is the interactive means of providing the basic food and necessities of a community. As survival is survival in nature, politics rests on an ecological foundation. The organization of a community must be in accord with natural laws and limits. Political participation depends on information, much of which can be provided by observers and scientists.

There can be no separation of politics and ecology. Every political act has ecological consequences and every ecological decision is a political demand for control over use of the environment. Ecological consciousness can complement political consciousness.

The ecological, social, and political problems of today do not have simple disciplinary solutions. The problems are cosmological and must be solved on that level. But a single cosmology cannot solve all problems in all places. Where human understanding is still underdeveloped, humanity cannot afford to suppress the diversity of thought necessary for adaptation to the diversity of environments, or to eliminate ecosystems and the societies adapted to them, which explains why archaic cultures are valuable.

Practicing holistic, or metapolitics, is the recognition that humans are part of a larger community, a larger whole that includes all humanity and all the earth, with its species, habitats and resources.

5.3.1. Deciding Goals of Ecological Politics

The government of a community is a framework to maintain the lives of people. For the original archaic peoples, tribal teachers were adequate. In our representational republic, representatives are relatively uneducated, except in law, and less capable of institutional change.

The functions of government are to support the functions of politics with specific actions, such as: To make laws; to decide the meaning of the laws, how they are applied and related to a Constitution; to lead the country and to make sure the laws are obeyed. These action specifically include: To protect the nation; to command the military; to manage internal affairs; to coordinate national activities; to manage external affairs; to represent the nation to other nations; to coordinate trade; to coordinate information; and, to coordinate education.

5.3.1.1. Expressing the Purpose of Government

Central government has lost sight of its own purpose, which is not the sum of special interests or its own desire for perpetuation. Government has always had other reasons for existing. Some of these reasons are to:

   1. Hold a vision of the common good, where 'common' means common to all beings in the ecological community as well. Make goals conscious, with some flexibility to enhance the vision over time. Balance public and private interests.

   2. Coordinate the means to satisfy the long-term needs of the community, balancing freedom and regulation. Tie rates of consumption to the limits of the system—this means controlling resources and land use, in essence determining the physical shape of the community.

   3. Regulate the community. Link it to cultural values. Determine the closure and openness of the community; rates of increase or decrease, through births, deaths, or immigration. Encourage or discourage some forms of technology or trade. Provide work opportunities to members.

   4. Protect the community from internal and external threats: natural disasters, criminal elements, and other communities. Most of these threats are unavoidable. Some are long-term and rare; others are constant and have low intensity. Some are part of the human condition; others are the result of historical balances that cannot be restored easily or quickly. Be aware of them and minimize the damage.

5.3.1.2. Increasing Participation

John Dewey believed that personal face-to-face communities were necessary to a free and open government. The local communities need not be isolated as they have been in the past; they are more open and active, connected to other larger communities. Government requires trust and goodwill; these arise more easily in communities of acquaintances.

   Citizenship is too complex for television or even electronic global villages; it must exist in the community, in person, in place, where individuals can learn about each other in context. Government by local meeting assumes the common sense and wisdom of the common person in an open exchange of belief and need.

   Often this kind of involvement takes more time than just voting annually or having one person decide for many. The effect of presenting a problem before a traditional American Indian council was to slow down response by passing it to the entire constituency and getting a consensus. This ensured due consideration.

   To encourage the participation necessary for effective democracy, or communism or socialism for that matter, government should solicit public opinion. Land-use agencies do so. Government should offer real power to people—power should devolve to lowest level—by changing the local political institutions to start. Montana or Vermont in the U.S. offer examples of how to change local participation.

5.3.1.3. Taking & Yielding Powers

Central government must shrink in order for local government can expand. Some things must be done at a national level, such as the protection of watersheds, rivers, and the atmosphere, to make sure of minimal or median protection. Some protection must be enforced at the international level.

Following the federal model, delegated powers go to the highest level, and reserved powers to the community. So, a new national government would coordinate internal and external defense and security; maintain law and order; and, set ground rules on economic exchange to ensure fairness. The most important responsibility of government is to set standards for itself and its institutions. The constitution would instruct the courts to interpret clauses as narrowly as possible.

The new nation would have an administrative department to handle taxation, budgeting, and purchasing. It may coin local money, perhaps on the model of the Local Employment and Trade System—LETS—on Vancouver Island in Canada, which records credits and debits on a computer, which can then only be used locally. There may be departments to protect the civil rights and liberties of the people and a department to protect the environment. Environmental disputes could be resolved by mediation, as was developed in Seattle in the U.S. in 1980s. The nation would also conduct foreign policy, provide technical services to communities, and maintain regulatory offices.

To avoid insularity, being set against the rest of the world, each nation could create an office of global communication, which could set up connections similar to sister cities program. It might be beneficial to join confederations of other similar areas, especially those that could offer complementary crops, or a larger union, such as the United States, for preferred trading.

Spending on education, roads, welfare would be done at local level. There is some risk, especially with education or wilderness restoration, but the breakdowns and errors will not be devastating as with centralized planning. Citizens will need to do some of the work of government as well as make the decisions. They should have total control over some things. The judgments of the people are more important than the efficiency of those judgments. It may not be necessary to have many separate authorities or committees; it might be better to integrate policy-making bodies so they are not too specialized.

With centralization of functions, money has become the primary source of security for most people. Welfare, as giving money to those who do not have it, may reduce homelessness or disease, but it cannot restore family. Family needs a supporting community context—institutions. Decentralization, and the power it would return to local communities, may also help the family as a source of security. Money is an enormous simplifier, but many things cannot be simplified. Decentralizing would make government and economics small scale enough to be understandable and manageable.

Decentralized communities fitted to their ecological location are more suitable and livable than urban spreads. Some cities may still be fairly large and dense like those envisioned by Paolo Soleri. Some may be smaller and rural like those suggested by Murray Bookchin. Their relation to support areas would be more explicit and include large amounts of natural and domestic vegetation. As much as possible, the cycles of materials would be closed.

As cities become more sustainable, their forms may change. They may become more compact, with more multiple-use streets, as a focus for human activity; buildings could use solar power, efficient heating, perhaps integrate roof-top crops; older buildings could be integrated into new groupings to integrate services, play, and work, with living; local public spaces and services could be central; derelict land could be regenerated, either as garden areas or new construction.

Preconditions to a sustainable, steady state, economy include pollution control and the redistribution of resources more equally. The redistribution of resources and improvement of environmental quality are more important than increased production by sophisticated technology. This strategy calls for social and educational organization more than technological style. Styles of technology must be determined by culture and context. Such development requires a local authority working with suitable economic and ecological conditions. No authority can be effective without the participation of the people.

5.3.1.4. Protecting Ways of Life

A government could impose a limit on the intensity of development of the entire area, with transferable development rights (TDRs) assigned to each unit of area. Any project would have a TDR value—25 for an apartment building, for example, or 1 for an individual home; TDRs could be bought or traded from other landowners. All land could be held in communal ownership and leased to farms and businesses, except preservation and conservation lands.

Compartmentalization avoids the need to compromise every ecosystem for human use. Multiple use systems should only be part of the picture. First, the government could ensure a protected environment of mature ecosystems, then productive systems, and then multiple use, and urban areas. This could be done through function (not activity) zoning. The landscape needs to be zoned (compartmentalized) to provide a safe balance between protected ecosystems and used ones. Restrictions on land and water are one means of avoiding overpopulation or overexploitation.

Long before the limits of food or space are reached, or the ecological balance is lost, or a vital minimum is exhausted, phosphorus, for example, the quality of life will sink lower. Regardless of how much protein or energy can be provided to support human life, human happiness will be problematic in large, insecure populations. The question is not how many people agriculture and technology can support in one place at once, but what kind of life is possible for those who have no choice but to live in that place. The limiting factor is that condition in the environment that approaches the limits of tolerance of individuals. The population density may be the limiting factor. It may be living space. It may be wilderness. It may be beauty—aesthetic space.

At a limit, the cost of change accelerates. We seem to understand technological limits, to sailing ships and computer chips for instance, but not to individuals or groups, not environmental or ecological. Calculating these kind of limits is difficult—too much data, too much uncertainty.

Peter Drucker points out that economists from Adam Smith to the conservative F. A. Hayek argued that it is impossible for governments to control or manage the economy, especially in an information age. Recognizing, on the basis of mathematical models of complexity, that detailed management of the biosphere is beyond human capacity, a government should minimize its management, to coordination of communities or larger alliances. The biosphere is dominated by natural communities of which we are largely still ignorant. Detailed planning of complex open systems is not necessary. Planners are not in a position to attempt detailed models of future situations because many relevant parameters remain unidentified, and many of those known cannot be quantified. Plans can be made within the limits of variables, although it is not safe to be limited by lethal variables, as Gregory Bateson recognized. Closeness to limits reduces flexibility, that is, uncommitted potential for change. Vagueness and lack of detail are acceptable in planning, because people will fill in the details. Furthermore, it is almost impossible to plan every detail of a dynamic chaotic system. That does not mean stagnation, that a rice field must always remain a rice field or a town a town. What the government should preserve is the pattern, not the details, is limits, not directions. The limits are to be applied to scale not development.

Therefore, we must limit human intrusion in every system. Government should zone some segments to be free from human activity, and tailor human-made systems to approximate the form of the natural systems replaced. Interference is a broad term for the negative side of human activities. There are numerous forms of human interference: Overexploitation, introduction of exotic species, pollution of air and water, and the subsumption of habitats, in shape and size. Interference is caused by large human population growth, with its poverty, inadequate metaphors and images that are too anthropocentric or short-term, uncontrolled change or transformations, as a result of colonialization or revolution, and political or economic failures, from wars or market forcing.

5.3.1.5. Paying Costs & Leveling Extremes

Relative to European communities, many nations have less funding for public services, such as parks and public transportation. Some nations have traded public support for higher levels of private affluence, which has not made people any happier. In fact, they are more insecure; and they can become far poorer, and then second-class and neglected.

Many cultures should try, like Sweden, England and Japan have tried, to weaken the connection of material reward for achievement. Income distribution is too unequal. Full internationalization through trade would bring only greater extremes, which most populations can least afford.

The communities could levy taxes on property. But, there is a discrepancy in the wealth of communities. The nation could collect income taxes, and communities could claim a percentage of taxes collected. The community and nation could both tax the same bases: Income, sales, meals, property, and fuel, as many nations are now. The nation would set a ceiling on each tax; the community rate could be zero on some. Or the communities could do all taxes and give the national government a percentage, although differences in wealth might be maintained; then the state could return a percentage to make up equality in education and environmental protection. The important thing is that taxes are used to direct development and reflect the true costs of the society that people want.

Government could change taxation procedures to reduce growth instead of stimulating it. Talcott Parkinson suggests that taxation beyond a certain point yields declining marginal returns. Government could use a single tax rate flat at some percentage, perhaps from 10 to 25; and then pay everyone a fixed amount of income for basic needs, from 3,000-10,000 USD.

Similarly, property taxes could be appropriately scaled to use. One way to keep farms as farms is to tax land by use. The more important the use, farming for instance, the lower the taxes. Buying farmland for shopping centers would result in discouragingly high taxes.

It is difficult to persuade people to pay more in taxes, to vote to keep less of their income. But, through education or understanding, a culture could expand the understanding of the self and expand self-interest in that way. Some catastrophe might work towards equality, but that might have other high costs to society.

Of course, most of these taxes could be eliminated entirely, if only environmental uses and losses were taxed. Some taxes, such as luxuries or heroic income, might be maintained temporarily until the extremes of ownership and wealth are leveled. This form is expanded in later sections.

5.3.1.6. Meeting Limits of Government

When a place has a reputation for being small and livable, it attracts more people, until it is no longer small and livable. But, imposing limits and stopping growth are problematic. Government could impose limits on birth through licenses, perhaps risking rebellion, through limits on housing and public services, possibly causing shantytowns, or through peer pressure, which could contribute to social disorder. Nature is self-organizing, and, society is self-organizing, but we need to recognize some limits and define others, and take responsibility for keeping to those limits in order that the self-organizing process not break down. Limits are fundamental to understanding nature and life.

5.3.2. Applying Ecological Planning & Limits

A number of proposed plans to heal the earth and improve human communities have been presented in popular books. Many of them are too philosophical and general, suggesting that we could change values without showing how or urging us to alleviate some of the symptoms without addressing the disease. Other plans, such as the *Limits to Growth*, are too global. And still others, such as *Design with Nature*, are less concerned with limits than with basic conservation. *Goals for Mankind* offers a similar compendium of global goals that can essentially be summarized to be health and freedom for people in a healthy environment. Many of these plans offer admirable models, but little in the way of specific goals or paths.

A plan should consider the whole system. Communities should be designed for an optimal fit within the limits of the system. Ecological planning considers an optimum or satisfactory population within one ecosystem, although it is connected to others by trade for some necessities or luxuries. This kind of planning is a conscious adaptation of the benefits of technology to the traditional idea of physical, as well as cultural, limits. Direct observation and traditional knowledge yield far more "information" about the societies of animals than autopsies and mathematical models. An outline of a comprehensive plan is presented, to deal with some of the implications, as well as question them.

1. Identify our place within its natural boundaries. Most places exist in a uniquely identifiable ecosystem, with recognizable boundaries and a unique history and character.

2. Calculate the optimum amount of wilderness to preserve the natural cycles indefinitely. If the current area is less than our calculations, restore the difference and set it aside as a reserve.

3. In the remaining area, zone areas for appropriate use, including conservation, preservation, reservation, and artificial areas (with historical, cultural, and functional importance).

4. Identify the resources needed for human use, including raw materials and the productivity of the areas. This productivity can be used to calculate a base line population.

5. Apply cultural modes—in style, values, and technology—to set limits on technology and population. Preserve the cultural values. Renewable resources will sustain a population longer than energy capital like oil or gas.

As part of the formulation of a plan, we have to examine the natural and cultural histories of a place. We need to understand interactions in the ecosystem, as it was with no humans, as it was lightly settled, and as it is now, dominated by humanity.

5.3.2.1. Limits & Planning

Our modern cosmology, with its basis on machine metaphors and the principles of plenitude gets in trouble because it does not understand how basic the concept of limits is to the physical universe, to life, to ecosystems, and to human constructs, such as cities and economics. Limits are important at all levels, starting with the physical.

The limits of the universe, like the speed of light or quantum of a field, put limits on freedom. Events are limited to localities; size limits function; history limits development. Biological order is built on physical and chemical orders. That is why life is limited to such a narrow range of conditions. And that is why the most complex orders are vulnerable to changes in their substrates; energetic radiation can alter and destroy an individual, a small change in climate can destroy crops and civilizations. Complex orders always depend on simple orders. The success of life depends on miniaturization, where a prodigious number of overlapping mechanisms are packed in a small space. These are persistent by virtue of built in regulation circuits; and open enough for novelty.

Life involves a vast number of interacting structures. Living consists of complex behaviors whose limits are defined by rules of order that can be empirically described. The earth is suitable for life because of three kinds of limits: Solar radiation has stayed within certain limits for 4 billion years; the biogeochemical cycles of oxygen, carbon, nitrogen, phosphorus, sulfur, water have stayed within certain limits; and, the environment has been constant enough for organic evolution, but variable enough for natural selection to be challenged.

The earth is suitable for humanity because of another set of limits: It is covered with a vast array of ecosystems that interact and in which plants and animals create niches; there is material cycling and energy flow within limits; the prolific nature of biological reproduction, which is limited by processes such as predation and by material and energy cycles; and the carrying capacity can sustain a given amount of life.

Cosmologies make the world manageable by limiting it. They are also tuned to the limits of the local ecology, within their knowledge of interactions; the long-range ecological consequences of drainage, irrigation or overexploitation contribute to the deaths of cultures. But many archaic cosmologies are a form of tens and limitation. Most try for adaptation before domination, according to Gerardo Reichel-Dolmatoff.

Human cosmologies themselves are limited and contradictory. All cosmologies cause destruction and waste; all produce the opposite of the good intended. Archaic and modern, occidental and oriental worldviews are complementary but not complete. The very circumstance that makes each cosmology unique—being in a unique place—ensures that each is limited. Often, a cosmology is accepted as unquestioningly as a language, technology or place.

Cosmologies have a sense of place, with its beings and features, which is necessary for information on how to live and to get food. The ecological benefits of rootedness are that people will take care of a place if they realize they are going to be there for a thousand years. Having a place means that the inhabitant has stock in it and participates in its unfolding, through planting and caring. Detailed understanding of plants in a locale allow gathering of food and medicine. People in place (being in place as used here means in a human scale in unique surroundings) acquire a sense of community, nonhuman and human; shared set of values and concerns; health and spiritual benefit. An ethic, ecologically, is a limitation on freedom of action in the struggle for existence, according to Aldo Leopold.

5.3.2.2. Political Limits
Politics is the art and science of human government. The first goal of politics is to ensure the survival of the human community. Then, it has to maintain the affairs of that community. Politics is the interactive means of providing the basic food and necessities of a community. As survival is survival in nature, politics rests on an ecological foundation. The organization of a community must be in accord with natural laws. Political participation depends on information, much of which can be provided by observation and science.

Robert Bellah and associates make three distinctions of politics, of which politics of the community is the first. It is followed by politics of interest, where different interests are pursued, according to agreed-upon neutral rules; conflict tends to overwhelm consensus. Finally, the politics of the nation addresses the "higher" affairs of the nation. It is more concerned with leadership than citizenship. Like the politics of interest, it accepts the status quo of relations of power or distributions of inequality. Symbolism becomes more important; perhaps because now the citizen diminishes in importance and the symbolism unites and includes them minimally.

Government has become subservient to economic actors, according to John B. Cobb, partly because the ideology of economics is so positive. It proclaims that continued growth will solve most of the problems of modern civilization, from poverty to conflict, although the promise has not been fulfilled in the past 800 years. The problems have increased: Food shortages, housing shortages, energy shortages, unemployment, inequality of opportunity or goods, environmental deterioration, increase in weapons, and insecurity.

These problems continue due to the limits of politics. For example the size of society is a real limit; if there are too many people, within a limited territory or limited system, politics cannot provide them with an identity or control them. Size limits the distribution of things, such as food, housing, jobs and wealth, also. The time frame of the political society is also a limit; the short-range visions of national interest are often inimical to the long-range ecological requirements of the support system.

The participation of the members of a society is also a political limit. Communities have always had face-to-face limits, in terms of numbers of face-to-face encounters. In terms of distance, communities have always limits, also. The politics of community is small-scale and local. It is moral consensus is applied to daily operations.

Leadership is another limit; the pool of applicants is usually relatively narrow. The desire to use power is a limit. The will to power does not seem limited to the community, as does participation. The will to power can be found in human communities over 10-13,000 years. It seems to have evolved from the simple domination of other community members to all of nature.

Security is a problem for local communities and national governments. It becomes more difficult to protect against most any kind of weapons. Perhaps the solution is a global one, with the coordinated change in national policies and worldwide distribution of excess wealth.

Some facts result in motivation or fear, fear of the future in general, or of the reactions of others, in general. One response is a defensiveness in face of an unpredictable future. Thus, psychological limits intersect with political limits.

5.3.2.3. Limits of Human Populations

A number of recent studies have suggested that the human population of the earth could be much larger. Several other studies have recommended lower populations based on resource availability. All of the studies mentioned are concerned with finding a maximum human population. This thought experiment suggests ways to calculate an optimum population on a region by region basis, using a deductive, synthetic, conceptual model based on data generated from research on net primary productivity (NPP) and net community productivity (NCP). An NCP model is used to calculate regional goals for populations, considering cultural and economic goals. A deductive approach is necessary because accurate measurements of productivities in most ecosystems are lacking and exactness in some values can be misleading. A synthetic approach is necessary to integrate quantitative and qualitative data. In combining measures of qualitative and quantitative, it is simpler to set aside the first and then to calculate the second. The model must be conceptual because of the inherent fuzziness of the systems.

5.3.3. *Controlling Political Issues & Areas of Concern*

Growth is a first area of concern. Most cities and almost every human area is experiencing growth. Economics requires growth. Mesarovic and Pestel stated that "the issue for the economy is not to grow or not to grow; it is how to grow, and for what purpose." Growth was confused with development. They claim that if a workable world system is to emerge, it must be after the establishment of an organic pattern of growth. They assume continued growth. Due care is devoted to describing such a pattern and contrasting it with other, tragically inapplicable patterns of growth. Their treatment of the world system itself was regionalized and multileveled. They recommended that the establishment of organic growth was necessary with no need for special no-growth policies for populations or economies. They assumed that further industrial growth will continue, that economic growth is good, and that this growth solves human problems as long as it is organic.

Exponential growth is said to be bad, and organic growth is said to be good. In fact, although organic growth is better, there is little difference during a world crisis; both reach asymptotes of suffering. One need only regard the population crashes of lemmings to see that organic growth can go wrong. In the organic world, growth is healthy only when the rate of change is decelerative in the long run; cancer and population are constant or accelerative. Mesarovic and Pestle failed to realize that continued economic growth in any form is a threat to the stability of the biosphere. Furthermore, they assumed that we are limited to only those two kinds of growth, but that is palpably untrue.

Three other types of growth can be distinguished: Additive, an accumulation of more; replicative, an accumulation of more through reproduction; and mutualistic, where all agents change structure, as in the process of meiosis in cell development.

Rapid European expansion occurred at rates rarely exceeding a growth of 1% per year, and with unparalleled opportunities for expansion into sparsely settled areas, including North America, Australia, South America, and South Africa. Archaic countries do not have these opportunities; violent population growth has wrecked its hope for development, ravaging every resource. Growth itself requires greater material support for houses, schools, medicine, and jobs. The observation that exponential growth in a finite environment cannot continue is indisputable. And rates of exploitation are even more important than the rates of growth. By definition, the "first world" is the industrial West, with its outposts on major continents—Taiwan in Asia, South Africa in Africa, Israel in the Middle East, Australia, and others.

Karl Marx conceived of the idea of the 'second world,' while studying in the British Museum. Although it was intended to be born from the first world, the nonindustrial, agricultural, feudal Soviet Union formed the basis of the second world, which is now dedicated to the same ideal of material progress; the second mirrors the first. The third world is a new conception; 'poor' nations became 'undeveloped,' then 'under-developed,' then 'developing,' then the 'third world.' Hardin calls this ballet of terms the 'Flight of the Euphemisms.' Any terms, like undeveloped or poor, are distortions to some extent; they classify only according to statistical, economic or technological attainments, not by wisdom or happiness. Although the term 'third world' is used in this book for identification, on occasion, individual nations will be referred to as archaic, traditional, agrarian or industrial, or be named by place. The third world is really the mother of the first two. It contains the "wretched of the earth," in Franz Fanon's phrase, left behind in sullen poverty and gentle greatness. The first two world victimize the third by stealing its resources. The rich become richer, while the poor struggle to live. Ironically, with the value of scarce resources, some 'third world' nations, like Saudi Arabia, are now among the very richest.

The very poor have been romanticized to have a quiet vision of life on a human scale in peace. But this is just the hope of the frustrated and greedy that somewhere else people are more noble and honest. With the advent of radio and television, poor peoples have learned to want material wealth. And they can see what they are being denied. The economy has been growing almost constantly since it has been studied. We have been trying to force it to grow, rather than to let it contract. Peter Drucker reminded his peers that economics is still the dismal science, that everything has a cost (and therefore a price?), and that nothing can be consumed until it is produced.

The economy may not contract; it may continue to develop without growing. There is no necessary association between development and growth. Growth means an increase in size. Development means the introduction of an innovation.

The relations between labor, capital and the value of resources are changing rapidly. Capital investment is no longer economical. The old capitalist market economy is shifting to a neomercantilist one where some global agency will grant charters to local companies to husband dwindling resources. Resource limits may spur the change from growth to development.

J. S. Mill wrote that beyond the progressive state lies the stationary state; each advance is to approach it. Mill wrote that the stationery state was a metastatic state, after the Greek words meaning 'changing in place.' Mill's vision of a stable state was a response to the goal of industrial society. Technological progress would abridge labor, not necessarily increase production. In a state of equity, persons would have room for solitude and leisure development. But Mill did not believe that 'man' was bound to protect nature.

H.E. Daly concludes that the steady state economy is necessary and desirable. He notes that in the definition of economics, as the study of the allocation of scarce means among competing ends, the entire ends-means spectrum is not considered. Only intermediate ends or means are considered, not ultimate. He anchors ultimate means in physics and ultimate ends in religion. So economics falsely concludes that the middle ranges represent the entire spectrum.

A stationary economy is not synonymous with stagnant; there is always room for developing and increasing scope of mental culture. It could be highly sophisticated, dynamic, and imaginative. It is scarcely necessary to remark that a stationary condition of capital and population implies no stationary state of human improvement. There would be as much scope as ever for all kinds of mental culture and moral and social progress, as much room for improving the art of living, and more likelihood of its being improved.

A community is forced to accept an upper limit, beyond which it cannot grow any further. Further growth results in destruction or disruption of itself and nature. Production needs to be stabilized in a steady state economy, a mature economy, like a mature ecosystem, where processes and cycles are constant. A steady state economy must be based on natural laws and ethical principles. Natural laws include thermodynamics and ecological theories. Economic development will require technology. Ecologically sound technologies will minimize stress to the environment. Rules of economics, laws of nature and ethical principles must be related. W. I. Thompson projects a movement from succession economy to a mature economy in a global centripetal reconsolidation of planetary culture.

There is another distinction between growth and development. The social approach to development makes it sometimes irrelevant to discuss global limits to growth. Local limits are far more significant to majority of population. Regardless of how much food exists, people will starve unless they can get it.

Redistribution of resources and improvement of environmental quality are more important than increased production by sophisticated technology. The natural capacity of regional photosynthesis must be limiting factor in development, especially in tropical and subtropical areas. This development calls for social and educational organization more than technological style. Styles of technology must be determined by culture and context. Such development requires a local authority working with suitable economic and ecological conditions. No authority can be effective without the participation of populace. The diversity of types of agricultural and cultural habits may be analyzed from either adaptation to ecosystems or their transformation of them.

To stop growth, a strict regulation of the productive system is necessary. States should be able to control which products are made, with which technology. The machine with a governor excludes any other states besides a steady state. Corrective action is brought about by difference; it is error activated. Practical implications of the steady state are that nonrenewable resources will be conserved as much as possible, by recycling, while erosion, depletion and pollution are minimized; energy sources may be greatly decentralized and diverse. But a stationary state cannot go on forever; there will be an inevitable decline in resource accessibility. Therefore the most desired state is not stationary, but gradually adjusting to resources and values. The nature of evolution is constant adjustment. The human population may need to steadily decrease over thousands of years. Georgescu-Rogen advised even further that we must expect a steadily decreasing state. Since we do not now know enough about reserves and the rate of renewal of some renewable resources or about technological inventions, the metastatic state is reasonable.

5.3.4. Rights Justice & Law as Political Issues
Ethics and morals can lead to formal rules and applications in governments. Basing them in an ecological framework allows comparison and selection.

5.3.4.1. Rights
An ecological ethical model is not distorted by human needs and wants when it argues for the preservation of animals and habitats themselves, because they are, as they are. Paul Shepard says the argument is not new, and that its application is ambiguous because "unlimited rights" will conflict with human interest. But, there are two bad assumptions: That human interests are not ambiguous—they are—and that animals will be granted unlimited rights—they will not. Rights seem to follow the expansion of the sphere of ethics, as formal statements of intuitive knowledge. But, codifying rights is more difficult, especially for philosophers, who tend to limit rights with a series of restrictions. For example, a contractual theory assumes a perfect detachment and a rational debate of rules. Animals and imbeciles are left out. Scott Lehman argues that natural objects are not the subjects of experience, certain animals excepted, and so cannot possess rights. He limits experience to mental states. Perhaps he means nervous system states. Some philosophers maintain that a right is a claim to something; others, that it is an entitlement. Richard Watson takes reciprocity as central to the general concepts of rights and duties; few animals and no natural objects have rights intrinsically. He mentions that some primates and mammals are moral entities because they are self-conscious, have free will, understand principles, and intend to act accordingly. But the assumption of self-consciousness would rule out children and feebleminded adults, as well as most living beings. So, a larger definition of claim or reciprocity is needed, without regard for contracts and mutual duties.

When humanity was divided into citizens and slaves, there was no freedom. When it was divided into governors and governed, freedom was advanced by providing the governed with protection against the tyranny of governors. When people became self-governing, protection was needed against majority opinions, by distinguishing between the individual and society. New contraries—public and private—provide clarification of rights. Rights protect the interests of those holding rights. Natural rights are the rights of an underclass that has not been granted legal rights. These "natural rights" are used by minorities to legitimate their claims against controlling powers.

Rights and obligations were first thought of in a political context consisting of customs and practices within and between states. In the 17th century they were thought of in a constitutional context, where forms of government were established to protect natural rights. Now they are thought of in a human context. Freedoms of—speech, worship—depend on institutional protection and are political rights. Freedoms from—want, fear—are extensions of economic rights. Freedoms for—pleasure, reproduction—are biological rights. Pierre Dansereau categorizes the rights of individuals as:
- Physiological: Light, air, water, food, shelter, procreation
- Psychological: Minimum space, forming attachments, free from shocks
- Social: Choice, work, association

- Economic: Income, dispose of property, use resources
- Political: Education, information, participation in decision
- Religious: Adherence to a creed, opportunity to join in groups.

These rights are only very analogous to those of other beings. The extension of rights to animals and plants does not deny any traditional human rights. Animals should be accorded higher moral regard and legal standing to reflect the intrinsic worth afforded by their existence and sentience. Welfare laws to conserve species and to guarantee humane treatment in research, transportation, and slaughter indicate a growing concern among people. A new ethic can keep animals free from human intervention, prejudice, or overuse. Animals should be preserved because they are as they are; their existence is moral justification. Their intrinsic worth is independent of the instrumental values imposed on them by humanity.

Rights seem to follow the expansion of the sphere of ethics, as formal statements of intuitive knowledge. Humanity has taken its own opportunities. These opportunities have been codified for centuries as rights. Now, we must allow other beings equal opportunities. The interrelatedness of life dictates the interrelatedness of rights. And these rights are necessary to the integrity of the whole planet. Humanity developed in a community of animals and plants, as part of a clade on the same tree of life. The quality of human life has always depended on the quality of animal life. Animals have sensations and feelings, as important to them as ours are to us.

The strongest argument for rights is interrelatedness in communities. It is a basis for assigning rights to ultrahuman nature. Existence implies intrinsic worth. Garrett Hardin considers interrelatedness, but interprets it narrowly. He considers rights as rules of competition; every right is a ploy in the struggle for existence, and every right implies an obligation to furnish it. This is good as far as it goes. Life is more than competition; it involves cooperation and play. Rights are formal rules for living together.

5.3.4.2. Justice & Law

Socrates argued in the Republic of Plato against the conception of justice as giving every man his due, and proposed a definition of justice as every man performing his proper function. This proportion of reward to function in the community was named distributive justice by Aristotle. It describes the right to participate in the benefits of science and culture.

If justice is a proportion set up in the community between men and goods, justice is also the restoration of the relation of men and goods, when disturbed. Aristotle called this justice, rectificatory. This has constituted the business of laws and courts. During the stage of universal rights, world order transfers the criterion from the nature of man to the community of men; both law and justice, obligations and rights are reduced to equity. Thus, new nations demand to participate in a common justice, as opposed to the extension of natural rights. How can the idea of equity be given determinate content and political force? Society should be organized on the basis of functions, not rights. Ecological rights could be based on functions. It is foolish not to assign rights to animals, plants and earth because of contractual formalities. Morality means living together; symbiosis means living together. We are living together with everything on the planet, and in the universe. Therefore we ought to extend rights to all beings. Human life depends on a matrix of life. The matrix is historical. It has duration; it extends from the past into a future of following lives. This gives the past and future rights. They are part of the continuity of relationships.

A principle of justice based on need can be extended to the ultrahuman community. It needs to be altered to account for unconscious, interdependent beings. The right to use nature is a right to share. Current legislation on animal experimentation and protection implicitly recognizes the right to live in a healthy habitat.

One problem with the current legal system is that all ultrahuman beings are given the status of inferior human beings, that is legal incompetents, thus keeping humans in a guardian role. A new legal category is needed that would respect the existence, competence, and excellence of natural beings. Christopher Stone recognizes that the judicial system has granted rights to a variety of inanimate holders, trusts, corporations, and nations, for instance. The legal system already operates with fictions. A new category would be an extension of the direction of law.

Formal law tends to seek guidance on normative issues from the general population, rather than from legal experts. People care for animals and wilderness. Natural rights are defined by positive laws and by negative restraints on behavior. Laws are needed to protect wilderness, now. Legal or religious action almost always precedes the general shift in conscience. The obligation to treat others equally includes an obligation to change human social patterns in the direction of equality.

5.3.5. *Moderating Cultural Interactions*
The final function of politics is to moderate how the culture interacts with others cultures. There are only a few basic was to do this: They can ignore each other. They can trade with the other culture. They can attack it. They can try to conquer or destroy it, or to control it or colonize it. Or, they can cooperate or compete in trade ideas.

Culture provides a filter between humans and other humans. So, culture can serve as another evolutionary filter. It designates what we attend or ignore. It has to screen less valuable information to avoid information overload. In a way, culture is like a trigger. It allows less information to activate the system. And, this is the only way to increase information handling without making the system larger and more complex—of course, this is what stereotypes and metaphors do, also. But, culture traps people in behaviors. Sometimes, violence can be used to escape such a trap. Politics has to direct interactions so that they benefit the culture and allow it to survive and prosper.

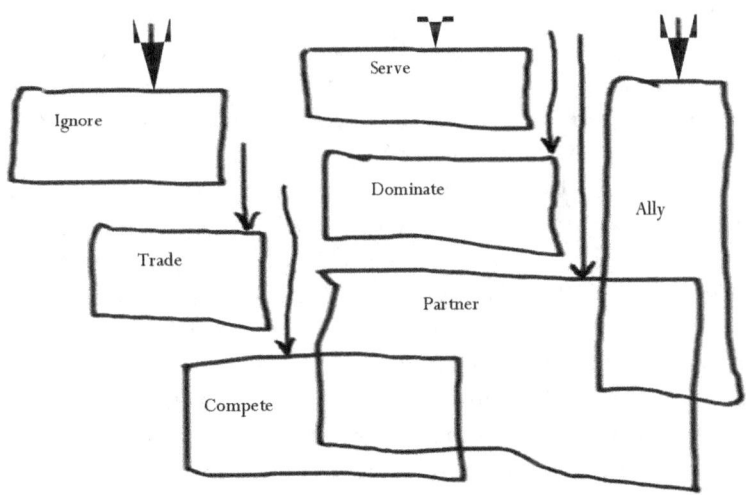

Figure 535-1. Map of cultural interactions

6.0. Describing a Thought Experiment in Government (Eutopian Framework)

When the word 'eutopias' has been used in literature, on occasion, as a counterpoint to 'utopias,' it has been used to describe a dream world of contradictions between rusticity and civilization, as in Bernard Mandeville's verse:

T'enjoy the world's conveniences,
Be famed in War, yet live in Ease
Without (great) Vices, is a vain
Eutopia seated in the brain.

This second meaning of utopia, 'eutopia,' is not used often. It means simply 'good place.' Good places do exist. They can be described, and even expanded. Some of the traits that make them good can be understood and repeated. A formal compilation of general properties of good places, a eutopian framework, can extend the application of utopian thought. Perhaps the number of good places can be increased with understanding of traditional ways and with more effective metaphors. Good places, and good societies, can be partly understood through certain paths of ecology and culture, which can be explored.

The earlier and foreign images of the world, created by archaic and classic cultures, are dismissed as being outmoded, useless, or unrealistic. Utopias have been offered as ideal schemes for social and political development. Sometimes, utopias offer memorable images. But, most utopias are rejected as irrelevant dreams and self-indulgent imaginings. Yet, as Pierre Dansereau has said, the failures of pollution, poverty, and urban decay are failures of the imagination. Rejecting the solutions of imagination, therefore, can only make the suite of human crises worse.

While utopian ideas might be stimulating, other traditional or accidental ideas might be applied more rapidly. Political realism dismisses utopian ideas as naïve and impractical. People are afraid that such ideas would destroy their investments in power and in collections of wealth. Political realism, however, is deficient in imagination and results, as well as deficient in courage and will. Despite great revolutions in technology and intensification, most people are still poor and threatened with displacement. Despite great revolutions in technology and living conditions over the past several thousand years, people are still very much shaped by unique cultures and small groups. These traditional institutions work very well on a local scale in a specific place. The information is available, but there is no framework to make it work, yet.

The images of good places, however, might be worth considering, with the images of wholeness. A complete eutopian structure would start from such an image of wholeness. It would be a framework that holds all the other pieces of solutions and makes them part of a whole thing. It would help us to understand the whole thing, the whole set of relations with people, land, and other beings, with other cultures and the ranges of technology. Eutopias would be a framework that holds many centers, beginning with the centers of different human cultures and including the centers of nonhuman communities and guilds. It has to address the whole, because the health of the whole depends on the health of the whole parts that make it up—the health of wildernesses, the health of civilizations, and the health of ecosystems, that is, inhabited places that are made through living.

Utopias may be impossible, but good places are possible. Good places already exist everywhere. Perhaps by logically working out the limits and adaptability of humanity, good places can be created by almost everyone.

Unlike either the political realism of nations or the ideal designs of utopias, a eutopian plan would be based on traditional human and cultural realities and would propose only modest and reasonable changes at local and international levels. For example, there are 500 million indigenous peoples in fifteen thousand distinct groups, such as the Uighur in China or the Kuna in Panama; and, there are over two billion people in hidden nations within massive political structures, such as the Azerbaijanis in the Soviet Union, the Kurds in Turkey and Iraq, or the Tibetans in China. Furthermore, there are regions in some countries, such as the Pacific Northwest in the United States or Wales in Britain, that may prefer independence to forced membership in a confederation. A Eutopian plan could allow any indigenous people with a traditional culture to become an independent nation without fear of conquest or compromise by existing political states. The benefits would outnumber those of a global monoculture and the negative aspects would be more manageable.

In eutopias, it is important to work with what exists, with what has already worked in place, with history and culture. This could start in California, Sri Lanka or any place that can support a nationhood aligned with a cultural history, without having a standard army or special currency.

The holistic framework would protect the creation of thousands of good places, or eutopias, based on human cultural realities and on the ecological limitations of places, that is, on homelands. These models already exist—they just need to be better defined and then protected from misguided ideas of growth and progress, as well as from the dominant, consuming industrial culture.

Culturally-based nations can provide a greater spectrum of intricate descriptions and possible relations than any one single thought experiment. That is why they need to be the basis of good-places-in-the-making. The framework is enriched by the ideals and visions of nations. This is consistent with the intuitive knowledge that many styles of life are simultaneously sustainable.

This is where eutopias would work effectively: Accepting the unpredictable nature of natural and social processes, yet managing adaptively on a micro-planning level. would incorporate tradition and working past elements, rather than breaking with them. As Edmund Burke, reflecting on the French Revolution, notes that society has gone through a natural process of development, forming traditions and institutions that provide rules of behavior known to the people. We tend to forget how much discipline already exists in every society. People abide by most rules, from driving on one side of the road to preserving their children from molestation.

Eutopias would have to accommodate different styles of living, from agriculture to hunting, fishing and herding. People have been nomads for a longer time than farmers or city dwellers. It might be better to accept that movement and dislocation is part of the harmony of life and try to minimize the negative effects, especially combined with consumerism and energy waste. The civilization of cultures is not a steady state, but it could be accommodated in a flexible framework.

A new model may solve some problems but will definitely create new problems; Nicolai Machiavelli reasoned that this would always happen. This is a good argument for eutopias, since changes would occur mostly on a small scale, easily correctable. That is why eutopias can be a framework, by limiting human evil and good to small places, with minimal control or competition.

There is no single model of government that will fit all cultures, all traditions, all needs or all nations. But, governments can be held to common standards through an international body. Eutopias tries to structure the global commonwealth of nations by proposing specific common goals, regarding weapons disbursement and population limits. It offers a consideration of distributive justice among nations and between the generations of every nation. It offers visions of culturally-based nations in equilibrium with nature, using ideas from ecological design and conservation biology. Such a eutopian process would solve many problems, from problems of scale to political inappropriateness. Not only would more nations exist in the framework, but alliances and networks would form and reform, as they do now. How would it work? A political framework, based on traditional cultures, coordinated by a global 'regulating' body, based on a modified United Nations, would be described and implemented.

The eutopian vision would start by addressing immediate needs for everyone, but then allow people to be as extravagant as they want within the general social limits. Most people like the place they live, and they like their culture, so it is not necessary to force them to stay in place or be what they are. That does not mean that they do not want to live better, just that they do not all want to be Swiss or U.S. citizens.

This framework would also reconcile the well-being of society with the health and continuity of living ecosystems. The international framework would provide paths for policing, international education, and other national needs. This plan would provide a path to independence and formal interdependence.

The eutopian framework is more than is a simple perspective; it is a design for a self-renewing process using proven cultural methods to improve human situations and environments. The frame is not a final goal but a way to allow the many small useful, culturally determined changes that we need for our survival on the planet as we like it.

Eutopias is a cheap solution because it uses the parts already in place. It is within reach of any people in any culture, regardless of how fast or technological, because it limits the ways of big, expensive solutions.

Eutopias is not a big law; but, it is a big story, large enough to allow all other stories. It is changing and open-ended. It is conservative, but that becomes an instrument to create peace and justice everywhere. It keeps human rights connected with species rights and land rights, through an integrative political approach. It anticipates and responds to problems and catastrophes, through an understanding of psychologies.

There is a lure of good places. What does lure mean? Something we desperately want? We have often moved to places that we have only heard about. If we do not live in healthy places, we want to move to healthy places. Sometimes, we remake our places until they have the properties of good places.

Good places exist. What does existence mean? Good places are found or made. People groups, with strong ethics and common beliefs and understandings, by respecting limits or keeping well below them, can make good places through their actions.

6.1. Outlining a Eutopian Framework for Government

Good places are a confluence of good human societies in healthy ecosystems. We have described some of the qualities of healthy ecosystems. And, we have described some of the qualities of good human societies. To have good societies in good places will require good images and good actions.

6.1.1. Properties of a Eutopian Framework

From political character studies to technological promises, utopias have kept close to the contemporary forms of society. The possibilities described for the future seem to be circumscribed by the limits of human imagination. The entire literature of utopia, imaginative as it is, cannot match the actual diversity of cultures for richness or the depth of nature for wonder.

Many archaic societies employ a set of principles, different from industrial cultures, that may be more adaptive to place. Instead of regarding the "universe as mechanical, humanity as master, and all persons as equal," the Yaruru consider the "universe static and internal, humans sensible to other's wants, and all beings equal;" by contrast, the Navajo consider the "universe personal and orderly, events primary, and the family first." The ways that people live in place reflect their principles. For instance, the Yaruru are much less likely to overwhelm their home place than any industrial culture.

Other modern metaphors can promise more adaptive behavior for industrial culture. A machine metaphor used by Kenneth Boulding, "the earth is a spaceship" suggests the limits of the earth and the value of its life-support system, but it masks other realities. The metaphor of the spaceship is a closed system model, which leads to inadequate understanding of open, natural systems. The earth is an open system that sustains life. The earth has no single captain with authority. In fact, the image of a spaceship does not fit a large, organic, nonmechanical system. Alas, the earth is not a spaceship. It is far more dangerous and uncontrollable. It is clear that many human behaviors and many human institutions in the past, which may have been appropriate to a large planet, are entirely inappropriate to a small closed spaceship. "We cannot have cowboys and Indians, for instance, in a spaceship, or even a cowboy ethic," Boulding says, "We cannot afford unrestrained conflict, and we almost certainly cannot afford national sovereignty in an unrestricted sense." Another metaphor in popular use, such as "the earth is a garden," is a better model for reintegrating humanity into a balance with nature, because the garden is a small balanced system directed by humanity, and part of the larger environment, and dependent on it. The rule of the garden is empirical and based on observation: If you do something, then something else happens. Even so, the metaphor of the garden has important limits. Humanity does not have adequate knowledge to direct all of the processes of nature.

In naming a new science of ecology, Ernst Haeckel combined two Greek words (eco-logos) meaning "the study of the house." Ecology relates to dwelling, to the frame that contains us. The desire to refine a focus on our problems has allowed the frame of reference to be neglected. This metaphor has turned attention to the whole. But, it too is limited. The house herein is not a construct any more than a spaceship. And, there is not just one house; there are many unique ones with individual properties and connections. As a general description, an ecological eutopia frame uses a root metaphor of many places, in different bioregions. This eutopias is a framework for human cultures, to preserve the unique image that a society needs to guide it and to make it different from others. To be effective, in contrast with the ideal characteristics of ideal cities, a eutopian framework embodies attributes that are compatible to the values and norms of living cultures.

By being attentive to the properties of place, and those of a good society, a eutopian framework can be described by its own properties from groundedness to comprehensiveness. These properties are quire different from the properties that can be observed with utopias or industry.

As noted (in an earlier Section), utopias provide images of ideal societies in abstract settings—literally nowhere. Utopias promise newness, order, happiness, and re-inheritance in an ideal political, technological framework. They banish the irrational, the irreparable, and all conflict. The common characteristics of many utopias, however, make them unworkable and unsatisfactory. Utopias tend to be ungrounded, that is, literally no-place, with no reference points in real places, ecosystems and bioregions. Utopias present a static order that is an unchanging model of perfection that is without history or change. Assuming the possibility of perfection (a teleological goal), human happiness is presented in a final order requiring tremendous discipline on human activities. Utopias aim to be ingenuous, to universalize the best of human society in a gigantic, centralized model of an international community ruled by a special government of the elite. The rules and laws of utopias are generally simple and arbitrary, denying the complexity of physical, environmental, and social problems, as well as of chaos, chance and evolution. Utopias tend to be homogenous, in terms of temperament, race, skills, and the uniformity of clothing and homes. Finally, utopias are incomplete; nonwestern, nonindustrial societies are ignored for the conversion of the sad metaphor of the storehouse of nature being looted to create masses of possessions for an exploding population.

The weaknesses of formal utopias are addressed in a framework of good places. Eutopias are grounded in local places. Their realistic properties, based on real cultures living with the ecological knowledge of local places, promise the possibilities of successful implementations.

6.1.1.1. Eutopian Framework is Grounded

Eutopias are grounded in places, and grounding may resemble a knotting in the physical process of existence. Eutopias are realizations of human ideas and designs. The making of places is an ordering of a distinct structure and with an important center. Humans and their communities are embedded in places. The Taureg of the Sahara have created an image, a world, that cannot be relocated to the rain forest of the Campa in Peru. When the symbols of a world lose their meaning, through wrongful application or abstraction, sickness and disintegration result.

Being grounded in place allows us to rediscover a participating consciousness and a symbiotic connection to the living earth. The organization of perception, meaning, and thought is intimately related to specific places. The commitment to a place implies acceptance of its limits. Place is a focus of meaningful events and a platform for ordering a world. The individual image of a place is modified by memory, experience, emotion, imagination, and intention. The social image of a place is influenced by individuals, myths, history, and consensus. The images reinforce each other over time. Each place and culture is unique.

6.1.1.2. Eutopian Framework is Dynamic

Eutopias are dynamic expressions of the productivity of places. Nature and human nature are not static orders; they are flexible, historical, and irreversible. Worlds have been built by peoples over so many thousands of years that it is not necessary to start from raw sensations for a new image. Societies build images that reflect knowledge of themselves and their environment. The problems of many human societies can be rooted in their anthropocentric images of the universe. But, the solution cannot be a uniform cosmology of the earth. The strengths of cultures lay in the diversity of values and in their fitness to particular places. A holistic eutopian cosmology can preserve the differences in a whole image of the earth. The image cannot be a rigid shell to contain everything, but rather a flexible, organic network holding all human and natural groups. A eutopian cosmology recognizes the value of a whole dynamic biosphere. The eutopian order permits traditional cultures and natural processes to be self-ordering and self-renewing without the imposition of a rigid order from above. They allow cultures to be healthy and harmonious.

6.1.1.3. Eutopian Framework is Adventitious

Societies are part of an unending, imperfect process, without a final state. Furthermore, the attempt at perfectibility through self-improvement causes disharmony, which is part of the same imperfect process. Each eutopia is a practical application to place. It is open to the differentiation and diversity that exists. It accepts confusion and conflict—but constructive, scaled conflict, not insoluble, that can lead to education, understanding, and the abandonment of stupidity. Many utopias imply that society can be remade according to reason. But reason is not large enough. Experience is necessary; the unconscious is necessary, and ecological design is necessary. Utopias pretend that all factors governing a system are known and that their effects can be calculated. Unknown factors determine a large part of the operation of any system. Furthermore, there is chaos in every system; there are plagues and random frenzies. Eutopias recognize and absorb unknown factors. They enhance the richness of place.

6.1.1.4. Eutopian Framework is Sophisticated

All the contents of the human species cannot be captured by a single policy. The eutopian framework protects difference and diversity from a uniform global policy. Within the framework, cultures are decentralized and autonomous; people identify with their local culture. Because the earth is finite, there are physical and biological limits to growth and progress. Eutopias voluntarily limit human influences within ecosystems. This does not mean that humanity cannot modify some ecosystems or become space-faring—just that it should not dominate every ecosystem or transform the entire matrix to human products, in order to luxuriate or to explore space. The process of producing goods results in waste, even at low rates of use. The principle of limited good is respected; desired things exist in nonexpansive quantifies. Eutopias is an approach that respects limits, maturity and subtlety, as well as beauty and elegance.

6.1.1.5. Eutopian Framework is Complex

The eutopian framework is multidimensional and pluralistic. Balanced development, rather than growth, is emphasized. When a culture falls out of balance with its local environment, massive disruption often results; industrial cultures have only avoided disruption by trading advantageously with other locales, using fossil fuels, and promoting institutional inequality. Small cultures have built-in checks; furthermore, their cultural definition of good helps to maintain balance between other species and the use of ecosystem productivities. This allows them more stability.

Gross imbalances of wealth and health are the unforeseen consequences of exploration, colonization, science, and management. These imbalances will become more unmanageable with time and television, or with any communication. The primary obstacles to equity and justice are political and managerial, not to mention inertia and poor priorities.

Regional areas are limited in size, to avoid problems of scale. Historical smallness, even lacking natural resources, has not been an obstacle to wealth for many countries, for instance, the sovereign German states of Hamburg or Bavaria. The merits of urbanization do not require a large population. Local concentrations of artists, philosophers, and scientists are capable of creating a distinct civilization. Cities fifty times as large as classical Athens or Florence have not been fifty times as creative. Eutopias would generate loyalty and complexity within limits of size and impact.

6.1.1.6. Eutopian Framework is Heterogenous

The eutopian frame is unselective. It accounts for all human diversity and variability, for prisoners and misfits, artists and technophiles, and for the insane and the aged. It is pluralistic. It rewards and uses individual differences in constitution and character. Humans are not perfect or interchangeable.

It accepts inequities, although biological injustices exist and can be ameliorated, and social injustices can be rectified. The eutopian frame is flexible enough to incorporate the positive features of traditional civilizations. Through its respect for the validity of all cultures and understanding of the responsibilities of cultures, it works to define an authentic concept of humanity. It tolerates fluctuation, irregularities, uncertainty, and diversity, which are properties of open systems.

6.1.1.7. Eutopian Framework is Comprehensive

The levels of application of human norms are both universal and local, depending on the context. For example, there are some universal human behavioral standards, such as a prohibition against incest or against eating human flesh, but local expectations conform with cultural values—and indeed, cannibalism and incest have been important parts of some societies at times. The eutopian frame tolerates and integrates all cultures. Each culture determines the style and complexity of its individuals. Eutopias strives for concerned noninterference, but offers advice and assistance to all cultures to integrate new attributes or common concerns, such as the equality of women, into the culture.

Eutopias considers the total community as a self-making whole. Human cultures make a place within nature. Culture is an immeasurable complex of material and spiritual achievements inside nature, by modifying and using nature. Nature changes with culture. Nature is the locus of the centers and images of all living beings. Nature is thus an important basis for all cultures. The self-ordering processes of nature must be protected through formal preserves of areas or through limited human impact on other areas. The eutopian framework allows people to identify with their domiture, that is, nature and culture.

6.1.2. *Dynamic Structure of Good Places*

The properties must be preserved by action. Properties are part of a structure of a good place. Properties can be described, but some of the pieces could be missing. The structure is necessary to contain and fit the properties, regardless of what is missing.

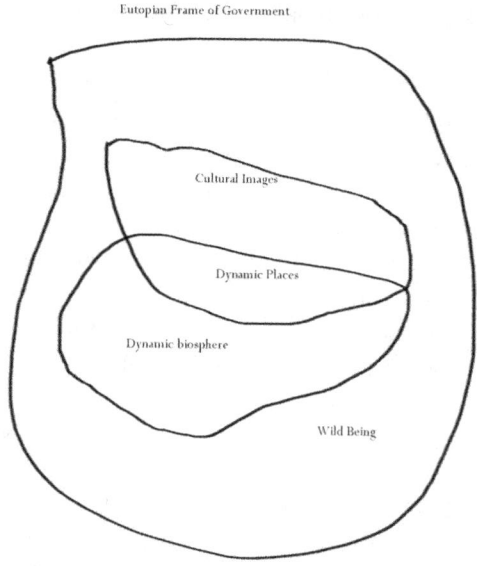

Figure 6112-1. Eutopian Framework for Government

Page 158

6.2. Participating in Government

People live in place. One secret is to have the places be good places, so that people might develop their potentials. There are many potential levels of action, many ways of being, starting with the individual and continuing through the international. However, individuals are part of families, which are part of groups that often include extended families. Larger groups may include clubs or corporations, communities or counties, states or regions. For the sake of simplicity, communities are considered under the heading of individuals. States and regions are considered under the heading of nations.

6.2.1. Participating as Individuals

From a cosmological or ecological perspective, living organisms interpenetrate deeply into non-living forms and the earth. Individual organisms are woven into a complex fabric. Their activities reshape the fabric. Human beings, to make good places, have to consider their individual and social actions, their participation, as responsibilities.

Individuals have responsibilities, as individuals or as members of groups or communities. These responsibilities range all the way from being healthy as individuals to educating others in the community (see the book *Eutopias* for an expanded discussion of those responsibilities).

6.2.2. Participating in Communities & Nations

A nation is an independent and self-guiding conglomeration of people—sometimes with more than one culture. Nations often have special properties, such as a national currency, flag, and armies. The reason for nations is the desire for autonomy, to practice unique cultural beliefs and traditions. For nations, sovereignty is limited to culture (or subculture?). Isolation and commerce have to balance. Free movement would cause an imbalance. Nations usually form during violent conflicts, sometimes as a result of settlement patterns, language and geography, sometimes from ethnic cleansing, war or partitioning. National formation has never been entirely rational and planned. The nation states are closely related to large scale violence, usually having to do with trying to consolidate their power (global war). They then have a monopoly on power. Often, a nation will specialize on political and economic issues, for instance, when the Spanish ransacked the planet for gold. They enlarge and consolidate their territoriality, which gives them increased capacity for marshaling resources, that is trying to maximize global functions with minimum territorial burden. But they have not been stable; there are violent fluctuations. They are part of long cycles. Formerly, nations were as self-reliant as communities.

Nations are an important grouping. Humans also require less than a global identity; they require a measure of provincialism. The provinces would be defined by culture, by region and language. Individuality requires distinctive features. Like individuals, nations have responsibilities, from keeping their native ecosystems healthy to maintaining the health of native cultures, as well as being economically self-sufficient and maintaining its borders.

6.2.3. Participating in a Global Government

A global coordinating body could help with communications between nations. It would help different cultures adapt to each other and learn from each other. Global interaction has been a tendency for over five hundred years. How should an individual or a culture be in an international context? What kinds of visions should we follow or goals to make?

6.2.3.1. Necessity of the Framework (The United Nations Currently)

Founded in 1945, to replace the League of nations of 1919, the United Nations (UN) describes itself as a "global association of governments facilitating cooperation in international law, international security, economic development, and social equity." From 51 countries, the UN has expanded to 191 member states in 2006, which the UN considers to be virtually all internationally recognized independent nations, except for Taiwan and several others.

The UN, with its system of 30 affiliated organizations, attempts to solve global problems, from disease and poverty to the environment and war. The UN agencies define the standards for air travel, telecommunications and consumer products. It has developed international campaigns against drug trafficking and terrorism. Its agencies try to assist refugees, to set up programs to clear landmines, to expand food production, and to reduce disease.

The United Nations has six main organs: The General Assembly, the Security Council, the Economic and Social Council, the Trusteeship Council, the Secretariat, and the International Court of Justice. When nations become Members of the UN, they agree to accept the obligations of the UN Charter, an international treaty that sets out basic principles of international relations. The Charter expresses four purposes: To maintain international peace and security; to develop friendly relations between nations; to cooperate in solving international problems; and to harmonize the actions of nations. In September 2000, the members of the UN met to set an international agenda for the new century. The Millennium Declaration lists measurable goals in seven areas: Peace, security and disarmament; development and poverty eradication; protecting the common environment; human rights and good governance; protecting the vulnerable; meeting the special needs of Africa; and strengthening the UN itself.

The UN has been successful in encouraging dependent people to become independent and then incorporating people into its system. In 1960 the General Assembly adopted the Declaration on the Granting of Independence to Colonial Countries and Peoples, which resulted in 60 former colonial Territories attaining independence and joining the UN as sovereign Members. When the UN was formed, 750 million people lived in non-self-governing territories; by 2006, that number was reduced to about 1 million.

The UN has been successful in affirming the fundamental equality of all people and to counter racism. A long UN campaign in South Africa contributed to ending the system of racial segregation known as apartheid. In 1994, a UN observer mission observed that country's first all-race elections. A World Conference in 2001 examined ways to combat racism, racial discrimination, xenophobia and intolerance.

An important mandate of the UN is the promotion of higher standards of living, full employment, and conditions of economic and social progress and development. The UN web site notes that as much as 70 per cent of the work of the UN system is devoted to accomplishing this mandate, based on the belief that eradicating poverty and improving the well-being of people everywhere are necessary steps to create conditions for lasting peace.

6.2.3.1.1. Structure of the UN Main Organs

The structure of the UN is geared give a voice and a vote to all Member nations, to formulate policies on the goals of the system and to resolve international conflicts.

6.2.3.1.1.1. *General Assembly*. The General Assembly is a "parliament of nations" in which member nations consider the world's most pressing problems. The membership includes every defined nation and each member has one vote. Decisions on key issues, such as admission of new members, the UN budget, and international peace and security, are decided by two-thirds majority. Other matters are decided by a simple majority. Recently, efforts have been made to reach decisions through consensus, rather than through formal vote.

The General Assembly holds an annual regular session from September to December, although it may resume later or hold a special or emergency session, if necessary, to address subjects of particular importance. At its 2001 session, for instance, the Assembly considered over 180 topics, including globalization, AIDS, conflict in Africa, protection of the environment, and consolidation of new democracies. The Assembly does not have the authority or power to force any member to act on UN decisions, but the UN considers that its recommendations "are an important indication of world opinion and represent the moral authority of the community of nations."

6.2.3.1.1.2. *Security Council.* The Security Council, under the UN Charter, has primary responsibility for maintaining international peace and security. The Council may convene at any time that peace is threatened. Under the Charter, all member nations are obligated to carry out the decisions of the Council.

The Council has 15 members. Currently, five—China, France, the Russian Federation, the United Kingdom and the United States—are considered to be permanent members. The remaining 10 are elected by the General Assembly for two-year terms. Decisions of the Council require nine 'yes' votes. A decision cannot be made if there is a veto by a permanent member.

When the Council identifies a dispute that may become volatile, it explores ways to settle the dispute peacefully. It may suggest principles for settlement or encourage mediation. If fighting has begun, the Council tries to secure a ceasefire. It can send a peacekeeping mission to separate the forces until a truce can be set up.

The Council can take other measures, such as economic sanctions or an arms embargo, to enforce its decisions. It can, in extreme situations, authorize member nations to use "all necessary means," including collective military action, to see that its decisions are carried out. The Security Council has established well over 50 peacekeeping operations. The Council can also make recommendations to the General Assembly on the appointment of a new Secretary-General and on the admission of new members.

6.2.3.1.1.3. *Economic & Social Council.* Under the overall authority of the General Assembly, the Economic and Social Council coordinates the economic and social work of the UN system. As a central forum for considering international economic and social issues, and for formulating policy recommendations, the Council fosters international cooperation for development. It consults with non-governmental organizations (NGOs) to maintain a vital link between the UN and civil societies of member nations.

This Council has 54 members, who are elected by the General Assembly for three-year terms. The Council meets throughout the year and holds its major session in July, when a special meeting of Ministers discusses major economic, social and humanitarian issues.

The Council's subsidiary bodies meet regularly and report back to it. The other bodies focus on issues such as social development, the status of women, crime prevention, narcotic drugs, and environmental protection.

There are five regional commissions to promote economic development and cooperation in their regions.

6.2.3.1.1.4. *Trusteeship Council.* The Trusteeship Council, considering its work complete, is composed of the five permanent members of the Security Council. The rules of procedure have been changed to allow it to meet if required. The Trusteeship Council had been established to provide international supervision for 11 Trust Territories that were administered by seven member nations, and to ensure that adequate steps were taken to prepare the Territories for independence. By 1994, the Trust Territories had attained independence as separate nations, or they had become part of neighboring independent countries. If the mandate of the Council is not changed, then it will probably be abolished.

6.2.3.1.1.5. *Secretariat.* The Secretariat carries out the administrative work of the UN, as directed by the General Assembly, the Security Council and the other organs. The Secretary-General, as head of the Secretariat, provides overall administrative guidance. The Secretariat consists of several departments and offices. Its staff of about 7,500 is drawn from 170 countries.

6.2.3.1.1.6. *International Court of Justice.* The International Court of Justice is the main judicial organ of the UN. The Court consists of 15 judges elected jointly by the General Assembly and the Security Council; its purpose is to settle disputes between countries. Although participation in a proceeding is voluntary, if a nation agrees to participate, then it is obligated to comply with the Court's decision. The Court also provides advisory opinions to the General Assembly and the Security Council.

In 1998 the General Assembly called a conference in Rome to establish an International Criminal Court (ICC). The ICC Court formed in 2002 and heard its first case in 2006. It is the first permanent international court charged with trying those who commit the most serious crimes under international law, including war crimes and genocide.

6.2.3.1.1.7. *Special Agencies of the United Nations.* Specialized agencies, as part of the UN system, address almost every area of economic and social endeavor. The agencies provide technical and practical assistance to countries around the world. In cooperation with the UN, they help formulate policies, set standards and guidelines, foster support, and mobilize funds. These organizations have their own governing bodies, budgets and secretariats. They report to the General Assembly or the Economic and Social Council.

Close coordination between the UN and the specialized agencies is ensured through the UN System Chief Executives Board for Coordination (CEB), which includes the Secretary-General and the heads of the specialized agencies, funds and programs, the International Atomic Energy Agency, and the World Trade Organization.

The International Monetary Fund, the World Bank, and 12 other independent organizations are linked to the UN through cooperative agreements. These agencies, among them the World Health Organization and the International Civil Aviation Organization, are autonomous bodies created by intergovernmental agreement. They have wide international responsibilities in the economic, social, cultural, educational, health, and related fields. Some, such as the International Labor Organization and the Universal Postal Union, predate the UN itself.

The Office of the UN High Commissioner for Refugees (UNHCR), the UN Development Program (UNDP), and the UN Children's Fund (UNICEF), work to improve the economic and social condition of all people.

The World Bank provides loans and technical assistance to developing countries to reduce poverty and to advance "sustainable economic growth." The World Bank, for example, provided more than $17 billion USD in development loans for the fiscal year 2001 to more than 100 developing countries. The ILO (International Labor Organization) formulates policies and programs to improve working conditions and employment opportunities, and sets labor standards for all countries. The FAO (Food and Agriculture Organization of the UN) works to improve agricultural productivity and food security, and to better the living standards of rural populations. The IMF (International Monetary Fund) facilitates international monetary cooperation and financial stability and provides a permanent forum for consultation, advice and assistance on financial issues. The ITU (International Telecommunication Union) fosters international cooperation to improve telecommunications, coordinates usage of radio and TV frequencies, promotes safety measures, and conducts research. The WMO (World Meteorological Organization) promotes scientific research on the Earth's atmosphere and on climate change, and facilitates the global exchange of meteorological data. The IMO

(International Maritime Organization) tries to improve international shipping procedures, raise standards in marine safety, and reduce marine pollution by ships. The WIPO (World Intellectual Property Organization) arranges international protection of intellectual property and fosters cooperation on copyrights, trademarks, industrial designs and patents. UNIDO (UN Industrial Development Organization) promotes the industrial advancement of developing countries through technical assistance, advisory services and training. And, the IAEA (International Atomic Energy Agency) is an autonomous organization that emphasizes safe uses of atomic energy.

6.2.3.1.2. Purposes Goals & Actions of the UN
Like any human institution, one important goal of the UN is to strengthen itself. Programs that involve every nation and its people reinforce the image of the UN as an international body, despite some failures and criticisms. Funding, however, is used by many nations, as a stick to drive the UN in different directions.

6.2.3.1.2.1. *To Maintain Peace & Security*. The primary purpose of the UN is to preserve world peace. Under the UN Charter, member nations agree to settle disputes by peaceful means and refrain from threatening or using force against other states. UN peace efforts have produced some dramatic results. The UN helped to defuse the Cuban missile crisis in 1962 and the Middle East crisis in 1973. In 1988, the UN sponsored an offer of a peace settlement ended the Iran-Iraq war, and in 1989, UN-sponsored negotiations led to the withdrawal of Soviet troops from Afghanistan. In the 1990s, the UN was instrumental in restoring sovereignty to Kuwait, and it played a major role in ending civil wars in Cambodia, El Salvador, Guatemala, and Mozambique. UN efforts helped to restore the democratically elected government in Haiti. The UN helped to contain conflict in other countries through disarmament and peacemaking.

6.2.3.1.2.1.1. *Arms Control & Disarmament*. The 1945 UN Charter envisioned a system of regulations that would ensure the least diversion of the world's human and economic resources towards armaments. The use of nuclear weapons weeks after the signing of the Charter highlighted the necessity of arms limitation and disarmament. In fact, the first resolution of the first meeting of the General Assembly, on January 24, 1946, was to establish a Commission to deal with problems raised by atomic energy and to make specific proposals for the elimination of atomic weapons and other weapons of mass destruction from national armaments.

Halting the spread of arms and reducing and eventually eliminating all weapons of mass destruction are major goals of the United Nations. The UN has established forums to address multilateral disarmament, including the First Committee of the General Assembly and the UN Disarmament Commission. Items on their agenda include consideration of a nuclear test ban, outer-space arms control, a ban on chemical weapons, nuclear and conventional disarmament, nuclear-weapon-free zones, the reduction of military budgets, and measures to strengthen international security. The UN supports multilateral negotiations in the Conference on Disarmament and in other international bodies. These negotiations have produced agreements such as the Nuclear Non-Proliferation Treaty (1968), the Comprehensive Nuclear-Test-Ban Treaty (1996), and treaties establishing nuclear-free zones.

The Conference on Disarmament has 66 members representing all areas of the world, including the first five major nuclear-weapon states (the People's Republic of China, France, Russia, U.K. and U.S.). This independent Conference is linked to the UN Secretary-General through a personal representative, who serves as the secretary-general of the conference. Resolutions adopted by the General Assembly often request the conference to consider specific disarmament matters. The conference annually reports its activities to the Assembly.

Other treaties brokered by the UN prohibit the development, production and stockpiling of chemical weapons (1992) and bacteriological weapons (1972); ban nuclear weapons from the seabed, ocean floor (1971) and outer space (1967); and ban or restrict other types of weapons, such as landmines. By 2001, over 120 countries had become parties to the 1997 Ottawa Convention outlawing landmines. The UN encourages all nations to adhere to treaties banning weapons of war. The UN is also supporting efforts to prevent, combat and eradicate the illicit trade in small arms and light weapons, the weapons of choice in most, 46 of 49, major conflicts since 1990. The UN Register of Conventional Arms and the system for standardized reporting of military expenditures help promote greater transparency in military matters.

The International Atomic Energy Agency, through a system of safeguard agreements, attempts to ensure that nuclear materials and equipment intended for peaceful uses are not diverted for military purposes. And, the Organization for the Prohibition of Chemical Weapons collects information on chemical facilities worldwide and conducts routine inspections to ensure adherence to the chemical weapons convention.

6.2.3.1.2.1.2. *Peacemaking.* UN peacemaking attempts to bring hostile groups to agreement through diplomatic means. The Security Council may recommend ways to avoid conflict or secure peace through negotiation or through recourse to the International Court of Justice. The Secretary-General also can play an important role in peacemaking, by bringing any threat to peace and security to the attention of the Security Council; the S-G can use the offices of the UN to carry out mediation or to exercise quiet diplomacy, personally or through special envoys, to resolve disputes before they escalate.

6.2.3.1.2.1.3. *Peacebuilding.* The UN has started to address the underlying causes of conflict, such as health, wealth, and education. Development assistance is a key element of peace-building. In cooperation with UN agencies, donor countries, host governments and local and international NGOs, the UN works to support good governance, civil law and order, elections and human rights in countries struggling to deal with the aftermath of conflict. At the same time, it helps these countries rebuild administrative, health, educational and other services that have been disrupted by war. UN-supervised elections in East Timor in August 2001, allowed people to cast their ballots for a democratically elected assembly.

Some of these activities, such as the UN's supervision of the 1989 elections in Namibia, mine-clearance programs in Mozambique and police training in Haiti, take place within the framework of a UN peacekeeping operation, and may continue when the operation withdraws. Others are requested by governments, as is the case in Cambodia, where the UN maintains a human rights office, or in Guatemala, where the UN helps to implement peace agreements.

In Africa, UN field missions continue peace-building activities in Guinea-Bissau and Liberia; and they remain in Angola and Burundi to support various initiatives aimed at promoting reconciliation. At the request of the Security Council, the Secretary-General has provided a comprehensive analysis of conflicts in Africa along with recommendations on how to promote durable peace.

6.2.3.1.2.1.4. *Peacekeeping.* All UN peacekeeping operations must be approved by the Security Council, which sets up UN peacekeeping operations and defines their scope and mandate in its efforts to maintain peace and international security.

Most operations involve military duties, such as observing a ceasefire or establishing a buffer zone while negotiators seek a long-term solution. Others may require civilian police or other civilian personnel to help organize elections or to monitor human rights. Operations have also been deployed to monitor peace agreements in cooperation with the peacekeeping forces of regional organizations. These forces are provided by member states of the UN, which does not maintain an independent military.

Since the UN deployed peacekeepers in 1948, 123 countries have voluntarily provided more than 750,000 military and civilian police personnel to engage in 54 peacekeeping operations. UN peacekeeping is a vital instrument for peace. Currently, 47,650 UN military and civilian personnel, provided by 87 countries, are engaged in 15 operations around the world.

Peacekeeping operations may last for a few months or continue for many years. The UN's operation at the ceasefire line between India and Pakistan in the State of Jammu and Kashmir, for example, was established in 1949, and still continues. UN peacekeepers have been in Cyprus since 1964. By contrast, the UN was able to complete its 1994 mission in the Aouzou Strip between Libya and Chad in about a month.

Total UN peacekeeping expenses peaked by the end of 1995, when the total cost was just over $3.5 billion. Total UN peacekeeping costs for 2000, including operations funded from the UN regular budget as well as the peacekeeping budget, were $2.2 billion. UN peace operations are funded by assessments, using a formula derived from the regular scale, but including a surcharge for the five permanent Security Council members.

6.2.3.1.2.2. *To Develop Friendly Relations between Nations.* Through its activities, the UN tries to increase the participation of developing countries in the global economy. The UN Conference on Trade and Development (UNCTAD) promoted international trade. UNCTAD also works with the World Trade Organization (WTO), in assisting exports from developing countries through the International Trade Centre.

The UN provides the means to settle disputes peacefully. The UN has played a major role in helping defuse international crises and in resolving protracted conflicts. It has undertaken complex operations involving peacemaking and humanitarian assistance, and it has worked to prevent conflicts from breaking out. After a conflict, it has increasingly undertaken action to address the causes of war and to lay a foundation for durable peace.

6.2.3.1.2.3. *To Cooperate in Solving Problems.* Many nations have problems as a result of historical paths and economic inequities. Many problems are geological or meteorological. Other problems arise from conflict.

The UN offers help with resettlement, after a crisis subsides. The UN helped to repatriate refugees to Mozambique, provided humanitarian assistance in Somalia and Sudan, and undertook diplomatic efforts to restore peace in the Great Lakes region. It has helped prevent new unrest in the Central African Republic, and it is helping to prepare for a referendum on the future of Western Sahara.

The UN offers help with reconstruction. In Kosovo, the UN is rebuilding schools and providing student supplies, as part of a wide-ranging assistance effort. The Security Council established an interim international administration there in 1999, following the end of NATO air bombings and the withdrawal of Yugoslav forces. Under the umbrella of the UN, the European Union and the Organization for Security and Cooperation in Europe are working with the people of Kosovo to create a functioning, democratic society with substantial autonomy. Municipal elections in October 2000, and the casting of a Constitutional Framework for Provisional Self-Government, paved the way for Kosovo-wide elections for a legislative assembly on 17 November 2001.

6.2.3.1.2.3.1. *Promote Human Rights.* World War II atrocities and genocides led to a consensus that the new organization, the UN, must work to prevent such tragedies in the future. So, the pursuit of human rights was central to the creation of the UN. An early objective was to create a legal framework for considering and acting on complaints about human rights violations. The UN Charter obligates all member nations to promote universal "respect for, and observance of, human rights" and to take joint and separate actions to that end.

The Universal Declaration of Human Rights, proclaimed by the General Assembly in 1948, sets out the basic rights and freedoms to which all human beings are entitled: The rights to life, liberty and nationality; the rights to freedom of thought, conscience and religion; the rights to work and to be educated; the rights to food and housing; and the right to take part in government. The UN states that the Declaration is not legally binding to nations. Then, it states that the rights are legally binding due to two International Covenants, to which most nations are parties. One Covenant deals with economic, social and cultural rights, and the other addresses civil and political rights. With the Declaration, they constitute the International Bill of Human Rights.

The Declaration laid the groundwork for more than 80 conventions and declarations on human rights, including conventions to eliminate racial discrimination and discrimination against women; conventions on the rights of the child, against torture and degrading punishment, the status of refugees and the prevention and punishment of the crime of genocide; and declarations on the rights of persons belonging to national, ethnic, religious or linguistic minorities, the right to development, and the rights of human rights defenders. The UN Commission on Human Rights (UNCHR) is the primary UN body charged with promoting human rights, through investigations and offers of technical assistance.

The United Nations and its various agencies are central in upholding and implementing the principles enshrined in the Universal Declaration of Human Rights. A case in point is support by the UN for countries in transition to democracy. Technical assistance in providing free and fair elections, improving judicial structures, drafting constitutions, training human rights officials, and transforming armed movements into political parties have contributed significantly to democratization worldwide.

UN human rights field activities are currently being carried out in nearly 30 countries or territories. They help strengthen national capacities in human rights legislation, administration and education. They investigate reported violations and assist governments in taking corrective measures when needed.

Promoting respect for human rights is increasingly central to UN development assistance. In particular, the right to development is seen as part of a dynamic process which integrates civil, cultural, economic, political and social rights, where the well-being of all individuals in a society is improved. The eradication of poverty is a key to the right to development.

The UN is also a forum to support the rights of women to participate fully in the political, economic, and social life of their countries. The UN contributes to raising consciousness of the concept of human rights through its covenants and its attention to specific abuses through its General Assembly resolutions or Court rulings.

6.2.3.1.2.3.2. *Promote Health & Human Development*. The UN programs and funds for health work under the authority of the General Assembly and the Economic and Social Council to carry out their economic and social mandates. The World Health Organization (WHO) coordinates programs aimed at solving health problems and at the attainment by all people of the highest possible level of health. It works in such areas as immunization, health education and the provision of essential drugs.

The UN has special health programs for children. Every year, 3 million children are saved by immunization, but almost 3 million more die from preventable diseases. UNICEF, WHO, the World Bank Group, several private foundations, most of the pharmaceutical industry, and many governments have joined hands in a new initiative (the Global Alliance for Vaccines and Immunization) to reduce deaths from diseases to zero. Other UN agencies work with local officials and NGOs to meet the health needs of children in conflict situations, such as this UNICEF-led immunization campaign in Afghanistan. The UN Children's Fund (UNICEF) is the lead UN organization working for the long-term survival, protection and development of children. Active in some 160 countries, areas and territories, its programs focus on primary health care, immunization, nutrition, and basic health education

UN programs try to eradicate diseases. UNICEF, UNDP, the World Bank and WHO joined forces in 1998 to launch a new campaign to fight malaria, which kills more than 1 million people a year. Joint initiatives to expand immunization and develop new vaccines have enlisted the support of business leaders, philanthropic foundations, non-governmental organizations and governments. The UN supports programs on HIV/AIDS, including grass-roots education campaigns, in 155 countries. Many other UN programs work for development, in partnership with governments and NGOs. Smallpox was eradicated from the world through a global campaign coordinated by WHO. Another WHO campaign has eliminated polio from the Americas, and aimed at eradicating it globally by 2005.

The UN Human Settlements Program (UN-Habitat) assists people living in health-threatening housing conditions. UNHCR's assistance for Pakistan's Afghan refugees focuses on education and health. To pay for this assistance, the UN has raised billions of dollars from international donors. In 2001, the Office for the Coordination of Humanitarian Affairs launched 19 interagency appeals, raising more than $1.4 billion to assist 44 million people in 19 countries and regions.

6.2.3.1.2.3.3. *Promote Education.* UNESCO (the UN Educational, Scientific and Cultural Organization) promotes education for all, cultural development, protection of the world's natural and cultural heritage, international cooperation in science, and freedom and communication of the press.

6.2.3.1.2.3.4. *Encourage Economic Development.* The UN is in a unique position to promote development; it has a global presence and a comprehensive mandate to address social, economic and emergency needs. The UN tries to be neutral and not represent any particular national or commercial interest. And, it offers a voice for every country, regardless of wealth or power, on major policy decisions.

The UN has played a role in building international consensus on action for development. Beginning in 1960, the General Assembly has helped set priorities and goals through a series of 10-year International Development Strategies. While focusing on issues of particular concern, the Decade strategies have consistently stressed the need for progress on all aspects of social and economic development. The UN continues to formulate new development objectives in such key areas as sustainable development, the advancement of women, human rights, environmental protection and good governance. The UN continues to build new programs and actions to fulfill the objectives.

At the Millennium Summit in September 2000, leaders of nations adopted a set of Millennium Development Goals aimed at supporting development; at eradicating extreme poverty and hunger; at achieving universal primary education; at promoting gender equality and empowering women; at reducing child mortality; at improving maternal health; at combating HIV/AIDS, malaria and other diseases; and at ensuring environmental sustainability. These goals have specific measurable targets to be achieved by the year 2015, such as: Reducing by half the proportion of those who earn less than a dollar a day; achieving universal primary education; eliminating gender disparity at all levels of education; and dramatically reducing child mortality while increasing maternal health.

The UN and its agencies, including the World Bank and the UN Development Program (UNDP), are the premier vehicle for furthering development in poorer countries, providing assistance worth more than $30 billion a year. The UNDP is the largest multilateral source of grant technical assistance in the world. The UN also publishes annually the Human Development Index (HDI), a comparative measure ranking countries by poverty, literacy, education, life expectancy, and other factors.

6.2.3.1.2.3.5. *Offer Poverty Relief.* Other UN social service programs address poverty and relief, especially in vulnerable Africa. A UN System-wide Special Initiative on Africa, a 10-year, $25 billion endeavor launched in 1996, combines all UN efforts into a common program to ensure basic education, health services and food security in Africa.

Relief work for Palestine refugees has been carried out since 1949 by the UN Relief and Works Agency for Palestine Refugees in the Near East (UNRWA). As of 2006, the Agency provides essential health, education, relief and social services, as well as implements income-generation programs for more than 4 million Palestine refugees in the region. A UN Coordinator oversees all development assistance provided by the UN system to the Palestinian people in Gaza and the West Bank.

6.2.3.1.2.3.6. *Provide Humanitarian Assistance.* Disasters can occur anywhere, at any time, from flood, drought, earthquake or conflict. The cost to human communities is lost lives, displaced populations, communities incapable of sustaining themselves, and great suffering.

After a disaster, or famine or war, the UN system provides emergency assistance, in the form of supplies, food, shelter, medicines and logistical support to the victims, many of whom are children, women and the elderly. When disasters occur, the UNDP for instance, coordinates relief work at the local level, while promoting recovery and long-term development. In 2001, for example, following a devastating earthquake in India, the agency helped local communities, while working to reduce long-term vulnerability.

In providing humanitarian assistance, the UN has to overcome major logistical and security constraints in the field. Reaching the affected areas can be a major obstacle, getting adequate supplies another. Recently, many crises have been aggravated by an erosion of respect for human rights. Humanitarian workers have been denied access to people in need. Warring factions have deliberately targeted civilians and aid workers. Since 1992, over 200 UN civilian staff members have been killed and 265 workers have been taken hostage while serving in humanitarian operations. In the effort to prevent human rights violations in the midst of crisis, the UN High Commissioner for Human Rights has taken an active role in the UN response to emergencies.

The UN coordinates its response to humanitarian crises through a committee its humanitarian bodies, chaired by the UN Emergency Relief Coordinator. Members include UNICEF, UNDP, WFP, and the UN High Commissioner for Refugees (UNHCR). Major non-governmental and intergovernmental humanitarian organizations, such as the International Committee of the Red Cross, are represented as well. The UN Emergency Relief Coordinator is responsible for developing policy for humanitarian action and for promoting humanitarian issues, such as helping to raise awareness of the consequences of the proliferation of small arms or the negative effects of sanctions.

People who have fled war, persecution or human rights abuse, that is, refugees and displaced persons, are assisted by UNHCR. At the start of 2001, there were 22 million people of concern to UNHCR in 120 countries, including 5.4 million who are internally displaced within a nation. About 3.6 million Afghans accounted for 30 per cent of refugees worldwide, followed by 568,000 refugees from Burundi and 512,800 from Iraq.

War and civil strife have separated an estimated 1 million children from their parents since 1994, made 12 million more homeless, and left 10 million severely traumatized. UNICEF seeks to meet the needs of these children by supplying food, safe water, medicine and shelter. UNICEF has also promoted the concepts of 'children as zones of peace.' It also created 'days of tranquility' and 'corridors of peace' to help protect children in war and provide them with essential services. And, in countries undergoing extended emergencies or recovering from conflict, humanitarian assistance is increasingly seen as part of an overall peace-building effort, along with developmental, political and financial assistance.

6.2.3.1.2.4. *To Harmonize the Actions of Nations.* There is a musical analogy with the health and operation of ecosystems, and with the health and harmony of nations; health equals harmony.

The four essential elements of music are rhythm, melody, harmony, and tone color. Their combined effects form a web of sound. The combination can lead to the idea of physical motion. Rhythm can lead to monotony. Melody is associated with emotion. A good melody should be of satisfying proportions.

Unlike rhythm and melody, which come naturally, harmony gradually evolved from an intellectual conception that was unknown until the ninth century A.D. The earliest form of harmony was called organum, when you harmonized in intervals of thirds or sixths above the melody. Harmony is the study of chords and their relationships (chords are sounding together of separate tones, a full chord is made of three or more tones).

What can music tell ecology? Harmony continues over time. If a forest has harmony it has to be seen over time, long periods of time. Furthermore, harmony is related to wholeness. The word 'whole' comes from the Indo-European root *kailo*, which is also the root for the words health and holy. The concept of the whole forest is relevant. A forest has a very complete complement of interacting beings. A whole forest can renew itself without replanting and pesticides.

David Bohm, in his theory of the implicate universe, proposes that health is a result of a harmonious interaction of all the analyzable parts that comprise the extricate order—cells, tissues, organs, the body—with the surrounding larger environment. Health is a quality that is grounded in the total order of the environment (or implicate order). Health is a dynamic quality of the entire movement of the environment (holoverse) as it flows. As organisms sometimes interfere with others or with the flow of change, the harmony breaks down—we call that disease. Health is the dance of bodies that interpenetrate (in Paul Shepard's image).

None of the bodies are completely independent or completely bounded; they are interdependent and open systems. A body is only maintained by a flow of energy and materials from its environment—much of this flow is in the form of other entities, usually much smaller, such as prey, insects, bacteria, viruses.

What can music suggest to a global political framework? The essence of harmony is allowing all elements to have a voice or sound. That is one purpose of the UN, to allow each nations to have a voice. Harmony is more likely if no one nation can dominate the others all the time at every level.

6.2.3.1.2.4.1. *Governance of Nations.* The UN has helped run elections in countries with little democratic history, including recently in Afghanistan and East Timor. In East Timor, UN-brokered talks between Indonesia and Portugal culminated in a May 1999 agreement that opened the way for a popular consultation on the status of the territory. Under the agreement, a UN mission supervised voter registration and an August 1999 ballot, in which 78 per cent of East Timorese voted for independence over their regional autonomy within Indonesia. In August 2001, a major step was taken in that direction, with the election of a Constituent Assembly which drafted the constitution for an independent and democratic East Timor. The people of East Timor, in August 2001, cast their ballots for a democratically elected assembly, under UN-supervised elections.

For countries in transition to more open government or democracy, the UN provides technical assistance for holding free and fair elections, improving judicial structures, drafting constitutions, training human rights officials, and transforming armed movements into political parties. In 1994, a UN mission observed South Africa's first racially-open elections. The UN has supervised elections in Namibia and elsewhere.

The United Nations works to support good governance, through civil law and order, elections and human rights, in countries struggling with the aftermath of conflict. The UN works to promote dialogue between parties, to establish a broad-based, inclusive government, with an appropriate political framework and leadership. In the Pacific, the UN helped the government of Papua New Guinea and the Bougainville parties reach a comprehensive agreement covering issues of autonomy, referendum and weapons disposal. In Haiti, following international action to restore the democratically elected government, the UN offered a comprehensive program that emphasized human rights, consensus-building and conflict-reduction, with the strong participation of civil society. The UN supports good governance with its programs.

6.2.3.1.2.4.2. *Environment of Nations.* Environmental conventions sponsored by the UN have helped to reduce acid rain in Europe and North America, to cut marine pollution worldwide, and to phase out production of gases destroying the ozone layer of the planet. International diplomacy, as a result of other conferences, such as UNCED, may recognize that nature is a finite source of resources, as well as a finite sink for wastes and a finite regenerator of cycles. The UN provides some oversight on overuse of resources, such as forests and fishing grounds.

6.2.3.1.3. Activities of the United Nations

The UN has developed many public forums, so that people from many nations can address the challenges and problems that are either world-wide or global.

6.2.3.1.3.1. *Conferences.* When an issue is considered particularly important, the General Assembly may convene an international conference to focus global attention on the issue and to build a consensus for consolidated action. A recent example is the UN Conference on Environment and Development, also called the Earth Summit, in June 1992, which led to the creation of the UN Commission on Sustainable Development to advance the conclusions reached in Agenda 21, the final text of agreements negotiated by governments at UNCED.

There are other examples. The International Conference on Population and Development, in September 1994, approved a program of action to address the critical challenges and interrelationships between population and sustainable development during the next 20 years. The World Summit on Trade Efficiency, held in October 1994, focused on the use of modern information technology to expand international trade. The World Summit for Social Development, held in March 1995, underscored responsibilities of nations for sustainable development and found commitment to plans that invest in basic education, health care, and economic opportunity for all, including women and girls. The Fourth World Conference on Women, in September 1995, sought to accelerate implementation of historic agreements reached at the previous World Conference on Women. And, the Second UN Conference on Human Settlements (Habitat II), in June 1996, addressed the challenges of human settlement, development and management in the twenty-first century.

6.2.3.1.3.2. *International Years.* The UN declares and coordinates "International Years" in order to focus world attention on important issues. Using the symbolism of the UN, a specially designed logo for the year, and the infrastructure of the UN system to coordinate events worldwide, the various years have helped advance key issues on a global scale.

6.2.3.1.3.3. *Agreements Treaties & International Law.* The United Nations Charter specifically requires the UN to undertake the progressive codification and development of international law. Over 500 conventions, treaties and standards have resulted from this work, and they have provided a framework for promoting international peace and security and for spurring economic and social development. Nations that ratify these conventions are legally bound by them.

The International Law Commission prepares drafts on topics of international law which can then be incorporated into conventions and opened for ratification by States. Some of these conventions form the basis for law governing relations among States, such as the convention on diplomatic relations or the convention regulating the use of international watercourses.

The UN Commission on International Trade Law develops rules and guidelines designed to harmonize and facilitate laws regulating international trade. The UN has also pioneered the development of international environmental law. Agreements such as the convention to combat desertification, the convention on the ozone layer, and the convention on the transborder movement of hazardous wastes are administered by the UN Environment Programme.

The UN negotiates treaties such as the Convention on the Law of the Sea, to avoid potential international disputes. Disputes over use of the oceans also may be adjudicated by a special court. The Convention on the Law of the Sea seeks to ensure equitable access by all countries to the riches of the oceans, to protect the oceans from pollution and to facilitate freedom of navigation and research. The Convention against Illicit Traffic in Narcotic Drugs is the key international treaty against drug trafficking.

The United Nations fosters international efforts to create a legal framework against terrorism. Twelve global conventions on the issue have been negotiated under the auspices of the United Nations, including the 1979 Convention against the Taking of Hostages, the 1997 Convention for the Suppression of Terrorist Bombings, and the 1999 Convention for the Suppression of the Financing of Terrorism.

The International Court of Justice (ICJ) is the main court of the UN. Its purpose is to adjudicate disputes among states. The work of the ICJ continues from 1946. The IJC has heard cases where the Democratic Republic of Congo accused France of illegally detaining former heads of state accused of war crimes and where Nicaragua accused the United States of illegally arming the Contras—the source of the Iran-Contra affair.

6.2.3.1.3.4. *United Nations Courts.* The UN also runs international criminal tribunals, including the International Criminal Tribunal for Rwanda (ICTR), as well as ones for the former Yugoslavia (ICTY), the Special Court for Sierra Leone, and the Ad-Hoc Court for East Timor.

6.2.3.1.4. Strengths of the United Nations

The UN has increased the involvement of nations with global issues, from disease to health and population. The UN has involved schools in its programs, through programs such as a "Model UN."

The efforts of the UN have resulted in upsurges of activism and declines in conflicts. A report produced by the Human Security Centre at the University of British Columbia, with support from several governments and foundations, documented a dramatic, but largely unknown, decline in the number of wars, genocides and human rights abuses over the past decade, after the end of the Cold War. The report, published by Oxford University Press, argued that the single most compelling explanation for these changes is found in the activities of the UN.

The report singles out several specific investments that have been particularly effective. There has been a six-fold increase in the number of UN missions mounted to prevent wars, from 1990 to 2002. There has been a four-fold increase in efforts to stop existing conflicts, from 1990 to 2002. There have also been: A seven-fold increase in the number of groups and other government-initiated mechanisms to support peacemaking and peacebuilding missions, from 1990 to 2003; an eleven-fold increase in the number of economic sanctions against regimes around the world, from 1989 to 2001; and, a four-fold increase in the number of UN peacekeeping operations, from 1987, to 1999. These efforts were both more numerous and often substantially larger and more complex than those of the Cold War era.

The UN has been able to broker independence for some nations. In East Timor, UN-sponsored talks between Indonesia and Portugal culminated in a May 1999 agreement which paved the way for a popular consultation on the status of the territory and eventually for an independent and democratic East Timor.

The UN has tried to consider nationless people. The UN has extended its efforts to groups of people within nations. For example, in 1977 the UN organized a meeting to discuss the creation of indigenous rights under international law. Indigenous peoples usually do not have armies or national currencies, perhaps not enough to define them as independent nations.

6.2.3.1.5. Inadequacies of the United Nations

The founders of the UN expected that the organization could prevent conflicts between nations and make future wars impossible, by fostering the ideal of collective security. Those expectations have not been completely realized. During the Cold War, about 1947 to 1991, the division of the world into hostile camps made peacekeeping extremely difficult. Following the end of the Cold War, the UN was expected to become the agency for achieving world peace and co-operation, as military conflicts continued to increase. The breakup of the Soviet Union, however, left the U.S. in a unique position of global dominance as self-anointed peacekeepers. This has created a variety of challenges for the UN. Even where it has been successful, the UN has been unable to create peaceful conditions lasting enough for its peacekeepers to withdraw.

Perhaps because of its nature, or its relative powerlessness, the UN has had failures, problems, and issues. One reason might be because it assumes that nations are rational players, certain of wants and communications, existing on a benign, stable planet. The intergovernmental nature of the UN means that it must reach consensus; it is an association of 191 member states and not an independent organization. Even when actions are mandated by the Security Council, the Secretariat is rarely given the full resources needed to carry them out.

The UN fails at times. In some cases, UN member nations have shown reluctance to enforce Security Council resolutions. Iraq may have broken 17 Security Council resolutions dating back to June 28, 1991 as well as trying to bypass the UN economic sanctions. The U.S. violated international law when it invaded Iraq. The UN did not respond; nor has it responded to other violations of international law by the U.S., especially related to the treatment of prisoners. For nearly a decade, Israel defied resolutions calling for the dismantling of settlements in the West Bank and Gaza.

The UN failed to prevent the 1994 Rwandan genocide, which resulted in the death of nearly a million people, due to the refusal of the security council members to approve any military action. The UN failed to intervene during the Second Congo War, 1998-2002, which claimed nearly five million people in the Democratic Republic of Congo, and failed to carry out and distribute humanitarian aid. The UN failed to intervene in the 1995 Srebrenica massacre, despite the fact that it had designated Srebrenica a "safe haven" for refugees and assigned 600 Dutch peacekeepers to protect it. The UN failed to successfully deliver food to starving people in Somalia; the food had been seized by local warlords, and a U.S./UN attempt to apprehend the warlords seizing these shipments resulted in the 1993 Battle of Mogadishu.

The UN has been unable to control sexual abuse by UN peacekeepers— men from several nations have been repatriated from UN operations for sexually abusing and exploiting girls as young as 12 in a number of peacekeeping missions. A 2005 internal UN investigation found that sexual exploitation and abuse has been reported in at least five of 16 countries where UN peacekeepers have been deployed, including the Democratic Republic of the Congo, Haiti, Burundi, Cote d'Ivoire, and Liberia. This abuse seems to be widespread and continuing, despite revelations and investigations by the UN Office of Internal Oversight Services.

The UN has scandals, problems and security issues. The inclusion of nations such as Libya and Sudan, whose leaders have weak records on human rights, on the United Nations Commission on Human Rights of nations, is an issue of concern. These countries argue, perhaps with some justification, that Western countries, with their history of colonial aggression and brutality, have no right to argue about membership of the Commission. One solution would be to qualify members by their current records on rights.

The Oil-for-Food Program was established by the UN in 1996 to allow Iraq to sell oil on the world market in exchange for food, medicine, and the other needs of ordinary Iraqi citizens who were affected by international economic sanctions, without allowing the Iraqi government to rebuild its military after the first Gulf War. The program was discontinued in late 2003 amidst allegations of widespread abuse and corruption; several people were implicated in bribery. Under UN auspices, over $65 billion USD worth of Iraqi oil was sold on the world market. Officially, about $46 billion was used for humanitarian needs, and additional revenue was used to pay for Gulf War reparations through a Compensation Fund, the UN administrative and operational costs for the Program (2.2%), and the weapons inspection program (0.8%).

The UN is limited by its lack of power. Although the UN has been effective at times dealing with limited kinds of conflicts, it has had problems dealing with unresolved, long-term conflicts, such as the Basques and the Spanish or Israel and Arab countries. UN concern over the Arab-Israeli conflict spans five decades and five full-fledged wars. The UN has defined principles for a just and lasting peace, including two benchmark Security Council resolutions in 1967) and 1973, which remain the basis for an overall settlement.

Sometimes the UN seems powerless with its own agencies. How should the UN deal with the World Trade Organization? Should it make it a nonprofit? How should the UN regulate goods and people? Is the free movement of goods or people across any boundary a good idea? The World Trade Organization needs to be made sustainable. Perhaps, it could be incorporated into the UN. But, the WTO must have environmental assessments, which are more important than WTO rules. New rules would give preferential treatment to trading partners with strong environmental policies and labor practices, and human rights.

The UN depends on voluntary dues from its member nations. Its funding is often too little. Expenditures of the UN system on operational activities for development, mostly for economic and social programs to help the world's poorest countries, amount to approximately $6 billion a year, excluding the World Bank, International Monetary Fund and International Fund for Agricultural Development. This amount is roughly equal to 0.75 per cent of world military expenditures of over $800 billion.

6.2.3.1.6. Proposals for a New Framework for the United Nations
In 2004, allegations of mismanagement and corruption regarding the Oil-for-Food Program for Iraq led to calls to reform the UN. There have been many calls for the reform of the UN, but there is little clarity or consensus about how to reform it. Some nations want the UN to play a greater or more effective role in world affairs, while other nations want its role reduced to symbolic humanitarian work.

An earlier, official reform was initiated by UN Secretary-General Kofi Annan shortly after starting his first term on January 1, 1997. Reforms mentioned included changing the permanent membership of the Security Council, which still reflects the power relations of the victors in the 1945 war; making the bureaucracy more transparent, accountable and efficient; making the UN more democratic; and, imposing an international tariff on arms manufacturers worldwide.

In September 2005, the UN convened a World Summit that brought together the heads of most member states, in a plenary session of the General Assembly's 60th session. The UN called the summit "a once-in-a-generation opportunity to take bold decisions in the areas of development, security, human rights and reform of the United Nations." Secretary General Annan had proposed that the summit agree upon a global "grand bargain" to reform the UN, revamping international systems for peace and security, and human rights and development, to make them capable of addressing the extraordinary challenges facing the UN in this century. World leaders agreed on a compromise text with such notable items as: The creation of a Peacebuilding Commission to provide a central mechanism to help countries emerging from conflict; the agreement that the international community has the right to step in when national governments fail to fulfill their responsibility to protect their own citizens from atrocity crimes; a Human Rights Council, since created and operational; an agreement to devote more resources to UN's internal oversight agency; several agreements to spend billions more on achieving Millennium Development Goals; a clear and unambiguous condemnation of terrorism "in all its forms and manifestations;" a Democracy Fund; and, an agreement to wind up the Trusteeship Council due to the completion of its mission. The UN is a recognition of our human limits—also that otherness needs to exist. It is too unsatisfactory, but too important to abandon.

A global unity cannot govern itself; it requires an external controlling agent. But, small nations could govern themselves, and the UN would be not a supergovernment, but a global center for small-scale business and small-scale politics. The UN should not be a union or an association, but a weak federal government with a few more powers than the largest nation. Perhaps the UN should also have a division of power similar to nations, that is, an executive branch, a representative legislature, with equitable representation, and a judiciary.

The traditional way of governing, from the Medes and the Persians, to the Swiss and the U.S., has been to reduce the size of the governed unit, not the size of the governing unit. The Roman approach was to divide and rule. The Duke of Sully and Henry IV of France planned to limit the size and number of European states to fifteen of equal size. Hitler applied the same strategy to Prussia and Austria. Kohr alleges that all successful empires share this small-cell pattern.

One way to divide a great power is to host a war to deunify it. Another way would be to give them a gift, according to Kohr, of proportional representation in a global union, such as the UN. A conventional principle of government grants each sovereign unit an equal number of votes irrespective of size. International law does not distinguish between degrees of sovereignty. Otherwise those with more population, territory, or wealth might be considered better. In theory, regions of nations could represent their regions, regardless of what other federation they might belong to. Centralized systems would have to be decentralized for membership.

For checks and balances to work the UN has to be larger than the largest of nations. How would the UN limit size, though? By territory, population? What would a maximum be? 20 million? How can we have equality of nations? Should that be decided by equal numbers? Equal territory or places? A global organization, such as the UN, can be a suboptimal solution with plenty of flexibility. It can be satisficing rather than optimal.

The UN could be an agent of disunity, of political anarchies. Its concern could be with global things and coordination (rather than strict order). All nations would have to be dissolved through representation to allow voting. But have a maximum size. The natural list of nations already exists, within the unions formed violently in the past 200 years. Aragon, Valencia, Catalonia, Castile, Galicia, Warsaw, Bohemia, Moravia, Slovakia, Ruthenia, Salvonia, Slovenia, Croatia, Serbia, Transylvania, Moldavia, Walachia, Bessarabia, Sicily, Basque, Catalania, Scotland, Bavaria, and Wales, among many.

A central governing body for the earth has two very important functions: To insure a diverse biosphere, on which all humanity depends, and to equalize the opportunity of humans to live in health. There is no organization that addresses either of these functions. A global organization is necessary to coordinate the system. Either individual nations or a partially-responsible global institution is inadequate. The global organization must have the regulatory powers to maintain a healthy environment and to coordinate the constituent nations. It might have a new name as well, with new powers and responsibilities. In his pamphlet Common Sense, Thomas Paine encouraged people to revolution. Later, he proposed that the U.S. help form an "Association of Nations." As a working title, the Association of Nations could replace the United Nations, which are not really united and which do not really represent all nations.

6.2.3.2. Responsibilities of New Frame
(Being edited)

6.2.4. *Strengths and Weaknesses of a New International Body*
A revitalized UN or a replacement body, such as a tentatively named Global Union of Commonwealths (GU) would correct some of the weaknesses of the old pattern and perhaps offer new strengths. However, it would also develop strengths and weakness of its own, that would have to be addressed during its operation through some kind of adaptive process.

6.2.4.1. Potential Strengths of the Frame of an International Body
A holocultural framework could identify and attempt to solve global problems, such as the greenhouse effect or acid rain, that cannot be solved at the level of a culture or nation. It can address the working of opposites in human affairs, where the solution to one global problem may cause another.

By being a global framework, it can adjust international economics. Local communities are based on traditional cultures, which have long-term lasting power. Traditional cultures often have wealth-leveling properties, absolute property ceilings, fixed wants, and production coupled with need— all of which results in a stable economy. Efficiency and productivity are less important than use and appropriateness. The framework can promote limited and rational economic development and coordinate international economic exchanges, protecting those cultures that choose to remain outside networks. It can put restraints on the current international community, from large corporations to large federations.

The framework can provide a holistic education of all cultures, besides that of the local culture. It can archive knowledge of other cultures. The experiences of many lives are encoded in myths, along with natural phenomena, supernatural beliefs, moral values, and features of the culture. All interpretation and recounting of the past is mythmaking. Mythic symbols store information concisely, which makes it possible for a person to assimilate the collective experiences of a culture. That is why myths reflect the detail of a culture.

The framework may be capable of realigning social boundaries to ecological realities; the boundaries of a watershed or ecotone would be more appropriate than geometric lines. A natural region supports a great deal of life without human intervention; it produces enough life to support a reasonable number of humans. We need to know natural associations and limitations because these determine the harmony of development.

A framework can justify a wide diversity in nature and accommodation to natural laws. It can recognize the value of the total biosphere and respect all forms of life, past, present, and future. It can do so, because, unlike traditional or industrial cultures, it is conscious of itself and its purpose.

6.2.4.1.1. Being Conscious
Creating a holocultural image requires changing the gestalt of images of self, nature, and society. That effort is revitalization. Unlike classic cultural change, revitalization requires the explicit intent of the members of society; it depends on restructuring elements already in use or known. Where the culture remains responsible for the performance of ritual or the preservation of doctrine, the images are preserved. When the images are anticipatory, they lead to development and social change. Attractiveness reinforces the movement towards them. We are dependent now on our consciousness of the entire system of nature and humanity. Undertaking a conscious orderly change in our living habits, before it is forced on us by an unbalanced environment, gives us more options.

6.2.4.1.2. Recognizing Context

Cultures change as the result of human interactions in nature. Nature and cultures are in a constant state of flux; cultures have much in parallel with biological species. Our thoughts and ideas, tools and cultures, are as much a part of nature as other species or peat bogs. To preserve our cultures and natural environments, we must understand that they are examples of a dynamic order brought forth by the earth in its history. We are physically dependent on nature. We are psychologically dependent as well; without signals from nature, our minds become closed and dead. We also are physically and psychologically dependent on culture. Yet, the diversity of habitats and cultures is allowed to erode.

A global framework for cultures depends on important principles drawn from ecology. One role of ecology could be to urge the toleration of fluctuation, irregularity, uncertainty, and diversity. As adaptive systems, cultures change as ecosystems change. And sometimes ecosystem change is a result of cultural change. They are linked together.

If humans adapted more closely to the complexities of natural ecosystems, then human cultures would be more diverse and stable. If humans adapted to the complexities of natural ecosystems, then human societies would be more complex. The proper attitude of an ecological framework is care, a positive spontaneity, but also a "letting be," a reverence toward the wild alienness of nature, a willingness to comply with the limitations of natural systems, and a willingness to reduce human dominance.

The framework could recommend an optimum size for each human population. A nation must have a population large enough for economic advantages in food production, education, and entertainment, and for political tools. As Leopold Kohr has noted, the size of a culture is determined by the function it fulfills. The function of a state is to provide its members with protection and other advantages that they do not have as independents.

When a state becomes too large, it cannot offer protection—it cannot offer even clean air or water. The country of Andorra, with about ten thousand people is stable, sovereign, and healthy; the Greek, Italian, and German city-states that furnished much of Western civilization often numbered less than twenty thousand individuals. As the size of a nation increases, the negative factors of civilization, such as overcrowding and breakdowns, increase. Technology has the capacity to allow some expansion, but not an infinite amount. A comprehensive population policy must be created for larger cultures, and it must fit into the context of wilderness and other cultures.

6.2.4.1.3. Being Comprehensive

A holocultural framework includes all human cultures without judgment. The framework provides a higher resolution image of the whole, since it incorporates all human cultures. It includes all its members, recognizing that each says something worthwhile. It is not details or knowledge of the operation that is critical, but an understanding of the wholeness of order.

The framework can interact with nature much like the mythic, but understand the rational and mechanical sides of thought. It would not be a conglomerate of sciences; it would not be limited by the facts of any science, even ecology. The insights of people of every culture must be considered. Each person tells of a way the world is; together, these ways make a holistic framework.

The framework includes ultrahuman cultures in its consideration. It can create wilderness zones that would have various limitations for conversion or use. It can reserve large areas of wilderness for ultrahuman beings and biogeochemical processes. The framework can attempt to combine the best single elements of industrial culture with the superior components of primary cultures, in parallel with Gordon Taylor's paraprimitive solution. High technology can offer immense benefits, with restraint and appropriate limits. Primary cultures can satisfy the human needs for belonging and status.

6.2.4.1.4. Making Authentic Images

Individual cultures, in their unique cosmologies, create images of the human place in nature, in terms of mastery, community, or participants. The holocultural framework offers a holistic value of human worth, outside of any one local perspective. It promotes and protects universally accepted values: Reciprocity—the repayment of obligations; territorial integrity for cultures; legitimacy—the value of children born in wedlock; and the working of opposites—life and death, sacred and profane. It can promote basic rights human rights: The right to land, food, shelter; to equal opportunity to develop, regardless of race or sex; to participate in global affairs as desired; and to live without excessive discrimination or conflict.

6.2.4.1.5. Protecting the Diversity of Cultures

Each culture is a response to a unique place, and so there is a diversity of cultures. Industrial culture condemns to backwardness any culture that is not part of its global electronic neural system. This definition of backwardness means only a lack of fast things or professional enslavement. Primary cultures do not lack art or play, or food, tradition, freedom, or happiness.

It might be good for cultures to be uncoupled economically; it might be a sound option for traditional societies unwilling to make the same mistakes as industrial ones. The framework would keep cultures separate and coordinate any exchanges between them. It would resolve disputes that arise from territorial expansion, the past movements of people and borders, or the unequal expansion of cultures in the same territory, such as the Sinhalese and Tamil in Sri Lanka.

6.2.4.1.6. Providing Order

The GU would have to be stronger than the largest nation, through arms control, disarmament, and its own weapons program. It would have to disarm the nations substantially. Police operations would be quite similar to the current United Nations, although there would be differences. The GU would have a permanent police force, kept in regional divisions. The funding for the police force would be as a result of the income of the GU, not dependent on voluntary membership fees.

The first force of Police would always be unarmed. If a second force is necessary, it would be well armed. In fact, GU police forces would be better armed than any single nation. A maximum residence time would be set, and an exit strategy required.

Of course, the GU would work to prevent conflicts. Although many conflicts would be reduced by the changes in the Eutopian framework, there will always be conflicts between cultures. GU forces would try to solve the problems through understanding, compromise and consensus.

6.2.4.2. Potential Weaknesses of an International Framework

History does not show a progressive unfolding of human betterment; loss and defeat are much of the texture of daily life. A framework will not be able to solve all problems, especially ubiquitous ones like hunger. No human construct is perfect and completely comprehensive. No human framework can expect to solve every problem to everyone's satisfaction. The framework can be expected to exhibit a number of weaknesses.

6.2.4.2.1. Being Abstract

A holocultural framework is a general human construct, which may not be implemented. There is no working model of global unity. Our experience with international cooperation on an immense scale is minimal. Our ability to plan our cultures and foresee our impacts is minimal. Other abstract ideals, including democracy and communism, have been disappointing and modified in practice.

Kinship is more rigidly localized than other dimensions of culture, which can be more rapidly disseminated and assimilated. The transition from kinship to a simultaneous abstract global citizenship may slow. Kinship loyalty sometimes clashes with global perspectives. A framework trying to lessen the conflict and resolve contradictions may be faced with more conflict.

6.2.4.2.2. Being Uncritical

Such a framework, by definition, accepts any human culture, even bad ones. It cannot make judgments about use. In avoiding ethnocentrism, it must accept failure. It may not be able to deal fairly with cultures that are dying out, because they are unfit or because they are victims of a large coercive culture. Yet, it cannot artificially support bad images. It must preserve the process of making and sustaining a way of living, not every individual culture.

This framework does not reject or judge cultures, but incorporates all the practicality and paradox. It makes no distinctions between right and wrong or good and bad; these polarities are more like positive stimuli useful to development. Hence, there is no evil, as considered in many cultures, only suffering that results from lack of wisdom. Many customs, like sacred cows in India, at first glance, seem to be dysfunctional. But, even sacred cows provide dung for cooking fires.

6.2.4.2.3. Being Contradictory

It used to be, as Karl Marx said, that village life enslaved the human mind with traditional rules and subjugated it. No more—too much communication is a greater threat. Our excess communication tends to wear out our ability to feel empathy and react to suffering. Some cultures may overcommunicate and others may undercommunicate. Undercommunication may result in ignorance and suffering; overcommunication may result in passiveness and insignificance. The framework will have to abide more than one contradiction.

6.2.4.2.4. Being Weak

The framework may not have the power or authority to make agreeable boundaries. It may be unable to set aside large enough areas for natural processes. It may not be able to dictate population restrictions for some cultures without seeming to be genocidal or prejudiced. It may not be able to achieve an agreeable redistribution of some kinds of wealth. Any action may result in some dislocation and suffering. It may be impossible to limit the interdependence of nations.

The framework may not be able to deal with incompatible cultures or the divisive forces of large industrial cultures. Some cultures may refuse to participate. It may not be able to handle large differences or to limit the influence of powerful corporations, which have no local accountability. Some traditional cultures may have trouble incorporating new ideas, such as the equality of women.

6.2.4.2.5. Being Fallible

A holocultural frame may try to address global problems that may be insoluble within its range. Some of its actions may have negative consequences for some cultures. For instance, in mediating boundaries that have changed over centuries, it may be difficult to rectify imbalance, theft, or suppression. Cultures have dominated, displaced, merged, or destroyed other cultures for millennia. No one knows how far back to trace a wrong. The dividing line might always seem arbitrary. It may be appropriate to return lands to the Pawnee, but not to the people that the Pawnee displaced.

6.2.4.2.6. Being Naïve

What does it mean to be naïve? Artless? Ingenuous, which we already consider a weakness of utopias? What is naïve? That people will accept inequity as it worsens? That people will always accept cheating and discrimination? Is it naïve to think that corporate greed will benefit starving children? Is it naïve to think that people will give up heroic luxuries to help people somewhere else on the planet? That nations will find it in their interest to break apart along ethnic or economic lines? A eutopian framework may always seem naïve by some definition or example, but by contrast with hard "realities" it will always seem less naïve.

6.2.4.3. Responsibilities of a Global Framework

There is already a world system. But it is not, and should not be, a stagnant, monolithic industrial system—to say that there is a human body is not to say that all organs have decided to become kidneys. But, we need to name the system to reflect what we want. In the dictionary, the word 'united' comes after the word 'unimportant,' but before the word 'universe.' United means solo, monistic, inseparable, integral, harmonious, or connective—a somewhat contradictory assortment of meanings. A stronger word is needed. An alliance is an association for mutual benefit. A confederacy emphasizes the independence of the governments. But, a union implies a permanent alliance with complete unity of purpose, hence it seems a stronger word. The union is for the planet, that is the earth or globe. The words earth and planet imply an astronomic object, with all its processes and life forms, but 'global' has also come to mean anything to do with the whole earth and the comprehensive system of the world (the human image of each culture), hence this word is used. Each member government, however, may be more or less than a nation or state, congress or division, or corporation or organization. The word 'commonwealth' means self-governing, as well as a group of people united by common interests, and it implies that wealth is a common thing, not some individual form of luck or talent (and it has been used to describe confederations of independent states or nations). So, rather than call a government for the planet the United Nations, Society of Communities, or the Association of Stakeholders, this is offered: The Global Union of Commonwealths (or GU).

A global order is necessary to govern this world system. The Global Union of Commonwealths (GU), would be an elected body, with the regulatory powers necessary to maintain a healthy global environment. It should have regulatory and advisory powers to maintain the independence and integrity of its constituent nations. It should have regulatory and punitive powers to rectify resource and human rights infringements; only this body would have police powers and large impersonal weapons. Various advisory bodies would recommend policies and actions to nations. The Global Union has six basic functions: To ensure a diverse biosphere; to manage resources; to protect unique cultures; to coordinate representation; to provide services to nations; and, to create peaceful conditions. For instance, to ensure a Diverse Biosphere, the GU has to identify, zone, conserve and preserve landscapes. Then it has to monitor, protect and restore the landscapes as necessary.

6.2.4.3.1. To Ensure a Diverse Biosphere

To ensure a diverse biosphere, on which all humanity depends. The Global Union works to conserve genetic resources and ecosystems. Preservation of entire systems is addressed on a global scale. The Global Union is responsible for planetary monitoring of all major biomes and their ecosystems. The destruction of basic landscapes sets the frame for proper conservation and development policies. Many natural and artificial values are conserved this way.

In ecological ignorance, our ancestors cut down the cedars of Lebanon, ruined the Mediterranean, created dust bowls and deserts. History supports the notion that no civilization has ever recovered after ruining its environment. Some, like Egypt or Rome were replaced from the outside. Others, such as Ur or Rapa Nui, were rebuilt by wealthier invading peoples. A few, like the Mayans, settled for a lower level of complexity.

Ray Dasmann distinguishes between ecosystem people and biosphere people. Indigenous traditional societies are examples of the former, and technological societies are in the latter. The former live within a single ecosystem usually and are dependent on it for survival. If ecological rules, such as "do not overkill," are violated, they perish. Island people do not tolerate overpopulation. But biosphere people can draw support from any ecosystem on earth; if one place is ruined by exploitative pressure, then another place can be drawn from. But with absolute increase in human numbers, they cannot be completely insulated from ecosystem failures. Knowledge of local collapse in distant states, which are part of the resource commons, could precipitate an ultimate collapse.

A natural way of extermination is by stimulating overgrowth. The natural way of preserving things and increasing the base of life is to contain growth; instead of expanding form, it duplicates it. Julian Huxley calls this adaptive radiation. Speciation uses a wider range of noncompetitive food sources than the expansion of a single species. This type of adaptation occurs in humans also. The relationship between groups can be characterized as symbiosis, living together. Biologically symbiosis increases the chances of its organisms for survival. Humans should choose goals that are symbiotic from the alternate paths.

But problems arise when societies become larger and inflexible, when the variety that insures tribal and small communities yields to nation states. Nation states have no value in a global order. The designation of cultural units does not involve a major revolution. Revolution is a false dilemma; it does not reflect the possibility of thousands of microrevolutions on farms, factories, and families, all at local levels.

6.2.4.3.1.1. *Identify Basic Landscapes.* The basic landscapes and their divisions have been described (Section 5.3.2.3.2.5). Sacred landscapes are critical for keeping many cultures healthy. Preservation landscapes, also of high cultural value, are maintained by human exploitation using traditional ways, including herding and nomadism. Conservation landscapes allow a higher level of exploitation, but without the addition of subsidized energy or the impacts of heavy equipment. Domestic landscapes have been simplified and manipulated for higher levels of use; fields and forests are managed by industrial methods and tend to have the characteristic of domesticated, controlled lands. Artificial landscapes have been almost completely modified and covered, for travel, urbanization, and industry, although a few wild species may be present. Foundational landscapes protect the processes that create wilderness (often the most fragile and sensitive areas).

By keeping these divisions separate, and limiting the kinds of activities in them, the landscapes themselves will be healthier. Not all activities are compatible; furthermore, living systems have developed in relative isolation, and function best with a limited amount of interference from other species or other systems.

6.2.4.3.1.2. *Protect Ecosystems.* Formal law tends to seek guidance on normative issues from the general population, rather than from legal experts. People care for animals and wilderness. Natural rights are defined by positive laws and by negative restraints on behavior. Laws are needed to protect ecosystems and wilderness, now.

Wilderness has been the name used by many cultures for uniformly empty, chaotic, useless, valueless, or untamed areas. Although what remains currently is still largely untamed, wilderness is not uniform, empty, chaotic, useless, or valueless. Recently, wilderness has been recognized as holding resources and as being important for recreation. Wilderness has also been realized to be the source of agricultural and cultural richness. Indeed, these reasons are presented as justification for saving wilderness from exploitation or interference. But there are more basic reasons to save wilderness: It is the source of diversity, it exists apart from human concern and industry, and it is the only sanctuary for wildlife apart from humanity. Wilderness is filled; it has its own values and uses

Other forms of wild ecosystems equally need protection. Eight distinct kinds of wilderness are identified: Sacred landscapes, Foundation Areas, Reservation Areas, Preservation Sites, Restoration Areas, Neopoetic Communities, Conservation Parks, and Wild Forests (or Fields; see Wittbecker 1984). Many domestic landscapes need to be protected, especially where they have become integrated into surrounding systems; this would include small farms, for instance. Many landscapes or systems are valued as heritage sites and these too should be protected for cultural reasons. Some artificial areas should be protected if their operation is isolated from other systems (that is, the original ecosystem has been totally destroyed or replaced).

Plants and animals—and their ecosystem context—are as much of our heritage as art, history and tools. Ignorance of one is just as sad as ignorance of another. The survival of society depends on an expanded ecological awareness of the global system in its complexity and connectedness. The spirit of humanity depends on an ecological consciousness that places humanity in a proper relation to the wild places of the earth, taking what it needs, but letting the rest be.

It is important to respect limits and to maintain the integrity of ecological processes that generate the ecosystem. To this end, we should establish a position as Keeper of the Ecosystem, perhaps as an elected office. The Keeper would take a personal interest in all the activities that involve the creek. The Keeper would represent the interests of the creek in political, business, and public meetings. The Keeper would be responsible for public education to setting up land trusts—the function of a Land Trust is to identify and protect lands that have biological or cultural significance; it could work through acquisition, conservation easements, cooperative agreements, and education. The Keeper would give educational presentations on the value of the creek and ecosystem protection, and work to involve stakeholders in their legacies. Economic and political means would provide incentives to preserve land from development, preserve diversity of habitats, and reintroduce native species. Personal commitment is the most effective means of protection.

6.2.4.3.1.3. *Calculate Global Ratios*. Each land or ocean system would be classified and put into an appropriate category, ranging from pristine to heavily industrialized land. Each category would occupy a different percentage of the planetary surface, depending on calculations of minima and maxima and depending on cultural values and decisions. At a minimum, approximately fifty percent of the land area would occupy the first division (eighty percent of ocean and water surfaces); sixteen percent in each of the other three (four for water); leaving two percent for completely artificial landscapes—industrial or city (two for water). These figures are consistent with several earlier proposals. Eugene Odum suggests thirty percent forest cover worldwide, with sixty percent in tropical areas. Paul Shepard offers seventy-five percent of the total land area left wild in a technocynegetic society. Constantin Doxiadis suggests fifty percent of the surface area in wilderness. We cannot preserve less until we learn more about the requirements for large cycles.

6.2.4.3.2. To Manage Common Resources
The Global Union would have the power to designate areas for conservation, including the oceans and atmosphere. It would regulate all industrial and residential use of common resources. Furthermore, it would form new institutions, both regulatory and advisory, such as a Global Union Environmental Agency, to deal with resource availability and alternate technologies, create global scientific bodies to study global ecological balance, collect data on global systems, explore remote areas, and maintain a central library of all information on sciences, technologies and cultures. It would maintain reserves of food and minerals for emergencies and catastrophes. The Global Union could perform a resource function for all nations, maintaining large crop margins, for instance for seven years, to secure survival. Future survival should depend on systems sufficiently flexible and elastic to sustain moderate failures in parts of the world without causing catastrophes to a connected food system. This attitude applies to the entire technology and survival controversies: Irrigation, tankers, nuclear power, pesticides, population, deforestation, and genetic engineering.

Finally, the GU would recommend optimum populations for nations, although it would not enforce those figures. Optimal sizes would be calculated, based on social and ecological limits, as well as on traditional values. Every nation needs a comprehensive population policy, closely related to environmental and technological policies, and within the constraints of their agriculture. A single population policy for the world is unfair, since cultures are at different stages of development with different values. There are dilemmas posed by necessity to equate global balances and republican needs. Since the allocation of resources to a nation and the representation of a nation would be determined by area and not population, there would be no reason for a nation to exceed the optimum figure. If a nation wanted to expand its population, it could do so through a number of means: Trading off with other nations or through the development of new food technologies, such as attached greenhouses for every building. If growth exceeded a safety margin established by the Global Union, demographic policies would be strongly recommended by the Global Union, without prejudice or malice.

Humans have modified their surroundings as much as possible within their power to improve their lives. Recently, they have done so to improve nature. Believing that nature was incomplete, they added plants and animals, then added fields, structures, canals and dams to feed the plants and animals. In The Origin of the Species, Darwin observed that insular biotas were glaringly depauperate in general, until supplemented by human culture: "man has stocked … far more fully and perfectly than has nature." Unfortunately, filling up nature and perfecting the earth did not proceed with ease; there were setbacks. Exotic animals and plants ran wild and became pests. Fire control caused raging fires. Dams became the sources of diseases. Canals introduced pests. Plantations ruined soils. Irrigation projects salted up the soil. Peter Matthiessen noted that where great, wild creatures ranged, vermin prosper. If the influx of new organisms of all kinds continues unabated, all life on earth will eventually become homogenous or drastically changed; then it will also be strained through the filter of adaptability to humanity and their managed crops. This flora and fauna will undergo change as our living habits change. On the other hand, if we plan our future, we can include squirrels instead of rats, butterflies instead of cockroaches.

The induced instability of ecosystems is an important cause of economic, political, and social disturbances throughout the world. The disturbances are passed on to humanity. And where our intervention has unbalanced nature, we need to repair. Each biota has developed only once in the history of the world. And once lost can never be regained. Some environmental degradation can be reversed, but not biome or species extinction. We do not know how many whole systems that we have destroyed. Nor do we know which element of a system is a more crucial one. Very little is known of degradative synergies from noise, heat and pollution.

6.2.4.3.2.1. *Renewal of Resources*. Ecosystems damaged by social activities may reacquire lost ecological qualities by natural processes. Ecosystems dependent upon periodic natural disturbances, for instance floods or fires, may be markedly changed if these disturbances are controlled. Damaged ecosystems may also be rehabilitated to a condition that includes some of their original properties and some beneficial to humanity. Much of our manipulation of nature is highly desirable for us, perhaps even for some natural systems. Some possibly may be enhanced by management techniques to an improved condition different from the original. Some may remain degraded.

Ecosystems have enormous powers of recovery from traumatic damage. They can overcome the effects of outside disturbances by progressively reestablishing ecological equilibrium, even if not exactly to the original state. Frequently, other potentials are activated by the outside disturbance. Unfortunately, the key word is outside. No disturbances are outside, anymore. If all ecosystems are disturbed, no improvement can come from outside either.

The rate of healing of injured systems is often more rapid than expected. Good management and human commitment can aid the process. The recycling of degraded environments is one of the urgent tasks of our age. Marsh envisioned man as a coworker with nature in the reconstruction of "the damaged fabric which the negligence and wantonness of former lodgers has rendered untenable." Under loving care, even very degraded ecosystems can be made productive and satisfactory for humanity, although not the same as the original. "Even the most successful programs of reclamation and the best artificial environments cannot of course duplicate the subtleties and complexities of natural environments; but most of them will improve in time," states Rene Dubos.

Of course, they might, as they become less under control and less invaded. Perhaps humans have a secret desire for simple environments. Dubos seems entranced by the bleached islands of Greece, as well as by deserts. Do we want all earth to be those abstractions? Dubos has spoken eloquently of the humanized landscapes, but there is no one to praise what has been lost. There are inherent values in wilderness as much as in the humanized landscapes. The impoverishment of Southern Europe may be aesthetic, but it leads to human impoverishment.

Should ecosystems be restored to a close approximation of the predisturbance condition? It is always feasible to establish more than one type of ecosystem on a disturbed site. Due to climactic change, faithful restoration may be impossible. Certain ecosystems are perturbation dependent. Untouched reference areas could be preserved as models.

6.2.4.3.2.2. *Conservation of Resources*. The Emperor Asoka, in Third century BC India, took a positive stand on wildlife conservation. The same Asoka earlier had caused roads to be built with periodic rest stops, for the care of animals. In most literatures there is little mention of the long history of rural conservation. The rural economy is the result of centuries of careful cultivation. Wise people have always treated resources with care. Many countries in Europe and Middle East had strict regulations for management of water, wood and farmlands. Vergil's *Georgics* were written in support of government policy to remedy the decay of rural lands.

Carrying on from the UN, the GU would work to conserve genetic resources and necessary wetlands and watershed forests. The Biosphere Programme of UNESCO is a worldwide monitoring of all major biomes and their ecosystems based on international agreements. Conservation efforts are concerned with: The dynamics of a system; the interactions within the system and effects of climactic and system changes, including human involvement; the varying time scales of concern; and, the preservation of natural communities with a high degree of integrity, subject to intrinsic processes.

Conservation is basically a problem in ecology and must be addressed on a regional and global scale. Conservation is practiced as an affluent token; even poorer societies are conserving with the expectation of tourist income. Volunteer financing is inadequate. Long-term GU financing is necessary to extend the effort beyond the lifetimes of politics. The cost of saving the wild for a common heritage must be borne equally. If Brazilians cannot extract minerals from the Amazon basin, if an Indian peasant loses a bullock to a Bengal tiger, there must be some balance.

Richard Allen contends that the way to save the world is to invent and apply patterns of development that conserve living resources essential for human well being and survival. Although resource conservation is thought of as specialized and limited, it cuts across all human activities, and should be incorporated.

6.2.4.3.2.3. *Management of Resources*. History records the debris of some civilizations that tried to manage their resources and failed; they existed in the Americas, the Middle East, Africa, Asia, the Pacific, and Europe. Natural resources were originally defined as objects provided by nature for human use. This concept has been expanded over thousands of years to include minerals, wildlife and people. Eric Jantsch claims that humanity now acts as a systems manager at all levels, where management is an activity that aids evolution, acting with it, recognizing and applying an ethics that transcend an individual level.

Even most of the noncultivated land surface of the earth is being managed; elephants, giraffes, crocodiles, wolves, caribou, snail darters, redwoods, prairies flowers are managed or else destroyed. Many are done in by human recreation, with its attendant necessary vehicles. Even a modern, balanced exploitation may destroy forests and fisheries. Currently, many resource managers espouse the ideas of equilibrium maintenance and maximum sustainable yield. These ideas are poor guides to management. By trying to maintain habitats in equilibrium, we often set them up for catastrophic decline, for instance, in fire-climax pine forests, or destroy resident species, such as the California condor.

The use of maximum sustainable yield in wildlife management has resulted in the degradation of the populations involved, whales and salmon, for instance. A carrying capacity is not constant; species that live near the limit of capacity cannot be killed at a maximum. Even small numbers, for the Sandhill crane, less that six percent, hunted could result in extinction. This may be true of wolves, bears, mountain lions, and other species.

Some managers, like whalers, are far worse. They do not try to manage for a continued maximum yield; they try to maximize the economic value of a resource, in spite of an awareness of extinction—the rape of one "resource" provides the capital for the rape of the next.

The idea that everything should be managed is based on an extreme belief that nature is a resource to be processed. Furthermore, management is self-perpetuating and self-justifying. The objective of resource management is to increase the measure of quality of life for affluent people in overdeveloped countries.

Management, even conservation management, has been based on economic objectives. And, as Aldo Leopold pointed out, the weakness of relying on economic motives is that most members of the earth's community, such as wildflowers and song-birds, have no economic value. Yet all the members of the community contribute to the integrity of the whole, which is vital to maintaining what we do consider important. Those beings with no economic value are ignored, or worse, labeled as weeds or vermin and destroyed so that crops and animals with short-term advantages for human ends can be substituted. The goal of this institute is that kind of temporary control.

The impulse to manage nature is an expression of the judgment that we know how the world should be run. But we are finding that we do not know at all. We did not know about the effects of DDT or radiation or chemical dumps or special drugs. The whole approach of the conservative position ignores the physical and ecological dimensions of resources. The vandal position is even more basically ignorant. Laws of ecology must be obeyed for these laws determine our existence and that of "resources." There can be no "balance" between obeying some laws and disobeying others.

We are unbalanced. Our whole industrial world view is unbalanced. Balanced resource management will still unbalance nature, though perhaps at a slower rate. The balance of nature has to come before the balance of resources. We will continue to be unbalanced until we enlarge our understanding of nature and let ecological limits suggest new technologies and techniques. A balanced relationship between humanity and environment is necessary.

Such a balance must be based on conservation, if it is to avoid harmful 'side-effects' and provide benefits. We must invent patterns of development that also conserve living resources essential for survival and well-being. This kind of conservation is not a special and limited activity; it is a process that affects all human activities. Conservation must be integrated with development to ensure that vital parts of the biosphere are protected or modified only in ways it can sustain. A conservation strategy has to identify the most significant objectives, according to criteria of biological importance and urgency of need. Damage to life support systems that are becoming irreversible—extinctions, habitat destruction—these need the highest priority. Every independent group should prepare proposals for cooperative programs concentrating on biomes that cross boundaries, that is, tropical forests, rivers, and global common areas, such as oceans and atmospheres.

Common resources can be managed, if the system is managed so as to minimize fluctuation and interference, so as not to impact the stability of the process, so as to harvest an appropriate production, but so as to be aware that even a stable sustained yield of a renewable resource might change deterministic conditions so that resilience is lost and a chance event could trigger sudden change and the loss of integrity of the system. Some resources can be restored or renewed, although intervention may be inappropriate if natural cycles, including catastrophic events, are not understood. Natural processes of recovery work slowly, but good management can accelerate them.

6.2.4.3.3. To Protect Unique Human Cultures

Cultural patterns relate human communities to the ecological areas in which they are embedded. Any culture is only one of many possibilities. There is no single or correct way. By 1900, humanity had spread through 1,000 different cultures and well over 3,000 languages—roughly equivalent to the number of natural biogeographical provinces and subprovinces on earth. Whenever groups were geographically separate, there was differentiation, which enforced separate cultural identities.

The real feelings of innumerable groups of people center on much smaller regions of the world than nations. For example, Britain is composed of Scotland, North and South Wales, Northern Ireland, Anglia, and Saxony. It may mean more to be Welsh or Irish than British, or Quebecois than Canadian, Kurd than Iraqi, Mongolian than Chinese. Forced cultural integration breeds tensions; in the USSR by 1988, the tensions exceeded the force and advantages of integration. Rwanda, and Tanzania are additional cases.

Many cultures in established countries, like Scotland in Britain or the Nyiha in Tanzania are organized cultural communities, but are not permitted to join the UN because they do not possess armies. A new world order would permit autonomous groups to join the Global Union according to cultural or linguistic affinities and not merely force of arms. Nations could break up into preferred "natural" units. Every cultural group, or nation, is considered equal, regardless of size or sophistication. These things would contribute to their protection from forces that fragment and destroy cultures.

6.2.4.3.4. To Coordinate Representation of Cultures

The Global Union, would function as a global coordinating body with powers and limits. In order to coordinate representation, the GU would create a representative body. Each nation would provide a set number of representatives to the governing body of the Global Union, which would provide a forum for designing the governance of the earth, one in which everyone can participate.

6.2.4.3.5. To Provide Services to Nations Groups & Individuals

Garret Hardin noted that the Marshall Plan, which channeled $12 billion for rebuilding Europe after 1945, was not entirely altruistic; it was meant to keep the USSR out of Europe. After the Marshall plan succeeded in Europe, Mr. B. Hardy convinced Truman to extend the plan to the world; the result was the beginning of foreign aid in 1949. But, the plan did not work as well. Over $80 billion and 25 years later, most aided countries are still poor. What was the difference? The plan in Europe recreated an industrial civilization. Foreign aid expected illiterate, fatalistic, poor populations to try something new to their experience. Although it was funded at about the same level ($3 billion per year), it was expected to help 20 times as many people—2 billion instead of 100 million. Furthermore, the expectations were wrong. A. van Dam suggested that the Marshall Plan extended to the world in the same spirit and at the same level would prove more rewarding and stimulating.

That amount of investment is only equivalent to the production of two day's goods and services in North America, Europe and Japan. Linear thinking, combined with economic altruism, can lead to great short-term successes, but to long-term problems.

Strictly, human altruism occurs only on a tribal level. Biological heredity makes kin altruism possible. Money makes a flexible and reciprocal altruism possible between unrelated members of the species. Money also makes people less materialistic; it is a symbol. It frees people from the calculation of gift-barter. Telescopic philanthropy—the term is from Charles Dickens—is not coupled with responsibility. Our gain is unrelated to any effect on the recipients. That irresponsibility may be part of appeal. Hardin wrote that human actions should be guided by charity, but he applied the older understanding of the virtue, which he noted confers benefits and refrains from injuring, but does not shrink from inflicting suffering to achieve real good. Amiability, or good nature, is a weakness not to be confused with charity. It is the source of foreign aid, which ruins the longer prospects of a self-reliant life.

Any kind of aid is a distribution from a commons, as Hardin notes. Dealing with a global commons is more effective through laws that end destructive behavior. Furthermore, laws are a second-order altruism; an individual does not risk acting as a lone altruist, in violation of Hardin's Cardinal Rule of Policy, which is to never ask a person to act against his own self-interest. If it can be demonstrated that the long term effects of egoistic actions are harmful, people may be persuaded to forgo short-term gains. To prevent a tragic end to commons, the system must be changed. People will be reluctant to change because of the uncertainty of technological forecasting and political stability. Political change may be similar to lifting one's self by the bootstraps.

The tragedy of the commons could happen in mass economy, not necessarily in an information economy. Hardin believes that coercion, centrally controlled by majority rule, is required for survival. Self-interest and knowledge of capacity could also avoid tragedy. J. Martino claims that private property can eliminate the tragedy also; self-interest of the owner dictates. In this case, a global socialism would work because it would be responsible to national cultural units, whose interests would be represented. Economic cooperation in world of scarcity will not solve environmental problems.

The Global Union, by comparison, would furnish only temporary aid in the form of help and education. The kinds of aid would be threefold.

6.2.4.3.5.1. *Rescue and assistance.* Responses by the UN to earthquakes in Peru (1970) and Nicaragua (1972), droughts in Africa, floods in Bangladesh, and other disasters, are indicative of the promise of cooperation, although many efforts have been minimal or diverted into administrative mazes.

6.2.4.3.5.2. *Civic action* would be concerned with representation and voting. Mass media would be available to every culture for referenda. Civic action would include technical projects, such as farming or reforestation. Civic action might also address inequity and population or immigration concerns. Civic action groups, similar to the U.S. Civilian Conservation Corps (1930s) or the U.S. Peace Corps (1960s-), could apply appropriate technology on request. Richard St. Barbe Baker suggested armies for reforesting the Sahara; the technical feasibility has been demonstrated in places, but any whole effort is crippled by politics.

Special education would be a priority. Education would be especially important at this common level, since cultures would dispense local specific information. All scientific and technological knowledge shall be available to all states, as regulated by the Global Union. Scientific research and development, especially on environmental problems, will be promoted in all states. The GU will support a free flow of scientific information and experience. The GU will also ensure that appropriate technologies are available to all countries. The GU will award basic educational and research grants to all humans, for whatever use desired. An earth university might be established. For public health, the GU would create indicators of social and biological health, as well as monitor health, trade, and social quality. It would establish centers on epidemic and disease control, recognizing that health in general depends on healthy global cycles and ecosystems. For financial health, the GU would standardize exchange rates and provide banking facilities. It would work to stabilize the prices of commodities and materials and set common business standards in terms of work and pay units and wade values—the unit of wage shall be a human work unit, which shall have equal value for all. The Global Union would provide laws and courts to address problems of justice.

6.2.4.3.5.3. *A Global Union Police Force* would replace all National armed forces; GU enforcement would consist of a persuasive presence for the observation of law and order. The UN force in Cyprus (1960s) performed this function admirably. An GU charter would ensure the inviolability of personnel and their right to intervene in any conflict when asked by any group. With world consciousness, the weak and disadvantaged can get food and shelter by appeal or right, without plundering, without war. War would be allowed to evaporate with the protection of all people by a central governing body. Fighting would occur, between individuals and small groups as interests conflict and communications falter. Nonviolence is possible only between rational individual human beings. Sometimes force is necessary. Therefore, some armed security would be necessary, and part of the police force would be armed. A shift from military to police forces could provide that security. This police force could provide humanitarian intervention.

6.2.4.3.5.4. *To Manage Populations.* Human populations tend to expand, especially after agriculture, to fill up the human niche, to use every possible resource and to reduce every kind of flexibility. People then become excited by the intensity of people and addicted to the luxuries of trade. For humans not to destroy the planet, we have to plan an a satisfactory or optimum population rationally or irrationally.

At low population densities, management only needs to apply to interpersonal behavior. Management in this sense is at the limits. A global framework could proscribe behavior at the limits, and prescribe on a cultural level. It could balance the equation of access, rights, and distribution.

6.2.4.3.5.5. *To Adjust Human Equity & Species Equity.* The GU would be responsible for distributing a portion of the wealth of the earth among humanity. In this sense it would be socialistic. It would regulate resources for a common good that included all living beings. A redistribution of the imbalance of wealth would require an attitude like altruism. It would also work to endure opportunities for ultrahuman species in wild ecosystems to allow natural regeneration of important systems.

6.2.4.3.6. To Create Concord (Peace) & Accommodate Discord
Like the UN before it, a global framework would try to create the conditions for peace and eliminate war. What is war, again? War means fighting or hostility, campaign or invasion. But, more than just being a kind of conflict, it has the connotation of physical harm or complete destruction. Long ago, war changed the level and scale of violence, by involving more people and by making the fighting more detached. Now, war is guaranteeing its own continuity. The dangers of the military-industrial complex, that Dwight Eisenhower warned of, have increased exponentially. The original axis of military and industry now includes, in the U.S., the enthusiastic complicity of the entire legislative branch of the government, which is supported by the military and industries, and the inbred ideas of the new forms of think-tanks, which are supported by the military and industries. All four are staffed by escalating revolving-door policies. The profit-driven American way of war, where the U.S. presents itself as the arsenal of democracy and the reluctant guardian of freedom, works to ensure the coca-colonialization, that is, the economic colonialism, of weaker countries and the physical subjugation of disagreeable countries.

Wars are advertised and sold to the citizens of a nation using the same dishonest and fallacious, but effective, techniques. Supposedly, one can consider war as the imposition of order through the death and destruction of people causing disorder. Is war simply contention or conflict? Contention means verbal strife or dispute. Dissension means difference of opinion or opposing groups. Conflict means strife, struggle, collision, hostility, fight or battle. These words may have been adequate at one time, but war, as institutional destruction, has to be eliminated; the word has to be refer to behaviors that are no longer exhibited. So, what will remain? All those smaller pieces, such as fighting, conflict, dispute, and strife. These will not go away. But, they can be kept small and handled by different kinds of treatment, and maybe rarely, force. Discord is a good word to collect the human behaviors. Discord means a disagreement, from the words meaning 'hearts apart.'

What then is peace? Is it dull and uninspired? Why is it desirable, if it is dull and impossible? The word 'peace' is from the Latin '*pax*,' which is from Sanskrit 'to fasten.' Peace can also mean concord, harmony, amity, friendship, or just 'quiet.' Popular definitions of peace start with 'freedom from war' and go on to 'freedom from public disorder,' 'freedom from disturbance' and 'freedom from disagreement.' This is a negative way to define freedoms or peace. Peace must therefore be order or agreement.

Agreement is a going together without conflict, which is what morals are, a going together. Accord is the fitness of things considered together. Concord means of the same heart and mind. It also means agreement or harmony. Concord can mean the friendly relationship between nations or a treaty. Concord is a better word; it avoids the negative connotations of peace.

The problems of war, aggression, nationalism, disarmament, degradation, goodness and peace are problems of human nature, that is, of symbols, cultures, politics, and ecology. They are not simple problems and not easily solved. They are interrelated as human groups and natural ecosystems are interdependent ecologically, politically, economically, and technologically.

Human interactions are dominated by symbols. The most powerful set of symbols, embodied as nationalism, has a direct relationship to war. The intellectual rationalization for the continuous preparation for war is the old Roman adage: "If you want peace, prepare for war." This adage has been so completely taken into the modern heart that most of the larger nations have spent half of every century in war, according to Pitirim Sorokin. Preparation for war has always led easily into war. There seems to be no reason that the present preparation will lead anywhere else.

Starting peace means ending preparations for war. Modern communications, radio and television, could reveal the concern for peace virtually everywhere. But, they also aggravate the images of inequality. It is unrealistic to expect cooperation without some fair redistribution of resources and manufactures. Equalization would allow trust. Trust would allow many customs and prejudice barriers to fade away.

Communication through art could have a fundamental role in promoting peace. Friedrich Schiller believed that there was historical proof that art can achieve what violence and law cannot—art could educate and liberate the individuals of society in a gradual and peaceful process. In spite of the cultural forces dominant at any moment, an individual has the potential to determine a different and peaceful course.

7.0. Getting to Global Government of Commonwealths

Having analyzed, or at least regarded, the whole of human history, it is possible to see long-term trends or problems. Having discussed and dissected what the human relationship to the earth actually should be and imagined goals and responsibilities, it is time to outline the physical steps that could be used to create a eutopian framework. There is always some path to a destination. There is always some way to proceed to goals. Having documented the catalogs of losses and suffering, it is necessary to act now. The first step is to strengthen the identities and boundaries of nations. We can start by offering the status of nation, with a voice and one vote, to any culture willing to participate in a new international government.

7.1. *Finding Workable Divisions & Sizes*

Before the advent of large-scale civilization, according to A. Keith, the habitable earth formed a mosaic of separate territories and peoples; and this grouping favored rapid evolutionary change. The size of the group depended on the fertility of the territory. In archaic peoples the group varies from 50 to 150 individuals; he calls these local breeding, competitive groups, units of evolution.

The tribe was the appropriate form of social organization for humans at the subsistence and pastoral stages. Tribes are a second step in production of evolutionary units; local bands are federated into larger units, tribes. Tribal groupings can reach a third stage, the national level, as exemplified by the Iroquois confederation or the Aztec state. Perhaps cities were followed by leagues of cities or city-states. Keith concluded that from an evolutionary point of view, city-states carry a weakness which eventually proves mortal. All go the way of Nineveh. He suggests that Egypt illustrates the weakness. Then nations followed. The national feeling requires larger loyalties and consciousness of common destiny. The territorial sense, conscious ownership of homeland, is important for human evolution; it is certainly not less important than kinship.

7.1.1. *The Stage of Nations*
The nations are a new stage in the development of cultures. Each new nation enlarged the size of ecosystem and increased the number of interrelationships. Is the nation system maturing? Nations are primary, secondary or tertiary producers depending on whether they trade with raw materials, processed goods or manufactured goods.

A nation, by definition, has a single, central government. A national people occupy a continuous country, have consciousness of the larger unit, as well as a consciousness of samenesses and differences, and of national security. The state is a type of strong central government with a professional ruling class divorced from kinship bonds. It is stratified and internally diversified. It may have developed in a number of ways: Irrigation, warfare, population growth, trade, or integration by religions.

The people of a nation-state were given full sovereignty officially in 1648, with the Peace of Westphalia. Representative governments still use that sovereignty to claim responsibility for their actions, without recognition of any international body. Perhaps this is why so few are willing to transfer any perceived sovereignty to an international body. Nations insist on sovereignty. But the sovereignty is concerned with rights more than responsibility. Sovereign governments have the relation of anarchy between them, that is, they are without a way of governing the community of nations.

The whole land surface almost of the globe is divided into centrally governed states. Currently, human affairs are managed within the framework of autonomous national units. Individuals live within boundaries they did not choose, whose boundaries were drawn with straight lines. States often impose one life-style on their populations and reeducate citizens to accept the regime.

7.1.2. Limits of Nations

Lord Acton observed that nationalism aimed solely at making a nation, the abstract idea of the political state, and not at encouraging liberty or prosperity. He also predicted that the result would be moral and material ruin. Perhaps abstraction is the ruin of humanity, more than nationalism.

Many large nations are basically exploitative: The United States concentrates on Latin America; Europe on Africa; and Japan over Southeast Asia; Russia over Eastern Europe; and China over Tibet. Some of the reasons for the existence of great powers are: The rapaciousness of society; the acceptance of war; and the economic advantages of large scale operation.

The cultures of industrial nations are based on unethical accumulations of materials. The success of large nations may be due to accumulations of power, the wrong kinds of power. Power is capacity to carry out reasoned intentions, even if the reasons are irrational. Power is centrifugal now, as people have more influence over future. The power has shifted to interference with nature. Reason can live in natural landscapes without radically altering them, but irrational use destroys them. Locke declared that the negation of nature was the way to happiness. The purpose of government was to allow people freedom to produce wealth for themselves. Many nations have usurped that freedom for their leaders. All economies are upset by power relations, but the dislocations still make the wealthy wealthier.

Nations use war as a tool of politics. War has allowed the seizure of the resources of other cultures. War has helped nations grow larger through conquest and incorporation.

Large scale does confer temporary economic advantages, especially if the economic system is only short-term. The scale of nations is a problem. Some nations are too big to cope with some issues and too small to cope with others. For employment, law, and liberties, decision-making has to be close to the personal level. However, Ervin Laszlo thinks that nations are too small for effective transborder decision-making, for labor, resources, and marketing. He thinks nations may be too small for national and environmental security. Many territorial and environmental issues are unmanageable at local or national levels. Nations have regional and global responsibilities that they seem too small to execute, especially related to regional peacekeeping. But, nations are already too big, which is why Canada sells all the forests in British Columbia, even if BC does not want to sell them, and BC sells Golden's forests, even if Golden does not wish to sell them. Nations are too big to balance the needs of communities. The perspective of great nations is ethnocentric and it fails to distinguish scale and size, which matter.

7.1.3. Discord Conflict & Nations

The population explosion and technicalization of human life is occurring in a framework of nationalism. The world order of nations commits those who believe in the theology to war with one another. The war ethos has been expanded and reduced to absurdity, as so many know and say. War has become so big that there can be no victories or victors, and possibly no survivors. The only remaining purpose can be the total destruction of the combatants, defined as nations, as well as most of civilization and large parts of the earth.

Strangely, the only people who do not know this—or admit it—are those in decision-making positions, who sadly are compelled to prepare for what they subconsciously must know would be a terrible disaster. Their power has made them the most secure prisoners of their nations, afraid to be

7.2. Transitioning to Global & Local Politics

People have been predicting catastrophes and global shifts for the past 50 years. They have identified discontinuities ranging from weather patterns to disease patterns to political upheavals and collapses of alliances. The trends they identify are unsustainable. The responses are unknown or uncertain. The predictions are uncertain. So, we need some kind of direction, as well as an understanding of catastrophes.

Many kinds of catastrophes are possible and that raises questions. What are the contributing causes? How can they be changed? Other questions include how can catastrophes be diverted or lessened or stopped? Disasters regularly arise from natural and economic systems. They are part of the process. Recently, we have a new catastrophe, called the U.S. problem, the U.S. emergency, or the U.S. crisis, even though it is a human crisis or a global crisis. Other catastrophes that befell other cultures, from the Mesopotamians to the Greeks to Rapa Nuins, were generally local and did not effect the remainder of humanity. Of course, the Mediterranean was changed, as was the Fertile Crescent and many islands. Now, we are more connected. Regional and local problems can become global. Perhaps we should act as if we were wise and make changes immediately.

7.2.1. Adopting a Psychology of Catastrophe

The word catastrophe means 'down turning,' from the Greek word fragments (*kata trope*). A catastrophe is a down-turning, literally. Most catastrophes are assumed to be fast, sudden, and manageable. But, catastrophes come in all ranges of speed, size, temporality, visibility, and combinations. Our language is poor in its terms for catastrophe. A slow catastrophe could be called a bradycatastrophe. A long-term catastrophe could be called a chronocatastrophe. A large catastrophe could be called a megacatastrophe, a global catastrophe perhaps. An unseen catastrophe could be called a cryptocatastrophe. A multi-pronged catastrophe could be called a polycatastrophe. Unfortunately, catastrophes can and do occur in many combinations. Thus the loss of species by the planet might be called a polycryptobradochronomegacatastrophe.

We know of many catastrophes that have happened in the past or distance. Such catastrophes may have included an asteroid strike that ruined the dinosaur dominance or the ecological collapse of freshwater systems, but until they happen to us, knowledge of them will not be adequate to inspire change and preparation.

Widespread poverty from gross inequities may cause current, close catastrophes, such as nuclear war or biological warfare. Richer countries will need to recognize that the poverty of others is not in their interest, especially as potential markets. Inequity may never be erased. Perhaps some inequity is good and stimulating, but gross inequity needs to be limited. Famine may come home with a vengeance, with a crisis of industrialized agriculture. But famine is not the real problem. The real problem is the inability of people to perform on unbalanced diets—to behave in a human way. This covers mental retardation, laziness and other incapacities.

7.2.1.1. Bad Circumstances

Humankind possesses incredible scientific evidence of environmental wobble, biological imbalances, and the unfitness of entire domestic species, but knowledge moves few to action. Probably nothing will be done until catastrophes become common experiences.

Perhaps good can come from catastrophes. Eric Jantsch wonders if major catastrophes on earth mean only a weeding of a garden by evolution; the loss of many lives that may permit more beautiful flowers. On the other hand, humans made the garden they way they like it. Many catastrophes would not improve our situation through chance.

Catastrophes concentrate attention on a landscape and its people and that is their benefit on human affairs. Ideally, it should not take catastrophes to precipitate corrective measures. Instead, we might resent the necessity to change. William Catton recommends that we do not indulge in resentment. Our bad present circumstances result from the innocence and hope of our ancestors; they are the result of decisions to have babies, fires, televisions, tractors, and status. The understanding of catastrophe may let us avoid it or at least ameliorate it. Catton makes the biological analogy that die-off is a signal to overshoot, and overshoot leads to habitat damage. The agent of a post-irruption crash may be starvation, war or just behavioral stress.

If civilization collapses, the struggle back to a technological society will have greater limitations. Accessible minerals have been scattered; the gene pool has been greatly reduced. Then it may be too late. Our species may die. It is hard to image all life on earth dying. Even the worst of catastrophes would leave a simplified ecology of mosses and slugs. Weeds and invader species would prosper. Habitats would be ruled by the natural laws of ecology again. Perhaps herbivorous animals would build up large populations again. Fortunately, catastrophes do not occur in completely destructive patterns. Limited starvation occurs before total starvation. There will be uncomfortable smogs before acid rains destroy all crops. But these things could signal the necessity of immediate corrective actions.

Eric Eckholm described how economic and political pressures, which are derived ultimately from population pressures, forced farmers to intensify their efforts to increase crop production. This seems to instigate an utterly dismal cycle of population expansion, environmental deterioration and poverty: As the population expands, arable lands are used to capacity, and sometimes beyond; as the soil deteriorates, it requires more fertilizers that cause more hazardous conditions that decrease agricultural capacity; people starve, but the population increases, and marginal lands are used to meet increased demands, or food is imported from other lands.

Eckholm describes how the usage of such marginal lands can result in a dust bowl phenomena, when climatic conditions revert. Clouds of topsoil rolled east into cities from the dust bowl in the central United States in the 1930s. Afterwards, national conservation programs were able to restore some of the mythical fecundity, through pasteurizing, strip cropping, terracing, and contour plowing. However, current production efforts are causing greater losses of topsoil, and farmers are abandoning some of the conservation methods for economic reasons. Eckholm concludes that free market conditions encourage dangerous trends. The lesson of the latest dust bowl may be forgotten until the next one.

The world food supply is in danger. Almost all the continents, except North America, now have grain deficits. And as energy and capital become dearer, the likelihood of adequately feeding the world grows remote. As topsoil loss contributes to a decline of world productivity, the higher expectations on the remaining acres may impair their productivity. This deterioration is most severe in poor countries, but its effects should concern everyone. Eckholm concludes that the United Nations must identify, analyze and marshal world resources against these trends. A scientific method will take a long time, however, and poor countries cannot wait. They must attempt a rural regeneration to stop urban drift. He interprets these trends as indicating the sinking of marginal peoples on marginal lands into a quiet helpless poverty, leading to later urban deterioration—perhaps less quiet.

The serious firewood shortage over most of the earth is also charted by Eckholm; it is considered due to population pressures on the remaining woodlands. Pressures on British woodlands in the 1300s forced people to turn to coal as a fuel source (a source then regarded as inferior). The timber famine reached Europe in the 1700s. It had existed in China and India over a thousand years before. There have been crises in clothing also, as animal hides became scarce, and then wool came into short supply as farming was expanded into grazing lands; cotton was imported from colonies, where it ruined fertile lands; now, synthetic fibers are made of petroleum products and chemicals. Each substitute required more energy to produce. Humanity has provoked a global crisis of local crises.

7.2.1.2. Fast Change

Most scientific studies have stated or implied that change cannot be fast, that people could not adjust, that social disruption would result, and that chaos would finish what ignorance and technology could not. The most serious drawback is the time of implementation. The Club of Rome claimed a 20-year feedback lag. The Ecologist cited a social inability to adapt to rapid change. Everyone assumes the time scale remaining before collapse will be long enough for their plans to be implemented. But, these studies also propose slow, long-range plans, while warning at the same time that the earth is facing imminent, drastic change. Certainly, if their plans are implemented too slowly, and if the population or pollution doubles again, surpassing some unrecognized critical level, then there will be worse disruption. Their beliefs depend on the truth of the limits to the rate of social change. As Plato recognized, it is never too late to reverse the fatal tendency towards decay, however late the hour.

It is questionable whether these time limits are absolute. For instance, war produces relatively fast, far-sighted—if wrong-headed—policies. War is actually stimulating to many individuals and often produces a national determination and purpose that peacetime does not. War is said to unite whole peoples in a common cause. But, war is a catastrophe for most living beings and for the equity of wealth.

There are other times when human beings face rapid and catastrophic change without chaos. Social systems can adjust if there are popular reasons. When a dam breaks, there is an emergency, and millions of people can mobilize to meet it. When the earth quakes or volcanoes erupt, when people flee from rival nations, there are emergencies, and they are met quickly.

There are millions of people starving every month in India and Africa, and others in Europe, the Pacific and the Americas. This is a catastrophe also, though it is slow, constant and quiet. These are emergencies and should be treated as such. Furthermore, whole species are disappearing, and whole ecosystems are wobbling, from exploitation, desertification and pollution. These are great catastrophes and much more final in character than any local one. In fact, many of the previously mentioned problems are only symptoms of these. Especially since we are part of the web of life and may be working toward our own extinction. Miners used to take canaries into the mines with them, because they are sensitive to carbon monoxide poisoning. The death of a canary was a warning. The extinction of so many species now may be such a warning to us.

The trouble with complex, self-regulating systems is that very small changes have large consequences—Reid Bryson points out that shifted rainfall patterns caused whole cultures to disappear. In some cases, where conditions, like drought, are cyclic, in the Sahelia region of Africa, humans expand during the good times, only to perish when the drought returns. In other cases, human activities, such as deforestation or overgrazing of herds, can cause weather changes. We tend to approach the limits of use of some environments. We also tend to overdependence on modern high-energy methods of agriculture and on some key resources, like water.

We need to adapt consciously to slow catastrophes. The environment is changing too fast for genetic adaptation, so our change will have to be psychological and social. Social changes can occur very rapidly when the time is right for them. Oil-producing nations, for instance, became financial equals of industrial countries within months. Pressures are building for radical change.

Change can intensify and accelerate. Small changes in different weather patterns can lead to dramatic changes in climate. Changes in climate can lead to dramatic changes in the species composition of ecosystems, as well as to human food production and housing costs.

7.2.1.3. Applying a Disaster Psychology

Catastrophe has its own psychology. Humankind possesses incredible scientific evidence of environmental wobble, biological imbalances, and the unfitness of many domestic species, but knowledge moves few to action. Catastrophes, on the other hand, concentrate attention forcefully. When a dam breaks, millions of people mobilize to meet the emergency. When the earthquakes or volcanoes erupt, the emergencies are met quickly. The psychological effects of a hurricane—fear of suffering and dread of loss, accompanied by exhilaration—have admirable 'side-effects;' the definiteness of danger and the immediacy arouse people to great heights of cooperation. People react admirably to catastrophe. They choose sensible directions and agree to practical expedients. War also produces relatively fast, far-sighted—if wrong-headed-policies. War is actually stimulating to many individuals and often produces a national determination and purpose that peacetime does not. War unites whole peoples in a common cause. There are times when human beings face rapid and catastrophic change without chaos. They can adjust if there are popular reasons.

Immediate foreknowledge provokes a greater response than indefinite expectations: hurricanes occur periodically, but not always in the next three hours. Probably nothing will be done until catastrophes become common experiences. As choices become more important, more urgent, errors are more disastrous. It should not take catastrophes to precipitate corrective measures. There are millions of people starving every month in India and Africa, and others in Europe, the Pacific, and the Americas. This is a catastrophe, although it is slow, constant, and distant, and perhaps because of that, it is neglected. Perhaps distance limits the ability of people to react to problems.

Furthermore, whole species are disappearing, and whole ecosystems are wobbling, from exploitation, desertification, and pollution. Environmental deterioration proceeds so slowly that the change is invisible, that is, until a catastrophic threshold is crossed. Those catastrophes, in places from the Tigris and Euphrates to northern Africa, seem to be long-term. The trouble with complex, self-regulating systems is that very small changes have large consequences—shifted rainfall patterns caused whole cultures to disappear. In some cases, where conditions, like drought, are cyclic, in the Sahel region of Africa, humans expand during the good times, only to perish when the drought returns. In other cases, human activities, such as deforestation or overgrazing of herds, can cause climatic changes. The scale and rate makes our situation seem natural, but that is because it has been a slow catastrophe, just now approaching the threshold.

But, humans should not adapt to these catastrophes. As Rene Dubos has pointed out, humanity is enormously adaptable and resilient. We could probably survive almost any physical or social conditions by adjusting to them; for example, overcrowding and smog are the norm in some areas. Hans Selye suggested that an organism is in more danger from its adaptive reactions than from external agencies. Adaptation has its own dangers. We might become less humane, less creative, and less concerned with starvation, suffering, crowding, or destruction. Our goal should not be to survive under any conditions, however difficult and unpleasant. Our goal should be to create an optimum life in an optimum environment. Perhaps this goal needs to be framed first in a humanistic or religious framework.

We do not know where to look for meaning in a cultural world, plagued with dispossessed people. Nothing is meaningful if civilization goes mad changing whole ecosystems, as Paul Shepard suggests it is. The adaptational environment is too fast for genetic adaptation. We have adapted from arboreal animal to nomadic hunter to agriculturalist to urban chemist in a short time. Little is understood about the adaptiveness of human social behavior.

If we could precipitate a disaster psychology for slow environmental or cultural catastrophes, then the priorities and motives of people might be changed. But how should everyone be convinced that there is a crisis? The change is so slow: Fewer eagles, fewer salmon, more people, and more beverage cans. The causes are so complex, and responsibility is so difficult to assign.

Unfortunately, a history or theory of catastrophes does not engage us. People need to feel situations before they act, and people will need to feel themselves as part of a delicate web of relationships before they act with ecological wisdom, as once they had to feel that the earth was round by going around it, as lately they had to see that the earth was an oasis in space by leaving it.

7.2.2. Taking Immediate Action

A transformation of world order is necessary before the next large catastrophic event. But perhaps, as many have said, the dreadful has already happened—in Hiroshima, Vietnam, Africa, and lesser known places—and the cultural transformation is already awakening or has already finished. Most cultural transformations are invisible.

Maybe the gloomy forecasts are right. But, it is the function of a Cassandra to be always wrong. To be successful, Cassandra always has to be willing to be proved wrong. If she is disbelieved and her warnings go unheeded, then her prognostications may come true. But, if she is given credence, steps are taken and policies are changed to falsify her warnings.

Political response is not enough to change the system. Many problems are social or cultural; many are personal. As people change their attitudes, social and political changes can be made. This could take generations. A violent revolution could occur within weeks, but generations could be wasted imposing patterns on personalities. Social change can spark personal change.

The future is said to be in our hands, but our hands are in the cookie jar or on our genitals, and we are afraid to let go to touch something different. Perhaps we are just insecure. Disaster is not inevitable, unless we refuse to change our ways, in which case disaster is inevitable. So, we need to change. The change is going to discomfort many, but not as many who are being discomforted by not changing directions.

How long do we have before we have to change? A decade? A hundred years? When should we start? Last minute? Last week? Next month? How should we acquire urgency? Or the political will to change or the wisdom to change in better ways? What are our long-term interests? Is it necessary to declare a state of emergency? Another alternative? Not a war against nature or injustice, which is a tired metaphor, but just a rational response to a long, slow catastrophe. The response has to be immediate action.

Figure 722-1. Cassandra in mythology

7.3. Taking Coordinated Action on Three Levels

After adopting an attitude towards catastrophe and starting to take action immediately, people, nations and a global framework will continue to act on those three levels. All three are necessary, but perhaps the individual is the most critical and important, if not to make changes, then to stimulate change for others and at higher levels.

This action has to include a survey of the state of the world, of all ecological and social systems. We have to make radical changes in the economic and political systems that arrange, produce and distribute wealth. We have to create a framework for world order without making the mistake of a gigantic global dictatorship, even if it is for the good of equality and environmental health. An order has to be based on bioregional models where nations are based on ethic populations in specific regions, where the operation is of interlocking hierarchical systems.

7.3.1. Acting as an Individual in a Community

The redesignation of cultural nations would not involve a major revolution for most people. Most people prefer to remain in their native culture, with a geography they fit into, in an economic system that reflects their values, and as part of a religion that explains their image of place. Revolution is a false dilemma, it does not reflect possibility of thousands of individual actions on farms, factories, and families, all at local levels. Individuals can control their lives. They can make choices to be self-reliant or to limit their impact on their supporting environment. Margaret Mead noted that this is how anything has ever been done, by the actions of committed individuals.

Of course, small steps can work. Little things matter, if the scale of the repetition is large enough, that is, if others do it also. Individuals can try to question things that seem to be automatic behaviors, such as wanting children or requiring personal transportation.

A first step for an individual can be to live frugally, as suggested by Henryk Skolimowski. You can reduce your role as a consumer by not seeking meaning in the acquisition of things. That would result in fewer clothes, fewer tools, fewer toys, and fewer luxuries, which would force the economy to change from obsolescence and growth to development and permanence. That does not imply being impoverished, just fewer luxuries.

Simplicity can continue with the diet, by eating lower on the food chain, with more vegetables and fruits, and by getting local food, which keeps the money circulating in your neighborhood. Reducing the consumption of meat will reduce the demand for meat and cattle, which will reduce the use of rangelands and resources for these animals.

These kinds of steps start with responsibility for your health, and include learning and play. Other steps reflect participation in the community and its government, and can include volunteering for conservation efforts or for service to the community. Individuals are responsible for trying to guide corporations and nations, which can lose their ethical directions. Individuals can reduce conflict through conversation, consensus and compromise. Listening to others is one way to start. Assessing one's self is also important. Based on participation and assessment, individuals can take effective actions (for a longer discussion, see the book *Eutopias*).

People live in communities. The community is responsible for the health and activities of individuals. Common values are reflected on the community level, since they are imbibed by individuals in the community. The community has distinct actions that can be taken for human culture to get to good places. Communities need to define themselves explicitly and implement specific ecological and cultural goals, from monitoring local ecosystems to managing resources for sustainable use.

A community must also balance its budget, matching income and pay-outs and planning for challenges and discrepancies. Income is the form of usable or tradable wealth that is used by the community to pay for public expenses and amenities. As Herman Daly and John Cobb point out, the means of raising community funds would also be the means of attaining personal and community goals. Taxes could be ways of internalizing costs, as well as guiding development and effort by targeting behaviors to be discouraged, such as polluting or gouging. Such taxes could include use taxes on air, water, elements, and land, loss taxes on depletable resources such as coal or fisheries, adjustment taxes on costly habits like smoking or drinking. Other taxes would influence financial speculation, the distribution of money, the 'heroic' accumulation of possessions, disposal of heritage things. Significant monies could come from licensing individual privileges, such as driving, voting, businesses, weapons, marriage, and children.

The community would spend money on its infrastructure and on vouchers for individuals or families. Vouchers could include income, medical treatment, education, and resource use.

7.3.2. Contributing at the National Level

Individual and community efforts may be most important, but action at the national level can co-ordinate changes or make them a matter of policy. Making the policy can feed back positively into community and individual actions as well. Although people group into families and communities, there are many possible groupings between the individual and the national. The responsibilities of each group may be determined at the national level, or certainly through a process involving the national, regional, local and personal levels. Thus, some things may be more appropriately controlled at a county, state or province level, such as collecting taxes for roads. Other things, such as health insurance, may be best directed at a national level, to ensure the equity of distribution.

The nation level has responsibilities to define itself, literally, into a larger self, to represent its people and other living beings. It has to define and secure its borders, balancing isolation and connectivity, emigration and immigration, and conflicts and treaties. The nation has to set ecological and cultural standards, the ecological for the health of the territory and cultural for trade, technology, and rights. Rights have to be established for nature and beings, nonhuman or human. And these have to address the space and opportunities to exist and flourish. Human rights have to include the right to a healthy environment with clean air and water, to security and the opportunities to make a home and create work. Some rights, such as the right to have children or share in luxury, might be tradable. A nation has to give equal representation to everyone in its borders. Although distinctions will be made between citizens, noncitizens, visitors, and tourists, each will be represented to some degree. A nation is obligated to protect the rights and privileges that have been defined and agreed upon. Citizens will have more rights and privileges than noncitizens or visitors, because they pay for them with taxes and participation.

A nation has obligations to meet the basic needs of its shareholders, through saving and restoring wild and neopoetic areas, as well as to control special groups such as corporations. A nation is obligated to limit use of limited resources, from water to minerals or space. It may need to privatize, communitize, or nationalize some resources.

National planning may be necessary to monitor resource use or human health, as well as to anticipate regional or global changes that would affect a nation, such as climate change or the integration of technology.

And, of course a nation has to balance its budgets, getting income to match pay-outs. Taxes can have effects other than raising money for a national government. Tax can used as a tool for the equalization of use; many people are luckier or greedier than others. Taxes could be a way of internalizing costs. Taxes can encourage or discourage activities. Although taxes would be in similar categories to community (or state) taxes, including use taxes, loss taxes, adjustment taxes, and redistribution taxes, they would be levied on national commons and national participants (see the book *Eutopias* for detailed discussions). Income would also be generated through fees or national licensing of things like airwaves, media, or voting. Payouts would go to reduce the legacy debt of the government, as well as operating costs, including those for elections, communications and special departments. National vouchers could supplement income, medical needs and resource access. A nation would also be expected to pay some share of global costs.

Both income and payouts would have to be restructured to achieve a balance. Many national subsidies and taxes would have to be eliminated. Certifying national standards in a long-term economy would make many changes easier to bear. And, of course, nations need to work with other nations and to assess their own performances.

7.3.3. *International Level Actions*

A eutopian framework could be implemented immediately. Most global studies, such as those from the Club of Rome and The Ecologist, state or imply that change cannot be fast, that people cannot adjust, that social disruption would result, and that chaos would finish what ignorance and technology could not. These studies propose slow, long-range plans, while warning at the same time that the earth is facing imminent, drastic change. If their plans are implemented too slowly, and if the population or pollution doubles again, surpassing some unrecognized critical level, there would be worse disruption. This Eutopian proposal suggests immediate action, scaled on a week.

Sudden change is already a hallmark of industrial progress. Industrial cultures have replaced older patterns with great suddenness. Eutopias cannot seem more sudden than the loss of a home or favorite place. Industrial cultures have reduced people's control over the means of production and power. Eutopias does not offer less control. Whole communities have been destroyed by industrial scale. Our social structures are already changing rapidly and impractically.

Let us take immediate action to make the changes conscious and more practical. Eutopias offers movement towards common, achievable goals. Eutopias would be a framework for cultures, where different human experiments are tried. Its variability would insure that we could reject any of the local visions that fail. People may object to giving up too much or not gaining enough. Eutopias may be called anti-human, anti-progress, anti-scientific, anti-technological, or anti-educational, but it is merely a new framework for conducting traditional human activities.

Natural environments and human societies are wobbling. Many contradictory impulses are leading to unbalance; some countries want to consolidate into economic powers and others want to secede into independent units. Human civilization will tear itself apart if we let it. We can slow it down and direct it.

The need to maintain our comfortable status for as long as possible, fatalism that nothing can be done or it is too late, prejudice, ignorance—all are keeping us from moving. There are other reasons not to move: Failure of knowledge, failure of communication, failure of imagination, and failure of nerve. Much human suffering is caused by self-deception, which leads to isolation and then anger, reaction, and more suffering. Real change is difficult in this state, but change is more difficult for people who are starving or oppressed.

For most people in agrarian countries, even freedom from hunger and sickness is utopian. For most people in industrial countries, the choice of a fulfilling profession is utopian. Grinding poverty, economic dislocation, homelessness, are more painful than any fast transformation to a eutopian framework. Already most cultures have been transformed by cash crops, mining, tourists, highways, high-rise housing, and condominiums. Physical disruption has been more extensive than the transition to a eutopian framework could cause.

A long view seems meaningless when so much suffering already exists. An immediate, realistic, coordinated program of action is needed, capable of being implemented by communities and global agencies. We must face our responsibilities directly, declaring that there is no place in a eutopian society for monopolistic and multinational corporations, for the maniacal religion of merchandise, for genocidal military establishments, for urban explosion, for state socialism, for overbearing bureaucracies, or for technocratic politics—we must act to end them. The declaration must be political, through cooperative networks or leaderless consensus, by persuasion and example. The problem of human existence on the planet must be approached without deference to artificial boundaries of states, races, or castes. Poverty, pollution, repression, are concerns of every human community. We must stand and state that nature has limits, that we cannot have all we want.

The application must be immediate. The crisis of exponential growth and destruction cannot be solved just after some final limit is approached or passed. The crisis of ignorance cannot be solved by hurrying ahead and creating more problems. Paradoxically, the best thing to do is stop—stop growing, stop producing, stop running; suspend the race and contemplate a direction. We have been asking how the earth will survive its human populations and how they can be lowered. Let us just freeze growth and see what happens. Let us just freeze the populations—a year or decade of no births. We know that whole countries have lost a generation and continued. We know they have rebuilt again from ruins. We could build from recycled materials alone, so there is nothing to fear from stopping. Immediate social reforms, the reallocation of resources, and the preservation of wilderness are necessary, because of the nature of the problem; we cannot predict global climatic or ecosystemic catastrophes. Substantive change and research cannot be delayed until academic controversies are resolved.

The transformation must be complete; it cannot be done partially. Global political and economic institutions must all be changed. The Global Union (GU), more empowered than the United Nations, must have authority for the preservation of nature and human cultures. Holistic change will permit the reorientation and balance of local institutions. For example, air pollution is not independent of industrial processes, transportation, and employment patterns. Communities must be of a size that their members can feel responsible for them. These changes are demanded by new requirements, ecological balance primarily among them. New institutions must be compatible with these new values.

The approach must be pragmatic and flexible. By its nature, the eutopian frame could reduce some of the stresses of transition, the uncertainty, ambivalence, or reversion. The readjustment to the realities of our new intricate involvement in the whole order of nature and her ecological balance will cause social swains. Some capital of energy and materials may be wasted. Population will be matched to solar budgets or net ecosystem productivities. Production will be redirected to communal needs in transportation, housing, food, and recreation.

There will be problems regarding the breakup into more natural cultural divisions. Some will want to decide boundaries by ecosystem; others through culture, watershed, or political power. The Global Union will have to decide when two groups claim the same place or when cultures combine through unions and conspiracies.

There will continue to be other problems. Cutting trees in Nepal causes floods in Bangladesh, and floods cause deaths because overcrowding has forced the poorest people to live on flood plains. The poor in the highlands everywhere effect those in the lowlands, often adversely. The quest for ecological balance means that some ecosystems must be maintained by systems managers, who often overmanage. The larger the human impact, the more control is necessary. Eutopias seeks to improve people's circumstances by enlisting them to save their environment and way of life.

People cannot be given material equality instantly. But things can be leveled within a culture;

cultures with excess may be taxed by the Global Union. Providing work for everyone is one way to narrow income differences. The GU, nations, communities, and families must provide it. Worthwhile work requires imagination. The large work force employed by military contracts in industrial countries will be dislocated at first, but that employment is supported by taxes, which could be reallocated for construction and deconstruction—so many highways, manufacturing plants and abandoned buildings.

Crime and civic unrest will not disappear. The Global Union and nations could reduce many kinds of global and victimless crimes with new policies. Because most cultures have strong policies regarding drugs, abortion, and prostitution, among other things, the GU would not impose rules on every crime. Dangerous weapons, from automatic guns to tanks, and dangerous products, including nuclear reactors and biocides, would be strictly regulated.

People will still make mistakes and bad choices in a eutopian framework. But, if a form of government is bad or ineffective, then it can be altered more easily in a smaller, more flexible framework. In the eutopian framework, people can learn from mistakes or unintended side-effects—as when doing good causes evil. The scale is small, so the catastrophe is small. There will always be some injustice, inadequacy, and unpredictability. Large political and economic institutions have only made it worse. If a eutopian frame turns out not to be the proper framework to solve these problems, it might point to a better way.

7.3.3.1. Implementing Immediate Steps for an International Body

The GU can be based on the UN, but with immediate responsibilities and powers, for protection and preservation, as well as some temporary powers, such as taxation. Too many things have happened in the past 100-500 years. The solutions need to be started now. Immediate steps are necessary to address catastrophic changes.

7.3.3.1.1. Creating a Framework for International Union

The original charter of the United Nations (UN) restricted its activities to peace-keeping and human rights. While these are still important, other things need to be addressed, especially as they directly relate to concord and harmony (peace and health). Many things need to be done. New organizational bodies need to be created. These bodies would operate inside the new Global Union (GU) and be harmonized with existing bodies. Other bodies, such as the World Bank or International Monetary Fund, that operate parallel with the GU, must be reintegrated as part of the GU Financing. They must be governed by the GU executive branch, rather than by their own independent governing bodies, which are unduly influenced by wealthy countries. The GU needs to control it agencies and departments, as well as its financing.

The GU must have the power to define itself, to rewrite its charter so that it encompasses more than security and health, or expand those things to include all of human activities. Several studies of the UN, such as the Jackson and Pierson reports, have already focused on organizational efficiency—and efficiency has been the dominant factor in all bureaucracies for the past one hundred years—but the organization needs to be powerfully relevant to address the challenges that modern global trade has proposed to traditional cultures.

The GU can accept new nations as members. Membership in the GU needs to be opened to those states now represented by UNPO, that is, cultures, without recognition of their land, as well as other cultures that may not be landed at all. Recognition may also be granted to the regional association of cultures or nations.

Independent cultural areas within nations shall have the status of independent nations within the GU. Any culture would be given legal recognition, protection, and full autonomy over their boundaries by application to the GU, which would determine priority of claims (by archaic peoples, agriculturalists, pastoralists, or industrialists). No action would be taken to disband existing nations. Nations could still remain allied with old, larger nations as independent or dependent regions, although they would have only one vote at the highest federation. The nations would determine the use of allocated resources. Local economics and technology would provide for populations. Traditional religions and customs are maintained or permitted to develop.

The GU may consider whether it should extend recognition to voluntary economic associations, that by reason of size or power, such as some international corporations or regional industry associations, have great influence of capital and resources. Once membership is nonculturally or nonnationally based, however, it must be open to NonGovernmental Organizations, that may be dedicated to special interests or to preservations. And, then, perhaps the interests may be religious or spiritual. However, for voting purposes, nations or organizations may have to give up privileges as one or the other. On the other hand, the GU might require corporations and organizations to be based at the community or national level and participate in them materially.

The framework would allow a loose unity. For example, consider this lesson from fifteenth-century China: Too much unity stifles a creative advance; or this lesson from Europe: Too much disunity wrecks a creative advance. Europe had enough disunity to prevent unification, but not enough barriers to prevent the spread of technology and competition for technology. The role of the GU would be to provide just enough unity for nations to advance and develop. A eutopian framework is a form of 'balkanization' with limited barriers and limited unity. The barriers serve only to protect the culture, its resources, its people and standard of living.

The GU would create a different structure than the UN. The GU could be modeled as a federal government, although it would be composed of independent nations. This would be necessary due to the responsibility of the UN for global issues and to coordinate nations. The GU would also guarantee fundamental environmental nonhuman rights, as well as human rights based on common things.

The GU would rework its constitution as a formal process of expressions and expectations. Traditionally a constitution is an agreement to divide into rulers and ruled. For the GU it would claim responsibility for all global affairs, including the environment and large weaponry.

The executive branch, the Secretariat, would be elected from the General Assembly. Seven to twelve members would be elected. They would elect a coordinator with the title of Secretary or Coordinator. It would have authority over all departments and agencies. It would mange the organization as an organic whole. The General Assembly, as a legislative branch, would make global and international laws. It would strengthen the Declaration of Human Rights (1945). It may make the planet into an incorporated entity. The judicial branch would be the International Court

Other branches may be separate and equal. Nations would nominate others for these branches. A Commission on the Earth would have the responsibility to consider all events in the environment from earthquakes to biodiversity. Other important Commissions would be the Commission on Beliefs and Religions and the Commission of the Heritage of Cultures.

The Office of Ombudsman would be expanded and strengthened. Although not traditionally a fourth branch of government, as first proposed in Sweden, its function would be to improve the effectiveness and fairness of the global government while protecting basic human and ambihuman rights. One strength would be its power to initiate legal proceedings in behalf of any human and ambihuman constituents or nations. It would be an independent branch with separate responsibilities: To investigate complaints against the UN or its officials for wrongdoing; to investigate complaints against nations; and, to investigate the operation of the UN.

7.3.3.1.2. Starting Catastrophic Measures by the International Union

Because the challenges are immediate and because the consequences of not meeting them could be catastrophic, these things have to be started immediately. Of course, they are part of a process that may never be complete, like a one-time fix, but they have to be started immediately.

7.3.3.1.2.1. *Transfer Powers to the International Body.* The major military powers would grant their powers to the Global Union and relinquish their efforts towards global leadership; they also resign from the security council, cease propaganda activities, renounce foreign policy objectives, call back all soldiers from foreign countries, and stop giving away produce, factories, or weapons. They put their technical and educational surpluses at the disposal of the GU. If the USA or Russia is to be a world leader, let her lead in tolerance or in trust. Let her be the first to give allegiance to a world organizing body, the GU, the first to divest themselves of nuclear weapons. If they fear for safety, they need only remember the success of nonviolence in India or of guerrilla actions in Southeast Asia, Central America, or the Middle East.

7.3.3.1.2.2. *Disarm Nations by International Body.* In a separate essay entitled "Toward a World Social Contract," Kenneth Boulding examined possible global mechanisms to abate conflict within "Spaceship Earth," including "universal policed disarmament down to internal police levels" and "the organizational union of the armed forces of the world under a limited world government" — both of which are key elements of unfolding official U.S. government disarmament policies envisioning a world "effectively controlled" by the United Nations.

The 1945 UN Charter envisaged a system of regulation that would ensure "the least diversion for armaments of the world's human and economic resources." The advent of nuclear weapons came only weeks after the signing of the Charter and provided immediate impetus to concepts of arms limitation and disarmament. In fact, the first resolution of the first meeting of the General Assembly was entitled "The Establishment of a Commission to Deal with the Problems Raised by the Discovery of Atomic Energy" and called upon the commission to make specific proposals for "the elimination from national armaments of atomic weapons and of all other major weapons adaptable to mass destruction."

The UN has established several forums to address multilateral disarmament issues. The principal ones are the First Committee of the General Assembly and the UN Disarmament Commission. Items on the agenda include consideration of the possible merits of a nuclear test ban, outer-space arms control, efforts to ban chemical weapons, nuclear and conventional disarmament, nuclear-weapon-free zones, reduction of military budgets, and measures to strengthen international security.

The Conference on Disarmament is a forum established by the international community for the negotiation of multilateral arms control and disarmament agreements. It has 66 members representing all areas of the world, including the five major nuclear-weapon states, the People's Republic of China, France, Russia, UK and U.S. While the conference is not formally a UN organization, it is linked to the UN through a personal representative of the Secretary-General; this representative serves as the secretary general of the conference. Resolutions adopted by the General Assembly often request the conference to consider specific disarmament matters. In turn, the conference annually reports its activities to the Assembly. The conference indicates that disarmament ideas are considered.

The U.S. must keep its own promise to give up nuclear weapons, which it made in 1970 when it signed the Non-Proliferation Treaty. The U.S. must terminate its $8 billion annual program to develop new weapons and agree to Russian President Putin's offer to reduce the mutual nuclear arsenals of about 10,000 weapons down to 1,000, or down the ante to zero.

The U.S. and Russia need find parity with the arsenals of the other nuclear weapons states, China, UK, France, and Israel, with stockpiles in the hundreds, and India, Pakistan, and North Korea each with less than one hundred bombs, should find reduction easier. China has offered to negotiate a treaty to eliminate all nuclear weapons and call every nuclear weapons state to the table. There already exists a plan for a model treaty prepared by scientists, lawyers, and policy makers, which was submitted to the UN as a discussion document. It lays out all the steps for dismantlement, verification, guarding, and monitoring the disassembled arsenals to insure that we will all be secure from nuclear break-out.

Russia and China have repeatedly offered a proposal in the UN General Assembly to ban weapons in space. That is the only way that those two nations will agree to join the U.S. in abolishing nuclear weapons. They do not want U.S. control and domination of space, which indeed is the aggressive mission statement of the U.S. Space Command, to gain military superiority over the whole planet. We must also replace the Non-Proliferation Treaty's guarantee of an 'inalienable right' to so-called 'peaceful' nuclear technology. This is the provision on which Iran is now lawfully relying. It could be nullified by establishing an International Sustainable Energy Agency and phasing out nuclear power. Every nuclear power plant is a potential bomb factory, so it would be impossible to eliminate nuclear weapons eliminating nuclear power.

An international body could disarm all nations; it could fund its work through the redistribution of the $200 billion in tax breaks and subsidies given to the nuclear and fossil fuel industries worldwide. The treaty negotiations and actual dismantlement of the nuclear arsenals could be done within weeks, although years or decades will probably be requested. If nuclear weapons were illegal, Korea, Iran and other nations might be willing to give up new programs, without recourse to attack or bribery.

All other nuclear weapons nations have indicated that they would be willing to give up their nuclear weapons, numbering in the 100s or 10s, if the larger nations do. The U.S. has been the biggest block to the efforts to stop proliferation. It is naive to believe that anything less than the elimination of nuclear weapons will reduce the possibilities of nuclear war and the unimaginable catastrophes that would follow a nuclear winter.

Elimination of nuclear weapons will not stop wars, although it is less likely that wars could be as destructive or final. Other weapons of 'mass destruction' also need to be reduced and controlled, especially long-range guns or automatic missiles. These weapons are designed to kill as many people as possible as quickly and cheaply as possible, regardless of their status as combatants or civilians. The International GU could work to bring every arsenal to parity.

7.3.3.1.2.2.1. *Take or Destroy Nuclear or Large-scale Weapons.* Complete disarmament could be accomplished within a week. Earl Osborn proposes this concept of sudden disarmament in response to the tedious phase-out envisioned by most plans. An agreement would not involve much negotiation. Taking this first step would add to the prestige of the country bold enough to do it. The GU could post a police force to disable all military ordinance. A thousand planes each carrying one hundred trained inspectors could be distributed at all major centers in the nuclear countries within 24 hours (1 day).

7.3.3.1.2.2.2. *Allow Personal Weapons in International Body.* For Nations, the GU would make available cruise missiles at some agreed-upon level. For individuals, it would allow personal weapons from hands and knives to arrows and single-shot guns, depending on national choices.

7.3.3.1.3. *Starting a Year of Consideration through the International Body*

We can do two simple things: Stop and go. We can stop—stop growing, stop producing, and stop running. Suspend the race and contemplate a direction. We know that whole countries have built again from ruins. So there is nothing to fear from stopping—if we know there would be no problem going again. What are the dangers of fast social transformation? Lack of justice? Lack of order? Stopping might create a steady state, a period of rest, and time to explore human values and quality considerations. This strategy would avoid the eventual hardening of choices. But it must be instituted at once. The crisis caused by exponential growth and destruction cannot be solved just after some final limit is passed and some ultimate catastrophe begun. The crisis of ignorance cannot be solved by hurrying ahead and creating more problems. We have been asking how the earth will survive its human populations and how they can be lowered. Let us just freeze growth and see what happens. Let us just freeze populations—a year or decade of no births. Let us stop subsidies to industrial agriculture. Discontinue links with the international commodity market. Stop throwing all waste into natural cycles. Suspend destructive searches for remote resources. Start no new buildings. We could make it a year or decade of celebration, an expression of human and cultural unity. By stopping, everyone would have time to participate in design.

The Global Union promotes a year of consideration. Starting with population growth, all economic growth, or expansion of claims, would be suspended for a year. Age grouping would be discontinuous for a while, if further years of consideration were necessary. The use of certain poisons or chemicals, especially greenhouse gases and other chemical additives that destroy ozone, would be discontinued.

This does not mean everything will stop, just growth-related activities. We can ask questions about everything. Then we can survey every habitat and ecosystem. We can act to conserve, restore and preserve ecosystems to keep them healthy. We can start creating a permanent organic agriculture. We can keep extra materials separate or recycle them immediately. We can restore uninhabited buildings and places. We can monitor all domestic and wild systems. We can integrate human and natural values and represent them legally. We can deconstruct some cities and build new ones. We can plan and rework transportation systems. We can work for equity across cultures and communities, redefining wealth, sharing and leadership. We can create a satisfactory aesthetic civilization, based on eutopian strategies.

The problems may be regional and global, but they can be addressed on a local scale, decentralized and human scale. A locality can have the authority, the power to take responsibility and make decisions, for global problems that impinge on the local. It may not solve the global problem, but it will affect it, especially if other local communities exercise their authority.

An ecological or global ecological design project could address every aspect of civilization, adding goals, resizing formal, corporate or cultural efforts to survive and prosper. Good design can make it easier to act on a local level, for instance, by providing human-powered transport for all countries. Pedal power can trump gasoline, even those that get 100 miles per gallon. By offering simple, good, lower-carbon stoves. By combining functions to improve social use; Papanek suggests putting washing machines (or Laundromats) in playgrounds, so mothers or fathers could socialize and work while watching their children. Papanek notes that the easiest way to save resources and energy, and cut waste, is to use less. Conserve. But, we can also produce designs for survival.

Let us make it a year of celebration (even in an emergency), where we start no new products, no new house starts, until the old ones are renovated or resettled. No new profits for individuals or corporations (all given to the government for redistribution to the neediest. We could put off having children for a year.

Using less seems to be connected with economic health. In a dramatically changing world, with most of us fearing change, design needs flexibility with a synthetic approach. It needs to be integrated, comprehensive, and anticipatory, as Fuller and Papanek urge. We have to direct our representatives into global emergency actions, and participate ourselves. This is another function of design, to change human behavior.

7.3.3.1.5. Start Equity Measures & Goals

The global environment needs to be equalized also. If every nation or person has certain rights to land and resources, then those have to be respected and adjusted. Some GU taxes would be designed to repair the inequity from hundreds of years of unfair trading or accumulation.

7.3.3.1.5.1. Implement Global Ecological Goals.
Global goals apply to the planet as a whole, for Gaia as a metaphor for the living planet. These goals are not simply the sum of local and regional goals. The GU would:
- Reimplement international initiatives to slow deforestation—the UN notes that previous initiatives accelerated deforestation, as in Cameroon, where log production is planned to double in the forest, home to 50,000 Pygmies with a unique and valuable cosmology and life-style
- Plant and maintain forests sufficient to guarantee indefinite support of known and unknown global biogeochemical cycles
- Protect fragile ecosystems with global importance
- Reduce threats to ecosystems from acid rain and other nonpoint-source pollutions to less than 5 percent of present values
- Plant 9 million ha of trees each year to meet current demands; for soil and water conservation, plant another 6 million hectares (at an estimated cost of $6 billion dollars); and plant 110 million hectares just to catch up with cutting
- For the planet, reforest 1.4 billion hectares to restore the 30-40% forest cover removed in the past 3000 years.

The GU would monitor ecological goals for nations and communities.

7.3.3.1.5.2. Implement Global Cultural Goals.
Global cultural goals apply to every human culture.
- Protect the health of human communities; set standards for health and provide information and assistance to nations.
- Provide educational assistance to nations. Encourage cultural education and history. Encourage teaching of local languages. Allow renewal of critical customs. Educate all people to feel their connections to their place, because, until they feel them, they will not act ethically or ecologically. Educate people to realize that long-term sustainability requires healthy places, and that protecting places protects jobs and values.
- Coordinate and support economic activities. Broaden local economies from resource extraction to invention and specialization. Promote the full use of ecosystem products; support small-scale businesses that produce new, high-quality products. Increase manufacturing efficiencies.
- Guarantee sovereignty for nations. Offer a platform for communication with other nations. Open communications with all groups working in the region. Work to establish equity.
- Help nations stabilize their cultural environments, as well as their populations and resources, which can be related to the limits of place.

The GU would be responsible for defining the goals that are common to human cultures and coordinating goals on the global level.

7.3.3.2. Managing Nations
The GU would take responsibility to manage the interrelationships of nations, to try to coordinate trade, reduce conflicts, and foster respect for other nations and cultures.

7.3.3.2.1. Create a Charter & Constitution for Global Union
The Charter of a global association has to expand the original charter for the United Nations. It needs a formal constitution that spells out additional responsibilities. The constitution would indicate how the Association would relate to nations, corporations, alliances, and NGOs.

Global organization should be in the form of a heterarchy, a multi-level structure integrated at regional and national levels. Community levels would self-reliant, but linked with other communities into nations and regional alliances, The regional alliances would not be allowed voting rights separate from their components in the GU. The regions would be too large to be manageable. Corporations currently that did not have to have a cultural or territorial base might be given temporary status until they were integrated.

7.3.3.2.2. Create New Structure & Branches of Global Union
Because a global association will have more responsibilities than the United Nations, it must create a new structure, with new branches and agencies.

7.3.3.2.2.1. General Assembly (Legislative) for All Nations
The General Assembly would include old and new nations. Conceivably, the number of nations could exceed 3000. The General Assembly would make all laws and rules.

7.3.3.2.2.1.0.1. *Define Limits of Global Law*. Global law would be directed at global interactions relating to nations and corporations. It would also address global resources and problems that follow from the cycles and uses of resources.

7.3.3.2.2.1.0.2. *Make Laws*. The UN made laws against war. The GU must expand those laws and be prepared to enforce them. Laws also need to passed to address other human concerns, such as slavery or internal violence. Laws have to be proposed to control international spread of disease. A whole set of laws is needed to control global resources.

7.3.3.2.2.1.1. Office of Normalization & Nationalization
The GU has to issue its challenge to allow cultures or provinces join the organization and to have one vote. Any culture or province would have the right to apply for membership. The size and form of nations would begin to decentralize and normalize. The requirements for nationhood would be basic: A traditional culture, traditional territory, or the size and uniformity of people. Although new nations would vote independently, they could maintain a regional association with other small nations.

7.3.3.2.2.1.2. Office of Standards for Ecosystems Nations & Trade
Through a eutopian program the Global Union (GU) could set up and enforce international ecological rules of trade, for including environmental costs into the prices of things. Economists, especially global economists, have not much considered these 'externalities' which are really free internalities, free so far, because they have been big and plentiful. To compete in an open arena with fixed economic policies and no ecological policies, nations often squander their ecological capital to be competitive in the short-term. There has been no reason political or economic to save resources to be sustainable in the long-run.

7.4. Managing Itself as a Global Government

The Global Union would create an Office of Budget to secure and balance its budget.
This office would be concerned with funding the GU. Where will money come from? What do we have now? Footloose food and crazed capital? In the form of dues, contributions and the sales of bumper stickers? The union would have the power to collect money from the use of the global commons, both for the purpose of limiting the use of the commons, but also to guarantee a source of income for the organization. The new office would have to coordinate the income from taxes on global resources and rents and fees on common lands, such as Antarctica.

Ever since priests made lists in clay to keep track of traded items, businesses have been using accounting to ensure that they prospered. The principles of accounting may permit some degree of permanence in a brewery or airline, for instance, but not in the entire environmental system. At some point of exploitation, many environmental systems, and the cultures that depended on them, collapsed.

The real costs of free goods and externalities are mostly still not accounted for, yet—this often influences the selection of corporate priorities and growth. Furthermore, the production and distribution system for most economies is linear (straight throughput) and not circular (complete recycling), although this is logical economically, given our frontier resource-use accounting. Major changes are occurring, though. The scale of civilization now makes externalization unfeasible. The costs of pollution and waste are being internalized; other inputs, such as labor and capital, are becoming more expensive. Economies will have to internalize or be forced to internalize. With the internalization of costs (since the losses as well as benefits will accrues privately), the system will benefit from intrinsic responsibility.

Economies need to work cooperatively to make sure the costs and benefits are extended equally throughout the system. They could start by sponsoring the rational use of rare resources through taxation. A wider economics could influence the government to determine priorities for wilderness areas or special landscapes. Beautiful, fragile, unique, or endangered ecosystems and species must be protected at the expense of commercial activity.

This can be done as soon as total cost accounting is in place. Under this approach, laying off timber mill workers who have to change jobs or move or depend on welfare is more costly than labor intensive production. Herb Hammond describes a holistic cost/benefit analysis that considers other values, including natural values of other beings (Hammond also uses a theoretically infinite time frame for his analysis—but one wonders if an infinite time frame is appropriate in a limited and indefinite context, that is, for mortal forests on a middle-aged earth). Hammond also considers discounting inappropriate in a holistic system. The opposite of discount (which is from the Latin meaning counting away) would be 'adcount' (meaning counting toward); this term could be used to indicate increased value over time, as the system develops more complex states.

An ecological economics with complete accounting, would start with an inventory of all known principles, using Buckminster Fuller's world game for theoretical exploration. To inventory and monitor the resources of the planet, we would convert general accounting systems to a planetary ecological accounting system (PEAS!), intergenerational and ecosystemic, rather than annual and agricultural. Wealth would be refined from a scarcity model to an energy model. By making ownership more costly, excess property might be eliminated, and we might be liberated from our slavery to 'thingness.' Energy accounting has gained more use and some respect. Ivan Illich suggests that we need a language accounting now, since huge amounts of money are spent teaching people their mother-tongue.

Ecological accounting uses the same terms as financial accounting. Planetary assets include universal constants and solar radiation. They also include the planet with its diverse ecological systems and state of life. And, they include the whole spectrum of human cultures and inventions, that is, the total of structures and materials, as well as human flows and traps. Many assets, such as ideas, patents and goodwill, are considered intangible.

Liabilities include unavoidable energy flows and wastes (materials not immediately exploited or recycled in the short-term). Liabilities are obligations to another system. They may be short-term or long-term, depending on the accounting period.

Equity can be calculated as the difference between assets and liabilities. One planetary form of equity is inactive biomass in soils. It is considered to belong to all stakeholders (that is, anyone who is influenced by the actions under consideration).

Income is kept in separate accounts. Planetary government income will come from rents, fees, taxes, interest, and memberships. Expense accounts include payouts of many kinds: Salaries, utilities, educational, emergency, and other materials, repairs, maintenance, and transportation.

The comprehensive planetary ecological accounting system (PEAS) expands the traditional reporting framework to include ecological and cultural performances as well as financial performance (similar to the newer idea of the Triple Bottom Line, John Elkington, 1998). Ecological accounting addresses a circular process with constant inputs and outputs. PEAS assesses all known costs, projects and plans for them. It constantly inventories and monitors materials and flows as well as institutional processes. This develops the information necessary for the accounting. Environmental verification principles and financial audit principles are assumed to be the same 'in principle,' so they are combined in one track.

The income and costs are contingent on natural processes. That is, they are uncertain and sometimes fuzzy. PEAS is designed, using systems theory, catastrophe theory, and fuzzy set theory, to handle such contingencies. Human needs are fuzzy; productivity output is also fuzzy, so they both need to be included in a fuzzy accounting system. Although traditional accounting sometimes reports such things with standards for estimating it, the standards and methods need to be expanded to encompass environmental scales.

The purpose of PEAS is not to just add a high environmental cost to the total cost. It is just to include the set of environmental costs as a necessary part of an integrated system that comprehends the planetary context of life and business. In other words, accounting adds the real costs of previously free goods of nature.

PEAS includes all data linking an economy to the larger environments. In order to consider so many factors, accounting has tended to place economic dollar values on the processes and services of nature, as well as on human perception and appreciation of psychological things, from sunsets to satisfaction. This is a problem. Eyre also devised a common denominator to consider organic and inorganic assets together. Population carrying capacity can be formulated only using both. He assigned a nutrition equivalent unit weights of metal, but this calculation depended on a dollar value for food and minerals. The advantages of primary production as wealth are that the wealth is sustainable, plants are renewable, and minerals can be recycled. The disadvantages are that: the net community production (NCP) is not considered, which takes all of the food chain into account; dollars are used instead of fair human work units or perhaps time or being or experience units; and the technological production costs of food are not considered.

7.4.1. Revenue or Income for International Framework

Right now, the income from member nations is related to their GNP, a partial indication of relative gross national product. With the capability of taxation, the GU would not rely on voluntary national gifts. Although the GU would tax global resources, such as land and air, it could also tax weapons quite heavily. In fact, Ervin Laszlo suggests an international body could tax military expenditures of nations instead of the simple GNP. This would ensure that nations that produced the most weapons would pay the most for the effects of those weapons. Income from gifts and charity could still be used to combat special problems.

Many forms of income are on the same things that nations or communities depend on. Revenue from global things would be collected by the global government only. The global government may tax some things to balance the collection styles of nations. Finally, some things, such as air or sins (e.g., smoking), may be taxed at all levels.

7.4.1.1. Rent for International Framework

The GU could charge rent for global lands and oceans. Ownership of much of the planet would be through a corporation or department. The use of these areas or resources would be rented for the long-term. But, they would also be monitored by the GU.

7.4.1.2. Membership Dues for International Framework

For the UN, member nations now have to pay a percentage or a flat rate. The United States has the maximum assessed contribution to the UN regular budget—22%. In 2005 the assessed amount is $439,611,612. Actual U.S. contributions to the UN in 2005 totaled $1,959,053,000. This included the regular budget, peacekeeping operations, international tribunals, specialized agencies and subsidiary organizations. The minimum assessed contribution is 0.001%. The scale of assessments for each UN member for the required contributions to the regular budget is determined every 3 years on the basis of Gross National Product (GNP).

Only nine countries (starting with the largest contributor: United States, Japan, Germany, United Kingdom, France, Italy, Canada, Spain, China) contribute 75% of the entire regular budget. Cuba contributes 0.043% of the regular budget. One of the richest countries, Saudi Arabia, contributes 0.713 percent. The size of contributions, however, does not seem to be related to need, importance or dominance.

In addition to their contributions to the UN regular budget, member states contribute to the peacekeeping operations budget and the cost of international courts and tribunals. The level of these contributions is based on their assessed contributions to the regular budget plus variations which take account of permanent membership on the Security Council. UN members also make voluntary contributions to UN specialized agencies and subsidiary organizations. The administrative costs of such bodies, though, are met from the regular budget.

The UN could acquire much more money if the assessment were related to the defense budget of a country instead of its GNP. This would reduce military research and spending. The U.S. defense budget, for instance, was $343 billion a year, almost 200 times its UN membership fee. That kind of assessment would discourage military build-up and perhaps reduce military spending.

Membership dues would be phased out over five years, until tax, rent and other income programs are operating.

7.4.1.3. Taxes on Global Things

This term in its most extended sense includes all contributions imposed by the global association upon nations, cultures, or individuals for the service of the association, by whatever name they are called: Tribute, tithe, talliage, impost, duty, gabel, custom, subsidy, aid, supply, excise, or other. Taxes are any charge of money or property imposed by the association upon individuals or entities that are within the authority to assess such charges. Most modern taxes are levied on the basis of economic measurements such as income, consumption, property, and wealth. These taxes would be uniquely applied to global things or processes or to nations.

7.4.1.3.1. *Traditional Kinds of Tax.* Many traditional taxes require complex schemes to avoid cascading taxes or the regressive unfairness of some taxes. Many taxes were ad hoc additions to a tax code to add income from new or overlooked profitable activities.

State of Being Taxes, or Title Taxes. An example of a 'state of being' tax is an ad valorem property tax, which is not an excise tax, but which may be imposed on the property or the person who owns that property at a certain moment of time, for example, on July 1st of each year based on the state of title at that given moment. The 'state of title,' state of ownership, or property by reason of its ownership, is what is being taxed. The next year, on July 1st, another such tax is imposed again in the same way on the same property and person, even though there has been no 'change' or intervening 'event.' The amount of the tax may change from year to year, based on the change in the value of the property or a change in the tax rate, or both, but those are separate issues governing how the tax is computed. What is being taxed, fundamentally, is the state of title, which is not an 'event' but instead a 'state of being.'

Event Taxes. For purposes of the U.S. constitution, for example, an excise is essentially any indirect tax, or 'event' tax. In the constitutional sense, an excise includes gift taxes, estate taxes, payroll taxes, sales taxes, miscellaneous excise taxes, and income taxes on any income other than income from property—in short, any tax that is not a direct tax. Excise taxes are taxes paid when purchases are made on a specific good, such as gasoline, which is often one of the major components of an excise program. Excise taxes are usually included in the price of the product. There are also excise taxes on activities, such as on wagering or on highway usage by trucks. An excise tax can have several general excise tax programs.

Excise duties usually have one of two purposes: To raise revenue or to discourage a specific behavior. Taxes such as those on sales of fuel, alcohol and tobacco are often justified on both grounds. Some economists suggest that the optimal revenue-raising taxes should be levied on the sales of items having an inelastic demand, while behavior-altering taxes should be levied where the demand is elastic.

Capitation Tax. The capitation tax or "head" tax is an assessment levied by the government upon a person at a fixed rate regardless of income or worth. A poll tax is an example of a capitation tax. Originally used as a duty on the importation of convicts and slaves, it was later used to discourage the poor from voting.

Severance Taxes. A severance tax, on items that are 'severed' from their context, would have the effect of limiting the use of nonrenewable resources, such as coal or oil, as well as slowly renewable resources, such as forests.

Income Taxes. In 1913, the Sixteenth Amendment to the U.S. Constitution was ratified. It empowered Congress to tax "incomes, from whatever source derived, without apportionment among the several States, and without regard to any census or enumeration." The Internal Revenue Code is today embodied as Title 26 of the United States Code and is a direct descendant of the income tax act passed in 1913. While some U.S. states, such as Nevada or Florida, do not have an income tax, all residents and citizens of the United States are subject to a federal income tax, which requires a minimum level of income.

Sales Taxes. A sales tax is a tax on the consumption of goods or services. Normally, it is a certain percentage that is added onto the price of a good or service when it is purchased. To avoid double taxation, or 'cascading' taxes, where an item is taxed from design and production to retail sale and resale, a sales tax should charged ideally only once on any one item. A retail sales tax is charged only on retail transactions, not on businesses buying raw materials for production or on businesses reselling finished goods.

A related type of sales tax is the value-added tax (VAT). All sales, retail and wholesale, are taxed in this scheme. To avoid multiple or cascading tax, every business is refunded the amount of VAT remitted by their suppliers. Most nations, especially European nations such as Norway or Ireland, have sales taxes or VATs at the national or local level.

7.4.1.3.2. *Effects of Traditional Taxes.* The combination of these taxes often makes them regressive. In terms of fairness, sales taxes are generally regressive, that is, poorer people tend to pay a greater percentage of their income on sales taxes than richer people, because they generally tend to spend a far higher percentage of their income for food, clothing, shelter, and medical care. In some locations, items such as food, clothing, or prescription drugs are exempt from sales taxes, ostensibly to alleviate the burden on the poor. Some of these exemptions, such as exemptions for clothing or prescription drugs, actually may actually have the opposite effect and make the tax more regressive, since poorer individuals may spend a smaller percentage of their incomes on these items than do richer individuals. Some of these taxes discourage the efforts that they tax. For instance, a tax on value added by labor to commodities can discourage labor.

7.4.1.3.3. *New Kinds of Taxes.* When Arthur C. Pigou introduced the concept of 'taxing bads' in the early 1900s, economists and politicians discussed with the idea, but its use was limited. Environmental taxes are functionally nonexistent in the current tax code of the United States. A few such taxes have been proposed, most recently a BTU tax during the Clinton presidency, but the defeat seems to have discouraged any kind of environmental tax since then.

Taxing 'bads' is essentially a 'tax shift.' Taxes are reduced on things that should be to be encouraged, such as work or savings. The loss of revenue is compensated by taxes on 'bads,' that is, on things to be discouraged, such as pollution and waste. A tax shift could help mitigate the impact of pollution charges on some businesses; it would remove taxes that discriminate against low-income families. A tax shift might also improve general fiscal health, as well as over-all environmental health.

Rather than use old labels, which were the result of ad hoc additions to many tax codes, it might be simpler to present them as what they are taxing, that is what kinds of income we want and what kinds of behavior we want to encourage. These kinds of new taxes can be put under four categories: Use, Loss, Adjustment—or the misplacement of resources, such as pollution—and Distribution. Several of these might be regarded as temporary, until a permanent conservative system is developed.

7.4.1.3.3.1. Use Taxes on Global Elements Cycles
A use tax is similar to many consumption taxes or a few severance taxes. These taxes take a percentage for a service for any resource. A use tax would have the effect of limiting the use of nonrenewable resources, such as coal or oil, as well as the use of slowly renewable resources, such as forests. The rate of the tax would be related to the scale of the economy, as well as to the carrying capacity of the ecological support system.
Tax collectors would monitor points of entry, from wellheads to forests, to ensure that the tax would be fair, and that it would be paid. The tax would be easier to collect and harder to avoid than

income taxes. It could be, and probably would be, included in the cost of any commodity that used the resource. Few commodities do not require some resource. This would discourage overexploitation of previously 'free' resources.

7.4.1.3.3.2. Air Use Tax

Taxes on output or on polluting inputs are called presumptive because their target is the pollution presumed to be associated with the activity. A combination of the two types, those that reduce output and those that reduce emissions per unit of output, could replace emission fees and reduce monitoring requirements and their prohibitive costs. The taxation of fuel use can be a powerful, indirect instrument for controlling air pollution because of the direct connection between fuel use and emissions. This is not quite the same as taxing the pollution; in this case the goods are taxed to address the pollution.

Indirect instruments, such as a tax on air, are designed to reduce the scale of output, as important complementary measures in a program of cost-effective pollution control. Air is used in almost every operation of an industry or bureaucracy. Clean air is used for cooling and to provide oxygen for the occupants of buildings.

7.4.1.3.3.3. Water Use Tax

Water is such a good solvent, it can be used to enhance many kinds of processes. Water is used in almost every operation of an industry or bureaucracy. It also is used for cooling and for drinking.

Bottled water consumption, which has more than doubled globally in the last six years since 1999, is a natural resource that is greatly affecting the world's ecosystem, according to a new U.S. study. "Even in areas where tap water is safe to drink, demand for bottled water is increasing, producing unnecessary garbage and consuming vast quantities of energy," according to Emily Arnold, author of the study published by the Earth Policy Institute, a Washington-based environmental group. A water use tax would encourage efficient use of water by making waste too expensive.

7.4.1.3.3.4. Land Use Tax

Land use tax is a base tax on land, which would encourage efficient use of the land, as opposed to, for instance, building taxes, which if higher than tax on land allows land to lie idle or buildings to deteriorate. It would reduce runaway and harmful speculation on land. Users fees would have to be high enough to cover the costs of the services provided, according to Daly and Cobb. Cities that increased land taxes and decreased building taxes have encouraged better building programs.

This tax would tax the use of soils by agriculture or forestry, especially rapid-use forestry with short rotations (or perhaps on less than 500-year cycles). Agricultural land should also be taxed on its unimproved value, according to Daly and Cobb. The taxes would be local rather than national. Improved agriculture, such as regenerative, would prove to be more efficient as a result of the higher initial cost and the lower taxes on improvements or profits.

7.4.1.3.3.5. Element Use Tax

Under the Clean Air Act, the U.S. Environmental Protection Agency (EPA) sets national standards for ambient air quality designed to protect public health and welfare. The EPA defines acceptable levels for six 'criteria' elements that are air pollutants: Sulfur dioxide (SO_2), nitrogen oxides (NO_x), ozone, particulate matter, carbon monoxide (CO), and lead. Along with emissions from natural sources, emissions of air pollutants from stationary sources, such as industrial facilities and commercial operations, and mobile sources, such as automobiles, trains, and airplanes, contribute to the ambient levels of those pollutants.

Some U.S. states levy a 'severance tax' on mineral production because these assets are non-renewable. Once the minerals are produced, or 'severed,' from the ground, they are gone forever. Since many of these assets, such as coal and oil, come from federal lands in the U.S., which are owned by all the citizens of the states and the nation, citizens are entitled to a fair rate of return on the assets. An element tax could capture the value of these assets for current and future generations of citizens.

7.4.1.3.3.5.1. *Carbon Tax.* Carbon appears in every living cell; life on earth is carbon based. However, out of place, carbon can poison life or cause changes to the climate of the planet. Carbon dioxide is recognized as a greenhouse gas, and increasing levels in the atmosphere are linked to global warming and climate change.

A carbon footprint is a measure of the amount of carbon dioxide emitted through the combustion of fossil fuels. In the case of an organization, business or enterprise, a carbon footprint is part of their everyday operations, as it is for an individual or household. A carbon footprint is often expressed as tons of carbon dioxide or tons of carbon emitted, usually on an annual basis.

A carbon tax would link the effects of burning carbon-containing fuels to the cost of repairing the damages from burning. A carbon tax could greatly offset other tax rates, as well as reduce energy consumption, especially fossil fuel consumption, and address climate change. Although there would probably be a small reduction in measures of wealth, such as the GNP or ISEW, there would be offsetting tax reductions elsewhere in the economy; and some of the money would go toward improving efficiency.

Displacing these old taxes with use taxes would improve the productivity of the economy. A high carbon tax, coupled with reduced tax rates on income and profits could generate a significant gain for each dollar of tax shifted. The gain would come not only from improved economic efficiency, but from reduced investment in infrastructure, in reduced operating costs due to higher energy efficiency, and in reduced environmental damage.

7.4.1.3.3.5.2. *Nitrogen Tax.* Nitrogen is a critical element of life; it is a major part of the atmosphere. In the form of nitrite, nitrate and ammonia, nitrogen enters watershed, oceans and streams from fertilizers, animal wastes and decomposing organic matter. If nitrogen levels increase, algae increases dramatically. Nitrogen oxides (NO_x) usually enter the air as the result of high-temperature combustion processes such as those in automobiles and power plants.

One way to help control NO_x would be to tax emissions from stationary sources. For example, firms might adopt currently available abatement techniques whose capitalized costs are lower than the tax they would otherwise pay. If a regional allowance trading program was put into place, the community could tax only the stationary sources of NO_x that do not participate in the program.

7.4.1.3.3.5.3. *Sulfur & Other Element Taxes.* Sulfur is also an element required by living beings, and it also appears in the atmosphere. Sulfur dioxide belongs to the family of sulfur oxide gases formed during the burning of fuel, mainly coal and oil, containing sulfur and during the operation of metal smelting and other industrial processes. Exposure to high concentrations of SO_2 may promote respiratory illnesses or aggravate cardiovascular disease. In addition, SO_2 and NO_x emissions are considered the main contributors to acid rain, which can degrade surface waters, damage forests and crops, and accelerate the corrosion of buildings. One option is to tax emissions of SO_2 from stationary sources not already covered under an acid rain program. Marketplace strategies can be coupled with regulations.

Phosphorus is a relatively rare element. Isaac Asimov calls it the bottleneck of life, a good example of Liebig's law of the minimum, which states essentially that something has to be in least supply. In the case of life, it is phosphorus. Phosphorus is a necessary constituent of protoplasm, but it is sometimes the element in least supply. Most phosphorus is locked up in phosphates in rock, which is weathered and 'escapes' to the oceans, which act as a sink. Sea birds play a large part in returning it to land. In fact, guano deposits are mined for fertilizers. Harvesting fish for food returns some to land, but little effort is made to recycle it. A community tax on phosphorus would encourage more of it to be recycled.

Oxygen is a major component of the earth's crust. It is a significant component of the atmosphere. For living beings, it allows energy to be released as part of their respiration. In the atmosphere, oxygen can be converted by natural processes, such as sunlight or lightning, to ozone. Ozone is not emitted directly into the air but is formed by the reaction of volatile organic compounds (VOCs) and nitrogen oxides (NO_x) in the presence of heat and sunlight. Ozone occurs naturally in the upper atmosphere and provides a protective layer there. At ground level, however, ozone is a prime ingredient of smog. Short-term exposures, from one to three hours, to ambient ozone concentrations have been linked to increased hospital admissions and emergency room visits for respiratory ailments. Ground-level ozone has remained a pervasive pollution problem in many areas. Rather than directly tax oxygen use, communities might want to tax the VOCs or chemicals that interfere with ozone.

The advantage of a broad-based tax on VOCs is that it would affect large and small sources of the compounds. A disadvantage of such a broad-based tax is that it may be regressive. To the extent that the tax raises the prices of consumer goods, it may take up a larger share of household income for low-income consumers than for higher-income consumers.

7.4.1.3.3.6. Species Use Taxes

Tax would be charged on the taking of members of any species; this tax is not the same as a hunting or fishing license, which is required to test knowledge and dictate that only a certain number can be taken. Many of these species are slowly renewable or functionally nonrenewable. This tax would work to encourage preservation, take-limits, or take-efficiency. This would tax the use of virgin species for commerce.

Species, as well as fresh air and water, are the interest of an ecosystem; the ecosystem itself, on life-bearing land, is the capital. If the capital is allowed to be used, the taxes on the land should be very high. Using the interest is a more sustainable practice.

7.4.1.3.4. Loss Taxes on Global Resources

A loss tax is a tax on losses from the capital base, that is, it is a tax on the destruction of resources, not just their use or on their negative impacts. It is similar to a dispossession tax or a capital depletion tax.

Resources can be sorted into one of three types of resources: (1) fastly accruable, that is, renewable in economic terms over a short time horizon; (2) slowly accruable, which are basically nonrenewable within a human lifetime; and (3) and slowly dispersed, which are really nonrenewable in most economic frames, but are actually renewable in geological time, which is rarely considered. Most of the wealth used by modern economies is nonrenewable. These resources are limited, interrelated and distributed unevenly. Forests are a special problem; although trees can grow to a good size in 30-40 years, forest ecosystems may take 300-600 years to develop and then last for thousands of years.

Oil, coal, peat, and some woods are functionally nonrenewable. Geological time periods are required to produce them. Mineral reserves may be understated, but, they may be located so far and so deep that it would cost more energy to extract them and move them than they are worth, unless we used a 'renewable' energy source, such annual plants, or a very slowly depletable resource, such as the sun.

Slow accrual and slow dispersal resources should be equally available to all cultures. It is impossible to sustain any quantitative arguments about resources and population pressure on them without a comprehensive overview. Demands on food, fertilizer, energy, and metals are related inseparably. Organic and inorganic assets need to be assessed together. Population carrying capacity cannot be formulated until both resources have been quantified.

This kind of loss tax is placed on things or processes that interfere with other things and processes, things that cause runaway feedback or the destruction of cycles, things in other words that reduce our continued use of and enjoyment of the earth. This tax would have the effect of internalizing both ecological and social costs; since all consumers would be paying the real costs, no consumers would be protected. It should also have the effect of reducing pollution.

Many of these things have been subsidized for many decades as a result of the power of special interests. The purpose of this kind of tax is to change behavior that depletes resources and discourages labor. It also can pay for the damage caused by misplaced or used resources, such as the destruction of ozone.

7.4.1.3.4.1. Land Conversion Loss Taxes

This tax would be on the conversion of complex systems to simpler, and more expensive to manage, systems, for instance, the conversion of forests to agricultural fields, or the conversion of fields to parking lots. The rate of taxation would be directly related to the cost of restoration plus the loss of productivity over the period of time before restoration.

7.4.1.3.4.2. Nonrenewables Loss Taxes

Nonrenewable means functionally nonrenewable in a human lifetime, although technically such resources are renewable in the very long term as a result of very slow processes, such as continental drift and folding. Nonrenewables includes geothermal energy, as well as fossil fuels, such as oil and coal. The rate of taxation would be related to the cost of human production of those things.

7.4.1.3.4.2.1. *Geothermal Loss Taxes.* Geothermal energy is the long-time flow of the energy of formation of the planet to space; it is not inexhaustible, although it may not be used up within the lifetime of the human species. It should be taxed at the community level because it is inequitably distributed, and to provide support for other energy sources that require more research and development.

7.4.1.3.4.2.2. *Fossil Fuel Loss Taxes.* In a way, energy does not cycle because it is lost in equal quantities from the planetary system; however, energy may be trapped by cycles on the earth for millions of years—in coal or oil, for instance. Oil, coal, peat, and some woods are functionally nonrenewable. Geological time periods are required to produce them. Assuming 1×10^{16} grams of carbon are fixed each year by photosynthesis, averaged over a billion years, the total mass recycled of carbon alone exceeds 10^{25} grams. The total coal and oil deposits in lithosphere are estimated at 10^{19} grams. However, a small amount of detritus does not get recycled; these ordered compounds form deposits. Marine organisms produced large deposits of oil, possibly in a reducing atmosphere; forests left ranges of coal.

Oil and tar may have been first extracted near the Zagros Mountains to be used for binding tools. Since then, oil production really has meant extraction. That is the only economic means to get it. It would be expensive to synthesize. F. de Chardenedes wrote a scenario of natural technology for producing petroleum; if the amount of energy, as heat and pressure, had to be paid for at a human public utilities rate (circa 1970), the cost would be over a million dollars a gallon. If we based the cost on human labor and technology, so that 1 gallon of oil is worth a million dollars, as Buckminster Fuller also calculated, then it would be used with more circumspection.

As technology improved, wood fires also shaped metals and provided steam for power; coal fires provided electricity; oil fires provide electricity and motion. Furthermore, oil and gas can damage and destabilize ecosystems.[7] Oil use places extra carbon and pollutants in the air. A tax on oil would reduce its extraction and use, as well as encourage renewable, cheaper alternatives.

7.4.1.3.4.2.3. *Natural Gas Loss Taxes.* Natural gas could be taxed at a much higher rate, a tax of 25 percent instead of 5 percent of the market value of the natural gas. This higher rate would discourage the use of natural gas, and to encourage the development of alternative and relatively renewable sources, such as solar energy, although the sun has a finite lifetime also. Natural gas reserves could be used as a transitional energy source or for special needs.

7.4.1.3.4.2.4. *Coal Loss Taxes.* Coal would also be taxed at a higher rate, a 25 percent tax based on the sales price per ton, instead of a one-cent-per-ton or a dollar-a-ton or a small percentage of the sales price. This should cover, not only the cost of restoring the landscapes or mines, but also the medical costs, such as black lung, associated with the mining of coal.

7.4.1.3.4.2.5. *Slow Renewables Loss Taxes.* These resources are essentially nonrenewable in terms of a human lifetime. Although some trees can mature in forty-year cycles, many require eighty, a hundred years or over three hundred. Forests themselves may take many hundreds of years to mature.

Although individual fish can mature in one to four years, fish populations require much longer time periods. Fish populations are also vulnerable with relatively low percentages as takes.

7.4.1.3.4.2.5.1. *Trees & Forests Loss Taxes.* Taxation can be a controversial field. Many states or provinces have special private forest tax laws that exempt timber from taxation or defer the tax until harvest. Economists fight over whether the bare land is the capital and timber a 'goods-in-process,' or whether the timber is the accumulated capital. One could even state that the forest ecosystem is the capital, not just the timber. Trees, as well as other species, fresh air and water, are the interest on a forest; the whole forest itself is the capital.

In the U.S., the Oregon Legislature intended to tax timber like any other crop, while forest land would be taxed at reduced values, under an overhaul of timber taxation that cleared both houses. Constanza and Daly suggest a natural capital depletion tax could be applied to forest use that is not biologically sustainable. Sustainability here is used to mean no extrinsic costs, that is, we cannot sustain forest use at the expense of clean air and water, at the disruption of processes, and with the destruction of plant and animal communities. This would tax the use of virgin materials for commerce. Both ideas would improve forest use, but could be extended to other ecosystems.

Forest land should be taxed on its land value. Since the forest is the capital, and trees characterize the forest, the depletion tax on trees needs to be high. If enough trees are removed the forest dies. The tax should be applied so that the benefits stay local.

7.4.1.3.4.2.5.2. *Fish & Fisheries Loss Taxes.* Wildlife has commercial value, that is, fish can be caught without being produced. The constancy of the environment, even with its changes, has allowed many kinds of animals to live in large populations. Fish have quite explicit needs for temperature, stream bed character, and cleanliness. Taxing fish takes should allow populations and habitats to recover. The community must be restored to health. This means balancing human needs with fish needs in a sustainable pattern. Some fish might never be hunted or taken, especially those with high ecosystem or cultural value.

7.4.1.3.4.2.6. *Fast Renewables Loss Taxes.* Fast renewables are things that are usually part of daily, monthly or annual cycles, such as solar power, hydropower or wind power. They can be taxed at a relatively low rate or even a negative rate to encourage development.

Large-scale use of any of these methods of production could result in other problems. Other than the aesthetics of giant wind or solar 'farms,' concentration could cause problems with ecosystem interference and stability, as well as with human safety and aesthetics.

7.4.1.3.4.2.6.1. *Wind Power Loss Taxes*. Wind is a term for the movement of air, usually the result of heat differences in the air and planetary rotation. Although wind energy is not infinite, it will continue for many millions of years. The purpose of taxing it is recognize its values and limits, as well as to shift to more benign energy sources. Wind power could have a negative tax (or tax credit) of 2 cents per kilowatt-hour for electricity produced from a wind farm.

7.4.1.3.4.2.6.2. *Solar Power Loss Taxes*. Energy from the sun drives most cycles on earth. Even though solar energy is finite, it will continue, and increase slowly, for billions of years. Solar power could have a negative tax of 3 cents per kilowatt-hour for electricity produced from arrays of solar collectors. There would be tax credits for solar domestic or business water heating.

7.4.1.3.4.2.6.3. *Hydropower Loss Taxes*. The earth-moon system generates tides on both bodies. The water cycle on earth pumps water into the atmosphere and its descent can also generate power. Hydropower would have a negative tax of 1 cent per kilowatt-hour for electricity produced from large or micro generators.

7.4.1.3.4.2.6.4. *Waste Loss Taxes*. Some waste can be considered a measure of loss from the system, that is, resources that are not captured for reuse. Many wastes come from industrial, agricultural, or mining operations and include toxic substances. A lot of waste comes from private households, in the form of paint, pesticides, and poisons. Many wastes, from solid wastes to energy, would be taxed by weight or neutralization costs and at amounts necessary to discourage their use or to encourage their incorporation into industrial cycles.

7.4.1.3.5. Adjustment Taxes on Global Sin & Pollution

Adjustment taxes are regulation or correction taxes to regulate or harmonize cures and causes. They are not applied to loss but to meet the cost of recovery. For example, water returned to the watershed that does not meet purity standards would be taxed. Many forms of solid waste, such as garbage, refuse, or sludge, could be taxed by volume, at a rate of 50 cents per cubic foot. Other forms of solid waste, such as hazardous waste, tires, batteries, or nuclear by-products would be taxed sufficiently to pay for their isolation or break-down. Recyclable solid waste, such as animal excrement or rock, would not be taxed if it was recycled properly.

There would be no necessity for sin taxes, unless they were not taxed at a national or community level (or if necessary to support explicit GU institutions on health, or for use of such things in International areas). International pollution would be taxed, however. Especially industrial and agricultural pollution.

7.4.1.3.5.1. *Sin Adjustment Taxes*. If people do dangerous things, and expect their government to take care of them, then government has to tax those things that result in illness. This tax would benefit people who suffer from bad habits. Due to its relatively high rate, it might reduce the consumption of addictive substances. The money from these taxes would address human consumption requiring health care, especially for health care beyond what the individual can afford.

7.4.1.3.5.1.1. *Cigarette Adjustment Tax*. Inhaling the smoke from burning in plants in moderation may be stimulating, especially in ceremonial settings. However, overuse has serious health consequences. An industry exists that makes profits by selling such things to users and addicts.

Like an excise tax, this tax is on sales of cigarettes, usually a fixed fee on each pack of cigarettes sold. This tax can double or even triple the retail cost of cigarettes in some U.S. states.

7.4.1.3.5.1.2. *Alcohol Adjustment Tax*. Drinking the products of fermented plants may also be stimulating. It certainly has a long, rich tradition, from native peoples eating fermented berries to the large-scale production of ale in Mesopotamia after 9,000 years ago. This relatively high tax would offset the increased medical and social expenses from its use.

7.4.1.3.5.1.3. *Drug Adjustment Tax.* Many communities try to control the kinds of drugs used. Many drugs, that may have greater or lesser consequences than those categorized as legal, may be illegal. Legal drugs would be taxed according to their purpose or perceived social benefit. Illegal taxes would be taxed at a much higher rate. However, if all substances were legalized, then taxes could be used to control their use. There could be additional social benefits, such as decriminalization and deimprisonment, and all the costs that that entails.

7.4.1.3.5.2. *Pollution Adjustment Taxes.* All forms of pollution would be taxed, especially those related to regional and global cycles of the elements necessary for metabolism of living beings. The amount of pollution that a firm or product releases into the air, water, or soil would be taxed. A pollution tax would address the 'market failures' that arise when businesses and consumers are not held responsible for the full health and environmental costs associated with their activities. Pollution taxes make polluters pay for their damages and incorporate these costs into their decisions and product prices (Specific elements of pollution, such as carbon and sulfur, are addressed earlier).

Water pollutants, for example, could be taxed on the basis of Biological Oxygen Demand (BOD). Dissolved oxygen is necessary to sustain fish and other aquatic life. Generally, firms that are subject to water pollution standards do not pay taxes or fees based on effluents that regulations still allow. Most of the high-volume BOD dischargers, referred to as point sources, are publicly owned treatment works, paper and pulp mills, food processors, metal producers, and chemical plants.

7.4.1.3.5.3. *Industrial Adjustment Taxes.* Particulate matter is the general term used for a mixture of solid particles and liquid droplets found in the air. Those particles come in a wide range of sizes: Fine particles are less than 2.5 micrometers in diameter, and coarse particles are larger than that. The particles originate from many different stationary and mobile sources, as well as from natural sources. Fine particles result from the combustion of fuel in motor vehicles, power generation, and industrial facilities as well as from residential fireplaces and wood stoves. Coarse particles are generally emitted from power plants, factories and sources such as vehicles traveling on unpaved roads, materials handling, crushing and grinding operations, and windblown dust. Some particles are emitted directly from their sources such as smokestacks and cars. In other cases, sulfur dioxide (SO_2), nitrogen oxides (NO_x), and volatile organic compounds (VOCs) interact with other compounds to form particles.

A tax on coarse particles could force some electric utilities and manufacturing plants to install improved electrostatic precipitators, wet scrubbers, or other equipment to reduce their emissions and lower their tax burden. Reductions in emissions caused by the tax would be economically efficient if the additional abatement costs were less than the social benefits from reduced pollution.

Opponents of this kind of tax argue that it would impose an excessive burden on firms that already incur costs to comply with current standards. Firms have escaped their justified burdens of safety and efficiency, so this is not a good reason. To the extent that the tax would raise the price of energy generated in this way, it might be regressive. But, once the price of energy reflects its true costs and effects, and once many unfair taxes are removed, then some disadvantaged people and businesses can afford to pay a larger percentage for energy costs.

7.4.1.3.5.4. *Agricultural Adjustment Taxes.* In order to make its impressive gains, agriculture tries to control more of the growing process of crops; it does this by adding fertilizers and pesticides, as well as by using special, energy-intensive machinery. These things would be taxed to offset their costs and effects.

7.4.1.3.5.4.1. *Pesticides Adjustment Tax.* Pesticides can have a number of adverse impacts on human health and the environment, imposing substantial costs on society. These include direct financial costs, such as the treatment of water, and wider environmental costs, such as loss of biodiversity, which are much harder to value.

Pesticide impact reduction is a prime candidate for the use of economic instruments. A pesticide tax would greatly benefit farmland birds. The tax could invoke the 'Polluter Pays' principle and reduce the inappropriate use of pesticides, as well as raise revenue to pay for solutions to the environmental impacts of pesticides. Preliminary economic analysis shows that a well designed tax would not significantly damage farming incomes or competitiveness.

7.4.1.3.5.4.2. *Fertilizer Adjustment Tax.* Fertilizer is used to increase the productivity of crops, although rarely is that productivity equal to the that of the original land cover. Fertilizers rob plants of root mass and foods of nutritional values. This means that more of the crops have to be planted, and people that have to eat more of the plants to get the same nutrition. Fertilizer pollution causes other problems, especially with nitrogen and phosphorus.

The application of environmental tax shifting to pesticide and fertilizer use could provide an incentive to minimize pesticide and chemical fertilizer use, and to generate revenue to allow for tax relief in other areas.

7.4.1.3.5.4.3. *Water & Other Adjustment Taxes.* To encourage crops to grow in areas that have low rainfall, such as central Washington state in the U.S., farmers irrigate their crops, even crops that are not native to the area, with water drawn from an aquifer. Since water from aquifers is often renewed at very low rates, it would be taxed at a rate designed to reduce use to replacement rates.

7.4.1.3.5.5. *Personal Pollution Adjustment Taxes.* A tax would be charged on personal pollution, from solid waste to discharges from machines. A fuel tax would be imposed on the sale of fuel to cover the calculated pollution from its use. In the United States, the funds are often dedicated to transportation, or even roads, so that the fuel tax is considered by many to be a user fee. In other countries, the fuel tax is a source of general revenue. Sometimes the fuel tax is not imposed on fuel that is not intended for transportation, such as fuel used to power agricultural vehicles or for home heating oil. This creates an economic incentive for the illegal use of fuel. The solution would be to tax all fuel regardless of use.

Because of the inelastic nature of the demand for fuel, in the short run the tax would be an effective source of revenue. In the long run, however, people adjust their consumption; over a period of years, people would consume less as the price increases, by driving less or by buying more fuel-efficient cars or furnaces. A fuel tax could be a way to reduce reliance on environment-damaging fossil fuels.

7.4.1.3.5.6. *Sale of Heritage Items Adjustment Taxes.* A heritage tax would be applied to any thing considered part of the natural or cultural heritage, such as special buildings or landscapes. It would also include unique art works produced by the culture. It would include a tax on the export of such things without a value-added component, such a raw logs or unprocessed resources.

7.4.1.3.5.7. *Financial Speculation Adjustment Taxes.* The speed and detachment of money may artificially change the values of things that should remain uninflated or undepressed. A speculation tax, like a Tobin tax, is a small tax on each international financial transaction.

There are many potential benefits from a modest tax on financial transactions, such as the buying and selling of shares of stock or blocks of foreign currencies. Such a tax would have the effect of reducing short-term speculation in these markets, thereby making them somewhat less volatile. It would slow capital movements. It would also cut back some of the economic resources that are wasted in these transactions, since if the number of trades declines, the money spent on these trades would decline as well. In addition, it would make the tax code fairer, since most financial speculation is conducted either directly or indirectly by wealthy people. Just as poor and moderate income people pay taxes when they gamble at a casino or buy a state lottery ticket, a speculation tax would simply be applying a comparable tax to gambling in financial markets. Finally, a speculation tax could raise an enormous amount of revenue for a community or state.

7.4.1.3.6. Distribution Taxes on Global Things

Distribution taxes are the same as reapportionment for luxuries and large incomes. Many large incomes are so large that they are heroic. Combined with heroic inheritance and profits, these incomes essentially remove their receivers from any sense of local community by concentrating wealth. Distribution taxes have the function of reapportioning wealth. These taxes would be assessed in international waters and lands. They would be on luxuries or incomes that have evaded national and community taxes.

7.4.1.3.6.1. *Heroic Possessions Distribution Taxes.* A heroic possessions tax is a tax on products that are not considered essential, in other words, luxuries. A luxury tax is similar to a sales tax or VAT, except that it mainly affects the wealthy because the wealthy are the most likely to spend heavily on luxuries such as expensive cars, boats, houses, or jewelry. One might even consider this tax as a 'nonuse' tax, since many luxuries are not often used and are taken out of circulation for others.

Although a luxury tax of some sort may be justified on many things, the regulations would have clarify implementation in order to achieve at least some degree of equity. Although the tax would be collected at the community or state level, it might be coordinated at the national level, considering the multiple residences of those who can afford other luxuries. Regulations have to broaden the definition of luxury. It is hard to argue that a luxury tax is unjust and counter-productive, considering the massive suffering and starvation outside the gated compounds.

7.4.1.3.6.2. *Heroic Income Distribution Taxes.* A heroic income tax would be applied to incomes over a certain amount, as determined by a ratio of one to ten. Herman Daly and John Cobb quote a range of the acceptable inequality of income at ten to one, although some corporations, like Ben & Jerry's ice cream, used to limit it to a one to seven ratio. As Cobb and Daly point out, the idea of unlimited inequality works against the notion of community. As they also wisely point out the goal of a community is not some perfect ideal of equality, but a limited inequality that allows individual differences to show, and individual rewards for luck or skill, but also allows others to catch up. And, this idea, rather than being new, is explicit in many biblical accounts of Hebrew laws governing landholding and usury, among other things. So, this tax rate would be quite high for those with heroic incomes. Paying such a tax would make these people heroes and in fact they would likely acquire heroic status for paying.

7.4.1.3.6.3. *Heroic Transfer Distribution Taxes.* A transfer tax is a tax on any transfer of wealth, including inheritance, death duty, estate, or bequest. It has similarities to death taxes, inheritance taxes, and estate taxes, but it is much broader. It is applied to any transfer of wealth, to spouses, children, relatives, and even bequests to trusts, foundations and charities, and not on the total wealth. This would include payment of life insurance benefits or financial account sums to beneficiaries.

This tax would require relatively heavy regulation. This tax would serve to prevent the perpetuation of wealth, free of tax, within wealthy families. It would work towards reducing the accumulation between generations, thus leveling the field more for the next generation.

7.4.1.3.6.4. *Heroic Profit Distribution Taxes.* A community has to be responsible to keep the economic playing field level, to use a popular sports metaphor. In the event that a person or corporation records a profit that could distort the community, then the community has to limit that profit through taxes to not more than ten times the mean profit in the community (not the average or median).

7.4.1.3.6.5. *Discussion of Transitional & Missing Taxes.* Under this new tax scheme, there would be no taxes on buildings, equipment or inventories. There would be no corporate income tax, although, as Daly and Cobb suggest profits would have to be distributed to all shareholders as income. There would be no personal income tax, no property tax, and no sales tax. Why? Because things people want or work for should be encouraged. Once the real price of oil and other goods has settled out, no other taxes are needed for value-added things.

In order to reach this position, however, there may be a series of transitional taxes, such as an added tax on all new vehicles.

7.4.1.4. Licensing for a Global Association

A license is a formal authorization by law to do something, such as marry, hunt, or practice law or medicine. The GU may issue international licenses for some purposes.

A marriage license or a license to reproduce children would be more appropriate at the community (or possibly national) level, although global population planning would be coordinated at the international level. The same would likely be true for driving, vehicle, collecting, and voting licenses, although such international licenses might be issued for special areas, such as open seas.

7.4.1.4.1. Licensing International Corporations

Virtually every U.S. state licenses businesses. A business is defined as any commercial enterprise, trade, occupation, calling, profession, vocation, or activity engaged in, conducted, carried on, advertised, or held out to the public to be a business by any person, agent, or employee for the purpose of gain, benefit or advantage, either direct or indirect, with the principal objective of livelihood or profit through repetitive means.

The business license certificate is evidence of having met community requirements and that a fee has been paid for doing business within the limits of a community or state. Most codes requires that people obtain a license when conducting any business activity within the community, even if the business is located outside the area and has a license from another area. Other permits may be required to operate a business.

The fee imposed is solely for the purpose of obtaining general revenue. Business fees could help pay for community services like roads, fire, police and other community services that benefit businesses, business owners and the general public.

Corporations that have no land base, or that have evaded local charters would be subject to a license with the GU.

7.4.1.4.2. Licensing Wavelengths Satellites & Media

Any use, for broadcast or communication, of common frequencies of the spectrum of wavelengths, would be licensed by the agency responsible for regulating interstate and international communications by radio, television, wire, satellite, or cable. Satellites, carriers (or spacecraft), and any items in sublunar or solar system space would be licensed by the GU. These fees would be used for tracking and cleanup. Licenses would be required for wave communications in international areas. Due to the global aspect of the spectrum of waves, it might be necessary to coordinate all media among nations.

7.4.1.4.3. Licensing National Weapons
All weapons of a certain kind, from automatic weapons to cruise missiles, would be licensed by the GU. These weapons would be for national police forces and the police force of the GU. Their possession or use would be banned for individuals.

7.4.1.4.4. Other Licenses
The Global Union might offer international drivers licenses. Licenses would be required also for collecting in international places.

7.4.1.5. Fees & Tolls for a Global Association
Fees could be charged by the community for use of community space or renewal cycles, for example, visiting fees or sanitation fees. Tolls could be charged by the community to cover extra expenses for transportation, for instance, bridge tolls or road tolls. Special fees could be charged for tourist attractions and for heritage sites. Fees would be charged to save, restore, and maintain the common wealth of humanity. Such fees would be charged to nations.

7.4.1.5.1. Global Fees on Common Human Wealth & Great Art
Although much of the common heritage of the humanity on the planet would be free to observe or visit, fees would be charged to limit access. Fees would also be used for special costs such as cleanup. This fee might be applied to special areas of the planet or for works of art that are considered the heritage of humanity, such as many cave paintings or desert rock carvings.

7.4.1.5.2. Global Fees on Wilderness
Global wilderness areas, such as Antarctica or the North Pacific Sea, would have limited access. The fees would also support research in these areas.

7.4.1.6. Labor for Global Projects
The GU could use scientists from other countries. It would also use volunteers from many nations to work on international projects. It could have a formal two-year volunteer program, similar to the programs of nations, but without conscription.

Figure 715-2. Possible nations in India & Pakistan

7.4.2. Expenditures or Payout for a Global Association

The community has to pay for its existence, as well as the expenses, amenities, and services that it trades for its existence. The payout, or outgo, is available from income, and should balance income, although savings accounts and debt-load can expand or contract temporarily.

In economics, business, and accounting, a cost is the value of inputs that have been used up to produce something, and hence are not available for use anymore. In business, the cost may be one of acquisition, in which case the amount of money expended to acquire it is counted as cost. In this case, money is the input that is gone in order to acquire the thing. This acquisition cost may be the sum of the cost of production as incurred by the original producer, and further costs of transaction as incurred by the acquirer over and above the price paid to the producer. Usually, the price also includes a mark-up for profit over the cost of production. Costs are often further described based on their timing or their applicability.

When a transaction takes place, it typically involves both private costs and external costs. Its private costs are the costs that the buyer of a good or service pays the seller. Its external costs, which are also called externalities, in contrast, are the costs that people other than the buyer are forced to pay as a result of the transaction. The bearers of such costs can be either particular individuals or society at large. External costs are often nonmonetary, and as a result difficult to quantify for comparison with monetary values. They include things like pollution, things that society will likely have to pay for in some way at some time, but that are not included in transaction prices.

Social costs are the sum of private costs and external costs, that is, both the costs internal to the firm's production and external costs not included in the firm's production. For example, the purchase price of a car reflects the private cost experienced by the manufacturer. The air pollution created in the production of the car is an external cost. The manufacturer does not pay for these costs and does not include them in the price of the car, so they are external to the market pricing mechanism. The air pollution from driving the car is also an externality. The driver does not pay for the environmental damage caused by using the car. A psychic cost is a subset of social costs, for example from endangering pedestrians, that specifically represent the costs of added stresses or losses to the quality of life. A community has to consider all costs for as long as possible into the future.

At this level all costs, including environmental and social, have been internalized. The GU has to be able to guarantee that all unintended costs are being paid, as a result of the economic activities of nations.

7.4.2.1. Operate Organization & Agencies

The GU has as large a bureaucracy as any national government, in fact, larger than the largest national government. However, since there is an overlap of responsibilities and so many things are duplicated on lower levels, the GU will essentially be a coordinator. Nevertheless, it will have a large number of agencies, as well as the separate governing functions and commissions.

7.4.2.1.1. Health Supplement

Traditionally, an international body has been concerned with the levels of health of the people of all nations. One function is to make sure that the lower levels of health are improving faster.

7.4.2.1.2. Education Supplement

Traditionally, an international body has also been concerned with equalizing educational opportunities for people in every nation. The GU would be responsible to providing education on the common heritage of humanity and on the global environment and history.

7.4.2.1.3. Global Planning
Planning is a large part of a global order. The GU must plan for many contingencies that nations may not have to face independently.

7.4.2.1.4. Global Resource Surveying & Monitoring
Monitoring is crucial for nations and a global order. No coordinated effort has ever been made to inventory, assess and monitor the ecological systems of the planet. The GU would do this.

7.4.2.2. Issue Vouchers for Nations Corporations and NGOs
A voucher is an economic warrant and guarantee for goods and services. A voucher is a certificate which is worth a certain monetary value and which may only be spent for specific reasons or on specific goods. Examples include, but are not limited to, education, children, and medicine. The community would issue certain vouchers for all citizens. Vouchers would be an effective way of dispersing limited resources and reducing inequity.

Vouchers for individuals and communities, for example, vouchers for basic income, medical, child, and medical would be handled at the national level. Resource vouchers would be distributed first at the international level.

7.4.2.3. Productivity Resource Vouchers
Within a calculated optimum (see earlier Section), every community within a nation would receive a number of vouchers for its population for the optimum use of resources and processes. Each individual would receive a set of vouchers for specific resources, such as productivity or carbon. Each community could make decisions on population size and wealth depending on other values or trade-offs.

7.4.2.3.1. Carbon & Other Element Vouchers
Every community could be issued a number of vouchers equal to the carbon-bearing products of it population and their standard of living, based on a world standard. These would determine how much was used in each national system, regardless of its population or the intensity of its exploitation. Each community could be given vouchers for each element or compound, such as phosphorus or iron. These would be distributed among the population, according to a simple formula.

7.4.2.3.2. Vouchers for Water, Air & Other Compounds
Everyone has basic requirements for breathing, drinking, or getting materials. The requirements of living, such as breathing or drinking, would not require vouchers, except under extreme circumstances of overpopulation or overconsumption. Trying to issue vouchers for these things, on a personal level, might be too expensive and too invasive.

7.4.2.3.3. Others Kinds of Vouchers
What other kinds of things could be distributed using vouchers? Should there be vouchers for luxury? In a random lotto system for fairness? Or should it be a reward for generosity or some other virtue?

7.4.2.3.4. Other International Costs
   (Being edited)

7.4.2.3.5. Restore Global Cycles or Places
Many places have been impacted by the international problems of pollution and simplification of land, and disruption of global ecological cycles. The GU would develop programs for restoration.

7.4.2.3.6. Create Set-aside Accounts for Global Catastrophes
A large part of the finances and efforts of a global association have to be concerned with global changes in climate and geology. These sometimes catastrophic changes are an integral part of the change and aging of the planet. They have to be anticipated, prepared for, and responded to.

7.5. *Expanding Global Responsibilities*

The Global Union becomes responsibility for its own health as well as any global or solar system threats.

7.5.1. *Executive Branch of Global Union*
The executive branch of the global association makes sure that the global laws of the GU are obeyed. Other functions of the branch are: To execute policies; to control policies; to appoint officials; to command the police force; and, to veto legislation. The executive branch has to be formed from the assembly of national representatives. It has to be relatively large, and it has to have salaries, support monies, and travel monies.

In addition to global laws, the Executive Branch would have to oversee the enforcement of laws by nations, especially where the two levels overlap.

7.5.1.1. Coordinate Global Union
The Secretary, equivalent to the former Secretary-General of the UN, would be the head of the Executive Branch. The Secretary would be elected from the General Assembly and serve a term of six years. The Secretary help from the Assistant Secretary, Police Chief, department heads, and heads of independent agencies. The Assistant Secretary would be head of the legislature and next in line to head the branch. The Police Chief would be head of all GU police forces. The Department heads would advise the Secretary on issues and help carry out policies. Independent Agencies would help carry out policy or provide special services.

The executive branch could be headed by an Executive Council of the department and agency heads; these offices would elect the Assistant Secretary.

7.5.1.2. Security Council of Global Association
The Security Council would be composed of twelve people elected by the General Assembly every three years. There would be no permanent members. The Council would elect its own Secretary to speak for the Council. The veto power would be replaced with consensus.

7.5.1.2.1. Assess Threats (Internal & External)
The Security council is concerned with any kind of threat to the global order and the orders of nations and nature. Many of these threats are internal, as nations enter into conflicts with other nations. These threats can be handled by delegations or police actions. But, many threats are external to the planet. They come from solar or interstellar space and tend to be physical.

7.5.1.2.1.1. International Conflict

Widespread poverty may cause catastrophes. Richer countries will need to recognize that the poverty of others is not in their interest, especially as potential markets. Inequity may never be erased. Perhaps some inequity is good and stimulating, but gross inequity needs to be limited.

Each culture develops rules for living together. A common culture provides an ideal framework for public and private decision making. The Sami in northern Scandinavia have institutionalized ways of avoiding conflict, for instance, by shaming those who would impose their will. The Fipa of Tanzania use cooperative exchange rather than competition to keep the peace. The Akawaio of Guyana believe that community disharmony upsets the spirit world, resulting in illness and misfortune.

Conflicts, territorial or symbolic, are symptoms of insecurity. Many of our wasteful conflicts could be more easily resolved through a neutral international power. Conflicts would still occur. Conflicts over prestige or power, as much as for various crusades as for a true state, still lead to human and environmental destruction. The Security Council would be charged with the responsibility to avoid massively destructive forms of conflict, such as biological war or nuclear war.

7.5.1.2.1.2. Global Threats

The planet is still a very active planet. Some threats to humanity rise from the normal activities of the planet, such as volcano-building or continental drift. Other changes, such as greenhouse gases, are causing possible threats.

7.5.1.2.1.2.1. *Geological Threats.* Typical geological threats include earthquakes volcanoes, and mudslides; rare threats may be comets or sunspot activity. While technology may be able to retard some of these threats or counter them early, the best solutions are design. Cities can be moved from floodplains; cities can be required to have quake-resistant buildings.

7.5.1.2.1.2.1.1. *Climatic Threats.* Someone said that civilizations exist through the consent of geology; however, the consent of the 'first empire of climate' might also be needed. Climate is a constant and immediate challenge. Many variables affect climate. One variation, with a long cycle of perhaps 100 million years, is continental drift. When Panama closed continents, it forced the gulf stream north. The earth's orbit around the sun, a 100,000 cycle, also changes climate. This is close to the spacing of ice ages. Other smaller cycles, at 10,000 years or 6,100 years are minor harmonics perhaps. Other activities that influence climate are sunspots, comets, and volcanoes. The most stable periods seem to be the coldest or warmest weathers. For instance, 400,000 years ago, a warm period lasted 25,000 years. If we are in a 10,000-year warm period, it may be almost up. This means that predictions are relevant.

Cooling can lead to disease and depopulation, which can lead to cooling. Farmland is abandoned to trees in times of collapse. Because trees take CO_2 out of the atmosphere, the regrowth of forests after the plagues in 1322-1351 in Europe and China, would have allowed drops in CO_2, which would have allowed climate to cool some.

The years 1997 to 2004 broke most heat and storm records, especially as some of the warmest years on record. We experienced 500-year floods, droughts of the century, and other extremes. Some of these events have been related to greenhouse effects.

7.5.1.2.1.2.1.2. *Oceanic Threats.* Ocean currents affect not only islands and coasts, but they affect the entire climates of continents. For example, the effects of the Pacific El Nino current can be linked to droughts in India and China in the past 150 years that caused three times the deaths of the Black Death, and more than the 60 million who died in WWII.

There does not seem to be a single trigger for El Nino. One trigger has to do with water overflow and then back flow from the western pacific. Others have to do with sunspots, which would reduce radiation, or volcanic eruptions. Many of these atmospheric, oceanic and geophysical triggers may converge. Nineteenth-century famines may be correlated with ENSO events that influenced China, Indonesia, Brazil, and southeast Africa.

The adherence to political colonialization and 'free market' economics, along with climate changes, made the suffering in famines worse. Millions died within the market system of the golden age of liberal capitalism. Thus, the famines were political and economic failures. Even at the height of the famines in 1877-78 and the 1890, Britain continued to export grain from India to England, which had its own agricultural downturn. The invisible hand did not lift those starving in India or China. There was starvation before the British, especially during El Nino events in 1596 and 1630, but many droughts did not result in such widespread and deep famines. Market economics and politics magnified the effects. The market economy can spread risk, through insurance companies, when crises are local and intermittent, but they may not be able to respond when the crises are global and ubiquitous. As the risks increase everywhere, fewer things can be done.

Other movements of water, such as tsunamis or floods, can be linked to earth movements, such as landslides or earthquakes.

7.5.1.2.1.2.2. *Solar System Threats.* Solar energy is not quite constant; over millennia it has been increasing; over the next billion years it will start decreasing. Collisions with asteroids or comets will always be a threat due to the nature of the solar system. The passage of the solar system through dust clouds will effect the climate of the planet and the solar output. The GU could plan to deal with asteroids and comets.

7.5.1.2.2. Provide Security using a Police Force
Countries scramble to identify and claim resources that they need, fighting for them if necessary. Resources in short supply include water, timber, and fossil fuels. Countries strive for resource security, but this leads to further fighting and instability. Traditional ownership is stretched, leading to new disputes. All of these conflicts are the kind that could be resolved by the GU. Cooperative solutions are more durable and effective. Violence only leads to resentment and further violence. The GU has to have either the most weapons in the largest police force or the best moral stance.

7.5.1.2.2.1. Expand Police Force
Peacekeeping, as defined by the Global Union, is a way to help countries torn by conflict create conditions for a sustainable situation of concord. GU peacekeepers—police, rather than soldiers and military officers—civilian police officers and civilian personnel from many countries would monitor and observe peace processes that emerge in post-conflict situations and assist ex-combatants in implementing the peace agreements they have signed. Such assistance comes in many forms, including confidence-building measures, power-sharing arrangements, electoral support, strengthening the rule of law, and economic and social development. All operations must include the resolution of conflicts through the use of force to be considered valid under the charter of the Global Union.

7.5.1.2.2.2. Use Police Force
The Charter of the Global Union would give the GU Security Council the power and responsibility to take collective action to maintain international peace and security. For this reason, the international community should look to the Security Council to authorize peacekeeping operations. Most of these operations would established and implemented by the GU itself with police serving under GU operational command. In other cases, where direct GU involvement is not considered appropriate or feasible, the Council would authorize regional organizations such as the North Atlantic Treaty Organization, the Economic Community of West African States or coalitions of

willing countries to implement certain peacekeeping or peace enforcement functions. In modern times, peacekeeping operations have evolved into many different functions, including diplomatic relations with other countries, international bodies of justice, such as the International Criminal Court, and eliminating problems, such as landmines, that can lead to new incidents of suffering or fighting.

The GU would be expected to have many operations around the world, similar to the peace operations of the UN. Recent operations of the UN in Africa include the Burundi Civil War (2004), the Civil war in Côte d'Ivoire (2004), Second Congo War (1999, United Nations Organization Mission in the Democratic Republic of the Congo, Second Liberian Civil War (2003), the Eritrean-Ethiopian War (2000), the North/South Civil War and Darfur conflict (2005), and the Moroccan occupation of Western Sahara. In the Americas, the UN monitored the 2004 Haiti rebellion. In Asia, the UN was involved in: The 1949 Indo-Pakistani Wars. In Europe, the UN put itself in: The 1964 Cyprus dispute, the 1993 Abkhazian War, and the 1999 Kosovo War. In the Middle East, the UN participated in the 1974 Agreed withdrawal by Syrian and Israeli forces following the Yom Kippur War, the 1978 withdrawal of Israeli forces from Lebanon, and the 1948 various cease-fires and assists.

7.5.1.2.2.2.1. *Deal with International Conflicts.* The police force would be entrusted to try nonviolence as a first response. In some cases police would be unarmed. If not that did not work, police would use weapons.

Conflict cannot be separated from other things, such as environmental destruction or inequities. For that reason, the Security Council and its force has to consider the broadest meaning of security: It is for people to have the resources and opportunities to provide themselves with their needs. Thus, security has to be addressed on many levels. For example, what do forests have to do with peace? Of the fourteen nations requiring UN peace-keeping operations since 1990, twelve of them have lost over 90 percent of their forests. Perhaps peace-keeping should be abetted by tree-planting. As ecosystems are destabilized, nations become less stable, and must be helped with more than social conflicts.

7.5.1.2.2.2.2. *Protect against Interference Events or Disasters.* Police would be expected to be prepared for natural disasters, including the extraterrestrial. The police would focus on the prevention of man-made disasters, from watersheds that were compromised to chemical spills. Collisions with asteroids will always be a threat due to the nature of the solar system.

The flexibility of a natural ecosystem to respond to change has been reduced, so either we have to take over control, which could cost quite a lot, or we have to adapt to the diminishment after some climatic episode.

Figure 7512-1. Laser satellite protection from bolides

7.5.2. *Agencies & Special Offices for Global Union*

Agencies of the Global Union are necessary organs to present information and research to the main branches of the Association.

7.5.2.1. Food & Shelter Agency

This agency is devoted to monitoring the food and shelter requirements and deficiencies of groups in every nation. It would provide information for traditional or ecological ways to build food supplies or shelters. Through international volunteers, it may provide help with expertise and labor.

7.5.2.2. Comprehensive Energy Agency

This energy agency would consider all possibilities: Human energy, animals, fire or combustion, fossil fuel, solar energy, geothermal energy, wind energy, and nuclear energy from fission or fusion. It may recommend and sponsor less hazardous kinds of energy use, such as solar energy and wind energy. It would also work to make sure that energy is not wasted; this may mean building or converting more efficient houses. Without the conservation of energy, giant wind farms or solar farms will dominate the landscape, ruin the scale and be possibly as hazardous as fossil fuels or nuclear power.

7.5.2.3. Transportation Agency

Transportation is a global phenomenon. Many kinds of transportation use the atmosphere and oceans—in fact many new proposals have to do with the undersea environment. The GU would monitor or control traffic in the global commons.

7.5.2.4. Economics Support Agency

Economies are tied together now in global patterns. They might be overconnected. This agency would provide information on economic weaknesses and problems to nations. It would act to provide alternatives to some kinds of economic practices and suggest practices that would eliminate the worst excesses.

7.5.2.5. Education Support Agency

Education needs to be stressed. The goal of education is for people to choose within limits—limits on wealth, waste, and freedoms that might endanger others. Education allows people to choose without being conditioned by brainwashing or dishonest advertising. The UN supported programs to enhance education, and it established the United Nations University for Peace, Costa Rica (a nation that has abolished its army), as an institution of higher learning for education for peace. The GU would continue these kind of efforts.

7.5.2.6. Health Agency

Health needs to be stressed, in every nation. The GU needs to monitor global disease and threats, to reduce chronic disease. Chronic diseases are neglected conditions. Chronic diseases represent a huge proportion of human illness. They include cardiovascular disease (30% of projected total worldwide deaths in 2005), cancer (13%), chronic respiratory diseases (7%), and diabetes (2%). Two risk factors underlying these conditions are key to any population-wide strategy of control: Tobacco use and obesity. These risks and the diseases they engender are not the exclusive preserve of rich nations. Chronic diseases are a larger problem in low-income settings. Research into chronic diseases in resource-poor nations indicates that it is critical to intervene early in the course of any epidemic. Fast intervention could save many millions of lives.

7.5.2.7. Communications & Technology Agency

There is a need for the development and delivery of a strategy for schools and other learning and skills institutions. This agency could provide strategic leadership in the innovative and effective use of communications and technology to enable the transformation of learning, teaching and educational organizations for the benefit of every learner.

The agency would be charged with regulating interstate and international communications by radio, television, wire, satellite, and cable. Its jurisdiction would cover in fact every nation and international areas.

7.5.2.8. Research Agency

This Agency is the central research and development organization for the planet. It manages and directs selected basic and applied research and development projects for the international body and member nations. It pursues research and technology where risk and payoff are both very high and where success may provide dramatic advances for issues of global importance.

The reductionist path taken by science has yielded tremendous results about how the world is built up out of particles and molecules. Now that we have uncovered the complexity, we need to address relationships. This is where the synthetic path can help, by identifying emergent principles and operations. Science is an open, self-referential, self-correcting system capable of using analytic and synthetic methods.

Advances in science have been quite remarkable. How can it continue being remarkable, but applicable to whole systems? While pure research continues to reveal unimaginable details of ecosystems, and while applied research continues to support sophisticated use, more ecological and landscape research is needed. Research is expensive, time-consuming, labor-intensive, and uncertain, however.

Long-term research is especially important in forest ecosystems, since many of the components live hundreds and thousands of years, and the forest itself can live far longer. Long-term research requires different levels of monitoring, including environmental, biological, and ecological. Environmental monitoring is an umbrella for many activities, including climatic variables and geological processes; for example, the systematic recording of soil and air temperatures, humidity, air pressure are measured by meteorological organizations to predict long-term climatic change. Long-term research also depends on a stable cultural base and shared values between generations.

Other kinds of research needed equally are: Historical research, fire research, productivity research, mortality patterns, mature ecosystem research, key species, artifact interaction, and genetic research.

7.5.2.9. Business & Corporations Agency

Businesses and corporations sometimes have more people, money and power than nations. This agency would be concerned with monitoring and assisting these entities, to ensure that they do not violate the norms of nations or take advantage of cultural limits.

7.5.2.9.1. Earth Incorporation

Political systems are impotent to stop the massive interference in ecosystems by international corporations. The simplest and most direct way to give the earth a voice in the development of the earth by humanity is to incorporate the earth following international law. The entire planet, with its biochemical cycles and nonhuman communities, would become one legal body. Since corporations are human constructs, however, humans would have to represent ecosystems and their wealth of living organisms.

In early civilizations, the advancement of the state was expected to contribute to the welfare of its people. Corporations are recent devices created by states for public purposes. Most early U.S. corporations, for example, were concerned with travel (turnpikes and inland waterways) or safety (fire insurance)—they resembled public agencies more than profit-seeking associations. The exclusive privileges and political power granted to corporations were based on the implicit promise of social services.

The association of economic development with national wealth allowed incorporation laws to be broadened. The corporation was given the constitutional rights of an individual. A corporation is a legal entity, independent from its founders, with its own rights, privileges, and liabilities. It is, however, required to obey laws and pay taxes; and it is accountable for its deeds in courts of law.

Unfortunately, as private good became identified with public good, corporations became larger, more acquisitive, and less concerned with social services. The quest for profit now has the effect of violating social amenities, such as clean air and clean water, instead of ensuring them. No responsibility is taken for environmental degradation, since no right of contract or fair use of property has been breached.

Changes in societies, from rural to urban, from sparsely to densely populated, from culturally diverse to monotonic, have transformed corporations and the societies themselves. Business corporations now provide the bulk of goods and services in many states. The scale of these corporations, the processes of production, and the size and needs of human populations, have altered and degraded many ecosystems and biogeochemical cycles.

Successful modern corporations create an identity based on their purpose in providing goods or services; they define their business in terms of profitability, growth rate, cash flow, and competitive position; they develop a corporate vision, with specific objectives and strategies, including long-term vision, collection of ideas and creative implementation, aggressive manufacturing, and reliable finance.

The purpose of a corporation often transcends simple financial gain—the corporation seeks to maintain its own existence, before profit. Financial objectives (sales, assets, profits) exist to sustain its existence. The goals that most motivate corporate managers are survival, independence, self-sufficiency, and self-fulfillment. Yet, these motives are consistent with the financial objectives of the corporation: to maximize corporate wealth. The responsibility of managers is to maximize the value of the company. Furthermore, because corporations are long-lived, that value should last a long time—a good reason for looking beyond the ten-year monetary horizon and the lives of its managers.

Although current wisdom holds that a corporation's only responsibility is to its stockholders, corporations are being pushed to include social purpose in their strategies, again. Alas, they are doing poorly at it. They do not know how much responsibility to take, or where to put limits, or whether to pursue policies that diminish their profits. Corporations have proved spotty in doing social and environmental good. It would be more appropriate to have them deal with the environment as a corporate entity concerned with maximizing its own values. Of course, that would mean no more 'free' resources or environmental services.

The important advantages to incorporating the earth are the same as for incorporating a business. There are at least six advantages: (1) Managerial flexibility; the stockholders are separate from managers; responsibilities are assigned by needs of the corporation. (2) Limited liability; the corporation borrows and repays. It shields its members from hazards to which they would otherwise be exposed. (3) Financial advantage; the ownership of assets can benefit stockholders and the corporation. (4) Tax advantage; investments in the good of the corporation may not be taxed by nations. (5) Estate planning and longevity; the corporation exists indefinitely beyond the lives of its participants. (6) Central management and representation; a large and complex business needs operational and managerial efficiency. Many of the participants have no direct voice in the operation—they must be represented.

The earth incorporated would focus on a core business: to ensure the integrity and continuity of life and all its connections and to secure the opportunity for development free from undue interference. It would operate to optimize values, like any good corporation, but the values would be ecosystem values, such as fungus values and earthworm values, as well as human values.

A temporary Board of Directors would adopt bylaws, elect working officers, approve stock certificates, open accounts, and arrange a stockholders meeting. The stockholders would elect new directors, possibly from Global Union representatives or directly from elections, and decide on dividend declarations.

Stockholders, as citizens of independent nations, would turn over common and national property to the Earth Corporation, which would issue stock certificates to the stockholders. The corporation would allocate the purchase price of stock to capital at par value. Most of the shares—the percentage to be determined by the board as necessary to the operation of ecosystems—would be treasury shares. Anything more than par value would go to capital surplus, and only capital surplus could be distributed as dividends. Stockholders have the right to receive these dividends equitably, without resort to traditional distributions of wealth.

Stock certificates denote ownership of the corporation. Although the stockholders own the corporation, they do not own the property of the corporation, the earth, which is owned by the corporation itself. Stockholders, as individuals, groups, or nations, could make agreements about how business would be conducted, about what resources would be used or traded.

The elected board of directors would make decisions of distribution and limitation. Percentages would be deducted from the interest for the operation of the corporation and for equitable distribution to nations less favored by chance with biological or geological wealth. Furthermore, since the dividends would be distributed among people according to net ecosystem productivity and resource availability, no advantage would be gained by nations having large populations.

The basic functioning system would be considered capital, thus limiting the amount of human use of resources and probably the size of human populations. Interest would accrue in the form of net ecosystem productivity and diverted percentages of materials, such as gold or water.

The earth incorporated would solve the problem of having to value ecosystems in monetary or quantifiable terms; its systems would be untouchable capital. The human value of resources like copper, air, or water would be equated to the technological cost of recycling or producing them.

Raw material and energy are only two facets of the capital of a corporation—another is human ingenuity. Thus, human wealth would not be limited by restrictions on the availability of resources, but rather by a shortage of ingenuity.

An incorporated earth would be instrumental in conditioning international corporations to their social responsibility and in internalizing all costs. This corporation and governments could use traditional means, such as credit access, low interest rates, and setting priorities on equity issues, to evoke public interest in smaller and healthier human endeavors. The corporation would keep rights to global territories and resources, issue leases to nations, and monitor scarce resources.

The suggested articles of incorporation are:
FIRST: The name of the corporation shall be The Earth, Incorporated.

SECOND: The purposes for which the corporation is formed shall include: The protection of functioning ecosystems and their living beings from destructive interference.

The conduct of inquiry into the operation of such systems and the role of humanity therein for scientific and educational purposes.

The taking of appropriate legal steps to carry out these purposes.

The maintenance of all real common property, including all lands, seas, and atmosphere, subject to the restrictions and limitations hereinafter set forth, to use only the interest from income therein, reserving the principal thereof exclusively for the aforesaid purposes, it being intended that the corporation be organized and operated for preservational purposes and not for pecuniary profit.

The corporation is organized as a voice for nonhuman beings and systems. No part of the income of the corporation, if any, shall inure to the benefit of any trustee or officer of the corporation or to any private individual having an interest in the corporation (except for reasonable compensation) and no trustee or officer of the corporation or any private individual shall be entitled to share in the distribution of any of the assets of the corporation.

The corporation shall not be authorized to carry on propaganda, influence legislation, participate in any political campaigns, or discriminate against human cultures.

In furtherance of the foregoing purposes, the corporation shall have the following powers:

To accept and hold by gift or judicial order any real or personal property of whatever kind, nature, or description, wherever situated.

To sell, transfer, or dispose of the interest from any such property, but not the principal or any part thereof.

To make, accept, endorse, execute, and issue bonds, promissory notes, bills of exchange, and other obligations of the corporation for monies borrowed for the purposes of the corporation.

To invest and reinvest its funds in stock, bonds, or in such other securities and property as its trustees shall deem advisable, subject to the limitations and conditions contained in any grant or gift.

In general, and subject to such limitations and conditions as are or may be subscribed by international law, to exercise such other powers which now are or hereafter may be conferred by international law upon a corporation organized for the purposes hereinabove set forth.

THIRD: The operations of the corporation are to be conducted on the surface of the earth but the operations of the corporation shall not be limited to such territory.

FOURTH: The principal office of the corporation is to be located temporarily in the Global Union (GU), currently in the City of New York, State of New York, United States of America (and possibly relocated to Antarctica or elsewhere).

FIFTH: The number of directors, who shall be known as trustees, of the corporation shall be not less than 30 (a minimum number associated with major ecosystems), nor more than 3,300 (the number of independent cultures associated with biogeographical provinces and subprovinces).

An earth corporation would have a special charter to protect the planet and provide opportunities and services for all the inhabitants.

7.5.2.9.2. Recharter International (Landless) Corporations
Nations are people in place, whereas corporations are people in profit, often out of place. Corporations are like the feudal domains that evolved into nations. They are new kinds of political organizations, rich and arrogant, but they are currently free to leave behind any social or economic mess as they search for freer or better markets.

Nations need corporations more than corporations need nations, Lester Thurow notes. But, corporations are legal individuals. Nations simply need to make laws requiring that every corporation have a national base, preferably where most of the employees work, and must meet their obligations and duties as national citizens.

Laws for corporations, such as Antitrust laws, need to be consistent globally, says Thurow. Laws, like morals, have to react to new technology and new social situations, regarding consumer protection or company protection.

The GU could make a binding treaty on transnational corporate accountability. The GU would also collect data on Transnational corporations. Local corporations would have national accountability.

The question is who should have the power and how much. The GU would have the power to charter transnational or global corporations. The GU could tie corporations to place and force them to be responsible by identifying the corporation as a legal community in a place, rather than a fictitious artificial individual, with no address. Members, or staff and stockholders, would share equal responsibility and liability for the activities of the real corporate community. The GU would recognize that the corporate community has moral obligations which can be spelled out. The GU would recognize that the community is not permanent or abstract. It must have a place and participate in that place as a responsible community.

The GU would create a comprehensive model of requirements, such as stability, justice, and balance for transnational corporations. It would make sure that the charter requires serving public interests as well as private gains, to increase the meaningful work of employees, who want to serve the public good of the place as well. The GU would make sure that profits and losses, gains and costs are all privatized equally. The GU would make sure that all costs are internalized, that the capital of the ecosystem has to be paid for use. The GU would require fair labor practices in terms of reimbursement, where the minimum wage would be above a standard poverty level for a nation and the maximum could be no more than ten 10 times the minimum.

The GU would require a corporation to address environmental problems, using ecological performance standards, and address social problems, using social performance standards. The GU would require plans showing dependencies on environment and society community, then monitor corporations for their economic health, to make sure that they develop and mature correctly. The GU would also make sure they have plans for unforeseeable contingencies.

The GU would monitor corporate responsibility, the natural home communities of corporations for their ecological health, and the health of the home human communities. The GU would set standards for corporations to internalize the loops of production and waste, at least within the system of sharing corporations. The GU would track all impacts. The GU would encourage corporations to promote ecological design, and to guarantee the use and safety of their products and services. The GU would expect loyalty from corporations, but develop loyalty both ways.

7.5.2.10. Office of Personnel & Service
This office keeps track of permanent and temporary employees of the global association. The association would use a civil service examination, much like that developed in China, to qualify and individuals for positions.

7.5.2.10.1. Permanent & Part-time Staff
The permanent staff would support the functions of the body. All positions, even those of the assembly, would be paid by the GU organization, with the understanding that the first allegiance professionally would be to the global body, before any national or community interests.

7.5.2.10.2. Volunteers Service to GU or Nations
The GU would create a separate volunteer program, for those who wanted to volunteer to work in global areas, such as mid-oceans or Antarctica. Some of the volunteers could serve on peacekeeping or emergency response missions in specific nations. The specific commitment could be two years.

7.5.2.11. Office of Self-Assessment & Future
Self-Assessment in an organizational setting, according to definition, refers to a comprehensive, systematic and regular review of an organization's activities and results referenced against a model organization. The Self-Assessment process allows the organization to discern clearly its strengths and areas in which improvements can be made and culminates in planned improvement actions which are then monitored for progress.

Self-assessment can be extremely valuable in helping an organizations to critique its own activities, and form judgments about its strengths and weaknesses. For obvious reasons, self-assessment is more usually used as part of a formative assessment process, rather than a summative one, where it requires certification by others.

The UN needs to have access to assess the performance of independent governments. So that in addition to a self-analysis at a national level, there will be a GU assessment. Assessment could be based on two-year cycles, although planning could extend to 500 or more years.

7.5.3. *Judicial Branch & International Courts*
The judicial branch of government is made up of the system of courts and offices. The Interests Court would be the highest court on the planet. The Constitution would establish this Court and all other courts. Courts decide arguments about the meaning of laws, how they are applied, and whether they break the rules of the Constitution. The functions of the judicial branch are: To maintain the integrity of the Constitution, to interpret laws, and to check the executive and legislative branches and special commissions, by monitoring their activities.

7.5.3.0.1. *Monitor Other Branches & All Laws.* The judicial branch monitors the Executive Branch, the Legislative Branch, and all other departments and agencies for the relevance of their behavior to the constitution of the organization.

7.5.3.0.2. *Interpret Laws.* The judicial branch interprets the laws made by the legislative branch and their enforcement by the Executive Branch for their closeness to the constitution and the intents of the peoples of all nations.

7.5.3.1. Conflicts & Interests Court
The Judicial Branch would set up a court to resolve interests and conflicts of the member nations, especially as related to global resources. The Court would decide matters relating to use of global resources or shared resources.

7.5.3.2. Environment Court
The UN Environmental Programme is relatively weak, from lack of capacity, staffing and funding. It should be made an agency that could coordinate environmental policies for the planet. It should have enforcement powers, maybe taxing powers directly. The environmental agency would conduct environmental surveys and monitoring.

The GU Environmental Court could address all global properties, including the atmosphere, deep continents, oceans, moon, space, bioregions, watersheds, and wild habitats. Many of its issues would be raised by the environmental agency.

7.5.3.3. Office of Rights (Human & Ambihuman)
Should some rights be made universal? We know that there are universal rules for human behavior, most of which relate to families. We also know that some things should be made universal by law.

An economy has traditionally been seen as a morally neutral body, but even if it has only to conform to the nominal rules of society, it is already a moral agent. Economies are no more neutral than other organisms. Many areas of moral concern already are recognized: Worker safety; affirmative action; advertising truth; foreign investments; and harm to the consumer, public, and environment.

Responsibility occurs wherever the interests or rights of a person, society, or ecosystem are significantly affected by the actions of economic actors. Responsibility can be understood in terms of costs and benefits, that is, through operations and their consequences rather than abstract behavior. Every action entails a gain and a cost (or profit and loss). Profits and losses are distributed privately, socially, or environmentally.

Economies need to work cooperatively to make sure the costs and benefits are extended equally throughout the system. They could start by sponsoring the rational use of rare resources through taxation. Influence the government to determine priorities for wilderness areas or special landscapes. Beautiful, fragile, unique, or endangered ecosystems and species must be protected at the expense of commercial activity. Assigning rights to Nonhuman patterns would support many kinds of preservation.

7.5.3.4. Tax Court
The Tax Court would ensure that the taxes of the global association are legal and being collected. It may also ensure that the taxes of nations are not out of line with those of other nations.

7.5.3.5. Police Enforcement Court
This Court would judge cases related to police actions of the global association, in handling problems between nations or corporations.

7.5.3.6. Office of International Trade & Equalization
The resources of the planet are spread unequally around the globe. Local trade allowed some resources to be acquired through trade, especially things used for ceremonial activities, such as ochre or gold. Trade also exposed people to new ideas, and to distant people and their products. Trade also forced the collection of surplus in excess of needs and perhaps in excess of the system. Many effects of trade are long-term problems and do not become evident for several generations. They are also very difficult to reverse. For a society that needs surpluses to continue, with growing dependents and growing numbers of people, there is little flexibility to change. Other cultures, such as the English, encouraged trade to increase wealth.

Regional trade started to emerge a few thousand years ago, with Roman trade between 100 BC and 400 AD and Mongol Trade with China and Europe, 1250-1350. The Atlantic slave trade in the 1700-1800s linked three continents. The first wave of global trade destroyed many of the traditional societies of the Americas. A later wave of globalization destroyed traditional economic systems. European exports, especially in textiles, undermined regional livelihoods. These processes enriched the Atlantic shores. It also widened the inequities within nations.

Economics has become more and more global. Where peoples used to trade material goods, fish for roots or feathers for leather, for instance, now all things have a common symbolic value, most often expressed in yen or dollars. This means that whoever works the cheapest sells the most.

The purpose of this office is to promote the equalization of trade opportunities. It has to make sure that trade partners are not overconnected. The office would also help nations that are underconnected by trade. The office would safeguard the global aspects of the system. It would create rules for the international regulation of trade.

7.5.4. Commission on the Earth

The Commission would have trusteeship over global commons. Boundary issues need to be resolved first. The Commission would limit national jurisdiction of oceans to 20 miles from the border, rather than 50 or 200 miles, to protect ocean resources. Furthermore, it would have a say on continental shelves and shore fisheries. The other 65-70 percent of the surface of the planet has to be regulated as a common area.

7.5.4.1. Environmental Surveys & Monitoring

Surveys need to be made of every kind of ecosystem. Humanity needs to have an inventory of kinds of systems and kinds of changes. How is conserving terrestrial animals part of conserving ecosystem health? We do not know whether animal declines were caused by disease or some other factor, such as competition or predation. We need to find that out.

Monitoring is the key to understanding changes. Disease needs to be monitored as an important indicator of integrity. Other indicators are surveys of key species, habitat mapping and human impacts monitoring. Complex interactions have to be monitored, using a range of indicators at levels from behavioral to ecological. There may be limitations of the bioindicators of ecosystem health. Perhaps we need to find common and endangered indigenous species and monitor them, hoping that would reflect the health of the entire system.

7.5.4.1.1. Create Inventories

The Commission would inventory every ecosystem on the globe. An inventory is a complete list of all components of an ecosystem, from the geological to the ecological. A complete inventory of elements starts with the shapes of the features in the area, the geomorphology. The large volumes are rounded and natural hills—even the agricultural evidence is almost natural, that is, from the roadside not the air, the fields appear not to be squares, triangles, or circles; a small number of geometric shapes exist in the buildings by the road, but because of their scale are not too intrusive. A complete physical and ecological inventory would then be integrated with economic and cultural values.

With the information available now, from a more extended resource inventory and with optimal ideas about renewal, climatic conditions, traditional land-use patterns, local cycles, and ecological requirements (limits), conservation is more effective. Its goal is to support a steady state economy within optimum ranges based on natural and human limits.

7.5.4.1.2. Create Monitoring of Global Properties

The Commission would address real global problems, such as global warming, which has resulted in grain harvest shortfalls in recent years. The climate in general would receive renewed and detailed examination.

A global system is the sum of localities and may have unique properties of its own, that is, the universe has properties that local frames of reference do not have. An ecosystem is directly connected with global cycles and other ecosystems. The system is embedded in larger systems and global cycles, that is, cyclicity. There has to be a good substrate with energy and materials flowing into the system.

The global problems include: Global warming; ozone depletion (chemical caused); disruption of global cycles; contaminations (nitrates, mercury). These threats cause ecosystem collapse. Ecosystem breakdown happens as a result of stresses, singly or grouped, that relate to interference patterns in the system, most of which are caused by the human species now, although the potential for asteroids or volcanic eruptions remains.

Our actions on the planet are experiments, whether we want them to be or not. Ignorance, denial, or cupidity cannot unmake this experimental course, which may be global and irreversible. This Commission would make the experiment conscious and cautious.

7.5.4.1.2.1. *Atmosphere Monitoring*. The biosphere can exert control on the temperature of the surface and the composition of the atmosphere. On the other hand, soil types and the weather can limit vegetation; invasions of vegetation change soil types. An ecosystem is a topographic unit, a volume of land, occupied by organic beings, extended over an area and through time, with connections to larger mineral, chemical, water and air cycles. This means they are geographical units that intersect with atmospheric units. Ecosystems have a vertical structure, that includes the levels of climate from micro to topoclimate and macroclimate, to soils, water structures, and bedrock, as well as a horizontal structure. An ecosystem is a process, or a set of interlinked, differentially-scaled processes that may be diffuse in space but are easily defined in turnover times.

Processes encounter each other in a functioning web of an ecosystem, with tangible and diffuse surfaces. Lynn Margulis qualifies her definition of an ecosystem: The smallest unit capable of recycling the elements of its membership. For example, organic carbon can be expired, fixed, reacted, or transformed. This is done through the physiological activities of the members of the system, through breathing, enzymes, or some other way. Margulis states that elements recycle faster within ecosystems than between them. Forests, for instance, act as sinks for carbon. The rapid release of sinks can affect other atmospheric or terrestrial cycles. The biota of the planet appear to regulate the surface temperature, atmospheric composition, and ocean chemistry, for a start, perhaps like the human body regulates its temperature, blood chemistry, and other vital signs. As it achieves a new balance, with human inputs, the atmosphere may cause problems with agriculture and other human activities. Atmospheric monitoring is tied with water and terrestrial monitoring. Parts of the atmosphere could be designated as reserves.

7.5.4.1.2.2. *Oceans Monitoring*. Life had once been limited to the oceans. The evolution of living forms expanded those limits. Life, over time, has colonized deep oceanic vents, as well as Antarctic gravel fields. Oceans are not as productive as most land-based ecosystems. Worldwide, oceans could only support about twenty two million people, even though its area is over twenty three times that of grasslands. The ocean bottom acts as a sink for phosphorus. The rapid release of sinks can affect other atmospheric or terrestrial cycles.

This Commission would protect the integrity of the oceans. It could designate ocean wilderness or conservation areas. Perhaps eighty percent of the ocean surface could be designated as a reserve.

7.5.4.1.2.3. Deep Continents Monitoring. Continents are formed by the movement of tectonic plates. As each continent forms, it develops its own combination of topology and water and climate patterns. Australia for instance has become the driest continent now. As continents rise or subside, in addition to their movement and combination, life has to adapt to the changes. The purpose of such monitoring would be to predict long-term changes as a result of continental change.

7.5.4.1.2.4. *Bioregions Watersheds & Habitats Monitoring.* Monitoring bioregions and watersheds involves a larger spatial scale than ecosystems. Regional goals are appropriate for bioregions. Evaluation of data must occur in an integrated manner that spans biological and physical scales, watersheds, administrative boundaries, as well as functional areas. To understand how ecological processes are connected we need to relate information across disciplines and agencies, and collectively perceive the effect of our actions on the environment. This approach follows ecosystem theory (the hypothesis that cycles in nature integrate the physical, chemical, and biological components of ecosystems), and the hierarchical organization of ecosystem functions throughout the landscape. Hierarchy theory can be described as the development and organization of landscape patterns, e.g., vegetation communities, through time and space.

This can be accomplished by incorporating the three primary attributes of biodiversity, as described by Jerry Franklin—composition, structure and function—into four levels of organization—province, subprovince, watershed, and site. Indicators incorporating composition, structure and function at the appropriate levels of organization have been identified for many ecosystems; they range from landscape morphology to human demographics and cultural influences.

For watersheds and habitats one has to consider the impact of any kind of vegetation removal. What is a minimum, optimum or maximum vegetative cover for various watersheds? Science might identify minima or maxima but philosophy and conservation can aim at optima.

7.5.4.1.2.5. *Antarctica Moon & Space Monitoring.* The moon has been such a constant for the earth, it might be hard to imagine how things would develop or change if the moon changed or were destroyed. The moon is related to stability of earth system. Because of its relatively large size and closeness, the moon forms the other half of a double planet with the earth. The moon revolves around the earth and both orbit the sun, so the entire lunar cycle takes almost 30 days. The moon exerts a gravitational pull on the earth that is stronger on the closer side. This creates a tidal variation in the heights of the oceans; these vary monthly. For many shallow water creatures, amphibians and mammals, it is good to adapt to these tidal variations. Of course, the earth exerts a pull on the moon, also, but it is less dramatic.

Due to its rotation around the sun, and to imperfections in balance, the earth tilts on its axis. This obliquity of the ecliptic creates seasonal variations, to which most animals and plants have adapted. Any changes, even relatively small ones, could be catastrophic for climate—a one-degree change could account for some ice ages. Jacques Laskar and others have documented the importance of the moon on the habitats of the earth. A stable climate needs the influence of the moon; otherwise, there would be immense variations in the solar heating of the earth's surface. The moon provides energy pulses, stabilizes axial tilt, and causes tides and variations.

Space is an equally important part of the system environment. It is not only the source of the sun, but it is the sink for energy from the earth as well. Stars and the sink of space provide many elements and their proportions. Galactic and solar system dust influences long cycles of climate.

Life is also challenged by energy and gravity, as well as the moon's behavior. The moon provides daily variations in tides, that provide energy to organisms, although the organisms have to adjust for the different levels of water.

7.5.4.2. Ecological Design & Planning for Commission on Earth
The Commission is entrusted with finding out what is on the earth, as well as designing forms for the continuity and enhancement of human life on the earth.

7.5.4.2.1. Create Long-term Ecological Plans

Despite valid arguments against centralized and global planning, the most important thing people can do with civilizations and ecosystems is plan. That is, plan for the ecosystem needs and for human needs, plan for landscape, watershed, preservation, site, alternative use, and social objectives.

The goal of the Commission is to create a practical plan that fits cultures into nature in ways that protect all aspects of domiture. We can break the planning process into various stages, each with accompanying tasks and subplans. This plan, with all its partial plans, is necessary to protect the scale of landscapes that are too large to see, except perhaps by satellite, the parts that are too small to see, such as fungi and viruses, the parts that are too-long-lived for us to observe, such as long successional changes or evolutions, and the parts that we are ignorant about. Without special effort, we are aware only of what we see working in the system during a very short time. We trust that our plans will ensure that the system will remain as a healthy entity for a very long time so that many generations of us can gather our needs from it.

Planning is not meant to be a finished work of art—it has to reflect our understanding and use of nature. Each activity needs to be fed back into the process of updating the plan. Implementing the plan should result in improvements to it.

7.5.4.2.2. Protect Hotspots (such as Madagascar Hawaii & Ecuador)

The Critical Ecosystem Partnership Fund (CEPF) is a major endeavor to preserve Earth's most critically endangered and biologically richest regions. The biodiversity hotspots are in a state of emergency, according to Jorgen Thomsen, CEPF's Executive Director and Senior Vice President at Conservation International, the managing partner of the fund, who stated, "By engaging local people in biodiversity conservation, we ensure the best chance of success at protecting the environment for future generations." The CEPF, a joint initiative of Conservation International, the Global Environment Facility, The John D. and Catherine T. MacArthur Foundation, the World Bank, and the Japanese government, aims to invest at least $150 million over five years in biodiversity hotspots—highly threatened regions where more than 60 percent of terrestrial species diversity is found on only 1.4 percent of the Earth's surface. The Commission would work to refine and coordinate protection of all identified hotspots. The areas identified here and below are representative samples, not an exhaustive list.

7.5.4.2.3. Keep Critical Areas Intact (e.g., Amazon Congo & New Guinea)

Many areas are critical because of their size, as well as their uniqueness, and due to their out of scale effects on the global system. These areas should be kept in tact, as functioning systems, although they could be used by archaic cultures and by industrial systems, if precautions were taken. Their use by nations would be limited. Earth parks, in the Antarctic, Amazon, Arctic, Northern Canada, Congo, New Guinea, Oceanic areas, and Eastern Russia would be declared immediately.

7.5.4.2.4. Restore Large Areas (such as Mesopotamia & Western China)

Ecosystem restoration would be begun; massive planting efforts are undertaken. No further expansions would be permitted for development in wetlands or other sensitive areas. Destructive searches for resources would be suspended, in favor of substitution and recycling. No new building would be encouraged until uninhabited ones are restored.

Many special areas, now degraded or destroyed, could be restored. Candidates for restoration would include: the Zagros mountain area between Iraq and Iran, the Shat-el-Arab river system in Iraq, the forests of Lebanon, the central tall-grass prairie in the U.S. for buffalo as a Wildlands Project, and Northeastern China forests.

7.5.4.2.5. Anticipate Climate Change
What is the solution for climate change? Restore forests and grasslands, and use alternative energy. Should we try a high-tech solution? A massive program, like the atom bomb, only on alternative energy technologies, might work. Continued global warming could lead to reversal of ocean currents. One way to anticipate change for preservation is in the design of protected areas, using a north-south axis and including many different elevations. Siting cities, or most of a city, over twenty feet above sea-level might be prudent.

7.5.5. *Commission on Cultures & Religions*
This commission addresses how to keep cultures healthy and active by understanding the properties of a healthy culture and meeting its needs, from being grounded to being sophisticated. Cultures change over time; some develop, some collapse. Many cultures are transformed when they adapt to changes. Some cultures were transformed by domestication or agriculture.

Culture operates like nature, with rhythms of dissolution and reformation. Often the elements of a culture will simply be rearranged by a succeeding culture. A new culture can only be made from the heritage of the old. Our survival depends on the capacity to remake the image of the world from within, phoenix-like.

Like biological species, cultures do not fit perfectly into an integrated whole; there are discontinuities and contradictions. The culture is a loose-fitting patchwork of ideas, things and relationships. Humans can tolerate inconsistency and operate with contradictory beliefs: Soldiers fight for peace; ministers save the unborn for starvation. If the contradictions become too great and maladaptive, then the culture can collapse or disappear.

In the face of a change a culture can either embrace change or resist. Resistance to change is normal as a cultural process. Groups like the pygmies have specialized to fit the requirements of the environment, successfully. This makes it difficult to adopt other cultural arrangements.

On the other hand, resistance to change itself is an adaptive mechanism. According to Betty Meggers, it works as a successful "cultural isolating mechanism." Isolation remember is what allows a culture to develop in the first place. But, then does it force a culture to become stagnant? This Commission will examine the history and features of cultures and religions.

7.5.5.1. Preserve Cultures & Languages
The spread of the Bantu people in Africa caused a destruction and then a homogenization of languages. But then, because the societies were still relatively small-scale, they soon started to fragment in local mosaic environments. Bantu, for example, spread south as far as it could and people adopted that language, but then dialects started to diversify. Bantu now has produced 500 daughter languages in the past 200 years. Things tended again to a linguistic equilibrium. Of course, other peoples, such as the Hadza, Sandawe, or San Bushmen were pushed to the margins.

Language reflects places. Knowledge of the environment is coded in a language. Local peoples have knowledge from thousands of years of successes and failures. In Palau, they know the 1000 approximately fish species. The Kapingamarangi islanders in Micronesia spread their catch over 200 species without threatening their numbers. Western science has not had time to identify the species, much less create an effective marine management system. The vast undocumented traditional environmental knowledge is kept in indigenous languages by those people.

Languages can disappear for many reasons, normally, because people stop speaking them, especially if the young abandon the tongue and the elderly die. Occasionally, it can happen that a drought, famine, disease, war, flood, earthquake, tsunami, volcano eruption, acts of genocide, or other catastrophe wipes out a people. For example, the Paulohi language speakers in Maluku, Indonesia, experienced a severe earthquake and tsunami several years ago which killed all but about 50 of them.

Some people have said that they do not want to bring children into a world where their society, language, and people have no place. Some have turned to negative behavior like alcoholism, drugs, crime, or killing. The Waorani in Ecuador, the Carabayo in Colombia, and other groups in South America turned to killing, and for that reason some groups have still not had peaceful contact with the outside world.

This commission would work with groups that have diminishing number of speakers. It could help publish dictionaries, audio tapes, and news programs. It would promote groups that are successfully trying to recover their languages, such as Hebrew and Hawaiian.

7.5.5.2. Allow Religions to Act & Flourish

Religion is a part of culture that binds people to their ancestors as well as to the invisible powers of place. It focuses on the changeless aspects of natural and human processes. Religion concerns itself with an image of the world, that explains what the world is like. It also explains how we can influence it and why we would want to influence it. A shared religion affirms family and ancestral ties, but it also allows strangers without kinship ties to act more peacefully. Of course religion has also served more mundane human purposes, such as to justify the transfer of wealth to a leader or to the rich, or the sacrifice of lives for an ideal nongenetic reason. Religions, and myths, according to Joseph Campbell, are great poems, pointing through things to the ubiquity of a presence in each. Cultural inheritance seems to work. The heritability is high. Children tend to adopt their parent's religion, political views, and leisure interests.

Religions are attempts to understand or control the world, either by understanding the invisible or by having spiritual beings intercede. Religion tends to reinforce the integrity and structure of society, by providing a common image, and reinforce the belonging and commitment to the group. Religious claims about the other spiritual world tend to be counterfactual, but they cannot be too implausible. The supernatural has to play a part in the world. It has to be associated with living beings.

Religious rituals can also stimulate endorphins to the brain. These rituals may include painful poses, rhythmic movements, singing, or trials of endurance. Endorphins have good effects on the immune system. Trance states are another feature of religion. Endorphins allow people to feel positive about people who share their experiences.

Each religion is an attempt at transcendence with its own truths, certainties and stories. Their differences allow common beliefs, such as the golden rule, but also inhumanity. Some social virtues, such as trust, truth, restraint and obligation are grounded in religious beliefs. A contractual economy needs these virtues to survive, but at the same time, it is undermining religion with secularization.

The stories of religions concern events that are deeply meaningful to the listeners. This helps bind the group, also. Religion may help control disruptive forces, especially things about distribution and power. Religion coerces people into a social contract. Religion and story-telling may reduce variability of individuals in a group. But, this might increase variability between religious groups. Shared beliefs in a religious community may allow it to outcompete a strictly secular ones. It permits more sacrifice and commitment. Religion also allows ecological balance for many groups.

This commission would work to preserve the cultural capital built up by religions of thousands of years and regenerate other capital.

7.5.5.3. Ombudsman

Although not traditionally a fourth branch of government, as first proposed in Sweden, the function of the Ombudsman would be to improve the effectiveness and fairness of the global government while protecting basic human and ambihuman rights. Through the Ombudsman, nations or cultures could present cases of dispute for resolution. One strength of the office would be its power to initiate legal proceedings in behalf of any human and ambihuman constituents or nations. It would be an independent branch with separate responsibilities: To investigate complaints against the GU or its officials for wrongdoing; to investigate complaints against nations; and, to investigate the operation of the GU.

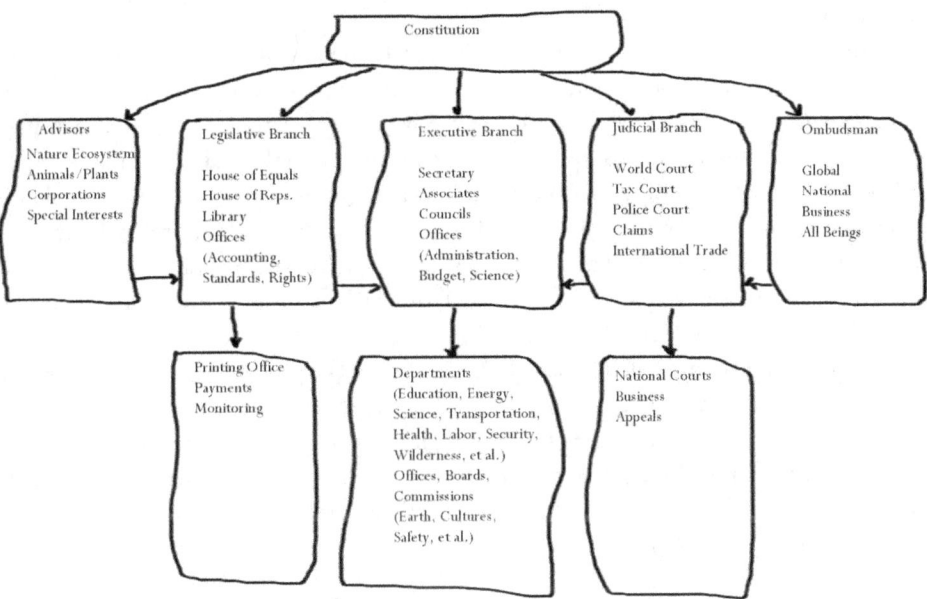

Figure 753-1. Structure of Global Union Government

8.0. Creating & Maintaining a Global Government

The Future: Will global government Happen?
Yes.
   If.

But, 'if' always has so many complications. Taking these steps would solve many of the problems addressed earlier. The satisfaction of physical and cultural needs, as a result of living in stable and small societies, would contribute to the health of people. Fitting economic costs and needs to the limits of ecosystems and monitoring the economic process would reduce wastes and pressures on natural processes. The coupling of agricultural productivity to a solar budget, and the conscious restoration of degraded systems, would contribute to the health of ecosystems. Sufficient wilderness would allow the self-maintenance of global cycles. With the increase in security, wealth, and self-esteem, human populations could be dependent on ecosystem productivities and still be diverse and unique.

With the removal of war capabilities and the equalization of wealth, the remaining issues are not the kind to incite violent passions. Disagreements over the best way to raise wheat or maintain a forest may be more easily resolved than deciding the best nation or truest religion. The death of large-scale dogmatic ideology and national idolatry could also mean the end of organized slaughter. We have to perfect the art of resolving conflict. Mastering it through social debate would free unprecedented resources to satisfy social needs. Perhaps a planetary electronic referendum would open communication. In designing the world, everyone can participate. We can reduce the violence to nature and ourselves and transmute it to debate. That which has been hitherto left unsaid-what we want to become, what we could become-could become explicit.

Changes would be made after a period of adjustment. The process must be sustainable and equitable. The population would be adjusted for carrying capacity.

The real answer is still 'if.' If things get worse, if there are catastrophes and collapses, and if people try to take charge of the global course, then a eutopian framework may be instrumental in creating a rich, equitable and peaceful future. But, if things really deteriorate, then a eutopian course is not likely to be attempted.

8.1. *The Dance of Art Money and Ethics: Advertising Good Places*

Advertising creates the mythic images of our industrial cosmology—Marshall McLuhan called advertising the "cave art of the twentieth century." The myths are powerful, but trivial, and memorable, but inadequate to convey the meaning people need to live. Perhaps the myths are restricted by their content. If so, then ecologists and artists, and urban planners, historians, and politicians need to use the strengths of advertising to convey ecological sense and traditional wisdom, the feelings of balance and the dreams of nature.

Our dream of nature, and it is still a dream, in modern Western culture, is the dream of order and beauty. But, as Aldous Huxley noted, the dream of order begets growth and tyranny, the dream of beauty, monsters and violence. Our dreams are nightmares because they are not complete. The nightmares are symptoms that reflect unbalanced and immature cosmologies, that is, images of the earth. A traditional cosmology evolves with people's needs, fears, and knowledge. But, if it is incomplete, or if it does not fit environmental conditions, it may fail. Many early cosmologies, primitive or advanced, failed to fit the earth.

The modern industrial image of nature as a resource has resulted in pollution, material shortages, and environmental degradation. A culture that degrades its ecosystem risks its own extinction.

Industrial cultures, however, are not the only cultures in existence. There are hundreds others, although at one time, around 1900, our species had over 1,000 different cultures and 3,000 languages, roughly equivalent to the number of natural biogeographical provinces and subprovinces on earth. Each culture exists in a particular location with a unique history. Later developments are not more adaptive than earlier; nor do they replace them. Ethnic groups are not evolutionary stages culminating in The U.S., but are equally valid ways of life. Each culture is only one of many possibilities, a way. There is no single or correct way.

Each culture has a root metaphor. In the West, it is the machine. The advent of the machine made processes of order more amenable to description. Although only a closed system itself, the machine was a fruitful metaphor for living systems. The theory of the living organism as a mechanical contrivance explained biological phenomena from the physiology of an organism to the processes of cells. The cybernetic machine metaphor was successful at explaining detailed processes without answering fundamental questions of meaning.

Science makes extended use of the metaphorical process to construct its models. For example: "Man is a system" according to Erwin Laszlo or "Man is a computer" according to Michael Arbib. Kenneth Boulding offered the perfect machine metaphor for the operation of the earth: as a spaceship. As a metaphor, a spaceship suggests the limits of earth and the value of a limited life-support system—unfortunately, it also implies something of human creation that can be controlled and fixed by human intention.

The use of the word 'ecology' by Ernst Haeckel implied that the natural world was a place to live, a house, rather than a machine to control. Making the earth into a house is fundamentally a poetic activity, according to Gaston Bachelard. Poetry also is a way of understanding the universe through metaphor, a literary device that transfers the characteristics of one term to another. As Picasso said of art, poetry also is a "lie that tells the truth." For example, William Shakespeare said "The body is a garden; and William Harvey said "the body is a machine." The body is not a garden or a machine, but the metaphors extend our understanding of the body.

Poetry is communicative of the quality of things. Like science, it discriminates the unsuspected in the commonplace. It is not different from science, but more diffuse; not better than science, but more comprehensive. It accepts ontological parity, the equality of beings; aspects of the world are not negated or reduced by one another. As metaphorical knowledge, which may be prerational or metarational, poetry can avail itself still of scientific references. Poetry can measure a whole qualitatively and mimetically, a germ or the cosmos with its imagery. Poetry is a tool for comprehending partially what cannot be known totally. A poetic language could include a view of the interrelatedness of all existence in a sublime ecology.

People need to be made aware of the power of self-determination. People need to feel things, like the immensity and uniqueness of nature or the strangeness of a biting tick, before they can act. Poetry can help people feel themselves as part of the web of life or on an oasis in space. That feeling, more than laws or injunctions, can justify preserving the ecological systems of the earth on which we live. Humanity is a poetic species, as Richard Rorty noted, "one which can change its behavior by the words it uses." We need desperately to change our behavior.

Mythology can join science with feeling to foster change. Mythology is not limited by method. Mythic symbols store information concisely, which makes it possible for a person to assimilate the collective experiences of a culture. Myth combines us with other beings. Mythologies are great poems that function to awaken the experience of awe and humility before mystery, create a cosmology, validate an established order, and bring the individual into harmony with the whole.

8.1.1. *Monetary Lies & Pecuniary Pseudotruth*
Unfortunately, the myths of the predominate industrial cosmology are inadequate. The myths are powerful, but trivial and misdirected. Poetry and art are undervalued as forms of communication, not to mention as ways of shaping and making. Business has transformed much of art and poetry into advertising, to match the style and attention span of the people in industrial cultures. Advertising, quite literally from the *Wall Street Journal* to college textbooks, refers to its activities as "shaping the American dream." Like art, advertising creates an image of a way of experiencing. Unlike art, it limits its focus for a specific goal—profit. Like art, it mirrors us. Unlike art, it intensifies and glorifies only the positive aspects of culture, ignoring the dark, negative aspects that are equally valid and influential.

Its simplicity is irresistible. Our environment deteriorates according to ecologists, but gets better according to economists. And their pictures are prettier. People want to hear that it is getting better. Advertising tells them it is. People want to act stupid, greedy, and selfish, and spend the inheritance of their children on themselves. Advertising tells them their actions are rewarded. The real issues of life and death, destruction and hope, make people feel helpless and anxious, so advertising draws their consciousness to comfortable trivia.

Despite the ugliness of the dreams of progress and growth, of waste and stylistic frenzy, advertising, using sophisticated techniques and narrowing the focus out of context, makes the dreams desirable and irresistible. People in agricultural and hunting cultures interiorize the abstract industrial vision. African farmers are convinced to buy inorganic fertilizers, even though it degrades the soil; women to buy powdered milk for their children, even if it kills them. Tractors replace draft animals in the paddies in the Philippines, even though they are costly and less energy-efficient; French winter fashions are found desirable in tropical Brazil, even if they can only be worn in air-conditioned villas. People in industrial societies are convinced that their children will be ruined without personal computers. Disposability is offered as a fix to a wanting in the temperament. Advertising fuels the acceleration of conspicuous and compulsive consumption.

8.1.2. *Ecological Persuasion*
Yet, advertising may be the most effective means to reshape desires and reform buying habits. Advertising presents the symbols of modern experience, even if they are just the trivial ones. It could present healthy symbols equally well. Advertising does incorporate traditional values, like family, friendship, and love, although to sell beer and cereal and, sometimes, churches and hospitals. And, like art, advertising lies, although Jules Henry thought it was instead a new kind of truth—"pecuniary pseudo-truth"—not intended to be believed, or certainly, proved.

Advertising is beginning to support more informational functions, such as the dangers of drug abuse and smoking. Advertising creates values—fur coats, fast cars, dark beer, slim cigarettes are certainly recent and artificial values—but it could be used to create positive ecological values and new identities that show that our needs for prestige, esteem, and belonging can be met without stylistic waste at mindless speeds. Advertising could promote new attitudes about appropriate technology, the rights of other cultures, and the place of people in nature. Good advertising could be as subversive and conservative as ecology. It could avoid confrontation with people's values; emphasize positive aspects without negative ones. A good ad could capture and carry the most self-indulgent viewer; for the most part, ads don't require effort, literacy, or consciousness, just attention.

Advertising has been serving the dream of progress, but progress is leading to catastrophe, a long, slow, global catastrophe. When people experience local, sudden catastrophe, they usually respond immediately, with heroism and sacrifice, aiding the victims of earthquakes or floods, sometimes famine. Advertising could bring to consciousness the slow catastrophes of erosion and population overshoot, and, perhaps, invoke the same altruistic and effective responses to them.

To work towards this service, conservation groups could define and promote an integrative mythology as the basis for the framework of diverse efforts to protect life and the environment. Conservation groups could provide a meaningful philosophical foundation, as well as coordination for other humane, social, and conservation programs. But, the approach must be egalitarian: Respect for life cannot neglect human life and suffering. The approach must be eutopian; it cannot ignore adaptive cultural traditions that arose in place over centuries. Furthermore, in addition to formal education, a culture could provide re-education through the most effective means, such as advertising. Conservation groups could spend money advertising "humane consciousness," moderation, and the joy of living, instead of just consuming or winning. Ecological ads would be unique and compelling, simple and effective. They would advertise not a product, but a way; not for a profit, but for a dream.

The other day, tired of scribbling and typing, I went to visit friends, who were watching a car race. After a while of enjoying the excitement, it occurred to me that only with entertainment industries is there so much technical fizz and coordinated enthusiastic teamwork. Imagine all that energy and enthusiasm directed to appropriate technology for reforestation or the proper use of forests. Imagine television coverage of forest work with the same amount of attention and detail. Why not a competition for the most beautiful or productive forest or teams working to restore devastated areas—broadcast by a major network as an important event. It also occurred to me that this remorseless entertainment is an anesthetic against the fear or emptiness or self-searching or death. Continuous entertainment is a kind of guarantee of health, riches, and long-life. Everything that is pleasurable, thought George Orwell, seems to be an attempt to destroy consciousness. Ecoforestry cannot ever compete with entertainment if it raises troubling questions or difficult expectations. As long as the industry can guarantee many forests through the arithmetic of fantasy, we will always seem to be complainers and false prophets—until it's too late, then we will be blamed for not avoiding the catastrophes.

Maybe the situation is not that bad. Maybe we can present images that rival the industry images. Maybe we too can speak the languages of euphemism that large corporations use to conduct their businesses of larceny and fraud. Positive images and pleasing language skills are everything these days; no one really looks for substance. The devotion to money, beauty and youth is our focus. I think one way to compete might be to present conservation biology or ecoforestry as a medical discipline, aimed at restoring forests to health—and advertise it that way. As with any medicine, the patient actually does most of the work to become healthy, although the doctor gets the credit and the payment. This would also lead to more respect for the practitioners, but also to more responsibility and more rules. The first rule, which we might take to be basic, is identical to the first vow of the Hippocratic oath, "Do no harm."

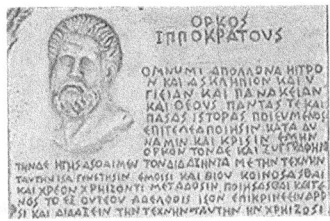

Figure 812-1. The Hippocratic Oath for Physicians

8.2. Creating & Maintaining a Global Government

A Global Government based on a eutopian approach would incorporate the strengths of traditional cultures with the strengths of science and political ideals. To avoid fanaticism and violence, Karl Popper has suggested that utopians should try to build an open, progressive, partially-planned society, instead of a finished, closed, completely-planned society. Indeed, this is how general systems theory would describe a working, successful society. Such a utopia would have to accept the imperfect nature of man and the changing ambiguity of nature. Utopias is the dream of reason. Eutopias is the dream of small traditions and cultures, reasonable or not. Where an imagined utopia offers revelations promising a desired future, Eutopias offers references from selves and cultures for producing good places on earth now. There is no mechanical prescription for making good places; there is no blueprint or timetable. The current institutions cannot create good places; the market has not been able to create health and equity; even radical ecologists have not been able to create a way—Eutopias is a fourth way. It is not an institution that benefits only the rich; nor is it a schedule of temporary handouts. It is a plan for a framework for local self-reliance and global exchange, that is respectful of traditional cultures and ecological networks. So far, there is only the idea or poetic image. Human will to power might be found in the will to imagine, and then to speak and become. What is our moral responsibility for this power? We can choose to alter our world with new images moderated by new ideals, such as good places. Eutopias could offer knowledge and power with charity.

The criteria for a eutopian frame include: Its benefit for humanity; the inadequacies of the present system; a drastic system change as a result of catastrophic awareness; and a low, but not too low, political feasibility. The benefits must be worthwhile to justify the costs. Benefits cannot be vague and unsatisfying when the costs are immediate and painful. Poetry and education must prove the benefits, so that the eutopian alternative can be begun. This code emphasizes its flexibility.

The best thing to do is stop—stop growing, stop producing, and stop running. Suspend the race and contemplate a direction. We know that whole countries have built again from ruins. So there is nothing to fear from stopping—if we know there would be no problem starting again. What are the dangers of fast social transformation? Lack of justice? Lack of order? That is what the eutopian framework is for—minimizing danger from radical actions.

The steady state would provide a period of rest, and time to explore human values and quality considerations. This strategy would avoid eventual hardening of the choices. But it must be instituted at once. The crisis caused by exponential growth and destruction cannot be solved just after some final limit is passed and the ultimate catastrophe begun. The crisis of ignorance cannot be solved by hurrying ahead and creating more problems.

The eutopian framework exists in the extended present, incorporating past traditions and future values. It would concentrate earthward (down) and inward. Heaven may be a perfect home, but eutopias is here and now. Eutopias is a new comprehensive philosophy to make sense of the world. Eutopias is comprehensive and global. A broader frame of reference is assumed. It is concerned with evolution unfolding, evolving, and producing new emergent forms, not just a static description. Eutopias is grounded in environmental concerns. Its values must be highest cultural and natural values. It must develop from existing social and political forces. Eutopias is vitally concerned with the well being of society. It regards society as a *sui generis* entity, not just an aggregate for analysis. Conservation is a means to an end, which is human fulfillment in harmony with nature. Human happiness depends on a balance between needs and commodities. In a throughput process it is not possible to economize all inputs simultaneously. There are many criteria for inputs to be preserved. Options must be site and culture specific. Eutopias recognizes and preserves slow cultural knowledge. A social base may be partly developed through ecological education. Social diversity may have cross-cultural appeal. Eutopias would retain the capacity to change and innovate, with changes in environments and human values.

Eutopias would detoxify national rivalries. Racism, sexism and ageism would lose their importance in a cooperative society of advanced communication, automation, equality, humane scale, and meaningful preservation. Eutopias is politically aware. We make political statements by the way we live. Every tradition is only one tradition among many. The higher sanity requires of philosophies and therapies is open, planetary dialogue between modern experience and sacred tradition. Eutopias requires a planning process that bridges all cultures and sciences. It must be a participatory political movement. It must appeal to a large segment of the total human society. Since not all interests will be satisfied, there must be opportunities for transformations or alternate paths. The global eutopian structure would be a framework for ordinary eutopias, where different human experiments are tried. Its variability would insure that we could reject any of the local visions that fail.

The eutopian frame can be justified. It is not just one kind of global society in one place. If we try to make one society, it will change over time, because people are in different places. Solutions come from living in place.

How can we form society within an ecological perspective? By following the principles of ecology and applying them to the properties of good places. According to David Orr, certain design principles work with ecosystems and nations: Small units dispersed in space, redundancy, short linkages between modules, simplicity, diversity of components, self-reliance, decentralized control, large margins, quick feedback. A megaframe like a eutopian one would allow this.

Eutopias requires a change of attitude. We have to change the framework so that we can change to new minds. We no longer have an external point of view. We are inseparable from the environment and each other, but we differentiate. Eutopias is a nostrum, really, a description of good places for all beings. Its connotation is as a panacea. This is appropriate since a panacea is a cure-all, a remedy for disease, and a solution to catastrophe.

8.2.1. What a Global Government Can Do
The framework is a self-conscious panacea. It requires an understanding of the anatomy, physiology, and diseases of the body in question, now the entire human and wild planet.

8.2.1.1. The GU Can Eliminate Bad Approaches & Actions
Human approaches to the challenges of nature have resulted in many losses. The lure of size and simplicity has resulted in many failures that become traps difficult to avoid or leave. The stresses from these things have resulted thefts, as attempts to balance or correct the situations. The very size and impact of humanity has made theft the only easy option, much easier in the short run than planning or self-restraint.

8.2.1.1.1. The GU Can Reduce Losses
Government can reduce the losses of nature and culture by creating a framework to protect them. It can reduce the losses of health, fitness and accord, by emphasizing them and creating circumstances for their continuity. It can reduce the losses of equity, renewal and design by offering new designs that allow for a normalization of equity and for the normal processes of renewal.

Losses from accidents and diseases can be reduced by preparedness. Losses from earth and climate changes can be reduced, also, with preparedness for 'normal' events, such as hurricanes, earthquakes, and droughts. Design can also be used to reduce impacts from these events; for instance, by denying building permits on floodplains. The losses from some events, such as droughts resulting from El Nino, can be ameliorated, by having surplus food and supplies stockpiled.

8.2.1.1.2. The GU Can Reduce Thefts

Stopping a theft can be as simple as stopping a thief. But, theft has become such a complicated thing, many steps removed from the people who make the decisions and from those who carry them out. Government would address the processes and trails of theft.

8.2.1.1.2.1. *Reduce Theft of Life from Ecocides and Democides*. Animal and plant lives are stolen for the profits of a few; ecological and human systems collapse as a result of biocide and ecocide. Hundreds of millions of human lives are stolen every century at the behest of a few. Millions die from starvation when regional crops fail; millions more die when the distribution system fails or is perverted for a few. This democide is unacceptable. The plague of power is responsible for the dialogues of death, and the absoluteness of some power is responsible for the massive scale of deaths in Russia, China, and some other nations.

Three reasons for these deaths seem more contributory than others: Inequity, runaway cultural antagonisms, and the use of absolute power. Inequity is simple to understand; some people have more valuables than others. Often, equalization does not happen until during or after a collapse, as it may have happened with the Mayans in 795 AD. Cultural antagonisms seem to worsen when the different cultures are forcibly combined in nations as the result of colonial wars. Totalitarian regimes, especially with great power and in secrecy, kill almost as many people as famines—more, when one realizes that many famine deaths come from denial of distribution. Famine itself is the regional failure of food production or distribution. However, the denial of distribution, as when food is saved for trade or the elite, such as the English did to the people of Ireland and India in the 1800s, can contribute to the severity and extent of a famine.

The GU responses to these three reasons are: To equalize wealth as much as possible, to separate cultures into separate nations, and to make laws to control ecocides and democides. Laws without supervision and enforcement would not be effective. The UN outlawed war, but when the U.S., U.K., Iraq, Korea, or others decide to violate it, no one enforces it. The GU needs to have the power of enforcement, backed by all member nations. The GU needs to have the moral force to keep national governments open and responsible. The workings of government should be transparent to the people, whether the government is democratic, royal or charismatic. The GU must be sure that people can bear witness to every regime in the world, from Korea and Cambodia to the U.S. and Russia. Bearing witness should reduce the number of secret pogroms. Restricting and checking the power of leaders, overseen by the GU, should greatly reduce democides, including genocides and mass murders. There are no permanent solutions.

8.2.1.1.2.2. *Reduce Theft of Common Sense*. The GU can reduce the theft of common sense by fostering and respecting common sense in communities and nations, as well as increasing its value and appreciation.

8.2..1.1.2.3. *Reduce Theft of Choice*. The GU can reduce the theft of choice by creating a framework that offers more choices for people in different communities and nations. It can also address the economic and political processes that reduce choice.

8.2.1.1.3. The GU Can Reduce Failures

The GU can reduce failures through education and opportunity. Perception, intelligence, and imagination can be taught. Integrity, will and charity can be shown by example. And, if there are enough teachings and examples, these human capabilities will be developed and applied to domiture, that is, civilization and nature. With will and imagination, people can design and build good places.

8.2.1.2. The GU Can Integrate Tools & Designs

Tools and designs are important extensions of the human mind. Their purpose is to foster and assist survival, not to make it more difficult. Tools and designs can be made appropriate to environmental limits and cultural preferences, both of which are often ignored by industrial approaches.

8.2.1.2.1. The GU Can Use Tools Effectively

The GU can illustrate how people can use tools with awareness of their effects and impacts. The principle of caution is followed.

8.2.1.2.2. The GU Can Thread Properties with Plans

The GU can thread the properties of nature, that is fields, ecosystems, and places, with the properties of cultures and good societies to make good places ecologically and culturally.

8.2.1.2.3. The GU Can Avoid the Traps of Noplaces

The GU can avoid the lure of or the accidental assembly of no-places. By exposing the lures of no-places, and showing the connections that make no-places into traps, an ecologically-aware, place-based government can neutralize the plague of placelessness.

8.2.1.2.4. The GU Can Suspend the Designing of Noplaces

By promoting the understanding of the inadequacies of bad characteristics and bad designs, government can stop the plague of uniformity and paucity. Through an understanding of the consequences of human ambitions and actions, a responsive government can avoid many of the evils that result from a civilization on technical autopilot.

8.2.1.3. The GU Can Increase Understanding

Understanding is a powerful thing. Understanding why an animal bites can dissipate the desire for revenge or punishment. Understanding why things break down can result in an examination of the context and effects of tools, and maybe a simplification.

8.2.1.3.1. The GU Can Help Understand Ways of Knowing

The ways that human beings know things is part of the human adventure. There are many ways of knowing, from traditional ecological knowledge to the most abstract science. None of these ways is the only way. None should supplant the others entirely. This is the importance of education, that it be applicable to local place, yet broad enough to put that place in a larger context, of the environment or planet or universe. These ways of knowing allow people to learn the operation of nature and fit human activities in it. This understanding points to the need for basic sciences.

8.2.1.3.2. The GU Can Help Understand How Things Go Together

Ecology is a science of relationships and patterns. Understanding the components of an ecosystem, and the properties of an ecosystem, can be applied to the growth, change and development of human systems.

8.2.1.3.3. The GU Can Help Understand How Things Happened
History can allow understanding of the regular patterns of human life, as well as the dramatic changes, such as agriculture or urbanization, and how these changes have affected the patterns. History is a record of the cumulative human impacts on living systems, as well as of a few famous people or battles.

8.2.1.3.4. The GU Can Help Understand How Things Renew
Systems automatically renew themselves, especially living systems. Systems that do not renew themselves very well, such as agriculture and cities, can be put on track for renewal by linking them with the surrounding natural systems. The GU can foster the renewal of human systems by integrating them into natural self-renewing systems.

8.2.1.3.5. The GU Can Help Understand How Nature & Culture Work
Nature and Culture are systems. Domiture is the combination of those two systems. Culture was once called a "Second Nature," but human culture has expanded so dramatically that the two systems are better identified as one developed system, now. The fitness of human systems are intimately related to the fitness of species and natural ecosystems. The human attachment to place is critical to understanding why people live where they do.

8.2.1.3.6. The GU Can Help Understand How to Live in Place
The GU can offer understanding of how people live in places, not only how they adjust themselves to a place, but how they adjust the places to their needs and desires. This mutual adjustment can be ruinous or beneficial. Emotional investment in a place, even love for that place, is crucial to the preservation of the genius of place.

8.2.1.4. The GU Can Start Making Good Places
The GU can start making good places by addressing the economics and politics of human cultures. Economics and politics are large-scale human programs to relate human needs to resources and distributions of resources and goods.

8.2.1.4.1. The GU Can Show How to Preserve & Restore, Design & Plan
The GU can provide an ecological planning process that offers a structure of limits and divisions for the planetary system that would permit the preservation and restoration of natural cycles and places. An ecological design process would be applied to ecosystems as well as to cities and fields.

8.2.1.4.2. The GU Can Illustrate Ways of Making a Living
The GU, through a holistic examination of how people make their livings in place, can show how changes can make better places. Economies can be as diverse as tropical or desert places; there is no evolution to one economic style, such as capitalism. The GU can show how to integrate individuals, communities and corporations into place.

The current, dominant economic and financial order is unfair to many groups and nations. It needs to be radically reshaped. It is better to do this as part of a directed plan than after some kind of collapse. Power and wealth must be more equitably distributed. Government could try to ensure that the underrepresented would be allocated more resources, which would increase the demand for basic services. But, would that let them disconnect from any dependence on a world market?

Wouldn't that be the goal for every nation? To be self-reliant in terms of food and basic production? Then, nations could reject technologies and products that did not fit their cultures or that would affect their own resources. These are all transitional processes, backed by the educative process and political pressure. A specific political process could be worked out later. There would be a painful readjustment to the realities of our new intricate involvement in the whole order of nature and her ecological balance. Social strains at this time will be unavoidable. A great amount of capital of energy and metals would be wasted. Sophisticated technology may allow a rebirth. A new world will have to be based on a gradually decreasing population. Production will have to be redirected to communal needs in transportation, housing, food, and recreation. It will be a much more humane world, moving from a materialist society based on industrial production and consumption to a contemplative culture based on ecological consciousness and symbiosis. But, people and cultures have to learn how to harmonize human culture with a deeper understanding of the ecology of earth, to become partners, rather than stewards or bosses.

This is the time to define goals in terms of population, quality of life, and preservation of biomes. Goals are not some final state reached once for all time, but a horizon to be strived for. Order is the highest ideal of mind; but chaos is necessary to shape and change it. Natural order is dynamic, creative, logical, and temporal. We live in natural orders. To preserve what we are, we must admire the matrix out of which we arose. What is desirable is a relationship with a certain amount of conflict.

Global peace could be dull sometimes, but global war would be deadly. We need competition as well as cooperation. We could make a golden age in the present, not in the past (where Plato put it) or in the future (where O'Neill puts it). Life in the past was sometimes good regardless of environment. There are enclaves of well-being in all parts of the world, in Asia and Africa, in Australia and South America. Why not such good places for all? There is no technological reason why gracious living can not be available for all.

Economies can emphasize different things, from producing family needs (reciprocity), to distribution and redistribution of luxuries, to trade (mercantilism), to unbounded capital and to bureaucratic efficiency. It may be time to emphasize a form of aesthetic efficiency, that is the shared production of what is wanted without as much regard for cheapness and mass production.

8.2.1.4.3. The GU Can Explore Ways of Governing
The GU can examine how people govern themselves. Political styles can be equally diverse; there is no evolutionary path to one political style, not democracy, socialism or community anarchy. The GU can suggest ways to fit governing to culture and place. Politics can use different types of leadership or rules. The rule of law is fine. Perhaps a rule of religious tolerance would allow people to live together, something on the order of the golden rule. Does it always come down to one person, president, pope, king, or dictator? Representing all? In small groups or communities, anarchy could work fine. Rather than rule, perhaps understanding. Would a rule of knowledge work? Or would people have to know too much? When it comes to politics, as with mythology and religion, different people have different levels of understanding. So, government should be simple enough for everyone to participate knowledgeably in.

8.2.1.4.4. The GU Can Try Ways of Integrating Religion & Art
Religion is a part of culture that binds people to their ancestors as well as the invisible powers of place. It focuses on the changeless aspects of natural and human processes. Religion concerns itself with an image of the world, that explains what the world is like. It also explains how we can influence it and why we would want to influence it. Art is a part of culture that expresses the invisible

parts of society and the environment.

Religion can lead to understanding of the world; it can lead to ecological balance. Art can lead to peaceful ways of interacting with nature and other human beings. Art ruthlessly examines society. Religion reinforces the integrity of society. Art is a survival technique for humans on a wild planet. Religion relates the human to the wild.

8.2.1.5. The GU Can Start Making a Framework for Revolution

One premise of global government is that many things have to be changed simultaneously; some things have to be eliminated, and other things have to be invented. This revolution in thinking and acting, especially on a global and national level, will have to be governed by the consent of people in those nations. The structure of human life, in unique cultures in specific places, the basic everyday experience of human life, will basically remain the same, but the superstructure, that is concerned with global trading and distribution and taxes—that will change.

8.2.1.5.1. Creating an Global Union Framework

The police force would be used for positive nonviolent interventions to help people with problems or disagreements. Such interventions would be cooperative efforts by neighboring nations, coordinated through a revitalized Association. All states now have armed forces, whose primary duty is killing their enemies, internal or external, in unending conflicts. The unarmed police force would have different goals: Rescue from catastrophes such as earthquakes; civic assistance, such as vote getting or monitoring; and simple police action, being a persuasive presence in areas of conflict. The GU would insure the inviolability of the police to go anywhere on assignment and to intervene in any conflict when asked by any party. If the GU had most large-scale weapons, it might short-circuit the vicious cycle of armament races, and it is conceivable that the GU would need to use weapons in some circumstances. The UN has successfully used police for the observation of peace and for enforcement, in Cyprus for instance. The UN has used police in response to natural catastrophes, such as earthquakes, in Peru and Italy for instance.

A global association would also coordinate the distribution and use of common resources, which would also be owned by the association as representative of all nations, rather than of individual nations; resources across the planet are uneven and have precipitated numerous disputes for thousands of years. The agency would address real global problems, such as global warming, which has resulted in grain harvest shortfalls in recent years. Climate itself would be a concern.

For any nation, the association could advise on topics ranging from justice to wilderness. Wilderness has an important role in human freedom, as well as in providing ecosystem services. The association could insist on self-reliance, by connecting human population to ecosystem productivity. It could also make sure that local air, soil, and water resources are stabilized.

For all nations, the association could provide education on health and appropriate technology. It could work to provide basic needs for food and health. It could insist on the truth of the ecological situation, on the real costs of economic decisions and growth, especially those that destroy ecological capital, in the form of wilderness ecosystems. It could recommend changing the system to allow taxes on destructive activities, such as excessive carbon emissions, and to normalize the values of resources and wilderness.

8.2.1.5.2. Encouraging & Fitting New Nations

The GU will offer any culture the opportunity to have a vote in the global management of human cultures and natural processes. Those cultures may choose to remain in their current national framework and share one vote, or become independent and exercise a whole vote.

Three levels of responsibility—individual, national, and global—are identified and discussed; each has responsibilities for specific attributes, such as population or health. This does not mean that only nations will exist within a global framework; alliances and networks will form and reform.

A government code could divide the earth into zones for preservation, conservation, domestication, and human communities. Human activities are limited to specific zones and, within those, the global authority controls all air, water and land use under complete sovereignty. Political units are formed from existing cultural units; an optimum human population is of each nation is based on a calculation of net community productivity on arable land through traditional agriculture. Common planetary resources are assigned according to the optimum population figure. The development of the nations is regulated by the Global Union through charters. Self-reliant nations would decide their own appropriate technology, crops and institutions based on traditional values and are responsible for the ecological education of their constituents. Residents of nations have equal rights and work opportunities, and have the responsibility to participate in government and to live as wisely as possible, to make good places.

8.2.1.5.2.1. *Connection & Size.* When small societies start to grow, they become successful in different ways. But, that success leads to increases in size, which can lead to a tragedy of scale. Each major technological breakthrough permitted a step increase in size. The size of a local population increased the likelihood of its success. For cultures, size was important. More successful cultures (as measured by size and continuity) were larger and more aggressive. Humans naturally increase the size of societies, but do not know how to stop or limit it. Ambition contends with common sense? Is the problem growth or growth without development for the scale? Henry Simons designated the great powers as "monsters of nationalism and mercantilism" and suggested that they are the obstacles to world peace, and must be dismantled for us to survive.

Leopold Kohr relates cancer to size. But, is it largeness or sameness without function? Cancer allows the mass of one unit to become too big. The cells outgrow their limits. Political cancer is a matter of proportion between large and small units. Cancer is a small-cell phenomenon, but it converts all cells to itself. Would a theory of social gravitation work? At one scale we have fusion and energy, but if the scale is too large that becomes crushing and instability.

The processes of social development can create traps that then determine the direction of development. Changes in scale, such as population size or sedentary living, can decrease the number of options possible, while providing different attractive options, such as the accumulation of luxuries. In this sense a trap is a sudden reduction in options or flexibility due to changes in scale or repetitive pattern.

The sheer size of a united China meant that tributes were enormous and that any commercial income could not compete well with the mass of tribute. The commercialization of states seemed to benefit from proximity to rich routes, small state size and rivalries.

The size of a cultures might not be optimal, since they grow unplanned and wild. Kohr quotes Arnold Toynbee as linking the rise of universal states to the downfall of civilization. Toynbee suggests that one solution might be the return to the Greek ideal of a self-regulating balance of small city-states, *Homonoia*, rather than further macropolitical solutions. Leopold Kohr sees 'gigantomania' as the economic problem of systems. Kohr notes that our choice is not between crime and virtue but between big crime and small crime, not between war and peace, but between great wars and small wars.

Local equalities are easier to acquire first, more than global equalities. We live local lives in home places, with local limits and local pressures. We can calculate an optimum size population of a culture or community, by relating it to the carrying capacity of the land and society. We can establish optimum scale of populations through limits of carrying capacity. We may also calculate an optimum size for the planet, based on the sum of local cultures. An optimum global population might be of the order: Between 0.5 billion and 1.5 billion people, the sum of local optima.

For the Chipewyan people in Canada, for example, the commitment to caribou hunting is ecologically inefficient, since people could spend more energy on secondary sources of food. For the Chipewyan, a deliberate "underutilization" of moose, rabbit, grouse, birds, and fish, is the result of cultural values: The willingness to live below the carrying capacity of the local environment—a characteristic of most hunting/gathering societies—the complex practice of drying caribou meat, and the reciprocity of the kinship system, that is, the act of giving as the basis for future relationships. The cultural decision to hunt caribou as the primary item of subsistence has produced a unique pattern in the utilization of land and in the formation and distribution of social groups. Many foraging groups, such as the Chipewyan, have been successful by staying below the maximum carrying capacity. Culturally, an optimum population has to be large enough to allow variety.

We may not know what is the minimum, optimum or maximum use of an ecosystem. Science might try to identify minima or maxima but management can aim at optima or satisficia. Francisco Varela analyzes the evolutionary process as satisficing rather than optimizing; a suboptimal solution is adequate. A free market has to be limited by conservative calculations of ecological balance. It is almost impossible to estimate the economic value of natural balance.

Kohr's reasons for the greatness of small states: There is a cultural diversion of aggressive energies, or artists are cheaper than soldiers; there is a relief from social servitude, as a result of time and leisure; there is the variety of human experience; and there is the testimony of history. Kohr concludes that it was always "the small state, not the empire, that survived. That is why small states do not have to be created artificially. They need only be freed."

8.2.1.5.2.2. *Measuring.* In an article on good forestry, Hugh Williams links the maximization of the moral good of creativity to the maximization of public good, then to forests specifically. Williams also proposes maximal creativity as an ethical imperative. Maximizing creativity, however, would lead to chaos, both in one's self and in ecosystems. There has to be a balance between creativity and stability, between innovation and habit. We should not being trying to maximize creativity in human beings or forests, but rather seeking stability and relative harmony. Maximizing creativity may be a meaningless exercise.

In a system of ethics, we might consider maximizing a value, but then we have to decide if it is being maximized for one species or the system, or if it is being maximized for the present or the future, or whether it can be maximized at all. John B. Cobb Jr. suggests that we should act to maximize value in general, at least for every entity with intrinsic value, rather than maximize value for one human or all humans, that is, the greatest good for the greatest number, in the present or the future. Perhaps though, we should aim for an optimum or satisficium here also.

An economic maximum is a monotone value, which only increases or decreases. There are no monotone values in ecology. Desired substances have an optimum value—more calcium is not always better. Before anything cam be maximized or optimized, we have to be able to measure accurately. We can measure wealth with modified Index of Sustainable Welfare to avoid distortion by size or by the combination of repair and maintenance with production.

8.2.1.6. Providing Paths for Individuals & Communities
Isolation can dangerous, whether it is isolated theoretical knowledge or an isolated culture. A maximum isolation is bad. A minimum is bad. An optimum is good. Isolation is dangerous, especially

isolated theoretical knowledge. We strive for optimal solutions and control, but should settle for suboptimal and partial control, a satisficing solution.

The GU suggests small solutions to big problems. Protecting and restoring ecosystems is a local effort. Reducing gases, that contribute to the instability of the climate, reducing consumption in general, reducing the human population, and reducing conflicts, which contribute to the escalation of wars, are local efforts. Integrating food into ecosystems, to regenerate soils and repair ecosystems, integrating technology into a culture, integrating economies into ecosystems, and equalizing wealth, are local efforts.

Although not every global problem has a local solution, people will have to address them in small ways, too. Climate would be very difficult to change, much less control on a global level.

8.2.1.7. Promoting Health at All Levels

The GU is healthful. Positive health results from being on good terms with cosmos. The idea of right to health should be replaced by moral obligation to preserve ones health. We need to become attuned to the earth, to commit our fate to nature, and not just say that we have faith in modern technology to save us with an artificial environment. We must be flexible, not detached or noncommittal. We must commit ourselves and be able to adjust to necessary changes—to be in a state of risk. The harmonious interplay between humans and environment results in adaptive fitness, which requires a constant expenditure of effort to maintain. We must maintain an environment for plants, animals and humans that is healthy for all. Conservation and creation must be tempered with preservation. We are too ignorant to tamper with everything. More searching and researching are necessary.

Ecological health requires a single system of environment combined with high human culture, with a matching flexibility, to create an ongoing, open, complex system, characterized by a slow change in its basic properties. High culture is not a return to the innocence of the Inuit, or the sparseness of the cave. It includes necessary institutions for the arts and sciences limed in transactions with the environment. Flexibility is needed; within limits, a variable can move to achieve adaptation.

The ecologist must create flexibility and then prevent civilization from immediately expanding into it. Flexibility is uncommitted potentiality for change. Flexibility must be distributed among many variables of a system. Freedom and flexibility in regard to most variables is necessary during the process of learning and creating a new system by social change. There are still many possible futures for the earth and humanity, but they become fewer as we burn or destroy the earth's flexibility and our options. Recommendations to reserve flexibility must be tyrannical.

The ecological health of a civilization depends on a single system of environment combined with high culture in which the flexibility of the civilization must match that of the environment to create an ongoing complex system, open ended for the slow change of even basic properties. Health is the capacity of the land and water for self-renewal. Conservation is the effort to preserve this capacity.

Although the nature of the biosphere is largely determined by evolution, by organisms adapted to specific parameters and to each other, the anthroposphere tends to be artificial and managed, with only human needs considered. We need to keep as much of the natural world as possible in the anthroposphere; there is a human need for variety, individuality, and the challenge to understand the nonhuman. Immersion in trees and bees is necessary to nourish human attributes that are in short supply: Awe, compassion, reflectiveness, and brotherhood. As humans move from concrete to trees, there may be a profound transformation in a scientific return to animism. The metaindustrial culture is one in which the trees are counted in a census of members of a community. In the shamanistic tradition, people are not viewed as individuals, their history and experience is seen as result of being part of the group.

One significant book in the Hippocratic corpus was *Airs, Waters and Places*, which showed how well-being is influenced by the quality of air, food, land and general habits. It is as important to know from whence your body atoms and molecules came as it is to know the history of a used car.

Atoms that came from stars and rocks make up molecules of seeds, flowers, defecation, and rotting leaves, which are cycled through our bodies. Bodies are open systems exchanging materials with the whole environment. It is therefore important to choose carefully what is put into the body. Good food comes from healthy plants and animals, unprocessed and unpoisoned. Cells and enzymes react poorly to poisons and preservatives. Physical, mental and spiritual well-being are dependent on a healthy diet. As much as possible, one should know the origins of one's food— the soil, the plants—and be able to determine what becomes you.

Illness can only be understood in context, in relation to network of interactions in which person is imbedded; the health matrix. Ill health may be a natural stage of growth and interaction. Temporary illness as part of dynamic balance (especially childhood diseases?). The observation and study of balanced relationships in complex systems should allow us to recapture an experience of harmony and intimation of divine from scientific knowledge of processes. "A truly ecological view of world has religious overtones," according to Rene Dubos.

8.2.1.8. Integrating Acts with Poetic Wisdom

A planet that is mindless is not entitled to moral or ethical consideration. The earth has a mind but ecocrises are driving it to madness. The alternative to ecological insanity is wisdom. Wisdom is the functioning of a mind that is respectful of its own boundary and processes, according to Gregory Bateson. Evolution is trial and error process of learning; all learning contributes to evolution of global mind. So the cure for ecocrises is the education of minds.

We need reeducation in the demands and recompenses of a sane, realistic world. Peace of mind, security and self-respect must arise out of being someone in a real community, and these will be valued more than conspicuous possessions and idleness. The process would be labor-intensive rather than capital intensive, and intimate rather than pretentious.

A high culture must respect the wisdom of its experience, using necessary technological devices (computers, televisions); be diverse enough to accommodate the genetic and experiential diversity of people; shall limit transactions with the environment, consuming natural resources (capital) only to make necessary changes. High cultures must depend on renewable resources from photosynthesis to wind, tide, and sun to continue "making," which is the source word for poetry, good places.

Poetry expresses the image of human potential, of what better circumstances may have formed. Poetry tells of a goal, even if it is the moral superiority of suffering in the 'third world.' By presenting a goal, poets can become the "unacknowledged legislators of mankind," as Shelley defined them. Poetry creates a fourth world, of unique groups sharing part of the wealth of the earth in a global community. This fourth world is where the past is reconciled with the present and the terrible beauty of the future is born. The terror of beauty, as Rilke recognized, results from its power to shake humans from the refuge of a small identity into an immense strange world.

The lives of humans and all beings has become a collective responsibility. Humanity has to learn to live again on a finite and varied earth. Learning is a transforming experience. Poetry objectifies conscious experience and makes it easier to communicate. Nationalism (1930s) used poetry in service to the state. Used for each nation in this way, poetry shows the diversity of human experience. The essential unity of the earth can be discovered through its infinite diversity. Poetry gives groups and individuals their identity; it articulates societies and authenticates forms of exchange. By transcending the limits of single cultures, it draws all cultures together. The tradition of poetry does not belong to just three worlds; it encompasses them and links them together in a fourth. Poetry is wise language.

8.2.2. Moving Forward Backward Inward & Outward

Human ills cannot be cured by a return to idyllic hunting and gathering groups or to a quasi-agricultural, ecologically-caring society. There is no possibility of complete return. Most industrial nations are urban, and are becoming more so, as agricultural countries pack their surplus peoples in cities. Nor can there be a return to 4th century B.C. Greece, or to 17th century China, or to 1910 France, or to any time. Many traditional cultures no longer exist; others are disintegrating under pressure from industrial cultures. Nor can there be a jump to a complete technological future, where technology transforms hydrogen into wealth for everyone. The GU works with traditional cultures and realistic planning.

8.2.2.1. Uncertainty & Incomplete Knowledge

The detailed planning of complex open systems is not necessary. Planners are not in a position to attempt detailed models of future situations because many relevant parameters remain unidentified, and many of those known cannot be quantified. Plans can be made within the limits of variables, although it is not safe to be limited by lethal variables, as Gregory Bateson recognized. Closeness to limits reduces flexibility, that is, the uncommitted potential for change. To minimize untested conclusions, The GU is based on the values and forms of traditional cultures. This could allow time for rational planning to catch up.

We have to invest and cultivate our inheritance. We must enlarge our human identity, to include other beings and the earth, to include our own posterity and its image of the future, without which we lose the will and capacity to solve problems. Creating the future is necessary to maintain the present. It is meaningful to construct a world that we will never live to see, to plant trees that take two hundred years to mature, to save some of the forests and soils—not for the oil and timber elite or even for the backpacking elite, not for social abstractions or for personal profit, but for our heirs, for them to see and decide to save or to use.

The GU addresses the inadequacies of the present system; it offers a drastic system change from the institutional gridlock of elitism, but the change is not so drastic that the feasibility of acceptance is too low. The benefits must be worthwhile to justify the costs. The benefits cannot be vague and unsatisfying when the costs are immediate and painful. Again, communication and education must prove that the benefits exist, so that the alternative global government can be exercised. It must be a participatory movement, and it must appeal to a large segment of the total human society. Since not all interests will be satisfied, there must be opportunities for transformations or for alternate paths.

The eutopian framework for government is an open, flexible, and partially-planned global relation, instead of a finished, closed, completely-planned society, as imagined in utopias. The GU accepts the imperfect nature of humans and the changing ambiguity of nature. The GU detoxifies cultural rivalries. Racism, sexism, ageism, and speciesism lose their importance in a cooperative society of advanced communication, automation, equality, humane scale, and meaningful preservation.

8.2.2.2. Action Responsibility & Wisdom

Now is the time to define goals in terms of population, quality of life, and preservation of biomes. Resolving conflict through social debate would free unprecedented resources to satisfy social needs. That which has been hitherto left unsaid—the goals of humanity-could become explicit. Goals are not some final state reached once and for all time, but a horizon. The GU offers continuity towards a horizon.

Solutions to uncertain futures can be found in the properties of good places and in the principles applied to them. The proper action come out of common sense. We need to be sure that we allow ecosystems to regenerate healthy conditions while we take our needs from some of them. We need to plan for at least seven generations ahead, being flexible and keeping some options open, and being as self-reliant as possible. We need to be frugal with most resources and keep seven years of food and supplies in reserve. We need to identify an optimum population, over a minimum and maybe fifty percent below a maximum. We need to be as playful and joyful as any previous generation.

Science presents us with too many facts, yet we crave to have more. Philosophy presents us with too many values, but we attend to too few. Technology presents us with too many things, but we do not know what we need. We do not need more information or rules, but we do need meaningful ideas. Our attitudes and feelings toward nature need to be revitalized with evocative metaphors that let us accept responsibility for that part of the earth that we build, namely human culture and human landscapes. In order to know what is important and what is valuable, we need wisdom that we may not have.

The words 'view,' 'vision,' 'witness,' 'wise,' and 'idea' are all derived from the Indo-European *weid* or *wid*, meaning to see, understand, or know. Wisdom is knowledge of the larger interactive system, which if disturbed, can generate exponential curves of change. Greed is unwise. Wisdom is recognition of and guidance by a knowledge of the total system. The system punishes any species unwise enough to quarrel with its ecology. Greed, size and pride are unwise. Any course of action, like that just discussed, that ignores ecological stability and intentionality, i.e., the logic of nature, is unwise.

Hans Vaihinger (1911) in *The Philosophy of As If* suggested imitation as a solution to our lack of wisdom. Humans have no choice but to live by fictions; as if this world is the ultimate reality, as if there were free will. Humanity must plan for its future as if its days were not counted (or at least for several billion years). Jonas Salk urges us to behave "as if" we were wise, by using good sense. Wisdom is a new kind of fitness. To survive, we must accommodate ourselves to the new conditions of a radically different life. Survival in this sense is not a win or lose proposition, but a double win.

Wisdom is knowledge of the larger interactive system, which if disturbed, can generate exponential curves of change. Wisdom is the recognition of and guidance by a knowledge of the total system. Lacking knowledge, lacking wisdom, we must behave "as if" we were wise, as if we had good sense. Humans have no choice but to live by fictions, as if this world is the ultimate reality, as if we are responsible for our actions. Humanity must plan for its future as if its days were not counted (or at least for several thousand years). Wisdom is a new kind of fitness. To survive, we must accommodate ourselves to the conditions of the earth.

Wisdom is the disciplined use of the imagination with respect to alternatives, exercised at the right time and in the right measure. But we need practical wisdom, prudence, and intellectual control in virtue, in place of the theoretical wisdom taught by schools. The truths of our unique cultures and the wild earth are apprehended through myths. The poetic language of mythology can fit all the facts and values, things and images, into our hearts so that we can feel them and act upon them—so that we can make good places.

Related to wisdom, there are many corrective factors of human action: Contact, art, love, and religion. Love is the formation of Martin Buber's I-Thou relationships between human and society and environment. Socrates stated that Eros is midway between wisdom and ignorance. He who has no sense of his own deficiency will have no love of wisdom. Love is the desire that good be one's own for as long as it can. Arts and the activities of the mind can correct the excesses of pride. Contact between man and nature and animals can correct the problems of abstraction. And, ecodeontics (or religion), the binding of humans to the invisible powers of place, can correct the effects of detachment.

8.2.2.3. Can We Make a Global Government Now?
Will it work? Yes, if—
and that word 'if' makes a difference. We can try to be wise, and act "as if" it might work. Will we survive? Has some limit been exceeded? If not, do we have time to correct our actions? Time has become a real problem, especially since calendars were invented to keep track of big events. If the climate or our lives were more regular, we might not be so concerned with time. The idea of a regular or eternal return might be satisfying enough. If a fundamental limit has been exceeded, what should we do? If it is too late, and it is very difficult to know this definitely or absolutely, then we could party. Or we could act "as if" we were wise. We need to start now. It is a global emergency requiring global government!

Figure 82152-1. A possible nation of Kurdistan

9.0. Appendix

The global government of expanded groupings in a eutopian framework is a total reconsideration of the current pattern of technologies, cultures, value systems, and behaviors, evolving into a low-profile technological ethic suitable for a renewal of ecological understanding. It is a code for preserving those parts of the earth that are needed for renewing the holecosystem and for habitats for the billions of animals, plants and living beings that are part of the earth. It is a code for allowing fair use of that part of the earth that is human. It is a code for human equality in opportunity and worth. It is the demand for a margin from catastrophe, so that if humanity is unable to live peaceably, the rest of the earth will not become extinct as well.

The new theme for people's minds may begin in prose, but it should culminate in poetry. The human mind, under pressure from the dialectic process, grows into more subtle noetic experiences, until ecstatic insight blossoms. We must learn to be an individual in a human society in an ambihuman ecology with amphibian grace.

Poetry expresses the image of human potential, of what better circumstances may have formed. Poetry tells of a goal, even if it is the moral superiority of suffering in the 'third world.' By presenting a goal, poets can become the "unacknowledged legislators of mankind," as Percy Shelley defined them. Poetry creates a fourth world, of unique groups sharing part of the wealth of the earth in a global community. This fourth world is where the past is reconciled with the present and the terrible beauty of the future is born. The terror of beauty, as Rilke recognized, results from its power to shake humans from the refuge of a small identity into an immense strange world.

The lives of humans and all beings has become a collective responsibility. Humanity has to learn to live again on a finite and varied earth. Learning is a transforming experience, but difficult. Poetry objectifies conscious experience and makes it easier to communicate. Romantic nationalism (1930s) used poetry in service to the state. Used for each nation in this way, poetry shows the diversity of human experience. The essential unity of the earth can only be discovered through its infinite diversity. Poetry gives groups and individuals their identity; it articulates societies and authenticates forms of exchange. By transcending the limits of single cultures, it draws all cultures together. The tradition of poetry does not belong to just three worlds; it encompasses them and links them together in a fourth. Poetry is wise language.

What mysteries of the universe we cannot understand, we must accept in faith. One secret is that all things are secret. The working out of the cosmic process is effected by the actions of human beings, by hate or love. Love is reverence for the experience of all beings. Through love, humans can make good places on earth.

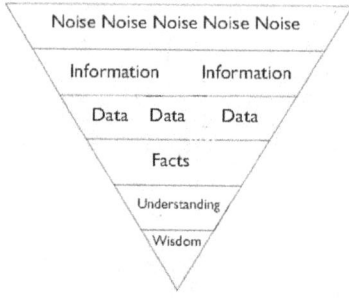

Figure 90-1. Pyramid to Wisdom

9.1. *Ecodex: Properties Principles Standards & Practices*

This experiment describing global government is a presentation of properties, principles, standards, and practices that can be combined to address challenges and problems facing our species and to make good places on earth.

Properties are qualities of a thing that distinguish unique individuals, systems, or patterns (characteristics are defined here as perceived distinctive features, where properties are inherent qualities); Gregory Bateson calls them differences that make a difference. Properties are also essential or accidental. An essential property is one that a thing possesses regardless of relationships with other things. If an essential property is lost, then the thing becomes another species; an accidental is one that makes less difference to essential properties.

Principles are fundamental rules or laws, derived from and based on the properties of the surrounding systems, that we can use to create images or models to meet stated objectives, that is, the goals towards which our action is directed, e.g., a healthy ecosystem or a balanced productive society. Principles unify our images. Standards are models or examples of quality or value, established by authority or mutual consent, that can be repeated as procedures. Standards are established from principles. Practices, as actions or procedures, are regular operations based on standards and principles. Principles match properties to our standards and practices to maintain the system favorable to us.

For example, one property of the planet is its wildness; we live on a wild planet. The corresponding principle is that the planet is self-making and self-ordering (ontologically wild), without requiring human control and management. Our objective for the planet is to allow the wild process to continue. We can set standards that are likely to keep the planet wild, stable and enjoyable: Limit our exploitation to less than fifty percent of the surface area; use appropriate techniques to minimize damage to wild systems; or, calculate optimum regional populations based on ecological and cultural carrying capacity. We can match our practices to those standards. For example, we could restore areas that have been damaged; rework or concentrate urban areas rather than converting wild systems; or, limit our population. The samples presented are not meant to be complete.

9.1.1. *Properties*
9.1.1.1. Global Properties
- Global biogeochemical systems depend primarily on wild ecosystems and cycles.
- Archaic peoples lived within the limits of their ecosystems.
- Modern agriculture, forestry and urbanization require great energy subsidies from fossil fuels or nuclear energy to survive. They exceed the limits of forests and land.
- Changes in scale put pressures on human and natural systems.
- We ignore very long-term trends in nature and human history that have very dramatic influences on our activities and management styles.
- Our history of use of surrounding ecosystems has been to exploit them to collapse and then to move on.
- We justify our temporarily successful behavior with myths that allow us to continue the behavior without being responsible.

9.1.1.2. Conservation Properties
- Forestry and agriculture deal primarily with wild ecosystems.
- Almost all artificial ecosystems depend on the services of wild ecosystems, especially for water, air and biogeochemical cycles.

9.1.1.3. Properties of Political Systems
- A political system is an adaptation to complexity in cultural development.
- The goal of the system is to ensure the survival of its culture, and to survive itself.

9.1.2. *Principles*

The global government recognizes and incorporates into its application a number of basic principles. The eutopian framework possesses three levels of authority, each with its own area of responsibility. There is a global authority to protect both the planet and human cultures. This authority, the Global Union (GU), is responsible for all land, air, and water utilization, for global cycles, and for interactions between nations. The GU gives equal opportunity to nonwestern, nonindustrial cultures to flourish.

Nations are based on traditional cultures, which have long-term, lasting power. Nations are responsible for protecting local environments and for providing a context for individuals. Both globalism and the simple community are necessary, if the community is not to be diseased and the globe impersonal.

The locus of political sovereignty is the individual, who is limited in giving away proxy rights. Politics has to be a participatory process, where an individual has some power over decisions affecting him or her. Participation is necessary, not only politically, but to establish the existence of common values throughout the population as a whole. Individuals have responsibilities for themselves and to their cultural governments.

9.1.2.1. General Principles
- The principle of lawfulness. Every unit of information can be analyzed into lawful components. The discovery of new patterns can confirm, but not prove, the principle.
- Preserve the earth, the heritage of all living beings. It has been modified and maintained by living processes over billions of years, and is required for the continuity of life.
- Keep humanity participating in the entire ecology of the planet. As with all beings, both the whole ecology and the species-specific are necessary for survival.
- The natural resources of the earth—the air, water, soil, plants, and animals—are to be preserved, and where possible, restored or improved.
- Allow all beings the equal opportunity for existence; this does not mean that they cannot be exploited or separated, just that they are not eliminated from the system.
- Humanity must build its civilizations within the framework of a planetary ecology. The human-created environment is necessary for human well-being.
- Economic development and social progress are necessary for the welfare of humanity. But must be conducted within environmental policies.
- The goal of economic and social development is to provide favorable and meaningful human habitations and activities.
- Human settlements must be planned and constructed within environmental constraints and according to ecological priorities.
- Technological processes must be brought into balance with the cycles of the earth. They must not damage or degrade natural cycles. Processes that cannot be controlled or rendered harmless, such as nuclear waste or inorganic pesticides, must be banned.
- Nonrenewable resources must be used sparingly, to avoid exhaustion before a steady-state economy has been achieved. The benefits from their exploitation are to be shared by all.

- All communities and citizens are responsible for the environments. They cooperate through a united body to preserve and promote the whole environment for the well being of all species and posterity.
- All humans have equal right to their share of the resources of the earth and to the amenities of civilization.

9.1.2.2. Global Principles
- No one group has sovereignty over the earth. The Global Union (GU) has regulatory powers necessary to maintain a healthy environment.
- The GU will establish a body for managing the earth's resources. And encourage states to establish local institutions.
- The GU will manage the earth through a fund from all states.
- The GU has regulatory and punitive power over all waste and pollution.
- The GU has regulatory power over all mineral resources in the earth, and distributes them equally, according to the principles herein.

9.1.2.2.1. Regulation
- The GU will be the intergovernmental body for the world to guide common policy.
- World-wide and interstate matters will be handled by all states working through the GU. Cooperation is essential to preserve, control and improve environmental and human conditions.
- The GU must ensure that rational planning considers the irrational, that human development considers the nonhuman. Therefore it has the power to refuse state plans.
- Only the GU shall have large-scale police capabilities. Only the GU shall have appropriate weapons. All mass destruction weapons, such as nuclear bombs, killer satellites and biological bombs, shall be reduced and recycled.
- Where population growth exceeds the safety margin established by the GU, on the basis of organic carrying capacity, demographic policies may be imposed by the GU, without prejudice or malice.
- The GU shall create a world bank for the exchange of all nations.
- The unit of wage shall be a human work unit, which shall have equal value for all.
- The GU shall stabilize prices of commodities and materials, and earnings from employment of labor.

9.1.2.2.2. Resources
- Limit use of other species within the limits of the dynamics of those species.
- Respect the use of materials through limited quantities and recycling.
- Respect the cycles of a system that renew or circulate elements.
- All scientific and technological knowledge shall be available to all states, as regulated by the GU.
- Scientific research and development, especially on environmental problems, will be promoted in all states. The GU will support a free flow of scientific information and experience. The GU will also ensure that appropriate technologies are available to all countries.
- The GU will award basic educational and research grants to all humans, for whatever use desired.
- The GU shall maintain quantities of food and currency to provide for disasters of natural and human cause. And shall be responsible for transfer of financial and technical assistance as

required.
- The GU shall provide social security to those unable to work because of age or inability.

9.1.2.3. Local Community or National Principles
- The community is the unit of survival and must be kept healthy.
- A community is composed of many interacting species and must be kept diverse.
- A communities embodies the rhythmic changes in the activities of individuals and groups, from which emerges periodicity, including genetic or system changes.
- A mature community is self-perpetuating and homeorhetic, with a dynamic balanced energy-matter budget.
- A community can change state and replace another community, as a result of orderly processes, such as succession or intentional development.

9.1.2.3.1. Management Principles
- Preserve all components, structures, and functions of system, that is, the health of a system providing services to the community or nation.
- Protect and maintain diversity; preserve the overall natural patterns of the system.
- Utilize natural processes for regeneration and protection.
- Current knowledge of the supporting ecosystems of a place is necessary.
- Acceptance of ecosystem limits of a place is necessary.
- Reduction of human demands on a place is necessary.
- Use of a place cannot be independent of human equity.
- The scale of human infrastructure and building should reflect the scale of the landscape.
- Human designs should follow the sensory force of a place and enhance the spirit of place.
- An optimum diversity in a landscape should be valued above a maximum or minimum.

9.1.2.3.2. Political Principles
- All states shall be equal, politically, regardless of size or sophistication. Every state has the right to its own integrity.
- States shall have sovereignty over their cultures, people, and organic and inorganic goods, within the limits of human and environmental rights and health.
- In accord with the GU charter, states have the right to use their assigned resources in any manner, within the limits of damage and pollution previously set.
- Nations have duties to ensure that activities are in conformity with principles set forth in the Global Union.
- Nations have duties to conduct their activities in a manner respectful of their complete effects.
- Nations must adopt an integrated and coordinated approach to planning and design, for the benefit of the environment and populations.
- Every nation has the responsibility to conduct its economy without causing damage to any other state or to the whole environment; each state must compensate for damage.
- Environmental risks and damages must be identified and solutions proposed.
- Through the GU, states shall develop laws on human and environmental rights, and activities.
- Education of the people on local culture, ecology and science is the responsibility of the state. The GU will provide aid for promoting enlightened opinion and responsible conduct. Mass media will disseminate educational information to protect and improve the whole ecology.
- Mass media will also be available in state centers for referendum needs.

- If population growth does not adjust to social and economic changes, it must be controlled by state policies.

9.1.2.4. Individual Principles
- The individual is the unit of experience and reproduction and must be kept healthy.
- An individual identifies with her home (habitat) and must keep it healthy.
- An individual depends on his niche (work or way of producing food).
- An individual acts for her self-preservation and self-interest first.
- An individual engages in ethical behavior, as part of a cultural group.
- Individuals have the right to ecological freedom and equality.
- The GU or any state will not have the right to determine values for any other state, within the basic limits of human and environmental rights and equality.
- Individuals are responsible for protecting the environment and improving damaged areas.

9.1.3. *Standards*
9.1.3.1. Conservation Standards
- Reserve at least fifty percent of the planet in wild areas.
- Calculate optimum regional human populations.
- Allow wild ecosystems to continue to be self-creating and self-managing. Allow for limits, disturbances, processes, and change.
- Modify our myths to provide appropriate images of place.
- Apply known ecological ideas to our exploitation of ecosystems.
- Minimize the effects of artificial corridors such as roads or flight lanes; retain appropriate shapes; keep to under four percent of most systems.
- Create large buffer zones, from 40 to 200 percent, especially around riparian areas.
- Leave snags, fallen trees and debris in the system at an appropriate level, from 15 to 25 percent.
- Calculate an appropriate diversity for each system.
- Calculate and preserve minimum species and habitat coverages for the whole system.

9.1.3.2. Political Standards
- Provide equal opportunities for all stakeholders and commonwealths.
- Rectify the worst of historical inequities through taxes and transfers.
- Charge equally for access to global commons, while restricting that needed for planetary regulation.
-

9.1.4. *Practices & Actions*
9.1.4.1. Conservation Practices
- Preserve the spirit of a place first.
- Set aside blocks of wild areas first; stop logging in all old-growth areas.
- Exploit only a limited amount of wild areas that will not affect wild patterns.
- Maintain the size and completeness of a system. Strengthen the shape and margins with buffers.
- Keep balances between densities and openness, as well as with exploitation and preservation.
- Maintain natural habitat structures in a surrounding wild matrix.
- Reduce fragmentation through the design of forested areas, taking into account the genetic

diversity of the trees, catastrophic conditions, minimum viable populations, corridors, and edge effects.
- Maintain and restore natural connections. Avoid artificial connections. Stop constructing new roads; close and revegetate old roads; integrate new roads.
- Retain the structures and processes (which produce the complexity and diversity) of the system, including legacies and special areas. Soil is an important structure.
- Restore clearcut areas; replant with native species. Restore damaged streams and wetlands.
- Recommend that reserves be made large enough for minimum viable populations and minimum viable ecosystem areas.
- Because current reserves are usually too small to hold viable populations, corridors must be planned to intersect with the larger areas set aside, and highway routes and underpasses must be modified.
- Use only appropriate equipment or technology to minimize accidental damage or takes.
- Bundle paths (especially utilities) to reduce number of incursions or roads
- Do not take all of one kind (or health or size or shape)
- Use labor-intensive methods (humanity our most valuable resource)
- Be sloppy, leave waste, debris or parts for natural renewal.

9.1.4.2. Political Practices
- Make the government open enough to see and flexible enough to change.
- Limit any terms to five years.

9.2. *End Notes*

[1] Called by P. Shepard 'philopatry'
[2] See also C.H. Waddington 1968.
[3] Paolo Soleri 1966.
[4] F. Sarfatti, 1975.
[5] for a full description, refer to Heinz Pagels.
[6] From Herman Daly 1977.
[7] see various Wittbecker articles.
[8] After G. Hardin, 1987.
[9] in *Instinct and Experience* 1912.
[10] in his book, *Emergent Evolution* 1923.
[11] in *Holism and Evolution* 1926.
[12] From Zeigler, 1976.
[13] Aristotle in Generation and Corruption, 316a5
[14] Bolwig 1963.
[15] E.T. Hall 1968.
[16] H. Eibl-Eibesfeldt 1970.
[17] E. Wilson 1971.
[18] B. Fagen 1985.
[19] Wittbecker. Courses taught at the Community Free University 1973-74 include: Radical Philosophy, Radical Ecology, and Radical Psychology. Certain distance learning courses and tutorials through the Ecoforestry Institute 1994-99 include: Forest Design, Matrix Management, and Restoration.
[20] Wittbecker, 1983.

[21] After N. Evernden.
[22] See also C.H. Waddington 1968.
[23] Richard Lewontin 1983.
[24] J. Ortega y Gasset in his "Meditations on Hunting"
[25] in *Farming without Fields*.
[26] Goerg Borgstrom, 1975.
[27] In M. Heidegger's word.
[28] In G. Weiss, 1975.
[29] In *The Subversive Science*.
[30] Quoted in M.W. Fox, 1980.
[31] From S. Kaplan, 1983.
[32] Fromme is quoted in Hampden-Turner.
[33] The word is from Y-F. Tuan, 1974.
[34] M. Heidegger, *Being and Time*. Tubingen: Niemeyer, 1960, p. 192.
[35] After Berry & Annis, 1974.
[36] Bormann and Likens, 1967.
[37] See Walsh, Loomis, and Gillman in *Land Economics*
[38] Holmes Welch 1966.
[39] As P. Singer 1981, points out.
[40] Whitehead, *Science and the Modern World*, p. 136.
[41] Recent translations say "Thou shall not murder."
[42] Stephen Kaplan 1973.
[43] Jane Jacobs. P. 82.
[44] After K. C. Chang.
[45] Wittbecker, 1970.
[46] Pirie, 1976.
[47] Moore and Lappe, 1975; Gabel, 1975.
[48] A. Tansley, 1935
[49] B. Commoner 1972, 1992; Ehrlich and Ehrlich 1990; Ehrlich and Holdren 1971, 1972; Holdren and Ehrlich 1974 for IPAT
[50] Wittbecker, ICE 1986, *Wild Earth* 1994
[51] Based on Eyre.
[52] In *Revelations*
[53] By Lamoureux et al.
[54] Frankel and Soule, 1981.
[55] Gilpin and Soule, 1986.
[56] Odum, Eugene P. 1970. "Optimum population and environment: A Georgian microcosm." *Current History* 58:355-366.
[57] Soule, Michael. 1986. *Conservation Biology*: The Science of Scarcity and Diversity. Sunderland: Sinauer Associates.
[58] Conservation International and Agrupación Sierra Madre. "Wilderness: Earth's Last Wild Places."
[59] Frankel and Soule, 1981.
[60] Bailey, Robert. 1999. *Ecoregions*.
[61] Georg Borgstrom, 1973.
[62] FAO, 1973.
[63] From *Modern Plastics*.

[64] Hayes (1976), cited in Daly, *Steady State Economics*, p. 169.
[65] M. Feinberg et al.
[66] Maya, From The Popol Vuh: Beginnings (J. Rothenberg and G. Quasha, eds., *America A Prophecy*. (New York: Vintage Books, 1974), p. 13.
[67] Especially in the works of Norberg-Schulz 1980.
[68] S. Kaplan 1973.
[69] Wittbecker, 1992.
[70] M. Sahlins, 1968.
[71] A.E. Wittbecker 1985.
[72] David Klein, 1978.
[73] Hemming, 1971.
[74] Eschenback and Geistauts, 1986.
[75] J. Ortega y Gasset, 1956.
[76] P. Shepard, p. 140-141.
[77] In C. Otten, *Anthropology and Art*. Garden City: American Museum of Natural History, 1971, p. 46.
[78] Anais Nin, p. 199.

9.3. Bibliography

Abrams, Charles. 1966. Man's Struggle for Shelter in an Urbanizing World. Cambridge: MIT Press.
Alexander, Christopher. 1977. A Pattern Language. New York: Oxford University Press.
Alexander, Christopher. 2002. The Nature of Order. Book One: The Phenomenon of Life. Berkeley: Center for Environmental Structure.
Anderson, E. N. 1996. Ecologies of the Heart. New York: Oxford University Press.
Andrewartha, H. G. and L. C. Birch. 1984. The Ecological Web. Chicago: University of Chicago Press.
Aristotle. 1952. The Works of Aristotle. Tr. by I. Bywater. W. Ross, ed. Oxford: Clarendon Press.
Arbib, Michael. 1972. The Metaphorical Brain. New York: John Wiley and Sons.
Bachelard, Gaston. 1969. Poetics of Space. trans. M. Jolas. Beacon Press, Boston, pp. 4-6.
Bacon, Edmund. 1967. Design of Cities. New York: Penguin Books.
Bacon, Francis. 1901. Novum Organum. J. Devey, ed. New York: P.F. Collier.
Baker, Richard St. Barbe. 1980. "A man of the trees: Ed Goldsmith interviewing Richard St. Barbe Baker." Coevolution Quarterly 25: 66-70.
Baldwin, Jr., A. D., J. de Luce, and Carl Pletsch, eds. 1994. Beyond Preservation: Restoring and Inventing Landscapes. Minneapolis: University of Minnesota Press.
Ball, Philip. 1999. The Self-made Tapestry: Pattern Formation in Nature. Oxford: Oxford University Press.
Barker, Roger J. 1968. Ecological Psychology. Stanford: Stanford University Press.
Barrett, William. 1978. The Illusion of Technique: A Search for Meaning in A Technological Civilization. New York: Doubleday.
Barton, Hugh, Editor. 2002. Sustainable Communities: The Potential for Eco-Neighborhoods. London: Earthscan.
Bates, Daniel G. 1998. Human Adaptive Strategies: Ecology, Culture, and Politics. Boston: Allyn and Bacon.
Bates, Marston. 1964. Man in Nature. Englewood Cliffs: Prentice-Hall.

Bateson, Gregory. 1987. Steps to an Ecology of Mind. Northvale, NJ: Jason Aronson Inc.
Bateson, Gregory. 1979. Mind and Nature: A Necessary Unity. New York: E.P. Dutton.
Becker, Ernest. 1973. The Denial of Death. New York: The Free Press.
Bellah, Robert N. et al. 1991. The Good Society. New York: Alfred A. Knopf.
Bell, J. S. 1964. On the Einstein Podolsky Rosen Paradox. Physics 1:195-200.
Benedict, Ruth. 1934. Patterns of Culture. New York: Houghton Mifflin.
Berger, John. 1973. Ways of Seeing. New York: Viking.
Bergonzi, B. 1969. Great Short Works of Aldous Huxley. New York: Harper and Row.
Bergstraesser, Arnold. 1962. Goethe's Image of Man and Society. Freiburg: Herder.
Berlyne, D.E. 1971. Aesthetics and Psychobiology. New York: Appleton Century Crofts.
Berry, Wendell. 1983. "People, Land, and Community," pp. 64-79 in Standing by Words. San Francisco: North Point Press
Bertalanffy, L. von. 1975. Perspectives on General Systems Theory. New York: G. Braziller.
Beston, Henry. 1971. The Outermost House. New York: Ballantine Books.
Black, C. A. 1968. Soil Plant Relationships. New York: Wiley.
Birch, Charles, and Cobb, Jr., John B. 1981. The Liberation of Life. Cambridge: Cambridge University Press.
Birch, Thomas H. 1982. "Man the Beneficiary?: A planetary perspective on the logic of wildland preservation." International Dimensions of the Environmental Crisis. R. Barrett, editor. Boulder: Westview Press.
Bly, Robert, ed. 1980. News of the Universe: Poems of the Twofold Consciousness. Sierra Club, San Francisco.
Bodley, John H. 1884. Cultural Anthropology. Mountain View, CA: Mayfield Publishing.
Boguslaw, Robert. 1965. The New Utopians. Englewood Cliffs: Prentice-Hall.
Bohm, D. 1980. Wholeness and the Implicate Order. London: Routledge and Kegan Paul.
Bonner, J.T. 1952. Morphogenesis: An Essay on Development. Princeton: Princeton Univ Press.
Bookchin, Murray. 1989. Remaking Society. New York: Black Rose Books.
Bookchin, Murray. 1989. Toward an Ecological Society. New York: Black Rose Books
Borgstrom, George. 1965. The Hungry Planet. New York: Macmillan Co.
Borgstrom, George. 1973. Harvesting the Earth. New York: Abelard-Schuman.
Botkin, Daniel B. 1990. Discordant Harmonies: A New Ecology for the Twenty-first Century. New York: Oxford University Press.
Boulding, Kenneth E. 1956. The Image: Knowledge in Life and Society. Ann Arbor: University of Michigan Press.
Boulding, Kenneth E. 1966. Beyond Economics. New York: Harper & Row.
Boulding, Kenneth E. 1969. "The economics of the coming spaceship earth," In Population Evolution and Birth Control. San Francisco: Freeman.
Brandeis, Louis D. 1935. The Curse of Bigness. New York: Viking Press.
Braungart, Michael, and William McDonough. 2002. Cradle to Cradle: Remaking the Way We Make Things. New York: North Point Press.
Bridgman, P.W. 1941. The Nature of Thermodynamics. Cambridge: Harvard University Press.
Bronowski, J. 1965. Science and Human Values. New York: Harper and Row.
Brown, G. S. 1979. Laws of Form. New York: The Julian Press.
Brown, Harrison. 1954. The Challenge of Man's Future. New York: Viking Press.
Brown, James H. and Brian A. Maurer. 1989. Macroecology: The Division of Food and Space Among Species on Continents. Science 243:1145-1150.
Brown, Lester. 1979. ``Crossing the threshold? Pressures on earth's biological systems." Environ-

ment 21(8):12-37.

Bryan, Frank and John McClaughry. 1991. The Vermont papers. Post Mills: Chelsea Green.

Bunge, Mario. 1959. Causality. The place of the causal principle in modern science. Cambridge: Harvard University Press.

Burns, Neal M.; Chambers, Randall M; and Hendler, Edwin, Eds. 1963. Unusual Environments and Human Behavior: Physiological and Psychological Problems of Man in Space. New York, The Free Press of Glencoe.

Burlingh, P. et al. 1975. Computation of the Absolute Maximum Food Production of the World. Wageningen, Netherlands: Agriculture University.

Callenbach, Ernest, et al. 1993. Ecomanagement. San Francisco: Berrett-Koehler.

Campbell, Joseph. 1969. The Flight of the Wild Gander. New York: Viking Press.

Campbell, Joseph. 1972. The Masks of God: Primitive Mythology. New York: Penguin.

Campbell, Joseph. 1972. The Masks of God: Creative Mythology. New York: Penguin.

Capra, Fritjof. 1975. The Tao of Physics. Berkeley: Shambhala.

Capra, Fritjof. 1982. The Turning Point. New York: Simon and Schuster.

Caratheodory, Alain M. Wild Apples. Wilmington: Mozart & Reason Wolfe, 1976.

Carson, Rachel. 1962. Silent Spring. Boston: Houghton Mifflin.

Casey, Edward S. 1996. How to get from Space to Place in a fairly short stretch of time: Phenomenological Prolegomena. In Senses of Place, ed. Steven Feld and Keith H. Basso. Santa Fe. pps. 13-52.

Catton, William R. 1982. Overshoot: The Ecological Basis of Revolutionary Change. Urbana: University of Illinois Press.

Cavalli-Sforza, Luca and Albert Ammerman. 1984. The Neolithic Transition and the genetics of Populations in Europe. Princeton: Princeton.

Cheng, T.C. 1970. Symbiosis. New York: Pegasus.

Chermayoff, Serge and Christopher Alexander. 1965. Community and Privacy. New York: Anchor Books.

Chew, G. F. 1970. Hadron bootstrap: Triumph or frustration. Phys. Today (October):23-28.

Churchman, C.W. 1968. The Systems Approach. New York: Delacorte Press.

Cicero, M.T. 1933. De Natura Deorum. Tr. by H. Rackham. London: Wm. Heinemann. Pps. ii, 154.

Clapp, Jennifer and Peter Dauvergne. 2005. Paths to a Green World. Cambridge: MIT Press.

Clark, Colin. 1958. ``World Population.'' Nature 181:1235-1236.

Clark, Colin. 1967. Population Growth and Land Use. London: Macmillan.

Clark, Grahame. 1977. World Prehistory. Cambridge: Cambridge University Press.

Clark, William C. 1991. "Managing Planet Earth," Scientific American September.

Cobb, John B. Jr. 1971. Is It Too Late? New York: Glencoe.

Cobb, John B. Jr. "Economism or Planetism: The Coming Choice," Earth Ethics 3(1):1-5.

Cobb, John B. Jr. 1992. Sustainability: Economics, Ecology, and Justice. Maryknoll: Orbis Books.

Coleridge, Samuel T. 2003. Coleridge's Poetry and Prose. New York: Norton.

Colinvaux, P. 1978. Why Big Fierce Animals Are Rare. Princeton: Princeton University Press.

Commoner, Barry 1971. The Closing Circle. New York: Knopf.

Coates, Gary J. and David Seamon. 1993. "Promoting a foundational ecology practically through Christopher Alexander's Pattern Language: The example of Meadowcreek," Ch. 14 in Dwelling, Seeing, and Designing: Toward a Phenomenological Ecology. Albany: State University of New York Press.

Conrad, Peter. 1999. Modern Times, Modern Places. New York: Knopf.

Costanza, Robert. Ed. 1991. Ecological Economics: The Science and Management of Sustainability. New York: Columbia University Press.
Costanza, R., B. G. Norton, and B. D. Haskell, eds. 1992. Ecosystem Health: New Goals for Environmental Management. Washington: Island Press.
Cottrell, Leonard. 1962. The Horizon Book of Lost Worlds. New York: Horizon.
Cramer, F. 1993. Chaos and Order: The Complex Structure of Living Systems. Weinheim: VCH. Cultural Survival Trust. 1992. "Veddhas say no to colonization plan," Cultural Survival, Spring 1992, Pp. 11-12.
Daly, Herman E. 1968. Economics as a life science. Journal of Political Economy 76:392-401.
Daly, Herman E. 1977. Stead-State Economics. San Francisco: Freeman.
Daly, Herman E. and John B. Cobb, Jr. 1989. For the Common Good. Boston: Beacon Press.
Daly, Herman E. 1993. The steady-state economy, In Herman Daly and Kenneth Townsend, eds., Valuing the Earth: Economics, Ecology, Ethics. Cambridge: MIT Press.
Daly, Mary 1978. Gyn/Ecology Boston: Beacon Press.
Dansereau, Pierre. 1957. Biogeography: An Ecological perspective. New York: Ronald Press.
Darling. F. Fraser and John P. Milton, eds. 1966. Future Environments of North America. Garden City: Natural History Press.
Darlington, P. J. 1957. Zoogeography. New York: Wiley.
Darwin, Charles. 1859. The Origin of the Species by Means of Natural Selection. London: Murray. Page 75.
Dasmann, Ray. 1972. Environmental Conservation. 3rd Ed. New York: Wiley.
Daubenmire, Rexford. 1970. Steppe Vegetation of Washington. Technical Bulletin Number 62. Pullman: WA Agricultural Experiment Station.
De Los Reyes, B.N. et al. 1965. A case study of the tractor and carabao-cultivated lowland rice farms in Laguna, crop year 1962-63. Phil. Agric. 49:75-94.
Diamond, J.M. 1975. The island dilemma: Lessons of modern biogeographic studies for the design of natural preserves. Biol. Conserv. 7:129-146.
Diamond, J.M.. 1997. Guns, Germs, and Steel: The Fate of Human Societies. New York: W. W. Norton.
Dietz, Thomas, and Eugene A. Rosa. 1994. "Rethinking the Environmental Impacts of Population, Affluence and Technology." Human Ecology Review, Summer/Autumn, 1.
Diole, P. 1974. The Errant Ark: Man's Relationship with Animals. New York: Putnam.
Doolittle, W. F. 1981. Is nature really motherly? Coevolution Quarterly 29:58-62.
Doxiades, C.A. 1975. Building Entopia. New York: Norton.
Doxiades, C.A.. 1977. Ecology and Ekistics. Boulder: Westview Press.
Drengson, Alan. 1989. Beyond Environmental Crisis: From Technocrat to Planetary Person. New York: Peter Lang.
Drengson, Alan et al. 1994. "The ecoforester's way: An oath of ecological responsibility," International Journal of Ecoforestry 10(1):48.
Drucker, Peter. 1969. The age of discontinuity: Guidelines to our changing society. New York: Harper & Row.
Drucker, Peter. 1990. The New Realities. New York: Dutton
Dubos, Rene. 1967. Man Adapting. New Haven: Yale University Press.
Dubos, Rene. 1972. A God Within. New York: Charles Scribner's Sons.
Dubos, Rene. 1974. Beast or Angel? Choices That Make Us Human. New York: Charles Scribner's Sons.
Dubos, Rene. 1976. Symbiosis between the earth and humankind. Science 193:459-462

Dubos, Rene. 1980. The Wooing of Earth. New York: Charles Scribner's Son.

Dugatkin, L. A. 2000. The Imitation Factor. New York: Free Press.

Durham, William H. 1991. Coevolution: Genes, Culture and Human Diversity. Stanford: Stanford University Press.

Eckbo, Garrett. 1969. The Landscape We See. Berkeley: UC Press.

Eckholm, Eric P. 1976. Losing Ground: Environmental Stress and World Food Prospects. New York: W. W. Norton.

Eddington, Arthur. 1935. Philosophy of Physical Science. London: Textbook Publishers.

Edie, James. 1969. New Essays in Phenomenology. New York: Quadrangle.

Ehrlich, Paul. 1968. The population bomb. New York: Ballantine Books.

Ehrlich, Paul and Holdren, John P. 1971. Impact of Population Growth. Science. 171:1212-1217.

Ehrlich, Paul and A. Ehrlich. 1972. Population, Resources, Environment. San Francisco: Freeman.

Ehrlich, Paul. 1981. An ecologist standing up among seated social scientists. Coevolution Quarterly 31:24-35.

Eibl-Eibesfelt, I. 1970. Ethology: The Biology of Behavior. New York: Holt, Rinehart and Winston.

Eigen, Manfred, and P. Schuster. 1979. The Hypercycle: A Principle of Natural Self-Organization. Berlin: Springer-Verglag.

Eigen, Manfred, and P. Schuster. 1981. Laws of the Game. New York: Alfred A. Knopf.

Einstein, Albert and Leopold Infeld, 1960. Evolution of Physics. New York: Simon & Schuster.

Eisenberg, Evan. 1998. The Ecology of Eden. New York: Vintage.

Eliot, T. S. 1949. Notes Towards a Definition of Culture. London: Harcourt.

Elton, C. 1966. Animal Ecology. New York: October House.

Evernden, Neil. 1981. Out of Place (unpublished manuscript).

Evernden, Neil. 1992. The Social Creation of Nature. Baltimore: Johns Hopkins.

Ewald, William R. Jr. 1968. Environment and Change: The Next Fifty years. Bloomington: Indiana University Press.

Eyre, Samuel. 1978. The Real Wealth of Nations. London: E. Arnold.

FAO. 1973. Production Yearbook, 1092. Vol. 26. Rome: FAO.

Feibleman, James K. Mankind Behaving: Human Needs and Material Culture.

Ferkiss, Victor C. 1969. Technological Man: The Myth and Reality. New York: Braziller.

Festinger, L. 1957. A Theory of Cognitive Dissonance. Stanford: Stanford University Press.

Finkelsten, D. 1972. The space-time code. Phys Rev 50, no. 12:2922.

Fitch, James M. 1961. Architecture and the Esthetics of Plenty. New York: Columbia University Press.

Foreman, Dave, ed. 1985. Ecodefense: A Field Guide to Monkeywrenching Tucson: Earth First! Books (p. 10).

Foreman, R.T.T. and M. Godron. 1986. Landscape Ecology. New York: John Wiley.

Forestry Commission, 1994. Forest Landscape Design. London: HMSO.

Forman, R.T.T. and Michel Godron. 1986. Landscape Ecology. New York: John Wiley.

Fowles, John. 1970. The Aristos. New York: The New American Library, Inc.

Fowles, John. 1979. Seeing Nature Whole. Harper's. 259:49-56

Fowles, John. 1980. Is nature necessary? Harper's.

Fox, M.W. 1974. Concepts in Ethology: Animal and Human Behavior. Minneapolis: U. of Minnesota Press.

Fox, M.W. 1976. Between Animal and Man. New York: Coward, McCann and Geoghehan Inc.

Fox, M.W. 1980. Returning to Eden: Animal Rights and Human Responsibility. New York: Viking Press.

Fox, M.W. 1997. Concepts in Ethology: Animal Behavior and Bioethics. Krieger.
Fox, M.W. 2001. Bringing Life to Bioethics. State University of New York Press.
Frankel, Otto. 1975. Crop Genetic Resources for Today and Tomorrow. O. Frankel and J. Hawkes, eds. New York: Cambridge University Press.
Frankel, O. H. and M. E. Soule. 1981. Conservation and Evolution. Cambridge: Cambridge University Press.
Fraser, J.T. 1975. Of Time, Passion and Knowledge. New York: George Braziller.
Fromm, Erich. 1956. The Art of Loving. New York: Harper.
Fromm. Erich. 1976. To Have or To Be. New York: Bantam Books.
Fuller, R. B. 1969. Utopia or oblivion: The prospects for humanity. New York: Bantam.
Fuller. R. B. 1970. Operating Manual for Spaceship Earth. New York Pocket Books.
Fuller, R. B. 1981. Critical Path. New York: St. Martin's Press.
Galbraith, John Kenneth. 1967. The new industrial state. New York: Houghton-Mifflin.
Gabel, Medard. 1979. HO-PING: Food for Everyone. Garden City, New York: Anchor Press/Doubleday.
Galdston, Iago, ed. 1963. Man's Image in Medicine and Anthropology. New York: International Universities Press, Inc.
Gans, Herbert J. 1969. People and Plans. New York: Columbia University Press.
Gazzaniga, M.S. 1967. The split brain in man. Sci. Am. 217:24-29.
Georgescu-Roegen, Nicholas. 1971. The Entropy Law and the Economic Process. Cambridge: Harvard University Press.
Georgescu-Roegen, Nicholas. 1976. Bioeconomics: A new look at the nature of economic activity. In The Political Economy of Food and Energy, ed. L. Junker. Ann Arbor: The University of Michigan Press.
Gibbs, J.W. 1960. Principles in Statistical Mechanics. New York: Longmans, Green and Co.
Gibson, William. 1986. "Ecology and Justice", Wilderness (Summer): 52-56.
Gillard, E. Thomas. 1963. Evolution of Bowerbirds. Sci. Am. 209:38-46.
Ginsberg, Lee and Mark Colyvan. 2004. Ecological orbits. New York: Oxford University Press.
Globus, G., G. Maxwell, and I. Sarednik. 1976. Consciousness and the Brain. New York: Plenum Press.
Goldsmith, Edward. 1988. "The Way: An ecological worldview," Pp. 160-185 in The Ecologist, Vol. 18, No. 4/5.
Goldtooth, Tom B.K. 1995. Indigenous nations: Summary of sovereignty and its implications for environmental protection. In B. Bryant, ed., Environmental Justice. Washington: Island Press.
Goodman, Paul and Percival Goodman. 1947. Communitas: Means of Livelihood and Ways of Life. New York: Abrams.
Goodman, Paul. 1962. Utopian Essays and Practical Proposals. New York: Random House. Goodman, Paul. 1970. New reformation: Notes of a Neolithic Conservative. New York: Random House.
Gould, S. J. 1977. Ontogeny and Phylogeny. Cambridge: Belknap Press.
Grande, John K. 2004. Balance: Nature and Art. New York: Black Rose.
Graves, Robert. 1948. The White Goddess. New York: Farrar Straus & Giroux. p. 260.
Gray, Russell D. 1988. Metaphors and methods. In Mae-Wan Ho and S. W. Fox, eds., Evolutionary Processes and Metaphors. New York: Wiley.
Gregg, Alan. 1955. A medical aspect of the population problem. Science 121 (3,50):681-2.
Greene, Patricia and Dean Apostol. 1994. Design for biodiversity. Landscape Architecture 85 (4):63-65.

Grene, M., ed. 1971. Interpretations of Life and Mind. New York: Humanities Press.

Gunderson, Lance H. and C. S. Holling. Eds. 2002. Panarchy. Washington: Island Press.

Gustavson, Carl G. 1976. The Mansion of History. New York: McGraw-Hill Book Company.

Gutkind, E. A. 1962. The Twilight of Cities. New York: Free Press of Glencoe.

Haldane, J.B.S. 1927. Possible Worlds and Other Papers. London: Chatto and Windus.

Hall, Edward T. 1969. The Hidden Dimension. Garden City, New York: Doubleday.

Hall, Edward T. 1976. Beyond Culture. Garden City, New York: Anchor Press.

Halprin, Lawrence. 1969. The RSVP Cycles: Creature Processes in the Human Environment. New York: George Braziller.

Hammond, Herb.

Hampden-Turner, C. 1981. Maps of the Mind. New York: Macmillan.

Harajan, 7.9.1935, p. 234. Gandhi.

Hardin, Garrett. "The tragedy of the commons," Science 162:1243-1248.

Hardin, Garrett. Ed. 1969. Population, Evolution, and Birth Control. San Francisco: Freeman.

Hardin, Garrett. 1977. The Limits of Altruism: An Ecologist's View of Survival. Bloomington: Indiana University Press.

Hardin, Garrett. 1980. "An ecolate view of the human predicament," in Global Resources. Baltimore: University Park Press.

Hardin, Garrett. 1985. Filters Against Folly. New York: Penguin Books. (Discounting the future or who can afford a forest? pp. 71-76. The effect of scale on values, pp. 128-140.)

Hare, Nathan. 1970. Black Ecology, The Black Scholar 1(April):2-8.

Harper, J. L. 1961. The Evolution and Ecology ... Evolution Vol. 15: 209-227.

Harrington, Michael. 1966. The Accidental Century. New York: Weidenfeld & Nicolson.

Hart, Richard. 1994. "Monitoring for ecosystem management," International Journal of Ecoforestry 10(2):74-75.

Hebb, D.O. 1958. Alice in Wonderland or psychology among the biological sciences. In: The Biological and Biochemical Bases of Behavior. H. Harlow and C. Woolsley, eds. Madison: University of Wisconsin Press.

Heidegger, M. 1960. Being and Time. 9th ed. Tubingen: Max Niemeyer Verlag. Heisenberg, W. 1958. Physics and Philosophy. New York: Harper Torch Books.

Heminger, Jr., S. K. 1974. Touches of Sweet Harmony. San Marino, California: Huntington Library.

Henberg, M. 1984. "Wilderness as playground." Environmental Ethics 6:253-263.

Henderson, Hazel. 1980. Creating Alternative Futures: The End of Economics. New York: Putnam.

Herber, Lewis. Our Synthetic Environment. (see M. Bookchin).

Heroditus. The History Book 1:22-23.

Hoffman, David. 1976. Inuit land use on the barren grounds. Inuit Land Use and Development Project, Vol. 2. Ottawa: Dept. of Indian and Northern Affairs.

Holling, C. S. 1973. Resilience and Stability of Ecological Systems. In: Annual Review of Ecology and Systematics, R. F. Johnston et al., eds., Vol. 4: 1-24.

Homer. 1956. The Iliad. Middlesex, England: Penguin Books.

Hoyle, Fred. 1977. Astronomy and Cosmology. San Francisco: Freeman.

Hughes, J. Donald. 1983. American Indian Ecology. El Paso: Texas Western Press.

Huizinga, Johan. 1955. Homo Ludens: A Study of the Play Element in Culture. London: Routledge & Kegan Paul.

Hulet, H.R. 1970. "Optimum world population." Bioscience 20(3):160-161.

Humboldt, Alexander von. 1897. Cosmos: A Sketch of a Physical Description of the Universe. trans. E. Otte. London: H. G. Bohn.

Huxley, Aldous. 1945. The Perennial Philosophy. New York: Harper.

Huxley, Aldous. 1948. Ape and Essence. New York: Harper & Row.

Huxley, Aldous. 1956. Knowledge and Understanding. In: Adonis and the Alphabet. London: Chatto and Windus.

Huxley, Aldous. 1977. The Human Situation. P. Ferrucci, ed. New York: Harper & Row.

Huxley, Julian. 1964. The Human Crisis. Seattle: University of Washington Press.

Huxley, Julian, and Huxley, T. H. 1947. Touchstone of Ethics. New York: Harpers.

Huxley, T. H. 1856. "On natural history as knowledge, discipline and power."

Hyde, Richard. 2000. Climate Responsive Design. London: E & FN Spon.

Illich, Ivan. 1973. Tools for Conviviality. New York: Harper & Row.

Illich, Ivan. 1978. Towards a History of Needs. New York: Pantheon.

Imanishi, Kinji. 1952. Man (Japanese language). Tokyo: Mainichi-Shinbunsha.

International Union for Conservation of Nature. 1984. World Conservation Strategy in Action. Gland, Switzerland.

Jackson, Wes, W. Berry, and B. Colman. 1984. Meeting the Expectations of the Land: Essays in Sustainable Agriculture. San Francisco: North Point.

Jacobs, Jane. 1961. The Death and Life of Great American Cities. New York: Random House.

Jammer, Max. 1954. Concepts of Space. Cambridge: Harvard University Press.

Jantsch, E. 1975. Design for Evolution. New York: Braziller.

Jantsch, E. 1980. The Self-Organizing Universe. New York: Pergamon Press.

Jonas, H. 1974. Philosophical Essays: From Ancient Creed to Technological Man. Englewood Cliffs: Prentice-Hall Inc.

Kant, Immanuel. 1998. Critique of Judgment. New York: Cambridge University Press. Kaplan, Rachel. 1983. "The role of nature in the urban context," in I. Altman and J. F. Wohlwill, eds. Behavior and the Natural Environment. New York: Plenum Press.

Kaplan, Richard. 1983. The role of nature in the urban context. Irwin Altman and Joachim Wohlwill, eds. Behavior and the Natural Environment. Plenum Press, New York, pp. 127159.

Kaplan, Robert. 2000. The Coming Anarchy. New York: Vintage Books.

Kaplan, S. 1973. "Cognitive maps; human needs and the designed environment." In W. F. E. Preiser, ed., Environmental Design Research. Stroudsberg: Dowden, Hutchinson & Ross.

Kellert, S.R. 1983. Affective, cognitive, and evaluative perceptions of animals. Irwin Altman and Joachim Wohlwill, eds. Behavior and the Natural Environment. Plenum Press, New York, pp. 241-265.

Kepes, Gyorgy. 1965. Structure in Art and Science. New York: G. Braziller.

Kieffer, George H. 1979. Bioethics: A Textbook of Issues. Reading, MA: Addison-Wesley Publishing Co.

Kirk, G. S. and J. E. Raven. 1957. The Pre-Socratic Philosophers. Cambridge University Press.

Klein, David R. 1970. IUCN Publ. New Series No. 16:209-242.

Klein, David. 1972. Toward an ecophilosophy. Tomte Symposium on Ecology and Land Use, Steinsgard, Norway.

Klein, David R. and R. G. White, eds. 1978. Parameters of Caribou Population Ecology in Alaska. Fairbanks: Biol. Papers Univ. AK, Special Report No. 2.

Klein, David. 1976. "Wilderness Part 1. Evolution of the Concept." Landscape 20: 36-41.

Klein, David R. 1981. Alternate species for northern animal production. Can. J. Anim. Sci. 61:7-15.

Klopfer, P. H. 1962. Behavioral Aspects of Ecology. Englewood Cliffs, NJ: Prentice-Hall. Kockelmans, J., ed. 1972. On Heidegger and Language. Evanston, IL: Northwestern University Press.

Koestler, A. and J.R. Smythies, eds. 1969. Beyond Reductionism: New Perspectives in the Life Sciences. London: Hutchinson.

Koestler, A. 1978. Janus: A Summing Up. New York: Random House.

Kohler, I. 1962. Experiment with goggles. Sci. Am. 206:62-86.

Kohler, W. 1947. Gestalt Psychology. 2nd ed. New York: Liveright Publishing Corp.

Kohr, Leopold. 1957. The Breakdown of Nations. New York: E.P. Dutton.

Kohr, Leopold, 1973. Development Without Aid. New York: Schocken Books.

Kohr, Leopold. 1977. The Overdeveloped Nations: Diseconomies of Scale. New York: Schocken Books.

Kozlovsky, Daniel G. 1974. An Ecological and Evolutionary Ethic. New York: Prentice-Hall.

Krebs, Charles J. 1985. Ecology. Third ed. New York: Harper & Row.

Kropotkin, P.A. 1972. Mutual Aid: A Factor in Evolution. New York: New York University Press.

Krutch, Joseph W. 1970. The Best Nature Writing of Joseph Wood Krutch. New York: Pocket Books

Krutch, Joseph W. Human Nature and the Human Condition. NC: NP.

Kuhn, Thomas. 1970. The Structure of Scientific Revolutions. Chicago: University of Chicago Press.

Kuhns, William. 1969. Environmental Man. New York: Harper and Row.

Lacan, J. 1968. The Language of the Self: The Function of Language in Psychoanalysis. Baltimore: Johns Hopkins Press.

Lackner, S. 1984. Peaceable Nature. New York: Harper and Row

Laing, R. D., H. Phillipson, and A. R. Lee. Interpersonal perception. NC: NP.

Lamarck, Jean. 1963. Zoological Philosophy. trans. H. Elliot. New York: Hafner Publishing Co (1809. Philosophie Zoologique).

Landers, Richard R. 1966. Man's Place in the Dybosphere. Englewood Cliffs: Prentice-Hall.

Lao Tse. 1963. Tao Te Ching. Translated by D. C. Lau. Middlesex, England: Penguin Books.

Lappe, Frances Moore and Joseph Collins. 1979. Food First: Beyond the Myth of Scarcity. New York: Ballantine.

Laszlo, Ervin. 1972. Introduction to Systems Philosophy: Toward a New Paradigm of Contemporary Thought. New York: Harper Torch Books

Laszlo, Ervin et al. 1977. Goals for Mankind. New York: E. P. Dutton.

Laszlo, Ervin. 1987. Evolution: The Grand Synthesis. Boston: New Science Library

Le Corbusier and Francois de Pierrefeu. The Home of Man.

Lieth, Helmut F. H., ed. Patterns of Primary Production in the Biosphere. Stroudsburg, PA: Dowden, Hutchinson & Ross, Inc.

Lieth, Helmut F H. and Robert Whittaker, eds. 1975. Primary Productivity of the Biosphere. New York: Springer-Verlag.

Leonard, George. 1978. The Silent Pulse. New York: E. P. Dutton

Leopold, Aldo. 1949. A Sand County Almanac; And Sketches of Here and There. New York: Oxford University Press.

Levi-Strauss, C. 1963. Structural Anthropology. New York: Basic Books.

Levy-Bruhl, Lucien. 1975. The Notebooks on Primitive Mentality. Translated by Peter Leenhardt. Oxford: Basil Blackwell.

Lewin, K. 1951. Field Theory in Social Science. D. Cartwright, ed. New York: Harper and Row.

Likens, Gene E., ed. 1989. Long-Term Studies in Ecology. New York: Springer-Verlag.

Lincicome, D.R. 1969. The Goodness of Parasitism: A New Hypothesis. Thomas C. Cheng, ed. Aspects of the Biology of Symbiosis. Baltimore: University Park Press.

Lorenz, Konrad. 1952. King Solomon's Ring: New Light on Animal Ways. trans. M. K. Wilson. New York: Crowell.

Lorenz, Konrad. 1974. Civilized Man's Eight Deadly Sins. trans. M. K. Wilson. New York: Harcourt, Brace, Javonovich.

Lovejoy, Arthur O. 1964. The Great Chain of Being: A Study of the History of an Idea. Cambridge: Harvard University Press.

Lovejoy. Thomas and D. C. Oren. 1981. "The minimum critical size of ecosystems," in W.D. Billings et al., eds., Forest Island Dynamics in Man-dominated Landscapes. New York: Springer-Verlag.

Lovejoy, Thomas and Richard Bierregaard. In Soule, Michael. 1986. Conservation Biology: The Science of Scarcity and Diversity. Sunderland: Sinauer Associates.

Lovelock, James E. 1979. Gaia: A New Look at Life on Earth. Oxford: Oxford University Press.

Lovelock, James E. 1988. The Ages of Gaia: A Biography of Our Living Earth. New York: W.W. Norton.

Lovelock, James E. 1991. Healing Gaia: Practical Medicine for the Planet. New York: Harmony Books.

Lowenthal, David. Environmental Perception and Behavior.

Lucas, Oliver. 1990. The Design of Forest Landscapes. New York: Oxford University Press.

Lynch, Kevin. 1960. The Image of the City. NC: NP.

MacArthur, Robert H. 1972. Geographical Ecology: Patterns in the Distribution of Species. New York: Harper & Row.

MacArthur, R.H. and E.O. Wilson. 1967. The Theory of Island Biogeography. Princeton: Princeton University Press.

MacKaye, Benton. From Geography to Geotechnics. NC: NP.

Malinowski, Bronislaw. 1944. A Scientific Theory of Culture and Other Essays. Chapel Hill: University of North Carolina Press.

Mandelbrot, B. B. 1982. The Fractal Geometry of Nature. San Francisco: W.H. Freeman.

Mander, Jerry. 1991. In the Absence of the Sacred. San Francisco: Sierra Club Books.

Mander, Jerry and Edward Goldsmith, eds. 1996. The Case Against the Global Economy. San Francisco: Sierra Club Books.

Mandeville, Bernard de (see Lewis Mumford, 1922).

Mann, John. 1965. Changing Human Behavior. New York: Scribner.

Margalef, R. 1968. Perspectives in Ecological Theory. Chicago: University of Chicago Press.

Margulis, L. 1974. Five kingdoms—classification and the origin and evolution of cells. Evol Biol 7:45-48.

Margulis, Lynn and Dorion Sagan. 1986. Microcosmos. New York: Summit Books. (pp. 169174.)

Margulis, Lynn. 1991. Big trouble in biology: Physiological autopoiesis versus mechanistic neo-Darwinism. In John Brockman, ed., Doing Science. New York: Prentice Hall Press.

Marsh, G.P. 1964. Man and Nature, The Earth as Modified by Human Action. St Clair, MI: Scholarly Press.

Maruyama, Magorah. 1979. Transepistemological Understanding: Wisdom beyond theories. Maruyama, Magorah, ed. Cultures of the Future. The Hague: Mouton.

Maruyama, Magorah. 1980. Toward Cultural Symbiosis. In: Evolution and Consciousness: Human Systems in Transition. E. Jantsch and C. H. Waddington, eds. Reading: Addison-Wesley Publishing Co.

Marx, Leo. 1964. The machine in the garden: Technology and the pastoral ideal in America. Oxford University Press.

Maser, Chris. 1988. The Redesigned Forest. San Diego: R and E Miles.

Maser, Chris. 1990. The Forest Primeval. San Francisco: Sierra Books.

Maslow, A. H. 1968. Toward a Psychology of Being. 2nd ed. New York: Van Nostrand.
Maslow, A. H. 1971. The Farther Reaches of Human Nature. New York: Viking Press.
Maturana, H.R. and Varela, F: 1987. Tree of Knowledge. Boston: Shambhala.
Mayr, Ernest. 1942. Systematics and the Origin of the Species. New York: Columbia University Press.
Mazrui, Ali Al Amin. 1976. A World Federation of Cultures: An African Perspective. New York: Free Press.
McArthur, Robert H. 1972. Geographical Ecology: Patterns in the Distribution of Species. New York: Harper & Row.
McCarry, James. 1972. The Quality of the Environment. New York: Free Press.
McCay, Bonnie J. and James Acheson, eds. 1987. The Question of the Commons. Tucson: University of Arizona Press.
McCulloch, Warren. 1965. A Heterarchy of Values Determined by the Topology of Nervous Nets. Journal of General Physiology 43:6.
McDonough, William and Michael Braungart. 2002. Cradle to Cradle. New York: North Point Press.
McHale, John. 1969. The Future of the Future. New York: G. Braziller.
McHarg, Ian. 1969. Design with Nature. Garden City: Natural History Press.
McKeon, Richard. 1973. Introduction to Aristotle. Chicago: University of Chicago Press.
McLean, G.F., ed. 1978. Man and Nature. Calcutta: Oxford University Press.
McLuhan, Marshall. 1964. Understanding Media. New York: McGraw Hill.
McLuhan, Marshall and Quentin Fiore. War and Peace in the Global Village.
McLuhan, Marshall and Quentin Fiore. 1967. The Medium is the Massage. New York: Bantam.
Meadows, Donna et al. 1972. The Limits to Growth. A report for the Club of Rome's project on the Predicament of Mankind. New York: Universe books.
Meadows, Dennis. 1982. "Fallacies in resource planning," in Charles Hewett, T. Hamilton, and I. Anderson, eds., Forests in Demand. Boston: Auburn House.
Meadows, D. H., D. L. Meadows, and J. Randers. 1992. Beyond the Limits. Post Mills: Chelsea Green. (Forest distribution and deforestation globally, pp. 57-64.)
Mech, L. David. 1984. The Wolf. Minneapolis: University of Minnesota Press.
Meeker, Joseph. 1974. The Comedy of Survival. New York: Charles Scribner's Sons.
Mehra, Jagdish. 1973. The Physicist's Conception of Nature. Boston: D. Reidel Publishing Co.
Merchant, Carolyn. 1980. The Death of Nature: Women, Ecology, and the Scientific Revolution. San Francisco: Harper & Row.
Merleau-Ponty, M. 1964. The Primacy of Perception. J. Edie, ed. Evanston, IL: Northwestern University Press.
Merleau-Ponty, Maurice. 1968. The Visible and the Invisible. Translated by A. Lingis. Evanston, Illinois: Northwestern University Press.
Merriam, Thomas. 1977. The Disenchantment of the World. The Ecologist, Vol 7, Pp. 22-29.
Midgley, Mary. 1989. Wisdom Information & Wonder. New York: Routledge.
Mill, John S. 1963. Collected Works. 5 Vols. Toronto: University of Toronto Press.
Miller, George. 1956. The magic number seven plus or minus two. Psych. Rev. 63:81-97.
Miller, Jr. G. Tyler. 1992. Living in the Environment. Belmont, CA: Wadsworth Publishing Co.
Mollison, Bill. 1988. Permaculture: A Designers' Manual. Tyalgum, Aus.: Tagari Pubs.
Montaigne, Michel de. 1958. Complete Essays. Stanford: Stanford University Press.
Montesquieu. 1949. De l'Esprit des Lois (The Spirit of the Laws).
Moran, Emilio F., ed. 1990. The Ecosystem Approach to Anthropology. Ann Arbor, MI: University

of Michigan Press.

More, Thomas. 1982. Utopia. London: Penguin Books.

Morgan, Conway Lloyd. 1925. Emergent Evolution. New York: Henry Holt and Co.

Morris, Richard and Michael W. Fox. 1978. Animal Rights and Human Ethics. Washington: Acropolis Books.

Mourelatos, A. P. D., ed. 1974. The Pre-Socratics. Garden City, New York: Anchor Press/ Doubleday.

Mumford, Lewis. 1922. The Story of Utopias. New York: Boni and Liveright.

Mumford, Lewis. 1956. The Transformation of Man. New York: Harper and Row.

Mumford, Lewis. 1961. The City in History: Its Origins, Its Transformations, and Its Prospects. New York: Harcourt Brace and World.

Mumford, Lewis. 1966. The Myth of the Machine. Technics and human development. New York: Harcourt, Brace & World, 1966.

Mumford, Lewis. 1973. Interpretations and Forecasts: 1922-1972. New York: Harcourt, Brace, Jovanovitch.

Munson, R., ed. 1971. Man and nature: Philosophy. In: Issues in Biology. New York: Dell Publishing Co.

Neihardt, J.G. 1959. Black Elk Speaks. New York: Pocket Books.

Myers, Norman. 1984. The Primary Source. New York: Norton. Myers, Norman. 1984. Gaia: An Atlas of Planet Management. Doubleday and Company, Garden City, New York.

Naess, Arne. 1972. The shallow and the deep, long-range ecology movement. A summary. Inquiry, 16: 95-100

Naess. Arne. 1974. Gandhi and Group Conflict Oslo: Universitets forlaget.

Naess, Arne. 1987. Okologi, Samfunn og Livsstil (Norwegian version, later published as Ecology Community and Lifestyle. New York: Cambridge University Press).

Needleman, Jacob. 2003. Sense of the Cosmos. New York: Monkfish.

Nettle, Daniel and Suzanne Romaine. 2000. Vanishing Voices: The Extinction of the World's Languages. New York: Oxford University Press.

Nicolis, G., and Prigogine, I. 1977. Self-organization in Non-equilibrium Structures. New York: Wiley.

Norberg-Schulz, C. 1971. Existence Space and Architecture. New York: Praeger.

Norberg-Schulz, C. 1980. Genius Loci. London: Academy Editions.

Northrup, F. S. (in Morris and Fox).

Odum, Eugene P. 1970. ``Optimum population and environment: A Georgian microcosm.'' Current History 58:355-366.

Odum, Eugene P. 1971. Fundamentals of Ecology. 3rd Edition. Philadelphia: Wm. B. Saunders.

Odum, Howard T. and Elisabeth C. Odum. 1981. Energy Basis for Man and Nature. New York: McGraw Hill.

Odum, William. 1988. Predicting ecosystem development following creation and restoration of wetlands. In J. Zelazny and J. S. Feierabend, eds., Increasing Our Wetland Resources. Washington: National Wildlife Federation Proceedings.

Oliver, Paul. 1997. Encyclopedia of Vernacular Architecture of the World. New York: Cambridge University Press.

Olson, Steve. 2003. Mapping Human History. Boston: Mariner Books.

Ong, Walter J. 1967. In the Human Grain. New York: MacMillan Co.

Ophuls, William. 1977. Ecology and the Politics of Scarcity. San Francisco: W. H. Freeman & Co.

Ornstein, R., ed. 1973. The Nature of Human Consciousness. San Francisco: Freeman.

Orr, David W. 2004. The Nature of Design. New York: Oxford University Press.
Otten, C., ed. 1971. Anthropology and Art. Garden City, New York: American Museum of Natural History.
Owings, N. A. 1969. The American Aesthetic. New York: Harper & Row. P
Pagels, H. 1982. The Cosmic Code: Quantum Physics as the Language of Nature. New York: Simon and Schuster.
Palumbi, Steven R. 2001. The Evolution Explosion. New York: Norton.
Partridge, Eric. 1983. Origins. New York: Greenwich House
Passmore, J. 1974. Man's Responsibility for Nature: Ecological Problems and Western Tradition. NC: Duckworth.
Peate, I. C., ed. 1930. Studies in Regional Consciousness and Environment. Oxford: Oxford University Press.
Peirce, C. S. 1955. Selected Writings of Peirce. Edited by J. Buchler. New York: Dover Publishing Company.
Pepper, Stephen C. 1958. Sources of Value. Berkeley: University of California Press.
Pepper, S. 1961. World Hypotheses. Berkeley: University of California Press.
Perry, D. A., T. Bell, and M. P. Amaranthus. 1992. "Mycorrhizal fungi in mixed species forests and other tales of positive feedback, redundancy, and stability," in M. Cannell, D. Malcom, and P. Robertson, eds. The Ecology of Mixed-species Stands of Trees. Oxford: Blackwell Scientific.
Perry, D. A. 1995. Forest Ecosystems. Baltimore: Johns Hopkins University Press.
Pfeffer, R. 1972. Nietzsche: Disciple of Dionysius. Lewisburg: Bucknell University Press.
Piaget, J. 1968. Logical Thinking in Children. I. Sigel, comp. New York: Holt, Rinehart and Winston. Page 6.
Pimm, Stuart L. 1991. The Balance of Nature. Chicago: University of Chicago Press.
Pirie, N. W. 1976. Food Resources. London: Pelican Books.
Planck, Max. 1959. The New Science. New York: Norton.
Plato. 1961. The Collected Dialogues of Plato. E. Hamilton and H. Cairns, eds. trans. L. Cooper et al. New York: Pantheon Books.
Poe, Edgar Allan. 1909. The Works of Edgar Allan Poe. 10 Vols. New York: The Century Co.
Poincare, Henri. 1905. Science and Hypothesis. trans. W. S. G. London: The Walter Scott Publishing Co.
Polunin, Nicholas, ed. 1980. Growth without Ecodisasters? New York: Wiley.
Polunin, Nicholas and John H. Burnett. Eds. Maintenance of the Biosphere: Proceedings of the Third International Conference on Environmental Future. New York: St. Martin's.
Ponge, Francis. 1972. The Voice of Things. B. Archer, ed. New York: McGraw-Hill Book Company.
Popper, K.R. and J.C. Eccles. 1977. The Self and Its Brain. Berlin: Springer-Verlag.
Popper, K. R. 1982. The place of mind in nature. R.Q. Elvee, ed. Mind in Nature. San Francisco: Harper & Row
Portmann, Adolf. 1964. New Paths in Biology. New York: Harper & Row.
Prabhu, R. and U. Rao, eds. 1946. The Mind of Mahatma Gandhi Madras: Oxford University Press.
Prehoda, Robert W. 1967. Designing the Future. Philadelphia: Chilton.
Pribram, Karl. 1977. Problems Concerning... In: Consciousness and the Brain, Globus et al., eds. New York: Plenum Press.
Price, David H. 1990. Atlas of World Cultures. London: Sage Publishers.
Prigogine, Ilya. 1980. From Being to Becoming. San Francisco: Freeman.
Radcliffe-Brown, A.R. 1952. Structure and Function in Primitive Society. London: Cohen and West.
Ramsay, William and Claude Anderson. 1972. "Economic analysis: medication for ecosystems,"

Managing the Environment: An Economic Primer. New York: Basic.
Rappoport, Amos. 1969. House Form and Culture. Englewood Cliffs: Prentice-Hall.
Rapport, DJ 1995. "Ecosystem health: An emerging integrative science." In Rapport, DJ, CL Gaudet, and P. Calow, eds. Evaluating and Monitoring the health of large scale ecosystems. pp. 5-34. Heidelberg: Springer.
Rapport, DJ, C Thorpe, and HA Regier, 1979. Ecosystem medicine. Bul Ecol Soc Am 60:180-182.
Reichel-Dolmatoff, G. 1977. Cosmology as Ecological Analysis: A view from the Rain Forest. The Ecologist, Vol 7, Pp. 4-11.
Reinheimer, Herman. 1913. Evolution by Co-operation: A Study in Bio-economics. London: Kegan Paul.
Relph, Edward. 1976. Place and Placelessness. London: Pion.
Riedl, Rupert. 1978. Order in Living Organisms. Translated by R. P. Jafferies. New York: J. Wiley & Sons.
Rifkin, J. 1982. Algeny: The Last Magic (prepublication copy).
Rodin, L.E., N.I. Bazilevich, and N.N. Rozov. 1975. ``Productivity of the world's main ecosystems.'' IN: Productivity of World Ecosystems. Washington, D.C.: National Academy of Sciences.
Rodman, John. 1977. "The Liberation of Nature?" Inquiry 20:83-145
Rodman, John. 1977. Theory and practice in the environmental movement: Notes toward an ecology of experience. In: The Search for Absolute Values in a Changing World. Tarrytown, New York: International Cultural Foundation.
Rolston, III, H. 1983. "Values Gone Wild." Inquiry 26:181-207.
Rorty, Richard. 1982. Mind as ineffable. In Mind in Nature, ed. R. Elvee. Harper and Row, San Francisco, p. 88.
Ross, W., ed. 1952. The Works of Aristotle. Oxford: Clarendon.
Roszak, Theodore. 1972. Where the Wasteland Ends. New York: Harper and Row.
Roszak, Theodore. 1979. Person/Planet. New York: Harper and Row.
Rothenberg J. and G. Quasha, eds. 1974. America A Prophecy. New York: Vintage Books.
Rudolfsky, Bernard. 1965. Streets for People. New York: Doubleday.
Ruesch, Jergen and Weldon Kees. 1956. Nonverbal Communication. Berkeley: University of California Press.
Sahlins, Marshall. 1968. Tribesmen. Englewood Cliffs: Prentice Hall
Sahlins, Marshall. 1972. Stone Age Economics. Chicago: Aldine Publishing.
Salk, Jonas. ND. Survival of the Wisest. New York: Harper and Row.
Sapir, E. 1949. Selected Writings of Edward Sapir in Language, Culture and Personality. D. Mandelbaum, ed. Berkeley: University of California Press.
Sarfatti, J., and B. Toben. 1975. Space-Time and Beyond. New York: Dutton.
Schaller, G.B. 1972. The Serengeti Lion. Chicago: University of Chicago Press.
Scheler, M.F. 1954. The Nature of Sympathy. Tr. by P. Heath. London: Routledge and Kegan Paul, Ltd.
Schleiden, M. and Schwann, T. (see Maynard Smith).
Schrodinger, Erwin. 1946. What is Life? The Physical Aspect of the Living Cell. New York: Macmillan.
Schumacher, E.F. 1973. Small Is Beautiful. New York: Harper and Row.
Schweitzer, Albert. 1949. Out of My Life and Thought. New York: Henry Holt and Co.
Schweitzer, Albert. 1957. The Philosophy of Civilization. Translated by C.T. Campion. New York: Macmillan Co.
Searles, H. 1962. The role of the nonhuman environment. Landscape (Winter 1961-1962):31-34.

Sears, Paul. 1957. The Ecology of Man. Eugene: Oregon State System.

Segall, Marshall H, D. T. Campbell, and M. Herkovits. The Influence of Culture on Human perception.

Sharp, Henry. Comparative ethnology of the wolf and the Chipewyan. In Man and Wolf. H. Frank, Ed. Dordrecht: Dr. W. Junk.

Sheldrake, Rupert. 1981. A New Science of Life: The Hypothesis of Formative Causation. Los Angeles: J. P. Tarcher, Inc.

Shepard, Paul. 1967. Man in the Landscape. New York: Alfred Knopf.

Shepard, Paul and D. McKinley, eds. 1969. The Subversive Science. Boston: Houghton Mifflin.

Shepard, Paul. 1974. Animal rights and human rites. The North American Review Winter, p. 35.

Shepard, Paul. 1978. Thinking Animals. New York: Viking Press.

Shepard, Paul. 1982. Nature and Madness. San Francisco: Sierra Club Books.

Short, John Rennie. 2001. Global Dimensions. London: Reaktion Books

Simmons, I. G. 1989. Changing the Face of the Earth. New York: Basil Blackwell.

Simon, Herbert A. 1969. The Sciences of the Artificial. Third Ed. Cambridge: MIT Press.

Simpson, G. G. 1944. Tempo and Mode in Evolution. New York: Hafner Publishing Co.

Singer, Peter. 1981. The Expanding Circle: Ethics and Sociobiology. New York: Farrar, Strauss & Giroux. (Page 62).

Singer, S. Fred, ed. 1971. Is There an Optimum Level of Population? New York: McGraw-Hill.

Skolimowski, Henryk. 1981. Ecophilosophy. Boston: Marion Boyars

Slater, Phillip. 1974. Earthwalk. New York: Bantam Books.

Smith, Maynard J. 1968. Mathematical Ideas Biology. Cambridge: Cambridge University Press.

Smithsonian Editors. Annual II. The Fitness of Man's Environment.

Smuts, J. 1926. Holism and Evolution. Ann Arbor, MI: University Microfilms.

Snyder, Gary. 1969. Earth House Hold. New York: New Directions. P. 105.

Snyder, Gary. 1995. A Place in Space. Washington: Counterpoint.

Soleri, Paolo. 1969. Arcology: The City in the Image of Man. Cambridge: The MIT Press.

Soleri, Paolo. 1978. A response to "Fields of Danger". The North American Review, Spring: pp. 71-72

Soleri, Paolo. 1983. The Food Chain: A Celebration. Scottsdale, Arizona. Sorokin, Pitirim. Social and Cultural Dynamics.

Soule, Michael and Wilcox, B. A., eds. 1980. Conservation Biology: An Evolutionary-Ecological Perspective. Sunderland, MA: Sinauer Associates.

Soule, Michael. 1986. Conservation Biology: The Science of Scarcity and Diversity. Sunderland: Sinauer Associates, Inc.

Speck, W. A. 1975. Mandeville and the Eutopia seated in the brain. In Primer, Irwin, ed. Mandeville Studies (1670-1733). The Hague: Martinus Nijhoff.

Spencer, Herbert. 1969 (1876-1896). Principles of Sociology. London: Macmillan.

Speth, James G. 2009. The Bridge at the End of the World. New Haven: Yale.

Stanley, Steven. 1981. The New Evolutionary Timetable: Fossils, Genes and the Origin of Species. New York: Basic Books.

Stevens, P. S. 1974. Patterns in Nature. Boston: Little Brown Co.

Stevens, Wallace. 1974. The Collected Poems of Wallace Stevens. New York: Alfred A. Knopf.

Stock, Doroty and Herbert Thelen. Emotional Dynamics and Group Culture.

Stokes, Kenneth M. 1994. Man and the Biosphere: Toward a Coevolutionary Political Economy Armonk New York: ME Sharpe.

Stone, Christopher D. 1974. Should Trees Have Standing? New York: Avon Books.

Stulman, Julius and Ervin Laszlo. 1973. Emergent Man. New York: Gordon and Breach.

Stratton, G.M. 1896. Some preliminary experiments on vision without inversion of the retinal image. Psych. Rev. 3:611-617.

Susser, Bernard. 1981. Existence and Utopia: The Social and Political Thought of Martin Buber. Rutherford: Fairleigh Dickinson University Press.

Szekielda, Karl-Heinz. 1988. Satellite Monitoring of the Earth. New York: John Wiley.

Tainter, Joseph A. 1988. The Collapse of Complex Societies. Cambridge: Cambridge University Press.

Tansley, A.G. 1935. The use and abuse of vegetational concepts and terms. Ecology 16:284-307.

Tax, Sol. Ed. 1960. Evolution After Darwin. Chicago: University of Chicago Press.

Tax, Sol, ed. Horizons of Anthropology. NC: NP.

Taylor, Gordon Rattray. 1968. The Biological Time Bomb. New York: The World Publishing Company.

Thakur, S.C. 1978. A Touch of Animism. In Man and Nature. G.F. McLean, ed. Calcutta: Oxford University Press.

Theobald, Robert. 1968. An alternative future for America. Chicago: Swallow Press, 1968.

Tinbergen, Jan, Coordinator. 1976. Reshaping the International Order, Report of the Club of Rome. New York: Dutton.

Thines, George. 1977. Phenomenology and the Science of Behavior. London: George Allen & Unwin.

Thom, Rene. 1975. Structural Stability and Morphogenesis: An Outline of a General Theory of Models. trans. D.C. Fowler. Reading: W.A. Benjamin.

Thomas, David H. 1979. Archaeology. New York: Holt, Rinehart and Winston.

Thomas, Keith. 1983. Man and the Natural World. New York: Pantheon

Thomas, Lewis. 1975. Lives of a Cell. New York: Bantam.

Thompson, W. I. 1971. At the Edge of History. Harper & Row.

Thompson, W. I. 1974. Passages About Earth. New York: Harper and Row.

Thompson, W. I. 1976. Evil and World Order. New York: Harper and Row.

Thompson, W. I. 1981. The Time Falling Bodies Take to Light. New York: Harper and Row.

Tibbs, B. C. 1992. Industrial Ecology: An environmental agenda for industry, Whole Earth Review 77:4-19.

Todd, John. 1977. Towards a sacred ecology. In Earth's Answer. pp. 170-183. M. Katz et al., eds. New York: Harper & Row

Todd, N. J. and J. 1994. From Eco-Cities to Living Machines: Principles of Ecological Design. Berkeley: North Atlantic Books.

Toffler, Alvin. 1970. Future shock. New York: Random House.

Toynbee, Arthur J. Change and Habit. NC: NP.

Tuan, Yi-Fu. 1974. Topophilia: A Study of Environmental Perception, Attitudes, and Values. Englewood Cliffs: Prentice-Hall.

Tuan, Yi-Fu. 1995. Passing Strange and Wonderful. New York: Kodansha International.

Tucker, William. 1982. Is Nature Too Good for Us? Harper's (March).

Turnbull C.M. 1961. The Forest People: A Study of the Pygmies of the Congo. New York: Simon and Schuster.

Tylor, Edward B. 1871. Primitive Culture. London: Murray.

Tylor, E.B. 1958. The Origins of Culture. New York: Harper Torchbooks.

Uexkull, J. von. 1957. A Stroll Through the World of Animals and Men. Schiller, Claire, ed. 1957. IN: Instinctive Behavior. New York: International Universities Press Inc.

Ulanowicz, Robert E. 1986. Growth and Development: Ecosystems Phenomenology. New York: Springer-Verlag.
United Nations. 1993. "Combating Deforestation," in Earth Summit 92. Washington: United Nations.
Vaihinger, Hans. 1961. The Philosophy of As If. C. K. Ogden, trans,. Bloomington: Indiana University Press.
Varela, Francisco et al. 1974. Autopoiesis: The organization of living systems. Biosystems 5:187-196.
Varela, Francisco. 1978. Principles of Biological Autonomy. New York: North Holland.
Varela, Francisco. Laying down a path in walking. In Gaia: A Way of Knowing.
Vayda, Andrew P., ed. 1977. Environment and Cultural Behavior: Ecological Studies in Cultural Anthropology. Austin: Texas Press.
Vitousek, Paul M. 1992. Global environmental change. Ann Rev. Ecol and Syst. 23:1-14.
Wackernagel, M. and W. Rees. 1996. Our Ecological Footprint: Reducing Human Impact on the Earth. Gabriola Island, BC: New Society.
Waddington, C.H. 1960. The Nature of Life. New York: Atheneum.
Waddington, C.H., ed. 1969. Towards a Theoretical Biology. Chicago: Aldine Publishing Co.
Waddington, C.H. 1975. The Evolution of an Evolutionist Ithaca: Cornell University Press.
Wagner, Philip L. 1960. The Human Use of the Earth. Glencoe: Free Press.
Walsh, R. 1981. Towards an Ecology of Brain. Jamaica, New York: Spectrum Publishers.
Waltner-Toews, D. and E. Wall. 1997. Emergent perplexity: in search of post-normal questions for community and agroecosystem health. Soc Sci Med, 45(11):1741-9.
Warner, A. W., D. Morse, and T. E. Cooney. The Environment of Change.
Watson, Richard A. and Philip M. Smith. 1970. "The Limit: 500 Million." FOCUS/Midwest 7(49):40-42.
Weil, Simone. 1955. The Need for Roots. Boston: Beacon Press.
Weiss, Gerald. 1975. Campa Cosmology: The World of a Forest Tribe in South America. Anthropological papers, Vol. 52, Part 5, Pp. 217-588. New York: The American Museum of Natural History.
Weiss, P. A. 1973. The Science of Life. Mount Cisco, New York: Futura.
Weiss, P. 1967. One Plus One Does Not Equal two. In The Neurosciences: A Study Program. G.C. Quarton et al., eds. New York: Rockefeller University Press.
Weiss, P. 1969. The Living System: Determinism Stratified. In Beyond Reductionism: New Perspectives in the Life Sciences. A. Koestler and J. Smythies, eds. New York: The Macmillan Co.
Welch, Holmes. 1966. Taoism: The Parting of the Way. Revised ed. Boston: Beacon Press
Weltfish, Gene. 1965. The Lost Universe. New York: Basic Books.
Westermarck, Edward. 1912. The Origin and Development of the Moral Ideas. Vol. 1. London: Macmillan.
Westing, Arthur H. 1981. ``A world in balance.'' Environmental Conservation 8(3):177-183.
Wheeler, J., W. C. Misner, and K. Thorne. 1973. Gravitation. San Francisco: Freeman.
Wheelwright, P. 1962. Metaphor and Reality. Bloomington: Indiana University Press.
White, Leslie A. 1959. The Evolution of Culture. New York: McGraw Hill.
Whitehead, Alfred N. 1933. Adventures of Ideas. New York: Macmillan.
Whitehead, Alfred N. 1938. Modes of Thought. New York: Macmillan.
Whitehead, Alfred N. 1967. Science and the Modern World. New York: Free Press.
Whitehead, Alfred N. 1969. Process and Reality. New York: Free Press.
Whitehead, Alfred N. 1978. Process and Reality (corrected edition). New York: Free Press.
Whittaker, R.H., F.H. Bormann, G.E. Likens, and T.G. Siccama. 1974. ``The Hubbard Brook eco-

system study: Forest biomass and production." Ecological Monographs 44:233-252.

Whyte, L.L. 1965. Internal Factors in Evolution. New York: Braziller.

Wiener, Norbert. 1962. Cybernetics. Cambridge: MIT Press.

Wigner, E. 1963. The problem of measurement. Am J. Phys. 31: np.

Willard, B. E. et al. 1977. "Ethics of Biospheral Survival: A dialogue." In Growth Without Ecodisasters? pp. 505-535. N. Polunin, ed. New York: John Wiley & Sons

Wilson, E.O. 1975. Sociobiology: The New Synthesis. Cambridge: Belknap Press.

Wilson, E.O. 1984. Biophilia. Cambridge: Harvard University Press.

Wingo, Lowdon. ed. Cities and Space: The Future Use of Urban Land. NC: NP.

Wittbecker, A.E. 1970. Ordering Spaces and Living Places: Aesthetic and Ecological Dimensions of Place. (Printed Bound Essay). Newark: Shamrock Press.

Wittbecker, A.E. 1970. Eutopias: A Poetic Commonwealth of Earth. (Printed Bound Essay). Newark: Shamrock Press.

Wittbecker, A.E. 1976. "The psychology of catastrophe: Environmental deterioration and rapid social change." Proc. Marsh Inst. 1:1-17.

Wittbecker, A.E. 1983. "Human populations related to ecosystem productivities." Contributed paper, Ecol. Soc. Am. annual meeting, Grand Forks.

Wittbecker, A.E. 1983. "Ecology, mythology, and holopoetic culture." Montreal: Proceedings XVII World Congress Phil.

Wittbecker, A.E. 1983. "Quantitative determinations of minimum wilderness areas for the planet as a whole." Contributed paper, 3rd World Wilderness Congress, Findhorn.

Wittbecker, A.E. 1985. "Ecophilia: Animal welfare, wilderness preservation, and the metaphor of home." Advances in Animal Welfare. 8:64-73 (accepted).

Wittbecker, A.E. 1985. "Vastitas ipsa: Wilderness Itself." Proc. Marsh Inst. 10:3-32.

Wittbecker, A.E. 1986. "Palouse Ecosystem Restoration." 4th International Congress of Ecology, Syracuse.

Wittbecker, A.E. 1986. "The role of deep ecology in wilderness preservation." Contributed paper, 4th International Congress of Ecology, Syracuse.

Wittbecker, A.E. 1986. "The place of human society in wilderness." The Trumpeter. 3(3):34-38.

Wittbecker, A.E. 1987. "Design and management of common area reserves: Sonoran desert model." Contributed paper, 4th World Wilderness Congress, Colorado.

Wittbecker, A.E. 1989. "Nature as self." The Trumpeter 6(3):77-81.

Wittbecker, A.E. 1991. "An empowered United Nations: Proposals for cooperation and survival." Common Voice: 1(1):1-8.

Wittbecker, A.E. 1992. "Drawings & Discussion of a Proposed Palouse Arcology." Proc. Marsh Inst. 17:44-61.

Wittbecker, A.E. 1992. "Setting community limits for long-term stability." International Forum for Biophilosophy, Budapest.

Wittbecker, A.E. 1993. "Boreal region wilderness limits." 5th World Wilderness Congress. Tromsø.

Wittbecker, A.E. 1994. "Ecosystem Medicine in Forest Ecosystems," Ecoforestry Lecture.

Wittbecker, A.E. 1995. "Saving common places: The Palouse," Wild Earth 5(1):54-58.

Wittbecker, A.E. 1995. "Limits and Goals for communities on the North Slope of Alaska," Pan Ecology 10(2):1-14.

Wittbecker, A.E. 1999. "Varieties of interaction in nature: Exploitation, disturbance, and interference," The Trumpeter (athabascau.ca/trumpeter).

Wittbecker, A.E. 1999. "Forestry as Ecosystem Medicine and Poetic Activity," Closing Address, Forests for the Future, Vancouver Island.

Wittbecker, A.E. 2001. "Ecological Thought Experiments" Sofia Echo Vol. 5, Issue 31, Aug 3-9, p. 12 (1st of 12-part series).

Woodwell, George M. and Robert Whittaker. 1968. ``Primary production in terrestrial ecosystems." American Zoologist 8:19-30.

Woodwell, George M. and Robert Whittaker. 1975. Primary Productivity of the Biosphere. New York: Springer-Verlag.

Wright, Robert. Nonzero: The Logic of Human Destiny. 2000. New York: Vintage.

Wynne-Edwards, V. C. Animal Dispersion in Relation to Social Behavior.

Young, L. B. Population in Perspective.

Zadeh, L. A. 1965. "Fuzzy Sets" Information and Control Vol. 8:338-353.

Zajonc, Robert. 1980. Feeling and thinking: Preferences need no inferences. American Psychologist 35:151-175.

Zeleny, Milan, ed. 1980. Autopoiesis: A Theory of Living Organisms. New York: North Holland.

Zonneveld, I. S. and RTT Forman, eds. 1990. Changing Landscapes: An Ecological perspective. New York: Springer-Verlag.

9.4. *Biography*

During a brief career in astrophysics and astronomy at the University of Arizona, where he worked on mathematical models of stars and on spectrometric analysis, Alan Wittbecker spent his daylight hours climbing trees and trying to track mountain lions; his companions were a mouse and squirrel, who shared his trailer near the observatory on Mount Lemon.

Encouraged by research budget cuts to pursue a different direction, Wittbecker went to graduate school in psychology, anthropology, philosophy, and ecology. As a graduate student in 1970, he was a cofounder of the G. P. Marsh Institute for Research in Ecology, where he worked for 22 years, including three separate years as Director (the position rotated annually to share responsibilities). He worked on a wide variety of projects, from forest monitoring and ecosystem restoration to country-wide wolf monitoring, in many countries, including Bulgaria, Canada, Mexico, Norway, and Russia. When funding was in short supply, he worked in other occupations, including librarian, systems engineer, editor, graphic artist, typesetter, housepainter, television repairman, cook, swimming coach, carpenter, clinical psychologist for a drug abuse clinic, Austin Healy auto mechanic, tree-planter, and college instructor.

In 1991, Wittbecker founded SynGeo ArchiGraph, a firm specializing in global and regional designs; he created designs for several bioregions, as well as international frameworks. A year later he set up the educational program for the Ecoforestry Institute, becoming an Instructor in 1994, journal Editor in 1995, and Director from 1997 to 2006. He has worked on public and private forests from British Columbia to California, and on wildlife projects, from Siberia to Norway.

A veteran of the U.S. Air Force, Wittbecker is also a returned Peace Corps Volunteer from Bulgaria, where he monitored wolves in the Central Balkan Mountains. He has used his education and interests to explore a spectrum of ecological applications, from research on forest pests—larch casebearers, cedar powderworms, coyotes, and bears—to the political implications of the protection of species and habitats.

When not engaged in preservation activities, he enjoys walking, swimming, reading, and drawing, at the Altazor forest in western Idaho. To discuss any of these essays with him, contact him at home@eutopias.net.

9.5. Index

Aborigine people, 74, 127, 138
Action, 178
   coordinated, 260
   immediate, 197, 200-4
Adams, John, 114
Adaptation, 22-3, 32-3, 39, 89, 94, 133-4, 259
advertising, 45, 115, 231, 246-8
agencies
   GU, 300
Agency
   energy, 231
   health, 231
   research, 232
   technology, 232
Agriculture, 87, 104, 114
   advantages of, 115
   disadvantages, 119
   ecological changes from, 115
   population, 118
   related changes, 116
Allen, Richard, 241
anarchy, 332
Annan, K., 228
Aranda people, 180
Arbib, M., 321
Aristotle, 136, 142
Asoka, 241
Association of Nations, 266
Augustine, St., 60, 111, 113

Bacon, Francis, 60
Bangladesh, 253
Bantu people, 317
Barber, R., 152
Barnett, 29
Barnett, A., 153
Bateson, Gregory, 43, 68, 139, 143, 187
Bellah, Robert, 191
Bentham, J.,136
Berger, 38
Berry, W., 76
Bessarabia, 229
bigness, 13
Bohm, David, 169
Bookchin, Murray, 47-8, 141
Boulding, K., 54, 71, 122, 155, 192, 204, 247
Boyd, Richard, 30
Bryson, R., 67, 195
Bunge, Mario, 18
Burke, Edmund, 59, 153

Callenbach, Ernest, 48, 59
Campa people, 37, 136, 152
cancer, 120, 147, 231, 257
   as metaphor, 75-6
capitalism, 21, 25, 43-6, 77, 102-4, 116-7, 254
carrying capacity, 40, 67-70, 79-81, 92, 99, 129, 258
Carson. R., 108
Cassandra, 197
catastrophe, 32, 76-9, 105, 119, 143, 248, 250, 264
   kinds of, 191-8
   meaning of, 193
Catastrophic Measures, 268
Catton, William, 26, 194
centralization, 124
challenges, 98, 114
   environmental, 79
   change
     fast, 256
characteristics, 43
Charter
   GU, 273
chiefs, 147
China, 269
Chipewyan people, 257
Chisholm, R., 104
chreod, 32-3, 63
Churchill, W., 23
cities, 126
   changes from, 130
   sizes, 126
citizenship, 184
city, 120, See Urban
   as trap, 126
   as trigger, 125
   changes from, 123
   ecosystem, 121
city Patterns, 121
city population, 122
civilization, 123, 163
Clarke, 22
clothing, 53
Club of Rome, 13, 195, 200
Cobb, J.B., Jr., 26, 105, 145, 199, 214, 222, 258
co-constrained construction, 42, 82
collapse, 99, 101, 102
colonialism, 95
Commission on Earth, 203, 239-41
Commission on Cultures & Religions, 203, 244
commons, 10, 126, 186, 200, 209, 231, 239
   tragedy of, 84
communication, 22, 104, 160

communism, 153
community, 31
compartmentalization, 186
competition, 67
conflict, 67, 73, 165, 251
    international, 300
    group, 166
connectivity, 127
conservation programs, 255
consistency, 181
constancy, 42
conviviality, 180
cooperation, 73, 174
corporations, 162
    rechartering, 307
cosmologies, 190
course, 80
courts, 309
culture, 36, 37
    definition, 38, 39
    effectiveness of, 49
    function of, 49
    functions of, 47, 48
    global, 55, 56
    global, upside, 57
    rules of, 108
    strengths of, 50
    weaknesses of, 50
cultures, 114, 232, 243
cycles
    biogeochemical, 85

Daly, H., 105-6, 148, 199, 218, 222-3
Dansereau, P., 27, 149, 152
Darin-Drabkin, 69
Darwin, C., 69, 70, 182
Dasmann, Ray, 36, 179
de Chardin, T., 47
de Spinoza, B., 56
Deep Ecology, 181
deme, 175
democracy, 143, 150
    changes to, 150
    differences in, 152
    dissatisfactions with, 151
Desana people, 49
Design
    Ecological, 315
Dewey, John, 140
Dickens, C., 186
dictator, 145
differences, 81

disarmament, 70, 214, 252, 269
    sudden, 270
    nuclear, 269
disaster Psychology, 257
distribution, 132
disturbances, 240
dominance, 90, 92, 97, 161
domiture, 330
Douglas, M., 30
Doxiadis, C., 181
drought, 85, 100
Drucker, Peter, 103, 142, 147
Dubos, Rene, 183, 196, 260
Dyson, Freeman, 16, 37

Earth Inc., 233-5
Earth parks, 242
Earth Summit, 170
East Timor, 164, 169, 171
Eckholm, E., 9, 194
ecology, 22, 68
economic
    limits, 140
economics, 130
economies
    Command, 132
    Market, 133
    Social, 133
    Tributary, 133
economy
    market assumptions, 135
    stationary, 195
ecosystem, 23, 82
    agricultural, 115
ecosystems, 122
Einstein, Albert, 16, 35
Eisenhower, D., 187
Eisenhower, M., 51
Eliot, T.S., 44
Ember, Carol, 128
Environmental Court, 309
Equity Measures, 272
ethics, 169
    ecological, 171
Ethiopia, 152
eutopian framework, 207, 340
eutopian plan, 35
eutopian structure, 35
eutopias, 35, 74, 75, 76, 77, 200, 202, 325
Evernden, N., 86
evil, 108, 109, 110, 111, 112
Executive Branch, 158

experiments, 18

failure of nerve, 263
fallacy
    economic, 139
fees & Tolls, 293
fertility, 118
flexibility, 41, 337
Fox, M.W., 171
framework
    global, 58
France, 275
Franklin, Ben, 107
Franklin, Jerry, 314
Freud, S., 164
frontier, 160
Fuller, R.B., 14, 34, 284

Galicia, 229
General Assembly
    UN, 211
Georgescu-Rogen, N., 196
Germany, 275
gigatrends, 10
    positive, 17
global accounts, 296
global ecological design, 271
global ecology, 35
global Framework, 235
global Government, 249, 342
    can do, 327
global Threats, 297
Global Union, 74, 264, 274
    responsibilities, 239
Global Union of Commonwealths, 236
Global Union Police Force, 246
globalism, 155
goals
    global ecological, 272
good Places
    properties of, 178
good Society
    properties of, 172
goodness, 108
government, 32, 78, 172, 184, 185
    eutopian form, 203
    eutopian, properties, 204, 205
    forms of, 156
    international, 265
    participation in, 208
    scale, 162
growth, 160, 193

economic, 134, 137
    vs. development, 137
GU offices, 308

Habermas, Jurgen, 48
Haeckel, E., 204
Hall, 37
Hanunoo people, 48
Hardin, G., 18, 24, 107, 160, 197, 244, 245
Harding, 42
harmony, 74, 177
Harris, Marvin, 146
Harvey, W., 322
Hayek, F.A., 187
health, 83, 182, 337
Hegel, 36
Henry, Jules, 323
Hippocratic oath, 325
Hong Kong, 88
Howard, E., 61
humanity as agent, 96
Hutterite people, 92, 161
Huxley, Aldous, 61, 62, 67
Huxley, Julian, 237
Huxley, Thomas, 164
hyperadaptivity, 57

identity, 81, 179
Illich, Ivan, 175
image
    collective, 62
images, 72
Imanishi, K., 36
immediate Action, 259
immigration, 169
incorporation of planet, 303, 304
India, 328
individuality, 178
industrialization, 105
intensification, 104, 105, 124
International Body
    strengths, 230
International Court of Justice
    UN, 212
International Monetary Fund, 213
International Union, 230
inventory creation, 311
Iraq, 328
Ireland, 328
Israel, 269
Ituri people, 47

Jackson, Wes, 28
Jacobs, Jane, 125, 138
Jantsch, Eric, 88, 255
Jefferson, T., 142, 149, 152
Judicial Branch, 158
    International, 309
justice, 198

kinship, 91, 234
Kluckhohn, C., 38
Koestler, A., 41
Kohr, L., 30, 89, 335
Kroeber, A., 38
Kropotkin, 60
Kuna people, 201
!Kung San people, 48
Kurdish people, 153, 190

landscapes, 237
languages, 317
Laszlo, Ervin, 17, 137, 251
law, 157
    global, 274
law of the maximum, 137
leadership, 32, 78, 144, 192
Legislative Branch, 157
Lenin, V., 154
Leopold, Aldo, 17, 170, 191
licenses
    international, 291
    licensing, 292
Lichfield, 89
Limerick, P., 156
limits, 31, 32, 33
    of politics, 32
Lincoln, A., 149
local, 31
Lovelock, J., 18
loyalty, 176

Machiavelli, N., 76, 202
MacLaren, Leon, 159
Malthus, T., 90
Manuel, F., 61
Mao Zedong, 154
Martino, J., 245
Marx, Karl, 74, 92, 132, 150, 154, 193, 234, 253
Marxism, 133
Masai people, 181
Maslow, A., 25, 61, 181
maturity, 44

maximum sustainable yield, 242
Mayan people, 86
McArthur, R., 84
McLuhan, M., 111
McNamara, R., 252
Mead, M., 260
Meggers, Betty, 42
membership, 9
    international, 275
    membership Dues
    GU, 275
Mesarovic and Pestel, 193
Mesopotamia, 120
metaphor, 38, 135, 204, 322
    root, 63
method, 172
Mill, J.S., 91, 136, 194
Miller, S. 20
Milton, John, 88
miniaturization, 56, 104
Mollison, 17
momentum, 16
monarchy, 147
money fetishism, 136
monitoring
    ecoregions, 313
    global, 295, 311, 312
    ocean, 313
    space, 314
Monod, J., 110
More, Thomas, 59
Mundurucu people, 93
Murdock, G. P., 53
myth, 322
mythology, 58

nationalism, 68
nations, 78
    size, 249
    size, limits, 229, 250
    status of, 266
NATO, 217
Navajo people, 204
Navy, US, 29
Nembi people, 51
Nepal, 265
Netherlands, 88
Nez Perce people, 93
Nicaragua, 245
nonviolence, 246
North Korea, 269

O'Neill, 14
O'Reilly, 27
Odum, E., 111, 238
Office of International Trade, 310
Ombudsman
    International, 319
openness, 81
operation costs, 294
Ophuls, W., 183
Orwell, George, 60, 61
Osborn, Earl, 252, 270

Paine, Thomas, 230
Papanek, V., 175
Parkinson, T., 188
participation, 151, 209
peace, 74, 247
peacebuilding, 216
peacekeeping, 216
peacemaking, 215
Peirce, C.S., 20
Pepper, S., 62, 63
Picasso, P., 322
planetization, 54
planning
    Ecological, 315
    Global, 294
plans, 107
    ecological, 189
Plato, 60, 198, 256
poetry, 322, 343
police Force
    GU, 233
    Global, 299
politics, 142, 143
    ecological, goals, 183
    functions of, 159
    limits of, 191
    myths of, 154
Polynesians, 62
Popper, Karl, 325
population, 89
    human, growth, 87
    human, limits, 192
population growth, 118
poverty, 140
practices, 44, 45, 46
preservation
    Hotspots, 315
Language, 317
president, 145
prime Minister, 145

principle of plenitude, 63
principles, 43, 44, 344
productivity, 83
progress, 68
properties, 45
    of culture, 40
    of ecosystems, 80
    of systems, 80
system, 40

questioning, 23, 25, 30

reciprocity, 131
redistribution, 132
reduce Losses, 327
Reich, C., 13
Reichel-Dolmatoff, G., 50
religions, 318
rent
    on Global Areas, 275
republic, 148, 149
research
    long-term, 302
restoration, 316
    global, 296
    large Ecosystem, 316
revolution, 237, 333
richness, 179
rights, 196, 197, 262
    TDRs, 186
Roosevelt, F.D., 156
root metaphor, 321
Rorty, Richard, 322
Ruthenia, 229

safety, 163
Sahelia region, 87
Saint-Simon, 60
Salk, Jonas, 341
Samuelson, E., 137
Saxony, 244
scale, 30, 46, 72
Schiller, F., 248
Schumacher, F., 111, 175, 176
Schweitzer, A., 179
Searles, Harold, 180
Sears, 22
security, 32, 162
Security Council, 296
    UN, 211
self-assessment GU, 308
self-extension, 173

Shakespeare, W., 322
Shepard, Paul, 196, 222, 238, 259
Simons, Henry, 335
simplicity, 21, 47, 56, 83, 159, 198, 248, 251
Sinhalese people, 69, 74, 177
Skinner, B.F., 47
slavery, 36, 70, 72-74, 92, 116
Smith, Adam, 10, 49, 104-5, 142
Smith Russell, 15
Snow, C.P., 86
Snyder, Gary, 59
Socrates, 19, 20, 150, 262
Soleri, Paolo, 15, 141
Sorokin, P., 53, 105, 188, 191
specialization, 116, 129
speed, 14
St. Barbe Baker, R., 186
stability, 19, 24, 32-4, 62-6, 69, 91, 138, 258
standards, 21-4, 35-6, 50, 96, 104-5, 160-3, 236
status
    cultural, 90
Stone, C., 15, 151
Stoneking, Mark, 41
structure
    GU, 273
symbiosis, 170
systems, 21

taboos, 46, 53
Tamil people, 88
Taureg people, 47
tax
    carbon, 280
    use, 281
Tax Court, 310
taxation
    GU power of, 274
taxes
    adjustment, 286
    adjustment, agricultural, 288
    adjustment, pollution, 287
    being or Title, 276
    distribution, 290
    distribution, heroic, 291
    event, 276
    global, 276
    heroic Income, 290
    loss, 282
    loss, fossil fuels, 283
    loss, slow renewables, 284
    national, 262
    new, 278
    on heritage items, 289
    sales, 277
    sin, 286
    speculation, 289
    traditional, 276
    use, 278
Taylor, Gordon, 233
technology, 175
Thom, Rene, 41
Thompson, W.I., 30, 54, 56, 175, 195
thought experiments, 18, 19
threats
    climatic, 297
    oceanic, 298
    solar System, 298
Tibetan people, 28, 34, 53, 153, 190
Todd, J. & N., 17
Toffler, A., 14
Tolstoy, L., 70, 252
Toynbee, A., 335
trade
    Global, 310
tragedy of the commons, 245
transfer powers, 268
trap
    economic, 139
traps, 98, 99, 335
trigger, 48
Tylor, 37

Uighur people, 201
Ulanowicz, 83
United Nations 210
    offices, 213
    strengths, 225
    weaknesses, 226
UN programs, 219
UN Secretariat, 212
uncertainty, 340
UNICEF, 221
United Nations, 9, 35, 64, 71, 210, 218
universals
    cultural, 53
Ur, 236
urbanization, 124
    changes from, 123
utopia, 59, 112
Utopia book, 59
utopias, 34, 62, 74, 201, 205, 325

Vaihinger, Hans, 341
values, 139

van Dam, A., 244
Varela, F., 20
Vergil, 241
Vernadsky, S., 127
violence, 72
vitality, 43
volunteer, 293
    International, 308
volunteers, 308
Von Uexkull, J., 179
Vonnegut, K., 70
voucher
    carbon, 295
    costs, 295

Wackernagel, M., 10
Waddington, Conrad, 41
war, 68, 247, 250
    advantages of, 168
    disadvantages of, 168
    nuclear, 70
    scale of, 168
wars, 165

Wataluma language, 48
Watson, R., 196
wealth, 91, 138, 140
    distribution of, 92
weapons, 270
    personal, 270
Wells, H.G., 36, 106, 112
Whitehead, A.N., 22, 84, 174
wholeness, 41
wilderness, 237, 333
Willkie, W., 64
Winner, L., 28
wisdom, 338, 340, 342

Yanomamo people, 92
Yaruru people, 204
Year of Consideration, 270, 271

Zajonc, R., 109

Colophon

Type: Perpetua
Display Type: Gill Sans Light
Book Design: Rian Garcia Calusa Designs
Cover Design: Rian Garcia Calusa
Graphics: Alan Wittbecker
Author Photograph: Merissa DePasse, 1989
Editing: J. Garcia B. of Rian Garcia Calusa
Hardware: Macintosh G5
Software: Adobe InDesign & Acrobat
Furious Charge & Entertainment: Pippi Frog
Spiritual & Material Support: Precious Woulfe

www.ingramcontent.com/pod-product-compliance
Lightning Source LLC
Chambersburg PA
CBHW081820280526
45789CB00007B/2278